CAMBRIDGE LIBRARY COLLECTION

Books of enduring scholarly value

Egyptology

The large-scale scientific investigation of Egyptian antiquities by Western scholars began as an unintended consequence of Napoleon's invasion of Egypt during which, in 1799, the Rosetta Stone was discovered. The military expedition was accompanied by French scholars, whose reports prompted a wave of enthusiasm that swept across Europe and North America resulting in the Egyptian Revival style in art and architecture. Increasing numbers of tourists visited Egypt, eager to see the marvels being revealed by archaeological excavation. Writers and booksellers responded to this growing interest with publications ranging from technical site reports to tourist guidebooks and from children's histories to theories identifying the pyramids as repositories of esoteric knowledge. This series reissues a wide selection of such books. They reveal the gradual change from the 'tomb-robbing' approach of early excavators to the highly organised and systematic approach of Flinders Petrie, the 'father of Egyptology', and include early accounts of the decipherment of the hieroglyphic script.

The Pyramids and Temples of Gizeh

A pioneering Egyptologist, Sir William Matthew Flinders Petrie (1853–1942) excavated over fifty sites and trained a generation of archaeologists. In 1880 he began the first ever systematic survey of the Giza Plateau, with perhaps his most important work being on the Great Pyramid. Theories abounded as to how the Great Pyramid had been constructed, yet few were based on close examination of the structure itself. Petrie's findings, still used as a reference today, enabled him to disprove prominent theories, such as the belief of Charles Piazzi Smyth that the Great Pyramid was a product of divine revelation and therefore flawless. This first edition of 1883 was not reprinted, and subsequent editions summarised some of the material. Petrie wrote prolifically throughout his long career, and many of his other publications are also reissued in this series.

Cambridge University Press has long been a pioneer in the reissuing of out-of-print titles from its own backlist, producing digital reprints of books that are still sought after by scholars and students but could not be reprinted economically using traditional technology. The Cambridge Library Collection extends this activity to a wider range of books which are still of importance to researchers and professionals, either for the source material they contain, or as landmarks in the history of their academic discipline.

Drawing from the world-renowned collections in the Cambridge University Library and other partner libraries, and guided by the advice of experts in each subject area, Cambridge University Press is using state-of-the-art scanning machines in its own Printing House to capture the content of each book selected for inclusion. The files are processed to give a consistently clear, crisp image, and the books finished to the high quality standard for which the Press is recognised around the world. The latest print-on-demand technology ensures that the books will remain available indefinitely, and that orders for single or multiple copies can quickly be supplied.

The Cambridge Library Collection brings back to life books of enduring scholarly value (including out-of-copyright works originally issued by other publishers) across a wide range of disciplines in the humanities and social sciences and in science and technology.

The Pyramids
and
Temples of Gizeh

W.M. FLINDERS PETRIE

CAMBRIDGE
UNIVERSITY PRESS

CAMBRIDGE
UNIVERSITY PRESS

University Printing House, Cambridge, CB2 8BS, United Kingdom

Published in the United States of America by Cambridge University Press, New York

Cambridge University Press is part of the University of Cambridge.

It furthers the University's mission by disseminating knowledge in the pursuit of
education, learning and research at the highest international levels of excellence.

www.cambridge.org
Information on this title: www.cambridge.org/9781108065726

© in this compilation Cambridge University Press 2013

This edition first published 1883
This digitally printed version 2013

ISBN 978-1-108-06572-6 Paperback

THE

PYRAMIDS AND TEMPLES

OF GIZEH.

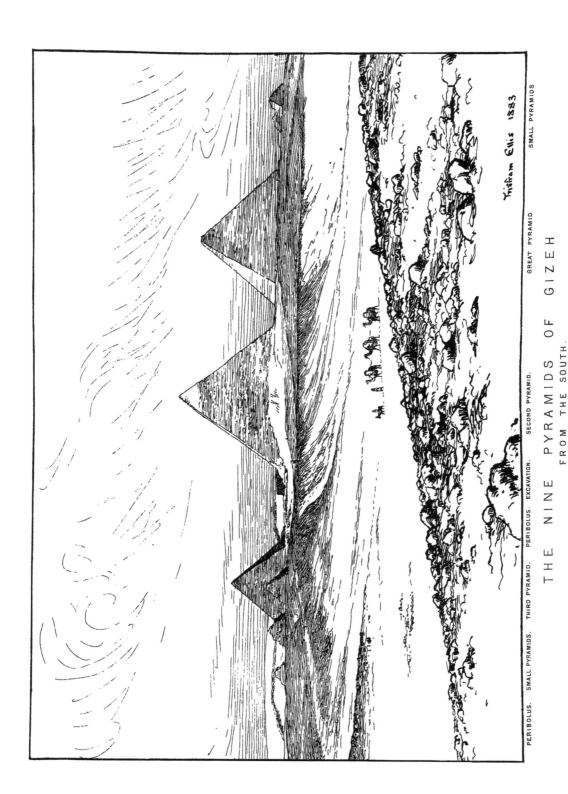

PERIBOLUS.   SMALL PYRAMIDS.   THIRD PYRAMID.   PERIBOLUS. EXCAVATION.   SECOND PYRAMID.   GREAT PYRAMID.   SMALL PYRAMIDS

Tristram Ellis 1883

THE NINE PYRAMIDS OF GIZEH
FROM THE SOUTH.

Thos Kell & Son. Photo-Lith. 40, King St. Covent Garden.

THE

PYRAMIDS AND TEMPLES

OF GIZEH.

BY

W. M. FLINDERS PETRIE,

Author of "Inductive Metrology," "Stonehenge," &c.

LONDON:

FIELD & TUER, Ye Leadenhalle Presse; SIMPKIN, MARSHALL & CO., Stationers'
Hall Court; HAMILTON, ADAMS & CO., Paternoster Row.
NEW YORK: SCRIBNER & WELFORD, 743, Broadway.

FIELD & TUER,
YE LEADENHALLE PRESSE, E.C.
T 3,224.

PUBLISHED WITH THE ASSISTANCE OF A VOTE OF

ONE HUNDRED POUNDS

FROM THE GOVERNMENT-GRANT COMMITTEE

OF THE ROYAL SOCIETY.

1883.

CONTENTS.

x   *CONTENTS.*

LIST OF PLATES.

ERRATA.

Page 30 ... *line* 7 *for* oonsider ... *read* consider.

,, 38 ... ,, 1 ,, case ... ,, core.

,, 41 ... ,, 2 ,, othe thers ... ,, the others.

,, 41 ... ,, 43 ,, $+$· ... ,, $+$·1

,, 42 ... ,, 33 ,, 0·9 ... ,, ·09

,, 43 ... ,, 13 ,, measurement ... ,, re-measurement.

,, 50 ... ,, 28 ,, ·24′ ... ,, 24′

,, 65 ... ,, 34 ,, ±3· ... ,, ±·3

,, 157 ... ,, 12 ,, dozen ... ,, dozens.

,, 212 ... ,, 1 ,, tweve ... ,, twelve.

,, 218 ... ,, 10 ,, Ibr ... ,, Ibn.

Plate xiv., *fig.* 7, the lithographer has drawn the lines wavy, whereas they really form a true spiral, as described p. 174, and in *Anthropological Journal.*

INTRODUCTION.

1. THE nature of the present work is such that perhaps few students will find interest in each part of it alike. The ends and the means appeal to separate classes : the antiquarian, whose are the ends, will look askance at the means, involving co-ordinates, probable errors, and arguments based on purely mechanical considerations ; the surveyor and geodetist, whose are the means, will scarcely care for their application to such remote times ; the practical man who may follow the instrumental details, may consider the discussion of historical problems to be outside his province ; while only those familiar with mechanical work will fully realize the questions of workmanship and tools here explained.

An investigation thus based on such different subjects is not only at a disadvantage in its reception, but also in its production. And if in one part or another, specialists may object to some result or suggestion, the plea must be the difficulty of making certain how much is known, and what is believed, on subjects so far apart and so much debated.

The combination of two apparently distinct subjects, is often most fertile in results ; and the mathematical and mechanical study of antiquities promises a full measure of success. It is sometimes said, or supposed, that it must be useless to apply accuracy to remains which are inaccurate ; that fallacies are sure to result, and that the products of such a method rather originate with the modern investigator than express the design of the ancient constructor. But when we look to other branches of historical inquiry, we see how the most refined methods of research are eagerly followed : how philology does not confine itself to the philological ideas of the ancient writers, but analyzes their speech so as to see facts of which they were wholly unconscious ; how chemistry does not study the chemical ideas, but the chemical processes and products of the ancients ; how anthropology examines the bodies and customs of men to whom such inquiries were completely foreign. Hence there is nothing unprecedented, and nothing impracticable, in applying mathematical methods in the study of mechanical remains of ancient times, since the object is to get behind the workers, and to see not only their work, but their mistakes, their amounts of error, the limits of their ideas ; in fine, to skirt the borders of their knowledge and abilities, so as to find their range by means of using more comprehensive methods.   Modern inquiry should never rest content with saying that anything was " exact ;" but always show what error in fact or in work was tolerated by the ancient worker, and was considered by him as his allowable error.

2. The materials of the present volume have been selected from the results of two winters' work in Egypt.   Many of the points that were examined, and some questions that occupied a considerable share of the time, have not been touched on here, as this account is limited to the buildings of the fourth dynasty at Gizeh, with such examples of later remains as were necessary for the discussion of the subject.   All the inscriptions copied were sent over to Dr. Birch, who has published some in full, and extracted what seemed of interest in others ; Dr. Weidemann has also had some of them ; and they do not need, therefore, further attention on my part.   Papers on other subjects, including the Domestic Remains, Brickwork, Pottery, and travellers' *graffiti*, each of which were examined with special reference to their periods, are in course of publication by the Royal Archæological Institute.   The mechanical methods and tools employed by the Egyptians were discussed at the Anthropological Institute, and are more summarily noticed here.   A large mass of accurate measurements of remains of various ages were collected ; and these, when examined, will probably yield many examples of the cubits employed by the constructors.   Of photographs, over five hundred were taken, on ¼ size dry plates, mainly of architectural points, and to show typical features.   Volumes of prints of these may be examined on application to me, and copies can be ordered from a London photographer.   The lesser subjects being thus disposed of, this volume only treats of one place, and that only during one period, which was the main object of research.   The mass of the actual numerical observations and reductions would be too bulky to publish, and also unnecessary ; the details of the processes are, in fact, only given so far as may prove useful for, comparison with the results obtained by other observers.

Though, in describing various features, reference has often been made to the publications of Colonel Howard Vyse* (for whom Mr. Perring, C.E., acted as superintendent), and of Professor C. Piazzi Smyth,† yet it must not be supposed that this account professes at all to cover the same ground, and to give all the details that are to be found in those works.   They are only referred to where necessary to connect or to explain particular points ; and those volumes must be consulted by any one wishing to fully comprehend all that is known of the Pyramids.   This work is, in fact, only supplementary to the previous descriptions,

* " Operations at the Pyramids," 3 vols. 1840.
† " Life and Work at the Great Pyramid," 3 vols. 1867.

as giving fuller and more accurate information about the principal parts of the Pyramids, with just as much general account as may be necessary to make it intelligible, and to enable the reader to judge of the discussions and conclusions arrived at on the subject, without needing to refer to other works. Colonel Vyse's volumes are most required for an account of the arrangements of the Second and smaller Pyramids, of the chambers in the Great Pyramid over the King's Chamber, of the negative results of excavations in the masonry, and of various mechanical details. Professor Smyth's vol. ii. is required for the measurements and description of the interior of the Great Pyramid. While the scope of the present account includes the more exact measurement of the whole of the Great Pyramid, of the outsides and chambers of the Second and Third Pyramids, of the Granite Temple, and of various lesser works; also the comparison of the details of some of the later Pyramids with those at Gizeh, and various conclusions, mainly based on mechanical grounds.

The reader's knowledge of the general popular information on the subject, has been taken for granted; as that the Pyramids of Gizeh belong to the first three kings of the fourth dynasty, called Khufu, Khafra, and Menkaura, by themselves, and Cheops, Chephren, and Mycerinus, by Greek-loving Englishmen; that their epoch is variously stated by chronologers as being in the third, fourth, or fifth millennium B.C.; that the buildings are in their bulk composed of blocks of limestone, such as is found in the neighbouring districts; that the granite used in parts of the insides and outsides was brought from Syene, now Assouan; and that the buildings were erected near the edge of the limestone desert, bordering the west side of the Nile valley, about 150 feet above the inundated plain, and about 8 miles from the modern Cairo.

3. One or two technical usages should be defined here. All measures stated in this volume are in Imperial British inches, unless expressed otherwise; and it has not been thought necessary to repeat this every time an amount is stated; so that in all such cases inches must be understood as the medium of description. Azimuths, wherever stated, are written + or −, referring to positive or negative rotation, *i.e.*, to E. or to W., from the North point as zero. Thus, azimuth −5′, which often occurs, means 5′ west of north. Where the deviation of a line running east and west is stated to be only a few minutes + or −, it, of course, refers to its normal or perpendicular, as being that amount from true north.

The probable error of all important measurements is stated with the sign ± prefixed to it as usual. A full description of this will be found in any modern treatise on probabilities; and a brief account of it was given in "Inductive Metrology," pp. 24–30. Some technical details about it will be found here in the Appendix on "The Rejection of Erroneous Observations"; and I will only add a short definition of it as follows:—The probable error is an amount on each side of the stated mean, within the limits of which there is as much chance of the truth lying, as beyond it ; *i.e.,* it is 1 in 2 that the true result is not further from the stated mean than the amount of the probable error. Or, if any one prefers to regard the limits beyond which it is practically impossible for the true result to be, it is 22 to 1 against the truth being 3 times the amount of the probable error from the mean, 144 to 1 against its being 4 times, or 1,380 to 1 against its being as far as 5 times the amount of the probable error from the mean result stated. Thus, any extent of improbability that any one may choose to regard as practical impossibility, they may select ; and remember that 4 or 5 times the probable error will mean to them the limit of possibility. Practically, it is best to state it as it always is stated, as the amount of variation which there is an equal chance of the truth exceeding or not ; and any one can then consider what improbability there is in any case on hand, of the truth differing from the statement to any given extent.

It should be mentioned that the plans are all photolithographed from my drawings, in order to avoid inaccuracy or errors of copying ; and thence comes any lack of technical style observable in the lettering.

As to the results of the whole investigation, perhaps many theorists will agree with an American, who was a warm believer in Pyramid theories when he came to Gizeh. I had the pleasure of his company there for a couple of days, and at our last meal together he said to me in a saddened tone,—"Well, sir ! I feel as if I had been to a funeral." By all means let the old theories have a decent burial ; though we should take care that in our haste none of the wounded ones are buried alive.

THE

PYRAMIDS AND TEMPLES OF GIZEH.

CHAPTER I.

OBJECTS AND MEANS.

4. THE small piece of desert plateau opposite the village of Gizeh, though less than a mile across, may well claim to be the most remarkable piece of ground in the world. There may be seen the very beginning of architecture, the most enormous piles of building ever raised, the most accurate constructions known, the finest masonry, and the employment of the most ingenious tools; whilst among all the sculpture that we know, the largest figure—the Sphinx— and also the finest example of technical skill with artistic expression—the Statue of Khafra—both belong to Gizeh. We shall look in vain for a more wonderful assemblage than the vast masses of the Pyramids, the ruddy walls and pillars of the granite temple, the titanic head of the Sphinx, the hundreds of tombs, and the shattered outlines of causeways, pavements, and walls, that cover this earliest field of man's labours.

But these remains have an additional, though passing, interest in the present day, owing to the many attempts that have been made to theorise on the motives of their origin and construction. The Great Pyramid has lent its name as a sort of by-word for paradoxes; and, as moths to a candle, so are theorisers attracted to it. The very fact that the subject was so generally familiar, and yet so little was accurately known about it, made it the more enticing; there were plenty of descriptions from which to choose, and yet most of them were so hazy that their support could be claimed for many varying theories.

Here, then, was a field which called for the resources of the present time for its due investigation ; a field in which measurement and research were greatly needed, and have now been largely rewarded by the disclosures of the skill of the ancients, and the mistakes of the moderns. The labours of the French Expedition, of Colonel Howard Vyse, of the Prussian Expedition, and of Professor Smyth, in this field are so well known that it is unnecessary to refer to them, except to explain how it happens that any further work was still needed. Though the French were active explorers, they were far from realising the accuracy of ancient work ; and they had no idea of testing the errors of the ancients by outdoing them in precision. Hence they rather explored than investigated. Col. Vyse's work, carried on by Mr. Perring, was of the same nature, and no accurate measurement or triangulation was attempted by these energetic blasters and borers ; their discoveries were most valuable, but their researches were always of a rough-and-ready character. The Prussian Expedition sought with ardour for inscriptions, but did not advance our knowledge of technical skill, work, or accuracy, though we owe to it the best topographical map of Gizeh. When Professor Smyth went to Gizeh he introduced different and scientific methods of inquiry in his extensive measurements, afterwards receiving the gold medal of the Royal Society of Edinburgh in recognition of his labours. But he did not attempt the heaviest work of accurate triangulation. Mr. Waynman Dixon, C.E., followed in his steps, in taking further measurements of the inside of the Great Pyramid. Mr. Gill—now Astronomer Royal at the Cape—when engaged in Egypt in the Transit Expedition of 1874, made the next step, by beginning a survey of the Great Pyramid base, in true geodetic style. This far surpassed all previous work in its accuracy, and was a noble result of the three days' labour that he and Professor Watson were able to spare for it. When I was engaged in reducing this triangulation for Mr. Gill in 1879, he impressed on me the need of completing it if I could, by continuing it round the whole pyramid, as two of the corners were only just reached by it without any check.

When, after preparations extending over some years, I settled at Gizeh during 1880-2, I took with me, therefore, instruments of the fullest accuracy needed for the work ; probably as fine as any private instruments of the kind. The triangulation was with these performed quite independently of previous work ; it was of a larger extent, including the whole hill ; and it comprised an abundance of checks. The necessary excavations were carried out to discover the fiducial points of the buildings, unseen for thousands of years. The measurements previously taken were nearly all checked, by repeating them with greater accuracy, and, in most cases, more frequency ; and fresh and more refined methods of measurement were adopted. The tombs around the pyramids were all measured, where they had any regularity and were accessible. The methods of workmanship were investigated, and materials were found illustrating the tools employed and the modes of using them.

5. For a detailed statement of what was urgently wanted on these subjects, I cannot do better than quote from a paper by Professor Smyth,* entitled, " Of the Practical Work still necessary for the Recovery of the Great Pyramid's ancient, from its modern, dimensions"; and add marginal notes of what has now been accomplished.

" As my measures referred chiefly to the interior of the structure, and as there the original surfaces have not been much broken, the virtual restoration of that part has been by no means unsuccessful ; and requires merely in certain places—places which can only be recognised from time to time as the theory of the building shall advance—still more minutely exact measures than any which I was able to make, but which will be comparatively easy to a scientific man going there in future with that one special object formally in view."

Notes of work, 1880-2.

The whole interior now re-examined and much remeasured, more accurately.

" The exterior, however, of the Great building, is exceedingly dilapidated, and I have few or no measures of my own to set forth for its elucidation. That subject is, therefore, still " to let " ; and as it is too vast for any private individual to undertake at his own cost, I may as well explain here the state of the case, so that either Societies or Governments may see the propriety of their taking up the grand architectural and historical problem, and prosecuting it earnestly until a successful solution of all its parts shall have been arrived at."

Total cost of present work £300.

" Size and Shape, then, of the ancient exterior of the Great Pyramid, are the first desiderata to be determined."

(A statement of the various measurements of the base here follows.)

" As preparatory, then, to an efficient remeasurement of the length of the Base-sides of the Great Pyramid, itself an essential preliminary to almost all other Pyramidological researches, I beg to submit the following local particulars."

" (1.) The outer corners of four shallow sockets, cut in the levelled surface of the earth-fast rock outside the *present* dilapidated corners of the built Great Pyramid, are supposed to be the points to be measured between horizontally in order to obtain the original length of each external, finished, 'casing-stone' base-side."

Sockets are not corners of base-side.

" (2.) Previous to any such measurement being commenced, the present outer corners of those sockets must be reduced to their ancient corners, as the sockets have suffered, it is feared, much dilapidation and injury, even since 1865 ; owing to having been then imperfectly covered over, on leaving them, by the parties who at that time opened them."

Sockets are apparently quite uninjured.

" (3.) The said sockets must be *proved* to have been the sockets originally holding the corner stones of the casing ; or showing how far they overlapped, and therefore and thereby *not* defining the ancient base of the Great Pyramid *to the amount so overlapped.*

By form of core, and by casing lines lying *within* the sockets, no others are possible.

* *Edinburgh Astronomical Observations*, vol. xiii., p. 3.

Notes of work
1880-2.

. . . . the ground should be cleared far and wide about each corner to see if there are any other sockets in the neighbourhood."

"(4.) Whether any more rival sockets claiming to be the true corner sockets of the ancient base are, or are not, then and in that manner, found,—the usually known or selected ones should further be tested, by being compared with any other remaining indications of where the line of each base-side stood in former days. Some particular and most positive indications of this kind we know were found by Col. Howard Vyse in the middle of the Northern side; and there is no reason why as good markings should not be discovered, if properly looked for, along the other three sides; and they are so vitally important to a due understanding of the case, that their ascertainment should *precede* any expense being incurred on the measurement of lengths from socket to socket."

Casing now found on all sides, and completely fixed.

Measures having been taken by triangulation, no extensive cuttings were needed.

"(5.) Col. H. Vyse found those invaluable markings of the line of the North base-side, or part of the very base-side itself, by accomplishing the heavy work of digging down by a cross cut, through the middle of the heap of rubbish, near 50 feet high, on that side. But he has published no records of how those markings, or that actual portion of the base-side, agree, either in level or in azimuth with the sockets. Indeed, he left the ground in such a state of hillock and hole, that no measures can, or ever will, be taken with creditable accuracy until a longitudinal cut through the rubbish heap shall be driven from East to West and all along between the two N.E. and N.W. sockets."

Casing - stones are not broken up, and the cutting is not necessary.

"(6.) The making of such a long and laborious cut, and then the 'lining' and 'levelling' of the bases of the Colonel's casing stones *in situ* (or their remains, for they are said to have been mischievously broken up since then), and their comparison with the sockets or their joining lines by appropriate and powerful surveying instruments, should be the first operation of the new measurers, to whom, it is fervently to be hoped, an intelligent Government will grant the due means for effecting it satisfactorily."

Sides now found by pits, and fixed by triangulation. Pavement traced on each side.

"(7.) A similar longitudinal cut, and similar comparisons are to be made in the other base-side hills of rubbish, together with a wider clearing away of the rubbish outside, in order to determine the form and proportion of the 'pavement' which is believed to have anciently surrounded the Pyramid; but of which the only positive information which we have, is based on the little bit of it which Col. H. Vyse cut down to near the middle of the North side."

Cuts, *if wanted*, might be made for a tenth of this sum.

Inscribed casing found, Greek.

"This work might cost from £12,000 to £14,000; for the material to be cut through is not only extensive but so hard and concreted that it turns and bends the hoes or picks employed in Nile cultivation, and which are the only tools the Arabs know of. But besides the theoretical value of such an operation for *distinguishing and identifying* the base to be measured, it would certainly yield practically abundant fragments of casing stones, and perhaps settle the oft-mooted questions of ancient inscriptions on the outer surface of the Pyramid."

" (8.) When the four sides of the base, and the corresponding sides of the pavement are exposed to view,—a new fixation of the exact original places of the precise outer corners of the now dilapidated and rather expanded corner sockets may be required ; and then, from and between such newly fixed points, there must be

    A. Linear measures of distance taken with first-rate accuracy.

    B. Levellings.

    C. Horizontal angles, to test the squareness of the base.

    D. Astronomical measures to test the orientation of each of the base sides.

    E. Angular and linear measures combined to obtain both the vertical slope of the ancient Pyramid flanks, and the distance of certain of the present joints of the entrance passage from the ancient external surface of the Pyramid in the direction of that passage produced—a matter which is at present very doubtful, but a new and good determination of which is essential to utilize fully the numerous internal observations contained in this and other books."

" (9.) When all the above works shall have been carefully accomplished, the men who have performed them will doubtless have become the most competent advisers as to what should be undertaken next ; whether in search of the fourth chamber, concerning whose existence there is a growing feeling amongst those who have studied certain laws of area and cubic contents which prevail among the presently known chambers and passages ; or for the more exact measurement of certain portions of the building which shall then be recognised by the theory as of fiducial character and importance."

" (10.) Should the next remeasurement unfortunately not be under sufficiently favourable auspices or powerful patronage enough to attempt all that has been sketched out above—I would suggest to those employed upon it the importance of endeavouring to operate in that manner on at least the north side of the Great Pyramid alone, where much of the work has been already performed, and where traces of the old base-side are known to exist, or did certainly exist 34 years ago."

" (11.) The levels as well as temperatures of water in the wells of the plain close to the Pyramid, and in the Nile in the distance, should also be measured through a full twelvemonth interval. A meteorological journal should likewise be kept for the same period at the base of the Pyramid, and the corrections ascertained to reduce it either to the summit or King's chamber levels above, or to the plain level below ; while no efforts should be spared to re-open the ventilating channels of the King's chamber and to prevent the Arabs from filling them up again."

" (12.) An examination should be made of the *apparent* Pyramid in the desert almost west of the Great Pyramid ; likewise of the

---

Marginal notes:

Notes of work, 1880-2.

Done.

Done.

Done.

Done.
Done.

Done.

Much of the interior now remeasured, with higher exactitude.

All results obtained without patronage.

Channels filled by wind, not by Arabs.

Done.

Notes of work,
1880-2.
_____

N.W.diagonal
done.
Done partly.

Done.

northern coasts of Egypt, where they are cut by the Great Pyramid's several meridian and diagonal lines produced ; also of the fourth dynasty remains in the Sinaitic Peninsula ; and of any monuments whatever, whether in Egypt or the neighbouring countries for which any older date than that of the Great Pyramid can reasonably be assigned ; including also a fuller account than any yet published of King Shafre's Tomb and its bearings with, or upon, the origin, education, labours and life of the first of the Pyramid builders."

6. To carry out, therefore, the work sketched in the above outline, and to investigate several collateral points, I settled at Gizeh in December, 1880, and lived there till the end of May, 1881 ; I returned thither in the middle of October that year, and (excepting two months up the Nile, and a fortnight elsewhere), lived on there till the end of April, 1882; thus spending nine months at Gizeh. Excellent accommodation was to be had in a rock-hewn tomb, or rather three tombs joined together, formerly used by Mr. Waynman Dixon, C.E. ; his door and shutters I strengthened ; and fitting up shelves and a hammock bedstead, I found the place as convenient as anything that could be wished. The tombs were sheltered from the strong and hot south-west winds, and preserved an admirably uniform temperature ; not varying beyond 58° to 64° F. during the winter, and only reaching 80° during three days of hot wind, which was at 96° to 100° outside.

I was happy in having Ali Gabri,* the faithful servant of Prof. Smyth, Mr. Dixon, and Mr. Gill ; his knowledge of all that has been done at Gizeh during his lifetime is invaluable ; and his recollections begin with working at four years old, as a tiny basket carrier, for Howard Vyse in 1837. He was a greater help in measuring than many a European would have been ; and the unmechanical Arab mind had, by intelligence and training, been raised in his case far above that of his neighbours. In out-door work where I needed two pair of hands, he helped me very effectually ; but the domestic cares of my narrow home rested on my own shoulders. The usual course of a day's work was much as follows : —Lighting my petroleum stove, the kettle boiled up while I had my bath ; then breakfast time was a reception hour, and as I sat with the tomb door open, men and children used to look in as they passed ; often a friend would stop for a chat, while I hastily brewed some extra cups of coffee in his honour, on the little stove behind the door; Ali also generally came up, and sat doubled up in the doorway, as only an Arab can,fold together. After this, starting out about nine o'clock, with Ali carrying part of the instruments, I went to work on the triangulation or measurements ; if triangulating, it was Ali's business to hold an

* Called Ali Dobree by Prof. Smyth. G is universally pronounced hard by Egyptians, soft by Arabs ; thus either Gabri or Jabri, Gizeh or Jizeh, General or Jeneral, Gaz or Jaz (petroleum).

umbrella so as to shade the theodolite from the sun all day—the observer took his chance ; if measuring, I generally did not require assistance, and worked alone, and I always had to get on as well as I could during Ali's dinner hour. At dusk I collected the things and packed up ; often the taking in of the triangulation signals was finished by moonlight, or in the dark. Then, when all was safely housed in my tomb, Ali was dismissed to his home, and about six or seven o'clock I lit my stove, and sat down to reduce observations. Dinner then began when the kettle boiled, and was spun out over an hour or two, cooking and feeding going on together. Brown ship-biscuit, tinned soups, tomatoes (excellent in Egypt), tapioca, and chocolate, were found to be practically the most convenient and sustaining articles ; after ten hours' work without food or drink, heavy food is not suitable ; and the great interruption of moving instruments, and breaking up work for a midday meal was not admissible. Then, after washing up the dishes (for Arab ideas of cleanliness cannot be trusted), I sat down again to reducing observations, writing, &c., till about midnight. Ali's slave, Muhammed the negro, and his nephew, little Muhammed, used to come up about nine o'clock, and settle in the next tomb to sleep as guards, safely locked in. Having a supply of candle provided for them, they solaced themselves with indescribable tunes on reed pipes ; often joining in duets with Abdallah, the village guard, who used to come up for a musical evening before beginning his rounds. Very often the course of work was different ; sometimes all out-door work was impossible, owing to densely sand-laden winds, which blew the grit into everything—eyes, nose, ears, mouth, pockets, and watches. During the excavations I turned out earlier—about sunrise ; and after setting out the men's work, returned for breakfast later on in the morning. On other occasions, when working inside the Great Pyramid, I always began in the evening, after the travellers were clean away, and then went on till midnight, with Ali nodding, or even till eight o'clock next morning ; thus occasionally working twenty-four hours at a stretch, when particular opportunities presented themselves. The tomb I left furnished, as I inhabited it, in charge of Ali Gabri, and not having been looted in the late revolt, it will, I hope, be useful to any one wishing to carry on researches there, and applying to Dr. Grant Bey for permission to use the furniture.

7. My best thanks are due to M. Maspero, the Director of Antiquities, for the facilities he accorded to me in all the excavations I required, kindly permitting me to work under his firman ; and also for information on many points. It is much to be hoped that the liberal and European policy he has introduced may flourish, and that it may overcome the old Oriental traditions and ways that clogged the Department of Antiquities. Excepting Arab help, I worked almost entirely single-handed ; but I had for a time the pleasure of the society of two artists : Mr. Arthur Melville, staying with me for a week in May, 1881, and

kindly helping in a preliminary measure of my survey base, and in an accurate levelling up to the Great Pyramid entrance; and Mr. Tristram Ellis, staying with me for a fortnight in March and April, 1882, and giving me most valuable help in points where accuracy was needed, laying aside the brush to recall his former skill with theodolite and measure. Thus working together, we measured the base of survey (reading to $\frac{1}{100}$th inch) five times, in early dawn, to avoid the sunshine; we levelled up the Great Pyramid, and down again (reading to $\frac{1}{100}$th inch); took the dip of the entrance passage to the bottom of it, and gauged its straightness throughout; took the azimuth of the ascending passages round Mamun's hole; callipered the sides of the coffer all over, at every 6 inches, and raised the coffer (weighing about 3 tons), by means of a couple of crowbars, to 8 inches above the floor, in order to measure the bottom of it. For the instrumental readings, in these cases, Mr. Ellis preferred, however, that I should be responsible, excepting where simultaneous readings were needed, as for the base length, and in Mamun's hole. To Mr. Ellis I am also indebted for the novel view of the Pyramids, showing the nine at once, which forms the frontispiece of this work.

To Dr. Grant Bey I owe much, both for occasional help at the Pyramid, in visiting the chambers of construction, the well, &c.; and also for his unvarying kindness both in health and sickness, realizing the conventional Arab phrase, " My house is thy house." Further, I should mention the kind interest and advice of General Stone Pasha, who gave me many hints from his intimate knowledge of the country; and also the very friendly assistance of our Vice-Consul, Mr. Raph. Borg, both in procuring an order for my residence and protection at Gizeh, and in prosecuting an inquiry into a serious robbery and assault on me, committed by the unruly soldiery in October, 1881; unhappily, this inquiry was a fruitless task apparently, as the military influence was too strong in the examination.

And now I must not forget my old friend Shekh Omar, of the Pyramid village, shrewd, sharp, and handsome; nor how anxious he was to impress on me that though some people of base and grovelling notions worked for money, and not for their " good name," *he* wished to work for fame alone; and as he had no doubt I should make a big book, he hoped that I should contract with him for excavations, and give him a good name. I gratified him with one contract, but finding that it cost many times as much as hiring labourers directly, and was not sufficiently under control, the arrangement was not repeated; but I will say that I found him the most respectable man to deal with on the Pyramid hill, excepting, of course, my servant Ali Gabri, who was equally anxious about his good name, though too true a gentleman to talk much about it. The venerable Abu Talib and the loquacious Ibrahim, shekhs of the Pyramid guides, also conducted themselves properly, and Ibrahim seemed honestly genial and right-minded in his words and acts, and knew what so few Arabs do know—how not to obtrude. The rank and file of the guides—so familiar, with their little stocks of *antikas* in the corners of old red handkerchiefs—reckoned that I was free of the place, having Ali for my servant; they never gave me the least trouble, or even whispered the omnipresent word *bakhshish*, but were as friendly as possible on all occasions, many claiming a hand-shaking and a hearty greeting. My impression of a year's sojourn with Arabs is favourable to them; only it is necessary to keep the upper hand, to resist imposition with unwearied patience, to be fair, and occasionally liberal in dealings, and to put aside Western reserve, and treat them with the same familiarity to which they are accustomed between different classes. With such intercourse I have found them a cheerful, warm-hearted, and confiding people.

CHAPTER II.

INSTRUMENTS.

8. THE list of instruments employed was as follows :

A*	Standard scale, steel		100	inches long, divided to	1 inch.
B*	Steel tape		1,200	„	50 „
C	Steel chain		1,000	„	20 „
D	Pine poles, a pair 1 inch diameter		140	„	10 „
E*	Pine rods, a pair 1 × 2 inches		100	„	1 „
F*	Pine rods, 10 of ½ × 1 „		60	„	1 „

(Jointing together into two lengths of 250 „ each.)

G*	Pine rods ⎱ ⎰ 3 of ½ × 2 inches		60	„	1 „
	for levelling ⎰ ⎱ 2 „ ½ × 1 „		60	„	1 „
H*	Pine rods, 2 „ ½ × 1 „ 40 and		20	„	1 „
J	Box on mahogany rods, 2 of 1 × 1		25	„	$\frac{1}{10}$ „
K	Boxwood scale,	1·25 × ·13	12	„	$\frac{1}{50}$ „
L	Steel scale,	1·07 × ·04	12	„	$\frac{1}{10}$ „
M*	Ivory scales,	2 of 1·18 × ·08	10	„	$\frac{1}{50}$ „
N*	Boxwood scale,	1·18 × ·08	10	„	$\frac{1}{50}$ „
O*	Gun metal scale,	1·06 × ·09	6	„	$\frac{1}{50}$ „
P*	Ivory scale,	1·0 × ·08	1	„	$\frac{1}{100}$ „

(The divisions of those marked * are all known to within $\frac{1}{1000}$ inch).

Q   Double calipers, 72 inches long.
R   Supports for catenary measurement by tape and chain.
S   10 thermometers for scale temperatures.

a	Theodolite ⎰ 10 inch circle, divisions 5′, vernier 3″ ⎱ telescope × 35.			
	by Gambay ⎱ 7 inch circle, „ 10′, „ 10″ ⎰			
b	Theodolite ⎰ 5 inch circle, „ 30′, „ 1′ ⎱ telescope × 6.			
	by King ⎱ 5 semicircle, „ 30′, „ 1′ ⎰			
c	Theodolite ⎰ 4 inch circle, „ 30′, „ 1′ ⎱ telescope × 8.			
	by Troughton ⎱ 4 semicircle, „ 30′, „ 1′ ⎰			
d	Box sextant ⎱ 1·64 inch radius, division 30′, vernier 1′.			
	by Troughton ⎰			

e   Hand level in brass case.
f   Gun metal protractor, by Troughton, 5·9 diam., divisions 30′.
g   Mahogany goniometer, 11 and 9 inch limbs.
h   Queen's chamber air channel goniometer.
j   Sheet steel square, 35 and 45 inches in the sides.
k   Folding wooden tripod stand, old pattern.

l Rigid tripod stand, 30 inches high, octahedral.
m Rigid tripod stand, 16 „   „
n Rigid iron tripod, 12 „   „
o 12 signals, with plumb bobs.

The above were all used, most of them continually ; a few other instruments were also taken out, but were not needed.

9. Several of these instruments were of new or unusual patterns, which—as well as various fittings adapted to them—require some explanation. The dimensions are all in inches.

A. The steel standard and straight-edge was on a new principle, employing the stiffness of a tube to maintain the straightness of a strip. It was skilfully executed by Mr. Munroe, of King's Cross. A steel tube, 102 inches long, 2·0 diam., and ·06 thick (see Fig. 1, Pl. xv.) was supported at the two neutral points, 20·8 per cent. from the ends, resting on two feet at one point and one at the other. This tube carried a series of 15 flat beds, all dressed exactly to a straight line when the tube rested on its supports. These beds supported the actual standard, which was formed of three independent strips of steel, each 34 inches long, 2·0 wide, and ·1 thick, butting end to end. These strips bore on the upper face, along the front edge, very fine graduations, the lines being about $\frac{1}{1000}$ wide. To ascertain the mean temperature throughout the whole length of the standard, a rod of zinc was screwed tightly to one end of the standard, and bore a scale divided to $\frac{1}{200}$ths at the other end ; the scale rising through a slot in the standard. The value of the divisions for various temperatures was carefully ascertained. As this standard was also a straight-edge, the edges of the three strips were all true straight lines, with a mean error of $\frac{1}{1200}$th inch ; and the edges were brought into one continuous straight line by adjusting screws set in the supporting beds, at the ends of the back edge of each strip. The object of having three separate strips was that they could be dismounted for independent use in measuring or drawing, and for testing each other's straightness ; that unequal heating of one edge should not cause as much distortion, in length or straightness, as if it were in one continuous piece ; and that the weight should not be too great for the rigidity, in handling it when detached from the supports. The principle of separating the stiff part from the actual scale was adopted in order to use the regular drawn weldless steel tube, which is the stiffest thing for its weight that can be had, and also to prevent any unequal heating warping the straightness, as the tube was boxed in by a thin wooden sheath, and so was sheltered far more than the scale could be. The minor details were that strips were held down by screws with countersunk heads, bearing on steel spring washers ; and they were pressed home against each other's ends, and also against the back adjusting screws, by diagonally acting springs. Along the front of the tube were projecting screws, nutted on and adjusted to form a right angle with the face of the strip ; so that the standard could be applied to any surface exactly at right angles.

The value of the divisions was ascertained by comparison with a brass standard scale. This scale was tested by Capt. Kater in 1820, 1824, 1830, and 1831 ; and by the Standards Department in 1875 (see a report on it in the Report of the Warden of the Standards, 1875, Appendix x., pp. 36–41) : as the steel standard was sufficient for comparisons, this scale was not taken to Egypt for fear of injury. The form of this brass standard is a bar, 42·14 long, 1·58 wide, ·17 thick ; bearing a scale of 41 inches in length, divided to ·1 inch, with a vernier of $\frac{1}{1000}$ths, and also bearing a metre divided to millimetres. The steel standard was ascertained, by means of this brass standard, to be exact at 19·6° cent. ; and the mean error of graduation and reading combined was ·0002, the greatest error being ·0005. By the intermediary of a steel tape, the steel standard was further compared with the public Trafalgar Square standard ; and according to that it was 1 in 60,000 longer, or true length at 17·8° cent., or a difference of ·021 on the length of the public standard, after allowing for the published error of ·019 inch. This is a guarantee that the length of the tape, which was used to transfer from the steel standard to the public standard, has no greater error than this ; and, on the whole, I should place as much, or rather more, confidence in the series of comparisons between the Imperial, the brass, the steel standard, and the steel tape, made under the best circumstances indoors, rather than in comparisons between the steel tape, the Trafalgar Square standard, and certain steel rod measures, made in the open air, with wind and varying temperature. The difference in any case is immaterial, in regard to any of the points measured, in the present inquiry.

B. The steel tape was over 100 feet long, ·37 inch wide, and 008 thick, and weighed just over a pound. It was coiled on an unusually large drum (4·2 diam.), to avoid any chance of permanent distortion. Etched divisions, in the ordinary style, being too ill-defined, I had an unmarked length of tape, and divided it by fine cut lines at every 50 inches ; the position of each line was shown by heating the steel to brown oxidation, and marking the number out of the brown by acid. It was found on trial that such lines did not weaken a piece of tape, even when it was violently twisted and wrenched ; and that the steel, being hard drawn and not tempered, nothing under red heat softened it. The cuts were not put on with any special care, as their exact value was to be ascertained ; but the worst error throughout was ·0098, the mean error ·0039 inch, and the total length true at 19·8° cent. This comparison was made when the tape was lying unstretched, on a flat surface, as ascertained by measuring successive 100-inch lengths on the steel standard. It stretched ·0127 per lb. on the whole length of 1,200 inches.

C. The steel chain of 1,000 inches I made on an entirely new pattern ; and it proved, both in Egypt, and, some years before, at Stonehenge, to be very handy in use. The links are each 20 inches long, made of wire ·092 diam., this being as thin as can be used with fair care. The eyes (see Fig. 3, Pl. xv.) are wide enough to fold up one in the other, without any intermediate rings. They are rhomboidal, so that they cannot hitch one on the other, but will always slip down when pulled ; and the internal curvature of the end of the eye is only just greater than that of the section of the wire, so that the linkage is sure when in use to come to its maximum length.* The junction of the eye is made with a long lapping piece, cut one-third away, and tinned to the stem. The whole was tested with 100 lbs. pull, to bring it to its bearings, before marking the divisions. The exact length of the links is unimportant, as, after the chain was made and stretched, a narrow collar of sheet copper was soldered about the middle of each link, the collars being adjusted to exactly 20 inches apart. Besides this, each link bore its own number, marked by a broad collar of copper for each 100, and a narrow collar for each 20 inches or link ; thus, at 340 inches there were three broad and two narrow collars by the side of the central dividing mark on the link. These collars were put towards one end of the link, apart from the dividing mark, and counted from each end up to the middle, as usual. The central eye of the chain was not tinned up, but was held by a slip clutch ; thus the chain could be separated into two 500-inch lengths if needed, each complete in itself, as for base lines for offsets. The handles were kept separately, hooking into any link at which accurate readings under tension might be needed. They were of the same wire as the chain, with wooden cross-bars. One of them included an inverted spring (see Fig. 2, Pl. xv.), so that the pull compressed the spring. When the pull reached 10 lbs., a small catch (not shown in the Figure) sprang out from the stem, and caught the coils. This left only a very small amount of play ; and hence, when using it, the regulation of the tension did not require to be looked at, but was felt by the finger when at 10 lbs. pull.

The advantages of this pattern are : (1) Great lightness and compactness of the chain, as it only weighs 2½ lbs., and forms a sheaf 1½ inch diam. ; (2) consequent small error by catenary curves, and ease of carrying it clear of the ground by its two ends ; (3) accuracy of the divisions ; (4) freedom from errors in the linkage ; (5) that no counting of the links is required, each being numbered ; and (6) that standard tension can be maintained by touch, while the eyes are used on reading the chain length. The worst error of division was ·03, the average error ·01, and the total length, with 10 lbs. tension, true at 15·8° cent. ; the stretching ·01 per lb. on the 1,000-inch total length.

D. The pine poles were only used for common purposes, being correct to about ·02.

E. F. G. H. All these rods were divided from the standard scale. I made

---

* This is preferable to the type of the standard chain of the Standards Department, as that has such a flat curve at the end of the eye that it is not certain to pull to the maximum length ; and in a light thin chain such a form would be liable to bend.

a right-angled triangle of sheet steel and stout brass tube, to slide along the edge of the standard. It was 13 in its bearing length, with a straight edge 4·3 long at right angles, for ruling by. It carried a fine line on inlaid German silver, by which it was adjusted (with a magnifier) to successive inches of the standard, for the successive cuts to be made. Altogether I divided 80 feet of rods into 1-inch spaces by this, with an average error of ·0015 inch.

The jointing rods were connected by a slip joint (see Fig. 4, Pl. xv.); a screw on each rod slipping through a hole in the other, and then sliding in a slot until the rod butted against the stop, S. Both the butt and rod ends were made by a screw in the end, sunk up to its head, the screw being screwed in until only slightly in excess, and then ground down to a true length, with a radius equal to the length of the rod. The levelling rods I made with similar jointing and fittings. A base-rod of 60 inches stood on the ground, having a flange against which the upper rods could be slid up or down by hand. It had also a block on the side, carrying a circular level, by which its verticality could be observed. The mode of work was for the staff-holder to hold the base-rod vertical, and slide the upper rods up or down, till a finely-divided scale at the top was in the field of the telescope; then setting the rods, so that one of the inch cuts on them should agree with the zero line on the base-rod, the fractions of an inch were read by the level telescope, and the whole inches reported by the staff-holder. This method enables a larger scale to be used for reading on than if there were similar divisions all down the rods; and yet it takes but little time for adjustment, as that is only done to the nearest whole inch or two, and it does not sacrifice any accuracy.

The other scales do not need any remark.

Q. The calipers (see Fig. 5, Pl. xv.) were made for gauging the thickness of the coffer sides; the arms were of equal length, so that variations were read on the scale of their actual value at the other end. The scale was the gun-metal scale, O, screwed temporarily on to the projection at the top, and read by a line on a brass plate, underlapping it, on the opposite limb. The zero of the scale was repeatedly read, during the series of measurements, by putting an iron bar of known length (±·0002 inch) and parallel ends, between the steel points at the bottom, in place of the side of the coffer. The limbs I made of pine, 71 × 4 × 1, lightened by holes cut through them. The hinge was of steel plates, with copper foil washers between them to prevent friction, and closely fitting on a stout iron pin. The readings of the scale value corresponding to the gauge-piece were four times 5·77, and once 5·76, showing that there was no appreciable shake or flexure in the instrument as used.

R. As the steel tape and chain were often used, suspended in catenary curves, two terminal supports were made to hold the ends six inches from the ground. One support was simply a wedge-shaped stand with a hook on it;

the other support carried a lever arm, weighted so that it balanced with 10 lbs. horizontal pull from the point where the tape was attached; hence the stand was drawn back until the arm swung freely, and then there was 10 lbs. tension on the tape. But transferring apparatus was needed, to transfer down from the marks on the tape to the station mark; and to be able to read as instantaneously as if the tape lay on the station mark, for simultaneous readings at each end. After several experiments I adopted a horizontal mirror, levelled in the direction of the tape length, and supported at half the height of the tape. The edge of this mirror being placed just beneath the tape, the reflection of the tape marks could be seen side by side with the station mark; both marks being at the same virtual distance from the eye, and therefore both in focus together. Motion of the eye does not affect the coincidence, except when the mirror is not level, or not at half the height of the tape; and even then only if large variations occur together. The mirror, its stand, and level, I arranged to pack inside the wedge-shaped terminal support.

S. The thermometers were common mercurial and spirit tubes. I graduated them by freezing point, and a hot bath with a fine chemical thermometer in it. Divisions are most easily and visibly marked on the tubes by coating one side with whiting and a trace of gum, then scratching the lines through that with a point; and then fixing, by dipping the tube in thick varnish. The tubes were mounted with the divisions placed behind, and thus much spread out from side to side, as seen through the tube. The wooden frames were thick enough to protect the whole bulb and tube sunk in them; and the numbering could be safely trusted to the frame, though the accuracy of the divisions was secured on the tube. This plan of seeing the scale through the tube, might be improved on by instrument makers flashing a thin coat of opaque white glass down the back of the tube, and then etching out the divisions through it.

10. *a.* The principal angular instrument was a splendid theodolite by Gambay, said to have been used by the French in their share of the Anglo-French triangulation. It was of a very unusual form, the support of the upper parts and altitude circle being a pillar formed of the cone axis of the lower or azimuth circle; and the 10-inch or altitude circle being set on a horizontal axis parallel to the plane of it, so that it could be turned over horizontal, as an azimuth circle, with its centre over the axis of the fixed or 7-inch horizontal circle. This was a bold device for making available the full accuracy of the finest of the circles for either altitudes or azimuths, and it was quite successful, as I could never detect the least shake in the converting axis, even though this was taken apart every time the instrument was packed The total weight was so small—being only 37 lbs.—-that I could freely carry it, as set up for work, from station to station; but to avoid straining it in

travelling, and to carry it easier over rough ground, it was usually packed in three boxes : one for the 7-inch circle and feet, one for the 10-inch circle, and one for the telescope, levels, and counterpoise. Its original case was ludicrously clumsy, heavy, and dangerous—a sort of thing to need two stout sappers to haul it about, and to take care that it never was turned over.

The 10-inch circle was very finely graduated on silver to 5′, the lines being so close as to show diffraction spectra. It was read by four very long verniers of 100 divisions each, one division equal to 3″. The magnifying power originally provided was quite inefficient,* being but single lenses of 1½ inch focus. One of these I retained for index reading, and then fitted four microscopes of ¼-inch equivalent focus (or magnifying 20 diams. on 5-inch standard, or 40 diams., as opticians are pleased to magnify it): with these the reading was excellent, the average error of a single reading and graduation being only ·4″; or, combined with errors of parallax, by the planes of the circles being about $\frac{1}{400}$ inch different, it was 7″. The circle errors were determined by repeating the quadrants of the verniers around it many times, and then going round the circle by stepping the length of each vernier; thus each quadrant was divided up by the mean stepping of four vernier lengths of 8¼° each. These four values were mapped in curves, and a mean curve was drawn through them; this mean curve was ever after used (along with corrections for level, &c.) in correcting all the observations of each vernier independently, so as to detect any extraordinary error or reading. The instrumental errors were all small: the eccentricity of the circles was in the 10-inch=4·8″, in the 7-inch=15·5″; the difference of axes of inner and outer cones of repeating motion=5·2″; the difference between the two ends of the transit level-bearing and the steel pivots sunk in them=6 6″; the difference of the diameters of the pivots, and their errors of circularity, inappreciable. The runs of the four verniers were ·42″, ·92″, ·25, and ·12″ on 5′ or 300″. Of course, in field work, the errors of pointing, of vibration of the instrument, and personal errors due to wind, sand, heat, glare, and constrained positions, increased the mean error of reading; and, on the average, it is 1·1″ for a single observation.

The 7-inch circle was scarcely ever used; the long cone of it was so finely ground that, on being set on an ordinary table (soon after I had thoroughly cleaned it), the whole of the upper part of the instrument (about 18 lbs. weight) was seen to be slowly revolving in azimuth, without any apparent cause. On

---

* Instrument makers seem to ignore the fact that there is a definite law for the power of reading microscopes; the angular width to the eye of a minute as seen in the telescope should equal the width of a minute as seen in the microscopes, else there must be a waste of accuracy somewhere. The formula is—focal length of object-glass : radius of circle :: focal distance of eye-piece : focal distance of microscope. Of course, in compound eyepieces and microscopes the equivalent focal distance must be employed, inversely to that deceptive term "magnifying power."

examining it, it was found that, not being quite level, and the counterpoise of 5 lbs. not being put on it, its centre of gravity was not at the lowest point attainable ; hence the rotation. The telescope was equal in character to the rest of the instrument, the object-glass being 1·66 diam., and 16¼ inches focal length, and the eye-piece of high power and large field ; thus it magnified 35 diameters. The form of the slow motions was far superior to that of English instruments ; all the tangent screws had a steel ball on the shank, which worked between two circular holes, in plates which were clamped together by a fixed screw ; the nuts were also spherical, cut into two separate halves, and also clamped between circular holes. Thus there was practically perfect absence of shake, and great working smoothness, even when stiffly clamped. Another excellent device was the use of spring steel washers to all screws whose tension was in question ; the screws were all made to run dead home on a seat, and to produce pressure through a curved washer, which they flattened, either for fixed tension, or for rotation of an axis. Thus a slight loosening of a screw made no difference or shake, and no delicate tightening up was needed ; if the pressure had to be altered, the washer was taken out and bent accordingly.

The three levels of the theodolite were suitably delicate, the value of one division being 2·47″ (altitude), 4·92″ (transit), and 12·8″ (cross level). For these and every other level used, I adopted a distinctive system of numbering. Every level had a different number for the mean position of the bubble end, and the divisions were numbered uniformly in one direction, and not simply on each side of the mean. Thus the ranges were respectively from 5 to 15, 16 to 24, 28 to 32, 40 to 60, &c., on the levels called No. 10, No. 20, No. 30, No. 50, &c. ; and when once a number was recorded (the mean of the two ends was always taken mentally), it showed which level was read, and in which direction, with any doubt, or further note.

Other adjuncts that I provided for this, and also for the other theodolites, were slit caps (see Figs. 6, 7, 8, Pl. xv.). It is manifest that objects seen through a fine hole are always in equally good focus, no matter what may be the distance ; hence, if an object-glass is limited to a small hole, it does not need focussing. But definition is commonly required in only one direction at once, either vertically or horizontally ; hence a slit—which admits more light—will be as effective as a hole. When a line is quite invisible, by being out of focus, placing a slit cap over the object-glass, parallel with the line, will make it clear ; and it will be well defined in proportion to the fineness of the slit. Each of the theodolites were therefore fitted with two movable slit caps, fine and wide, to cover the object-glasses. As focussing is always liable to introduce small errors, by shake of the tubes in each other, these slit caps were adopted to avoid the need of changing focus continually from near to distant objects ; they also serve to bring near points in view, at only a foot or two from the glass. To be able to place the slit-cap on the end of the telescope, without shaking it, was essential. This I did by making the slit of thin steel spring; soldered to brass clutches, so as to grip the telescope by three points; provided also with a projecting tongue above, and another below it, whereby to bend it open for clipping it on (see Figs. 6, 7, 8, Pl. xv.). The smaller theodolites were also fitted with diagonal mirrors clipping on to the object-glass; these enabled the instruments to be very accurately centred without a plumb-line.

b. The 5-inch theodolite, by King, was an old one, and was obtained for rough work; but it had never been adjusted, so I had to take it in hand; and on finding its errors, after correction, to be even less than those of the 4-inch Troughton, I generally used it for all small work. I corrected it in the rectangularity of cones to the circles, of transit axis to the cones, and of cradle axis to transit axis; also in adjustment of verniers for run. The telescope was of long focussing-range when I got it, and I increased the range from infinite down to $5\frac{1}{2}$ feet focus, which made it very useful in near levelling, as in buildings; also I did away with the mere fit of sliding tubes for focussing; and made the inner tube run on four points, slightly punched up in the outer tube, and pressed in contact with them by a spring on the opposite side of it. The old level I replaced by a good one of Baker's, running 41·5″ to ·1 inch. Microscopes of $\frac{1}{4}$-inch equivalent focus were fitted to two arms, which were slipped together when required for use, and rode round on the compass-box; with these the average error of reading on the 1′ verniers was 7″.

The spider lines in this, and the next theodolite, were somewhat different to the usual pattern. When either a single vertical line, or a diagonal cross, is used, it blocks out any very small signal; and I have even heard of an engineer hunting in vain for his signal, because the line exactly hid it. To ensure greater accuracy, I therefore put in two parallel lines, crossed by one horizontal (needed for levelling); the lines being about $\frac{1}{400}$ inch apart; if closer they may cling together if vibrated, and it is awkward to separate them while in the field. Thus the interval of the vertical lines was about 1′, and signals could be very accurately centred between them.*

c. The 4-inch theodolite by Troughton was not often used, except where lightness was important; I fitted it with two microscopes, similarly to the 5-inch; and its mean error of reading was about 8″ on the 1′ vernier.

Though neither of these were transit theodolites, yet in practice I used them as such for all accurate work. By reversing the telescope, end for end, and upside down, and turning the circle 180°, all the errors are compensated as

* Spider line from webs is useless, as it is covered with sticky globules to catch small flies; the path-threads of the spider are clean, but thick; so that the best way of all is to catch a very small spider, and make it spin to reach the ground, winding up the thread as fast as it spins it out, dangling in mid-air.

in a transiting instrument ; the only extra source of error is irregularity in the form of the rings, which can be tested by revolving the telescope in its cradle.

h. For ascertaining the angles of the Queen's Chamber air channels I needed to measure as long a length of slope as possible, at about 8 feet inside a passage which was only 8 inches square. For this I pivoted an arm on the end of a long rod (see Fig. 9, Pl. xv.), and passed it into the passage in the dotted position at A ; on reaching the slope it turned itself up to the angle by pressure, the main rod touching the passage roof. The arm carried an index, which touched a scale attached to the main rod. This scale was divided by actual trial, by applying a protractor to the limbs and marking the scale. To read it, a candle was carried on an arm, which shaded the direct light from the eye ; and the scale was inspected by a short-focus telescope. Thus the readings were made without needing to withdraw the goniometer from the narrow channel, and hence the arm of it could be much longer than would be otherwise possible.

j. A large square, 35 and 45 inches in the sides, of sheet steel strips, 2 inches wide, and tinned together, I made for testing angles ; it was not exactly adjusted to squareness, but its angles were very carefully fixed, by triangulating a system of fine punched dots on the face of it ; and the edges were adjusted straight within about 003 throughout their length. It could be used for the absolute value of slopes of about 51° 50′ and 26° 20′, by means of a rider level placed on one edge of it, and reading by means of a divided head screw at one end. To render the square stiff enough sideways, it was screwed down (with round projecting screw heads, not countersunk) to a frame of wooden bars, 2 × 1 inch in section. I generally found, however, that it was best to measure a slope by theodolite and offsets.

k. l. m. n. These stands were used for the theodolites. Generally the 10-inch theodolite could be placed directly on the rock, or on a stone ; but when a stand was needed I used one about 30 inches high, that I made of 1 × 1 pine rod ; the top was stouter and about 12 inches triangle, and the feet about 30 inches apart, connected by cross bars. Thus it was of the octahedral pattern, a triangular face at the top, another at the base, and six faces around ; this being the only form absolutely free from racking. The screw feet of the theodolite rested on leaden trays on the top of the stand, which allowed free sliding for adjusting its centring. A similar octahedral stand about 16 high, was made of ½ × 1 inch pine, for the 5-inch theodolite ; in order to stand it in chambers or on stones. The instrument was clamped on to the stand by a screw from beneath, passing through a plate under the triangular top of the stand, and screwing into the base plate of the theodolite, which rested upon the top of the stand. Thus it could be slid about on the stand, to adjust its centring, and then clamped tight afterwards. The iron stand was of just the same pattern, but made of ¼ inch iron rod ; the rods were bent parallel where joined, and passed into sections of iron tube, the whole filled up with tinning. These small stands would stand on the top of the large one when required.

o. For signals in the triangulation, to show the places of the station marks, I made a number of short wooden cylinders, 1¼ diam., painted white, and standing on three legs of wire (see Fig. 10, Pl. xv). In order to enable these to be centred over the station marks by a plumb-bob, the cylinder was cut in two across the middle ; a diaphragm of thin card was then put in it, with a hole truly centred by adjusting a circle on the card to the outline of the cylinder ; and the two halves of the cylinder were pegged together again. Then, having a plumb-bob hanging by a silk thread through the hole, at whatever angle the cylinder could stand the bob would be always beneath its centre. The bob was fixed to hang at the right height, according to the irregularities of the rock, by drawing the thread through the hole, and pressing it down on a dab of wax on the top of the cylinder.

The plumb-bobs are all of a new pattern (see Fig. 11, Pl. xv). The point of suspension is generally too near to the centre of gravity, so that a slight shift in it would move the position of the lower end a good deal more. Hence the suspension and the end of the bob are here made equidistant from the middle. To avoid the complication of screw plugs to each bob, there was a large horizontal hole through the neck, to hold the knot ; and a smaller vertical hole in the axis of the bob for the thread to pass.

The finest white silk fishing line was found to be the best thread for plumb-lines, or for stretching for offset measures ; it does not tend to untwist, or to spin the bob ; it is only $\frac{1}{60}$ inch diam., well defined and clean, and very visible. Wax is invaluable for hanging plumb-lines in any position ; and a piece of wood an inch square, well waxed, if pressed against a stone warmed by a candle, will hold up several pounds weight.

For station marks on rocks or stones, I entirely discarded the bronze and lead forms. They may be very good in a law-abiding country, but I found that half of those put down by Mr. Gill, in 1874, were stolen or damaged in 1880. The neat triangular stones in which they were sunk also attracted attention. I therefore uniformly used holes drilled in the rock, and filled up with blue-tinted plaster ; they are easily seen when looked for, but are not attractive. To further protect them, I made the real station mark a small hole 15 diam. ; and, to find it easier, and yet draw attention from it if seen, I put two ½-inch holes, one on each side of it ; usually 5 inches from it, N.E. and S.W. Thus, if an Arab picked out the plaster (which would not be easy, as the holes are 1 to 1½ inches deep) he would be sure to attack a large hole, which is unimportant. Where special definition was wanted, as in the main points round the Great Pyramid, a pencil lead was set in the middle of the plaster. This cannot be pulled out, like a bit of wire, but crumbles away if broken ; and yet it is imperishable by weathering. To clean the surface of the marks, if they become indistinct, a thin shaving can be taken off the rock, plaster, and central graphite altogether. Where I had to place a stone for a station mark, I sunk it in the ground ; and for the base terminals I took large pieces of basalt, and sunk them beneath the surface ; thus a couple of inches of sand usually covers them, and they cannot be found without directions.

On reading this description of the instruments, it might be asked what need there could be for doing so much in adjustment, alteration, and manufacture, with my own hands. But no one who has experienced the delays, mistakes, expense, and general trouble of getting any new work done for them, will wonder at such a course. Beside this, it often happens that a fitting has to be practically experimented on, and trials made of it, before its form can be settled. And, further, for the instinctive knowledge of instruments that grows from handling, cleaning, and altering them, and for the sense of their capabilities and defects, the more an observer has to do with his own instruments the better for him and for them.

CHAPTER III.

METHODS OF MEASUREMENT.

11. FOR the general questions of the principles of the arrangement of a triangulation, and of the reduction of the observations, we must refer to the two appendices on these subjects. They are so purely technical, and uninteresting to any but a specialist, that they are therefore omitted from the general course of this account. We begin here with lineal measure, and then proceed to angular measure, including theodolite work in general.

For lineal dimensions, I always used the system of a pair of rods butting end to end, and laid down alternately, instead of making marks at each rod length. In testing measures, the value of the sum of two rods can also be obtained more accurately than the exact butt length of either of them alone. But for the more important points, the direct measurement of a space by a rod has been often abandoned for the more accurate method of referring all parts to horizontal and vertical planes of known position. This is a necessary refinement when precision is needed, and it specifies a form in every element of size, angle, and place. In the passages, where the use of horizontal planes was impracticable, a plane at a given angle was adopted, and the roof and floor were referred to that.

In the Great Pyramid, the King's Chamber was measured by hanging a plumb-line from the roof in each corner of the room ; and measuring the offsets from the lines to the top and bottom of each course on each side of the corner. Then the distances of the plumb-lines apart were measured by the steel tape on the floor. The heights of the courses were read on a rod placed in each corner. For the levels, the 5-inch theodolite was placed just about the level of the first course ; then at 24 points round the side a rod was rested on the floor, and the level and the first course read on the rod.

The coffer was measured by means of a frame of wood, slightly larger than the top, resting upon it ; with threads stretched just beyond the edges of the wood, around the four sides. The threads gave true straight lines, whose distances and diagonals were measured. Then offsets were taken to the coffer sides from a plumb-line hung at intervals over the edge of the wood ; its distance from the straight stretched thread, being added to the offsets, thus gave the distances of the coffer sides from true vertical planes of known relation to each other, at various points all over the sides. Similarly, the inside was measured by a frame, slightly smaller inside it than the coffer. The bottom was measured by raising the coffer 8 or 9 inches ; the theodolite was placed to sight under it, and offsets were thus read off to the outside bottom from a level plane, also reading the height of the plane of sight on a vertical rod ; then the theodolite was raised so as to sight over the top of the coffer, the height of its plane on the same fixed rod was read off to give its change of level, and then long offsets were taken to points on the inside bottom of the coffer. Thus the thickness of the bottom is determined by the differences of level of the theodolite, *minus* the two offsets. Besides this, a check on the sides was taken by a direct measurement of their thickness with the pair of calipers already described.

The antechamber was measured in the common way ; but the granite leaf in it had a bar placed across the top of it, with a plumb-line at each end of the bar, *i.e.*, N. and S. of the leaf. The distances of the lines apart were taken below the leaf, and offsets were taken all up the leaf on each side ; this was done at each end and in the middle of the leaf.

In the Queen's Chamber two plumb-lines were hung from the ends of the roof-ridge, their distance apart observed, and offsets taken to the side walls and to the ends. Offsets were also taken to the niche, which was, beside this, gauged with rods between its surfaces all over. The heights of the courses were also measured in each corner. The angles of the air channels were read by the goniometer already described.

The subterranean chamber was measured in the common way, with rods along the sides, but the irregularity of the floor, and the encumbrance of stones left by Perring made it very difficult to measure.

12. Turning next to measurements made with the theodolite, these generally included some determination of angular as well as lineal quantities. The straightness of the sloping passages was uniformly observed by clamping a theodolite in azimuth, pointing along the passage, and having a scale held as an offset against the wall at marked intervals ; thus variations in azimuth of the passage were read. On reaching the end, the assistant holding the scale stopped, the theodolite was clamped in altitude instead of in azimuth, and the assistant returned, holding the offset scale to the floor or roof ; thus variations in slope of the passage were read. The whole length of the entrance passage, and the ascending passage and gallery in one length, were thus measured. For the air channels on the outer face, where the floor is unbroken, a slip of board carrying a perpendicular mirror was let down the channel by a string, in lengths of 10 feet at a time ; and the dip to the reflection in the

mirror was noted by a theodolite at the mouth. It is then a matter of mere reduction to obtain the variations from a straight mean axis.

The horizontal measurements outside the Pyramid were entirely performed by triangulation; and this included in a single system the bases of the three larger Pyramids, the pavement of the Great Pyramid, the trenches and basalt pavement on the E. side of the Great Pyramid, and the walls around the Second and Third Pyramids. The Great Pyramid was comprised in a single triangle. This triangulation by means of the 10-inch theodolite occupied some months in all; some angles being read 14 times, and the fixed stations being about 50 in number, besides about as many points fixed without permanent marks. The first-class points were fixed with an average probable error of ·06 inch; and the least accurate points, such as those on the rough stone walls, were fixed within 1 or 2 inches. For fixing the points uncovered by excavation, a rod was placed across the top of the hole, and a plumb-line dropped from it to the point to be fixed. A theodolite was then placed near it, and was fixed in the triangulation by reference to known stations; the distance of the plumb-line from the theodolite, was then measured by the angle subtended by divisions. on the horizontal rod which supported it.

For connecting together the inside and outside measurements of the Great Pyramid, a station of the external triangulation was fixed on the end of the entrance passage floor, thus fixing the position of the passage on the side of the Pyramid. From this station the azimuth down the passage was observed; thus fixing the direction of the passage. And levelling was also carried up from the pavement and casing stones of the N. face to this station; thus fixing the level of the passage, and hence that of all the interior of the Pyramid. The positions of the passages of the Second and Third Pyramids, on their faces, were also fixed in the triangulation.

The base of the survey was thrice measured, with a probable error of ± ·03 inch (or $\frac{1}{280000}$ of the whole) by the steel tape. To avoid the need of a truly levelled base line, a series of blocks of stone was put between the terminals of the base, which are 659 feet apart; a stone was placed at each tape length (1,200 inches), and at each chain length (1,000 inches); and a sufficient number of stones were placed also between these, as to support the chain or tape in catenary curves throughout, with the usual 10 lbs. tension. The stones thus varied from 140 to 393 inches apart. Then, the distances and levels of the stones being known, the reduction to be applied to the tape as it lay on them to ascertain its horizontal length, were easily applied. No attempt was made to place a mark at exactly each tape length on the stones; but a scale of $\frac{1}{50}$ths of an inch was fixed temporarily on each stone at which the tape lengths joined; then the two ends of the tape were read simultaneously on the scales several times over, slightly shifting the tape each time in order to equalize the friction of its support : thus the distances of the zeros of the scales placed all along the base were ascertained, and hence the total length of the base.

For the height of the Great Pyramid a line of levelling was run up the S.W. corner, across the top, and down the N.E. corner, stepping 15 to 20 feet at each shift. Separate lines of level were twice run round the Pyramid, (including the basalt pavement, &c.), and the differences were under $\frac{1}{4}$ inch, both between them and from the levels of Mr. Inglis, excepting his S.E. socket. Thus a complete chain, from N.E. to S.E., to S.W., to top, across top, and to N.E. was made ; and the difference was only $\frac{1}{4}$ inch on the return, the total run being 3,000 feet distance, and 900 feet height. Besides this, an independent measurement by rods had been carried up each of the four corners of the Pyramid to the top ; generally two, and sometimes three or four, steps were taken in one length, and levelled to the nearest, $\frac{1}{10}$ inch, from the upright rod to the upper step, by a reversible horizontal rod with level attached. The intermediate courses in each length were also measured off. This gives all the course heights, and is regulated at every 10 or 20 courses by the accurate levelling on the N.E. and S.W. The same point was always used on each step, both in the measuring and the levelling, so as to avoid errors of levelling and dressing in the steps ; and each tenth course has a cross scored on the stone, at the point used in the levelling. The Third Pyramid was only measured by rods up the courses.

The angles of the ascending passages were not retaken, as Professor Smyth had already done that work fully ; but the angle to the bottom of the entrance was observed by the 10-inch theodolite, placed on a shelf across the mouth of the passage. The levels of the horizontal passages were taken with the 5-inch theodolite, placed in the middle, and reading on both ends. The level from the entrance passage to the ascending passage was read off on a single vertical rod placed in Mamun's Hole ; a theodolite being put first in the lower and then in the upper passage to read on it.

As a general principle, in observing down a passage with a theodolite, no dependence was placed on measuring the position of the theodolite, which was usually outside the passage in question ; but in all cases a signal was fixed in the passage near the theodolite, as well as one at the farthest point to be observed, and the azimuths of both were noted ; the distances being roughly known, the minute corrections to be applied to the azimuth of the further signal could be readily determined. The azimuth observations of Polaris always included a greatest elongation. For the dip of the entrance passage the 10-inch theodolite was clamped in altitude, at closely the true angle ; an offset was taken to the roof at the bottom, and the theodolite was reversed and re-read as usual to get the dip, reading level at the same time. Offsets were then read to points all up the roof, keeping the telescope clamped in its second position ; thus

E

it was not necessary to know the exact height of the plane of the roof above the theodolite. The azimuth of the entrance passage was determined down to Mamun's Hole, by connection with the triangulation, whose azimuth is otherwise known; and it was also determined down to the bottom by Polaris' observations. The azimuths of the horizontal subterranean passages were read by the 5-inch theodolite, placed at the bottom of the entrance passage, and reading on a signal at the top, and on candles placed in the passages;* the S. end of the S. passage being invisible from the theodolite, its candle was sighted on in line with its N. end candle, and the line measured off in the chamber. The azimuth of the ascending passages was measured by three theodolites used together; all of the telescopes were set to infinite focus, so as to see each other's cross wires plainly when a candle was held behind the telescope observed on. The 10-inch was put in the entrance passage, reading on a signal at top, and on the 5-inch; the latter was placed on the rubbish in Mamun's Hole, reading on the 10-inch and 4-inch; and this last was placed just above the granite plug blocks, reading on the 5-inch and on a signal at the top of the ascending passage. Thus a chain of angles was formed from signal to signal, quite free from any errors of centring the theodolites or station marks. For the angle of the Great Pyramid casing stones *in situ*, the 10-inch theodolite was placed on the steps above; the dip was read to points on the top of the casing stones, and on the pavement in front of them; and then offsets were measured from these points to the face of the stone. The Second and Third Pyramid casing was measured by goniometer and protractor.

Thus it will be seen that several fresh methods of observation have been introduced, in order to obtain greater accuracy and more information : in particular the methods of plumb-lines and optical theodolite-planes, with offsets from these, have yielded good results. A fresh feature in the discussion of observations is the introduction of "concentrated errors;" on the principle of showing all the divergences from regularity on their natural scale, while reducing the distances of the parts so that they may readily be compared together. This is the essential basis of the method of graphic reduction, described in the Appendix (shown in Traces of Observations, Pl. xvi); and it renders possible the use of graphic methods in work of any delicacy; it is also exemplified in the diagrams of the King's Chamber walls (Pl. xiii), and of the relation of the casing and pavement (Pl. x).

---

* Naked candles are good objects for observing on, where there is no wind ; the spot of flame, the white candle, or the thin wick, serving at different distances ; offset measurements can also be taken accurately to the wick. Lanterns were only used for outside work.

CHAPTER IV.

EXCAVATIONS.

13. IN Egypt all excavations are forbidden, and a special permission is required for any such researches, the law of treasure-trove being the same as in England. Having in 1880–1 done all the triangulation of my station marks, it was requisite in 1881–2 to connect them with the ancient points of construction. For this, therefore, I needed permission to excavate, and applied to M. Maspero, the courteous and friendly director of the Department for the Conservation of Antiquities; Dr. Birch kindly favouring my request. In order to save delay and needless formalities, M. Maspero at once said that he would permit me to work under his firman, on all the points that I had indicated to him in writing; the Bulak Museum being formally represented by a reis, who would observe if anything of portable value should accidentally be discovered, though such was very unlikely and unsought for. Under this arrangement, then, I carried on excavations for about six weeks, having during most of the time about 20 men and boys engaged. The total expense was only about £18, or £22 including the reis of the Museum. He was a son of old Reis Atweh, who worked for Prof. Smyth; a very polite man, who quite understood that his presence was a formality.*

The first work that needed to be done (and that quickly, before the travellers' season set in) was to open the entrance passage of the Great Pyramid again to the lower chamber. The rubbish that had accumulated from out of Mamun's Hole was carried out of the Pyramid by a chain of five or six men in the passage. In all the work I left the men to use their familiar tools, baskets and hoes, as much as they liked, merely providing a couple of shovels, of picks, and of crow-bars for any who liked to use them. I much doubt whether more work could be done for the same expense and time, by trying to force them into using Western tools without a good training. Crowbars were general favourites, the chisel ends wedging up and loosening the compact rubbish very easily; but a shovel and pickaxe need a much wider hole to work them in than a basket

---

* A notice of these excavations appeared at the time in the *Academy* of 17th December, 1881.

and hoe require ; hence the picks were fitted with short handles, and the shovels were only used for loose sand.   In the passage we soon came down on the big granite stone which stopped Prof. Smyth when he was trying to clear the passage, and also sundry blocks of limestone appeared.   The limestone was easily smashed then and there, and carried out piecemeal ; and as it had no worked surfaces it was of no consequence.   But the granite was not only tough, but interesting, and I would not let the skilful hammer-man cleave it up slice by slice as he longed to do ; it was therefore blocked up in its place, with a stout board across the passage, to prevent it being started into a downward rush.   It was a slab 20·6 thick, worked on both faces, and one end, but rough broken around the other three sides ; and as it lay flat on the floor, it left us 27 inches of height to pass down the passage over it.   Where it came from is a complete puzzle ; no granite is known in the Pyramid, except the King's Chamber, the Antechamber, and the plug blocks in the ascending passage.   Of these sites the Antechamber seems to be the only place whence it could have come ; and Maillet mentions having seen a large block (6 feet by 4) lying in the Antechamber, which is not to be found there now.   This slab is 32 inches wide to the broken sides, 45 long to a broken end, and 20·6 thick ; and, strangely, on one side edge is part of a drill hole, which ran through the 20·6 thickness, and the side of which is 27·3 from the worked end.   This might be said to be a modern hole, made for smashing it up, wherever it was *in situ ;* but it is such a hole as none but an ancient Egyptian would have made, drilled out with a jewelled tubular drill in the regular style of the 4th dynasty ; and to attribute it to any mere smashers and looters of any period is inadmissible.   What if it came out of the grooves in the Antechamber, and was placed like the granite leaf across that chamber ?   The grooves are an inch wider, it is true ; but then the groove of the leaf is an inch wider than the leaf.   If it was then in this least unlikely place, what could be the use of a 4-inch hole right through the slab ?   It shows that something has been destroyed, of which we have, at present, no idea.

Soon after passing this granite, we got into the lower part of the entrance passage, which was clear nearly to the bottom.   Here a quantity of mud had been washed in by the rains, from the decayed limestone of the outside of the Pyramid, thus filling the last 30 feet of the slope.   This was dug out and spread on the passage floor, to save having to carry it out up the long 300 feet of the narrow passage ; no truck arrangement could be easily worked, owing to the granite block lying in the passage.   Work down at the bottom, with two lanterns and six men, in the narrow airless passage, was not pleasant ; and my visits were only twice a day, until they cut through to the chamber.   Here I had the rest of the earth piled up, clear of the walls, and also of the well, and so re-established access to these lower parts.

In the well leading from the gallery to the subterranean passages, there is a part (often called the "Grotto") cased round with small hewn stones. These were built in to keep back the loose gravel that fills a fissure in the rock, through which the passage passes. These stones had been broken through, and much of the gravel removed ; on one side, however, there was a part of the rock which, it was suggested, might belong to a passage. I therefore had some of the gravel taken from under it, and heaped up elsewhere, and it was then plainly seen to be only a natural part of the water-worn fissure. This well is not at all difficult to visit ; but the dust should be stirred as little as possible. One may even go up and down with both hands full, by using elbows and toes against the sides and the slight foot-holes.

14. The next business was to find the casing and pavement of the Great Pyramid, in other parts beside that on the N. face discovered by Vyse : the latter part had been uncovered, just when I required it, in 1881, by a contractor, who took the chips of casing from the heaps on the N. face to mend the road. Thus the tourists to the Pyramid actually drive over the smashed-up casing on their way. On the three other sides the Arabs had some years ago cut away a large part of the heaps of casing chips, in search of pieces which would do for village building. Thus the heaps were reduced from about 35 to only 20 feet in depth, over the middle of the base sides of the Pyramid ; though they were not touched at their highest parts, about 40 or 50 feet up the sloping side of the Pyramid.

The shafts for finding the casing were then sunk first of all about 100 feet from the corners of the Pyramid ; and then, finding nothing there but rock (and that below the pavement level), places further along the sides were tried ; until at last the highest parts, in the very middle of the sides, were opened. There the casing and pavement were found on every side, never seen since the rest of the casing was destroyed a thousand years ago. Thus for the North casing four shafts were tried ; but no casing was found, except where known by Vyse. On the East side four shafts were sunk, finding casing in the middle one. On the South four shafts were sunk, finding badly preserved casing in one, and good casing in another, entirely eaten away, however, just at the base (see Pl. xii.). On the West side five shafts were tried, finding casing in one of them, and pavement within the casing line at the N.W. The East and South casing was seriously weathered away ; on the East it was only defined by the pavement being worn away outside its ancient edge ; and on the South it was found to be even hollowed out (Pl. xii.), probably by the action of sand whirled up against the base, and scooping it out like sea-worn caves. The shafts were cut as small as possible, to avoid crumbling of the sides ; and they were steined with the larger blocks where the rubbish was loose : ledges were left at each six feet down, for the men to stand on for handing up the baskets and larger stones. The Arabs never would clear away the loose stuff from around the shafts, without having special directions ; and often there was a long slope of 15 feet high of rubbish, just at the angle of rest, over one side of a shaft : this needed to be cut away and walled back. Both the excavators and myself had narrow escapes from tons of stuff suddenly slipping in, sometimes just after I or they had been at the bottom of the shaft : the deep Southern shaft no one but Negroes would work in at the last. As I did not uncover the casing on the North side, I did not oonsider it incumbent on me to cover it over again ; and the casing down the shafts is safe from damage, as it is too troublesome and dangerous for the Arabs to try to break it or carry it off : it would be far easier for them to work out more loose pieces from the rubbish.

Besides these shafts, many pits and trenches were dug to uncover the outer edge of the pavement. For the basalt pavement, the edge of the rock bed of it was traced on N.E. and S. ; but no edge could be found on the West. It was cleared at the centre, where the trenches converge, and was there found to be all torn up and lying in confusion, along with many wrought blocks of red granite. Further out from the Pyramid it was perfect in some parts, as when first laid. The trenches were cleared at the ends, where necessary ; the North trench was dug into as far as nine feet below the sand at present filling it, or about eighteen feet below the rock around it, but nothing but sand was found ; the E.N.E. trench was cleared by cuttings across and along it, so as to find the bottom of each part, and make certain that no passage led out of it ; the N.N.E. trench was cleared by pits along it, and traced right up to the basalt pavement. The trench near the N.E. corner of the Pyramid was cleared in most parts, and the rock cuttings around it were also cleared, but re-filled, as the carriage road runs over them. Thus altogether 85 shafts, pits, or trenches were excavated around the Great Pyramid.

15. At the Second Pyramid it was not so necessary to find actual casing, as it was arranged differently : the bottom course of casing had an upright foot 10 or 12 inches high, at the bottom of its slope, not ending in a sharp edge, like the Great Pyramid casing, which was very liable to injury. The end of the slope being thus raised up already some way, the pavement was built against the upright face, and to get depth enough for the paving blocks, the rock outside the casing was cut away. Thus the casing actually stood on a raised square of rock, some few inches above the rock outside it (see Pl. xii.), and the edge of this raised square was further signalized by having holes along it (5 to 10 inches long and about half as wide), to receive the ends of the levers by which the blocks were moved. This arrangement is very clearly shown near the W. end of the S. side, where a block of casing remains, but slightly shifted ; and therefore, where this raised edge was

found in other parts, it was accepted as being equivalent in position to the foot of the casing slope, without needing to find actual casing in each place.

At the N.E. corner the raised edge was found, scarcely covered over. On the E. side two pits were sunk, and the edge was found in one at the S. end. The edge was cleared at the S.E. corner. On the S. side the edge was found at the E. end, and the casing *in situ* cleared at the W. end. The S.W. corner of the edge was cleared. On the W. side the edge was found at the N. end. The N.W. corner was cleared, but no edge was found there. On the N. side the edge was found at the W. end. Thus the raised edge was found and fixed at eleven points around the Pyramid. The joints of the platform of huge blocks on the E. of it were partly cleaned to show the sizes of the stones. Three pits were tried on the N.W. of the Pyramid, and the edge of the rock bed of the pavement was found in two of them. Two trenches were made to examine the edge of the great rock cutting on the N. side of the Pyramid.

Twenty-three trenches and sixty-seven pits were dug to uncover parts of the great peribolus walls of this Pyramid. Thus it was found that all the heaps and ridges, hitherto called "lines of stone rubbish," were built walls of unhewn stone, mud plastered, with ends of squared stone, like *antæ*. The great barracks, consisting of a mile and a half length of galleries, was thus opened. Many fragments of early statues in diorite, alabaster, and quartzite, were found, as well as early pottery, in the galleries ; though not a five-hundredth of their whole extent was uncovered. The great hewnstone wall, built of enormous blocks, on the N. side of the Pyramid, was examined by pits ; and quarry marks were found on the S. sides of the blocks. Two retaining walls of unhewn stone, like those of the galleries, were found in the large heap of chips, which is banked against the great N. wall. These retaining walls contained waste pieces of granite and basalt. The great platform of chips, tipped out by the builders beyond the S. peribolus wall, was cut into in two places. Some early pottery was found ; and it was evident, from the regular stratification, that it had been undisturbed since it was shot there in the time of Khafra. Altogether, 108 pits and trenches were opened around the Second Pyramid.

16. At the Third Pyramid it was necessary to clear the casing at the base level ; and this was a more troublesome place to work on than any other. Howard Vyse reports that he abandoned his work here on account of the great difficulty and danger of it. The material to be removed consists entirely of large blocks of granite weighing a ton and upwards, which lie embedded in loose sand ; hence, whenever the sand was removed in digging a hole, it ran down from the sides, and so let one of the large blocks drop into the hole. The most successful way of getting through it was to bring up other stones and place them so as to form a ring of blocks wedged together around the hole, and

thus supporting one another. As there is no clear setting for the casing here as there is in the Second Pyramid, and as the substratum had been removed at the eastern corners, it was necessary to find the casing foot near each end of the sides, and not to trust to the corners. There was no difficulty in finding casing stones, as the casing still remains above the rubbish heaps on every side ; the work was to get down to the foot of it. This was done at the E. end of the N. side, at both ends of the E. side, at both ends of the S. side, and at the S. end of the W. side. The N.W. corner was very deeply buried, and several trials were made to get down, but without finding any place sufficiently clear of the great granite blocks ; here, therefore, I had to be content with fixing the edge of the fifth course of casing, which stood above ground, and projecting this down at the observed angle by calculation. Seven points in all were thus fixed, of the intended finished surface of the original casing at the bottom course. Besides this, eighty-four pits were made along the peribolus walls of this Pyramid; these holes showed that the walls were all built like those of the Second Pyramid, but less carefully. Ninety-one pits in all were made around the Third Pyramid. This makes a total of 284 shafts, pits, or trenches, sunk in the hill of Gizeh ; and in almost every case the objects sought were found.

17. Some few details may be useful to future explorers. The tools used were the ordinary native forms, with a few English tools for special purposes, as have been described. Of supervision the Arabs require a good deal to prevent their lounging, and Ali Gabri looked well after them, proving zealous and careful in the work : I, also, went out with them every morning, allotting their work for the day ; then visiting them generally just before noon ; and again before they left off, in the afternoon. Going thus round to six or eight places some way apart, and often stopping to direct and help the men, occupied most of the day. It is particularly necessary never to put more men on a spot than are absolutely needed to work together ; generally each isolated party was only a man and one or two boys ; thus there was no shirking of the individual responsibility of each man to get through his work. Every man was told what his party had to do, and if they were lazy, they were separated and allotted with good workers, where they would be closely watched. The men were allowed to choose their work somewhat, according to their strength and capabilities ; and if any man grumbled he was changed to different work, or dismissed. A very friendly spirit, with a good deal of zeal to get through tough jobs, was kept up all the time by 'personal attention to each man, and without any extra stimulus of bakhshish, either during or after the work. The wages I offered, and freely obtained labour for, were rather above what excavators are required to work for by the Museum ; but were far less than what had been paid there before by Europeans. For ordinary work the rate was 10d. a day, and 6d. for boys; for work inside the Pyramid, 1s. a day, and 7½d. for boys. The men were paid

weekly, and no attempts were made to impose, as I kept a daily register of the number employed. Ali received what I always paid him while I was living there, £1 a week, and 4s. for his slave and nephew sleeping in the next tomb as guards ; for this he was always at my disposal for work (though I did not occupy half of his time), and he made all purchases and arrangements with the neighbours, besides keeping me quite free from molestation or black-mailing by the other Arabs.

CHAPTER V.

CO-ORDINATES OF STATION MARKS AT THE PYRAMIDS.

18. THE station marks of the triangulation consist of holes drilled in the rock or stone, and filled with blue-tinted plaster, as already described (sec. 10). Where great accuracy was needed a graphite pencil lead was put vertically into the plaster. Thus the mark may be scraped clean, if bruised or defaced, without destroying the mark. To enable the station-mark holes of about $\frac{1}{8}$-inch diameter to be readily found, and at the same time to draw off attention from them, two $\frac{1}{2}$-inch holes, similarly filled, are drilled, in most cases one on each side of each station mark, at 5 inches from it, to the N.E. and S.W. I also utilized some few of Mr. Gill's bronze station marks, that had escaped the attention of the Arabs. The less important stations, of the rock trenches, are merely marked by a single $\frac{1}{2}$-inch hole, filled with blue plaster. The general position of the station marks are shown in the plan of the triangulation on Pl. i.

19. The co-ordinates of the station marks, &c., are reckoned from a line beyond the N. side of the whole area, and from a line beyond the E. side of the area : thus there are no minus quantities. The azimuth of true North on the system of co-ordinates is East of the approximate North of the system, or the azimuth of its Eastern boundary, by

$$+ \ 1^\circ \ 12' \ 22'' \pm 6''$$

and the value of the unit of co-ordinates in British inches is

$$00508259 \pm 00000003 \qquad \text{log. } \cdot7060853 \pm \cdot0000017$$

or the number of units in the inch

$$196\cdot750 \pm \cdot001 \qquad \text{log. } \cdot2939147 \pm \cdot0000017$$

TABLE OF CO-ORDINATES OF MARKED STATIONS.

Place.	Letter	From North.	From East.
S.W. corner of the 9th Pyramid	A	3 987 140	935 234
N. side of 2nd Pyramid Temple	B	5 393 798	3 411 980
N. side of 3rd Pyramid Temple	C	8 382 255	5 839 239
Top block of 5th Pyramid	D	9 143 054	6 836 560
N. side of 3rd Pyramid	E	8 072 225	6 840 249
Rock of hill, W. of 1st Pyramid	F	4 246 813	8 132 966
Tomb, No. 17, Lepsius	G	3 000 000	6 000 000
Hillock S.E. of 3rd Pyramid	H	10 092 621	5 571 047
Top of large building E. of 3rd Pyramid . .	J	7 828 554	1 491 863
Pile of slabs N.E. of 1st Pyramid . . .	K	1 300 292	1 425 399
Slab in ground N. of entrance of 1st Pyramid (Gill)	L	908 159	2 242 158
Tomb N.W. of N.W. corner „ „ .	M	1 483 587	3 431 388
Tomb W. of „ „ „ „ (Gill)	N	1 848 869	4 136 068
N.W. socket of „ „ (Gill)	O	1 844 679	3 173 572
Edge of floor of passage of „ „ .	P	1 993 386	2 221 893
N.E. socket of „ „ (Gill)	Q	1 880 871	1 381 354
Staff on top of „ „ . .	R	2 756 484	2 298 662
W. side of 7th Pyramid	S	3 007 571	915 729
E. side rubbish heap of 1st Pyramid . . (Gill)	T	2 706 202	1 477 899
S.E. socket of „ „ . . (Gill)	U	3 672 518	1 417 048
S. side on masonry of „ „ . . .	V	3 523 071	2 369 777
S.W. socket of „ „ . . .	W	3 634 188	3 206 895
W. side rubbish heap of „ „ . . (Gill)	X	2 745 956	3 073 389
Tomb, No. 44, Lepsius „ „ . . (Gill)	Y	2 926 171	3 863 947
E. end of base line, on block of basalt . .	Z	4 415 043	1 704 140
W. „ „ „ „ „ „ . .	α	4 306 415	3 255 538
Masonry above, and W. of, door, 2nd Pyramid .	β	4 732 762	4 900 971
N.W. corner of rock cutting round „ „ .	γ	4 146 945	5 968 245
N.W. corner „ „ .	δ	4 592 901	5 758 968
N.E. corner „ „ .	ε	4 632 817	4 092 173
S.E. corner (on masonry) „ „ .	ζ	6 251 313	4 157 284
S.W. corner „ „ .	η	6 262 182	5 785 021
W. side of rock cutting round „ „ .	θ	5 950 148	6 000 994
Wall W. of 3rd Pyramid	ι	7 563 291	8 109 839
N. side of 4th Pyramid	κ	9 054 182	7 586 701
N.W. corner of masonry of 3rd Pyramid . .	λ	8 035 816	7 200 134
S.W. „ „ „ „ . .	μ	8 761 575	7 230 130
S.E. „ „ „ „ . .	ν	8 786 405	6 488 386
N.E. „ „ „ „ . .	ξ	8 038 069	6 485 183
Masonry below door, 1st Pyramid . .	π	1 935 512	2 249 041
N. end of North Trench	ρ	2 082 608	1 180 207
S. end of „ „	σ	2 514 650?	1 175 360?

TABLE OF CO-ORDINATES OF MARKED STATIONS.

Place.	Letter	From North.	From East.
N. end of South Trench	τ	3 051 826	1 184 632
S. end of „ „	υ	3 463 988	1 180 826
W. end of E.N.E. „	ϕ	2 678 581	881 168
E. end of „ „	χ	2 648 862	568 721
S. end of Trial passages	ψ	2 549 708	721 984
N. end of „ „	ω	2 350 481	718 038

RESULTING CO-ORDINATES OF POINTS OF ANCIENT CONSTRUCTION.

Place.	From North.	From East.
Existing. { Casing edge on N. side of 1st Pyramid . .	1 866 612	2 281 355
„ „ E. „ „ „ . .	2 671 090	1 401 430
„ „ S. „ „ „ . .	3 646 300	2 515 643
„ „ W. „ „ „ . .	2 664 836	3 185 923
N.E. corner of casing of „ „ . .	1 884 598	1 385 776
S.E. „ „ „ „ . .	3 668 168	1 421 276
S.W. „ „ „ „ . .	3 632 521	3 205 195
N.W. „ „ „ „ . .	1 848 772	3 169 668
Centre of „ „ „ . .	2 758 515	2 295 478
N.E. corner of casing of 2nd Pyramid . .	4 630 771	4 089 656
S.E. „ „ „ „ . .	6 297 958	4 121 664
S.W. „ „ „ „ . .	6 265 598	5 789 181
N.W. „ „ „ „ . .	4 598 359	5 756 193
Centre of „ „ „ . .	5 448 171	4 939 173
N.E. corner of casing of 3rd Pyramid . .	7 998 215	6 437 758
S.E. „ „ „ „ . .	8 814 325	6 457 924
S.W. „ „ „ „ . .	8 793 987	7 275 727
N.W. „ „ „ „ . .	7 976 980	7 255 560?
Centre of „ „ „ . .	8 395 877	6 856 742

CHAPTER VI.

OUTSIDE OF GREAT PYRAMID.

20. THE materials available for a discussion of the original size of the base of the Great Pyramid are :—(1) the casing *in situ* upon the pavement, in the middle of each face ; (2) the rock-cut sockets at each corner ; (3) the levels of the pavement and sockets ; and (4) the mean planes of the present core masonry.

Since the time of the first discovery of some of the sockets in 1801, it has always been supposed that they defined the original extent of the Pyramid, and various observers have measured from corner to corner of them, and thereby obtained a dimension which was—without further inquiry—put down as the length of the base of the Pyramid. But, inasmuch as the sockets are on different levels, it was assumed that the faces of the stones placed in them rose up vertically from the edge of the bottom, until they reached the pavement (whatever level that might be) from which the sloping face started upwards. Hence it was concluded that the distances of the socket corners were equal to the lengths of the Pyramid sides upon the pavement.

Therefore, when reducing my obervations, after the first winter, I found that the casing on the North side (the only site of it then known) lay about 30 inches inside the line joining the sockets, I searched again and again for any flaw in the calculations. But there were certain check measures, beside the regular checked triangulation, which agreed in the same story ; another clue, however, explained it, as we shall see.

The form of the present rough core masonry of the Pyramid is capable of being very closely estimated. By looking across a face of the Pyramid, either up an edge, across the middle of the face, or even along near the base, the mean optical plane which would touch the most prominent points of all the stones, may be found with an average variation at different times of only 1·0 inch. I therefore carefully fixed, by nine observations at each corner of each face, where the mean plane of each face would fall on the socket floors ; using a straight rod as a guide to the eye in estimating. On reducing these observations to give the mean form of the core planes at the pavement level, it came out thus :—

	Case Plane Sides.	Azimuths.	Socket Sides.	Azimuths.
N.	9002·3	− 4′ 35″	9129·8	− 3′ 20″
E.	8999·4	− 5′ 26″	9130·8	− 5′ 21″
S.	9001·7	− 5′ 23″	9123·9	+ 1′ 15″
W.	9002·5	− 5′ 39″	9119·2	− 7′ 33″
Mean	9001·5	− 5′ 16″	9125·9	− 3′ 45″
Mean Difference }	1·0	20″	4·4	2′ 42″

Here, then, was another apparently unaccountable fact, namely, that the core masonry was far more accurate in its form than the socket square. It is, in fact, four times as accurate in length, and eight times as accurate in angle. This forced me to the conclusion that the socket lines cannot show the finished base of the Pyramid.

The clue which explains all these difficulties is—that the socket corners vary from a true square in proportion to their depth below the pavement, the sockets nearer the centre being higher.

This means that the sockets were cut to receive the foot of the sloping face, which was continued right down to their floors, beneath the pavement. (See Pl. xi.)

Hence the sockets only show the size of the Pyramid, where it was started from varying levels, which were all under the pavement ; and its true base upon the pavement is therefore 20 or 30 inches inside the lines of the sockets.

This exactly explains the position of the casing found on the N. side, as it was found to be inside the line of the sockets.

The test, then, of this explanation, was to find the casing on the other sides, fix its position, and see if it was likewise within the lines of the sockets. The shafts were accordingly sunk through the rubbish, two or three feet inside the socket lines ; and the casing was found on each side, just in the expected alignment. Without this clue, the narrow shafts might easily have missed the casing altogether, by being sunk too far out from the Pyramid.

Now having found the casing foot on each side of the Pyramid, it is settled that the faces must have passed through these fixed points, and when the casing was duly projected down at its angle of slope to the socket floors, it was found to fall on an average 4 inches inside the edges of the socket corners. This is what might be expected, as the socket sides are neither straight nor square ; so that this margin would be much less at a minimum than it is at their corners ; and it would be natural to allow some free space, in which to adjust the stone.

21. Having, then, four lines passing through the middles of the sides, what is to define the junctions of those lines at the corners? Or, in other words, what defines their azimuth? Was each side made equidistant (1) from its socket's sides? or, (2) from the core side at each of its ends? Or was a corner made equidistant (3) from the sides of its socket corner? or, (4) from the sides of its core corner? The core may be put out of the question; for if the sides followed it exactly in any way, they would run outside of the sockets in some parts. Which, then, is most likely: that the sockets were placed with an equal amount of margin allowed on the two ends of one side, or with an equal margin allowed at both sides of one corner? The latter, certainly, is most likely; it would be too strange to allow, say, 6 inches margin on one side of a socket, and only 2 inches on its adjacent side. It seems, then, that we are shut up to the idea that the socket corners lie in the diagonals of the Pyramid casing.

But there is another test of this arrangement, which it ought to satisfy. Given four diagonals, as defined by the socket corners; and given four points near the middles of the sides of the Pyramid, as defined by the existing casing: if we start from one diagonal, say N.E.; draw a line through the E. casing to S.E. diagonal; from that through the S. casing, to the S.W. diagonal; and so on, round to the N.E. diagonal again; there is no necessity that the line should on its return fall on the same point as that from which we started: it might as easily, apart from special design, fall by chance anywhere else. The chances are greatly against its exactly completing its circuit thus, unless it was so planned before by the diagonals of the socket corners being identical with those of the square of the casing.

On applying this test to the diagonals of the sockets, we find that the circuit unites, on being carried round through these points, to within ·1 inch; far closer, in fact, than the diagonals of the sockets and the line of the casing can be estimated.

This is, then, a conclusive test; and we only need to compute a square that shall pass through the points of the casing found on each side, and having also its corners lying on the diagonals of the sockets.

This square, of the original base of the Great Pyramid casing on the platform, is of these dimensions :—

	Length.	Difference from Mean.	Azimuth.	Difference from Mean.
N. . .	9069.4	+ ·6	– 3′ 20″	+23″
E. . .	9067·7	– 1·1	– 3′ 57″	– 14″
S. . .	9069·5	+ ·7	– 3′ 41″	+ 2″
W.. .	9068·6	– ·2	– 3′ 54″	– 11″
Mean .	9068·8	·65	– 3′ 43″	12″

Thus the finished base of the Pyramid had only two-thirds of the irregularity of the core masonry, the mean difference of which was 1·0 inch and 20″ ; this is what would be expected from a final adjustment of the work, after the rougher part was finished.

But it must always be remembered that this very small mean error of ·65 inch and 12″ is that of the sockets, and not that of the casing stones ; these latter we can hardly doubt would be adjusted more carefully than the cutting of the sockets with their free margin.

Also it must be remembered that this result includes the errors of survey. Now the probable errors of fixing the plumb-lines in the triangulation were about ·2 on E. side, ·2 on S. side, ·1 on W. side, and the casing ·1 on N. side ; the probable errors of the triangulation of the points of reference is in general much less than this ; we may then say ±·3 for the absolute places of the plumb-lines. The exact amount of this is not of so much consequence, because the errors of estimating the original points of construction are larger. They are, on the N., ±·04 ; on the E., ±·2 ; but another less satisfactory estimate differed 1·1 ; on the S., ±·2 ; on the W., ±·5, taking the mean of two points that differed 1·1 inches. Besides this, the estimation of the socket diagonals cannot be put under ±·5 by the bad definition of the edges and want of straightness and orientation of the sides. If we then allow that the probable errors from all sources of our knowledge, of each of the original sides of the Pyramid amount to ±·6, we shall not over-estimate them. Hence it is scarcely to be expected that our determinations of the sides should agree closer than ·65 inch, as they do on an average.

So we must say that the mean errors of the base of the Great Pyramid were somewhat less than ·6 inch, and 12″ of angle.

22. In computing the above quantities, I have used my final determination of the socket levels below the pavement ; these, with the first approximate results, and Inglis's figures, stand thus :—

	Accurate in 1882.	Approximate in 1881.	Inglis in 1865.
N.E. . .	− 28·5	− 28·7	−28·6
S.E. . .	− 39·9	− 39·9	−42·2
S.W. . .	− 23·0	− 22·9	− 23·0
N.W. . .	− 32·8	− 32·6	− 32·8

the level of the pavement being zero. The approximation was very roughly done, and it is strange that it should agree as well with the accurate determination as it does. From Inglis's measures I have subtracted 28·6, in order to reckon them from the pavement level ; by the exact agreement of my two levellings at the S.E. (which was taken second in the series each time, and hence is checked by othe thers), I conclude that Inglis is there in error by a couple of inches ; and his other work, in measuring the steps, contains much larger errors than this.

The relations, then, of the core masonry, the base of the casing on the pave-ment, the edge of the casing in the sockets, and the socket edges, are shown in Pl. x., to a scale of $\frac{1}{50}$. The position of the station marks is also entered. The inclinations of the various sides of sockets and casing are stated ; and it is noticeable that the core masonry has a twist in the same direction on each side, showing that the orientation of the Pyramid was slightly altered between fixing the sockets and the core. The mean skew of the core to the base is 1' 33", and its mean azimuth − 5' 16" to true North. The diagram also shows graphically how much deformed is the square of the socket lines ; and how the highest socket (S.W.) is nearest to the centre of the Pyramid ; and the lowest socket (S.E.) is furthest out from the centre of the socket diagonals, and also from the mean planes of the core.

23. For ascertaining the height of the Pyramid, we have accurate levels of the courses up the N.E. and S.W. corners ; and also hand measurements up all four corners. The levels ·were all read to $\frac{1}{100}$ inch, to avoid cumulative errors ; but in stating them in Pl. viii., I have not entered more than tenths of an inch, having due regard to the irregularities of the surfaces.* The discrepancy of ·2 inch in the chain of levels (carried from the N.E. to S.E., to S.W., on the ground, thence to the top, across top, and down to N.E. again), I have put all together at the junction of levelling at the 2nd course of the S.W., as I considered that the least certain point. It may very likely, however, be distributed throughout the whole chain, as it only amounts to 1·8" on the whole run.

These levels, though important for the heights of particular courses, have scarcely any bearing on the question of the total height of the original peak of the casing of the pyramid ; because we have no certain knowledge of the thick-ness of the casing on the upper parts.

The zero of levels that I have adopted, is a considerable flat-dressed surface of rock at the N.E. corner, which is evidently intended to be at the level of the pavement ; it has the advantage of being always accessible, and almost in-destructible. From this the levels around the Pyramid stand thus :—

	N.E.	E.	S.E.	S.	S.W.	W.	W.N.W.	N.W.	N.
2nd Course	+ 107·7	...	+ 105.5	...	+ 111·2	...	...	+ 106·6	+ 107·4
1st ,,	+ 58·6	...	...	...	+ 57·6	...	...	+ 58·0	+ 58·9
Levelled ⎰	0	E.N.E.	...	...	...	...	...	...	...
rock ⎱	− ·15	N.N.E.	...	...	...	...	...	...	...
Pavement		− ·6?	...	− 5·5 ?	...	+ 1·1 ?	− 1·2 ?	...	+ ·
Socket	− 28·5	...	− 39·9	...	− 23·0	...	...	− 32·8	...

* Owing to mistaking (in a photograph) the rock bed of the pavement for the pavement

The pavement levels, excepting that on the N. side below the entrance, are not of the same accuracy as the other quantities ; they were taken without an assistant, merely for the purpose of showing that it really was the pavement on which the casing was found to rest on each side. The differences of the 1st course levels, probably show most truly the real errors of level of the base of the Pyramid.

24. To obtain the original height of the Pyramid, we must depend on the observations of its angle. For this there are several data, as follows ; the method by which the passage and air channels determine it being explained in detail further on, when the internal parts are discussed :—

				Weight.
Casing stones, *in situ*, N. side, by theodolite . .	51° 46′ 45″	± 2′ 7″		7
(To three points on top and three on base.)				
„ „ „ „ by goniometer and level	51° 49′	1′		2
„ „ „ „ by steel square and level	51° 44′ 11	23″		0
„ „ 5 overthrown by goniometer . . .	51° 52′	2′		0
„ „ 18 fragments, all sides, „ . . .	51° 53′	4′		0
(All above 2 inches in shortest length.)				
N. face, by entrance passage mouth	51° 53′ 20″	1′		10
N. face, by air channel mouth	51° 51′ 30″	20″		5
N. face, weighted mean	51° 50′ 40″	1′ 5″		
S. face, by air channel mouth	51° 57′ 30″	20″		

In assigning the weights to these different data, the reason that no weight is given to the angles of shifted casing stones is that there is no proof that the courses did not dip inwards somewhat ; on the contrary, I continually observed that the courses of the core had dips of as much as $\frac{1}{2}°$ to 1°; so that it is not at all certain that the courses of the casing were truly level to 5′ or 10′, and occasional specimens showed angles up to 54°. The angle by means of the large steel square was vitiated by the concretion on the faces of the stones being thicker below than above, 1 inch of difference making an error of 6′. The small goniometer was applied to the clear patches of the stone, selected in nine different parts. These three casing stones *in situ* have not as much weight assigned to them as they would otherwise have, owing to their irregularities. One of them is 0·9 in front of the other at the top, though flush at the base—a difference of 4′. The datum from the air channel, though far more accurate than that by the passage mouth (being on a longer length), is not so certainly intentional, and is therefore not worth as much. (See sections 32 and 33 for

itself, Prof. Smyth has entered all the levels in his works (both of his own measures and those of others) from a datum 20 inches below the true pavement level. This has led him to reckon the first course as two ; hence all his course numbers must have one subtracted, and all his levels about 20 inches subtracted, to reduce them to a true start from the pavement surface.

details.) From all these considerations the above weighting was adopted. It is clear that the South face should not be included with the North, in taking the mean, as we have no guarantee that the Pyramid was equiangular, and vertical in its axis.

25. The staff which was set up by the Transit of Venus party in 1874 on the top of the Pyramid, was included in my triangulation ; and its place is known within ± ½ inch. From this staff, the distances to the mean planes of the core masonry of the Pyramid sides, were determined by sighting over their prominent edges, just as the positions of the mean planes were fixed at the lower corners of the faces.   Hence we know the relation of the present top of the core masonry to the base of the Pyramid. The top is, rather strangely, not square, although it is so near to the original apex. This was verified carefully by an entire measurement as follows :—

		Mean of four readings, 1881.	Mean of three readings, 1882.	Mean of all.	
Centre of Pyramid base	N. side .	226·0 ± ·5	223·7 ± ·2	224·5	± ·7
	E. side .	214·4 ·4	213·8 ·6	214·1	·3
horizontally to the	S. side .	215·0 ·6	215·0 ·4	215·0	·4
	W. side .	216·4 ·5	218·7 ·5	217·6	1.0

Now, at the level of these measurements, 5407·9 at N.E., or 5409·2 at S.W., above the base, the edges of the casing (by the angles of the N. and S. side found above) will be 285 3 ± 2·7 on the North, and 301·6 on the South side, from the vertical axis of the centre. Thus there would remain for the casing thickness 60·8 ± 3 on the N., and 86·6 on the S. ; with 77·6 for the mean of E. and W.   Or, if the angle on the S. side were the same as on the N., the casing thickness would be 69·2 on the S.   This, therefore, seems to make it more likely that the South side had about the same angle as the North.

On the whole, we probably cannot do better than take 51° 52′ ± 2′ as the nearest approximation to the mean angle of the Pyramid, allowing some weight to the South side.

The mean base being 9068·8 ± ·5 inches, this yields a height of 5776·0 ± 7·0 inches.

26. With regard to the casing, at the top it must—by the above data— average about 71 ± 5 inches in thickness from the back to the top edge of each stone. Now the remaining casing stones on the N. base are of an unusual height, and therefore we may expect that their thickness on the top would be rather less, and on the bottom rather more, than the mean of all.   Their top thickness averages 62 ± 8 (the bottom being 108 ± 8), and it thus agrees very fairly with 71 ± 5 inches.   At the corners, however, the casing was thinner, averaging but 33·7 (difference of core plane and casing on pavement) ; and this is explained by the faces of the core masonry being very distinctly hollowed.

This hollowing is a striking feature; and beside the general curve of the face, each side has a sort of groove specially down the middle of the face, showing that there must have been a sudden increase of the casing thickness down the mid-line. The whole of the hollowing was estimated at 37 on the N. face; and adding this to the casing thickness at the corners, we have 70·7, which just agrees with the result from the top (71 ± 5), and the remaining stones (62 ± 8). The object of such an extra thickness down the mid-line of each face might be to put a specially fine line of casing, carefully adjusted to the required angle on each side; and then afterwards setting all the remainder by reference to that line and the base.

Several measures were taken of the thickness of the joints of the casing stones. The eastern joint of the northern casing stones is on the top ·020, ·002, ·045 wide; and on the face ·012, ·022, 013, and ·040 wide. The next joint is on the face ·011 and ·014 wide. Hence the mean thickness of the joints there is ·020; and, therefore, the mean variation of the cutting of the stone from a straight line and from a true square, is but ·01 on length of 75 inches up the face, an amount of accuracy equal to most modern opticians' straight-edges of such a length. These joints, with an area of some 35 square feet each, were not only worked as finely as this, but cemented throughout. Though the stones were brought as close as $\frac{1}{500}$ inch, or, in fact, into contact, and the mean opening of the joint was but $\frac{1}{50}$ inch, yet the builders managed to fill the joint with cement, despite the great area of it, and the weight of the stone to be moved—some 16 tons. To merely place such stones in exact contact at the sides would be careful work; but to do so with cement in the joint seems almost impossible

The casing is remarkably well levelled at the base; the readings on the stones of the North side, and the pavement by them being thus :—

	W. End.	Middle.	E. End.	Pavement by Casing.	Core 40 ft. E. of Casing.
Casing { Front...	+58·83	+58·84	+58·90	−·01	...
Casing { Back ...	+58·84	...	+58·85	−·03	...
Core ...	...	...	...	+·02	+58·87
Pavement ...	[−·56]	[−·30]	[−·05]	·00	...

The pavement levels in brackets are on decidedly worn parts, and hence below the normal level, as shown in the fourth column. The average variation of the casing from a level plane of + 58·85 is but ·02; and the difference to the core level, at the farthest part accessible in that excavation, does not exceed this. The difference of pavement level out to the rock at the N.E. corner is but ·17 on a distance of 4,200 inches, or 8″ of angle.

27. The works around the Pyramid, that are connected with it, are :—(1) The limestone pavement surrounding it; (2) the basalt pavement on the E. side; and (3) the rock trenches and cuttings on the E. side, and at the N.E. corner.

The limestone pavement was found on the N. side first by Howard Vyse, having a maximum remaining width of 402 inches ; but the edge of this part is broken and irregular, and there is mortar on the rock beyond it, showing that it has extended further.   On examination I found the edge of the rock-cut bed in which it was laid, and was able to trace it in many parts.   At no part has the paving been found complete up to the edge of its bed or socket, and it is not certain, therefore, how closely it fitted into it ; perhaps there was a margin, as around the casing stones in the corner sockets.   The distances of the edge of this rock-cut bed, from the edge of the finished casing on the pavement (square of 9068·8) were fixed by triangulation as follows :—

N.N.W.   616·9 near the corner ; corner itself not found, nor any W.N.W. side.

615·9 at 570 E. of probable N.W. corner of pavement.
618·7 at 670 „ „ „ „
616·2 at 890 „ „ „ „

N. side $\left\{ \begin{matrix} 564 \\ \text{to } 568 \end{matrix} \right\}$ very rough and irregular, opposite entrance.

N.N.E.   529·0 at N.E. corner, N. side of it.

E.N.E.   538·8 „ „ „ E. side of it.
533·9 at 586 from N.E. corner.

No cutting found at S.E. corner.
536·5 at 846 from S.W. corner.
533·0 at 520 „ „
534·6 at 206 „ „

S.S.W.   529·6 at S.W. corner, S. side of it.

W.S.W.   536·0 „ „ W. side of it.
627·9 at 751 from S.W. corner.

From these measures it appears that there is no regularity in the width of the cutting ; the distance from the casing varying 99 inches, and altering rapidly even on a single side.   The fine paving may possibly have been regular, with a filling of rougher stone beyond it in parts ; but if so, it cannot have exceeded 529 in width.

The levels of the various works around the Pyramid are as follow, taken from the pavement as zero :—

Flat rock-bed of pavement W. of N.W. socket			...		−	23·7
„	„	„	beside N.W. „	...	...	− 21·6
„	„	„	N. of N.W. „	...	...	− 17·0
„	„	„	N.E. of N.W. „	...	...	− 15·9
„	„	„	before entrance	...	...	− 27·1
„	„	„	inner end of E.N.E. trench		− 26·9
Basalt pavement, E. side of it		...	...	...	...	+ 2·0
„	„	W. side, in excavation		...	...	+ 2·0

The Pyramid pavement must then have varied from 17 to 27 inches in thickness; it was measured as 21 inches where found by Vyse.

28. The basalt pavement is a magnificent work, which covered more than a third of an acre. The blocks of basalt are all sawn and fitted together; they are laid upon a bed of limestone, which is of such a fine quality that the Arabs lately destroyed a large part of the work to extract the limestone for burning. I was assured that the limestone invariably occurs under every block, even though in only a thin layer. Only about a quarter of this pavement remains *in situ*, and none of it around the edges; the position of it can therefore only be settled by the edge of the rock-cut bed of it. This bed was traced by excavating around its N., E., and S. sides; but on the inner side, next to the Pyramid, no edge could be found; and considering how near it approached to the normal edge of the limestone pavement, and that it is within two inches of the same level as that, it seems most probable that it joined it, and hence the lack of any termination of its bed.

Referring, then, to the E. side of the Pyramid, and a central line at right angles to that (see Pl. ii.), the dimensions of the rock bed of the basalt paving are thus :—

NORTH TO SOUTH.

From mid-line of Pyramid	{ 1046·0 to N.E.	1061·9 to N.W·
	{ 1077·7 to S.E.	1062·8 to S.W.
Total length	2123·7 E. side.	2124·7 W. side.
S. corner of opening on E. side	321·0 to mid.	756·7 to S.E.
N. „ „ „	693·3 „	352·7 to N.E.

EAST TO WEST.

Width traced	1006·6 + *x.*
E. side, from Pyramid base	{ 2153·0 N. end.
	{ 2148·0 S. end.
S. corner of opening on E. side to base	2169·0
N. „ „ „ „	2160·0

Next, referring this pavement to the trench lines :—

NORTH TO SOUTH.

N. trench, inner end from basalt	318·1
S. trench, inner end from basalt	327·9

EAST TO WEST.

{ N.E. corner to N. trench axis	1073·2
{ N. trench axis *there*, to Pyramid	1079·8
{ S.E. corner to S. trench axis	1022·6
{ S. trench axis *there*, to Pyramid	1125·8
{ S.E. corner to N. trench axis, continued	1075·0
{ N. trench axis *there*, to Pyramid	1073·0

Hence the plan of the basalt pavement seems to be two adjacent squares of about 1,060 inches in the side; the N. trench axis being the boundary of them, and there being a similar distance between that and the Pyramid. The outer side of the paving was laid off tolerably parallel to the Pyramid base; but the angles are bad, running 15 inches skew.*

29. Next, referring to the rock-hewn trenches alone, the dimensions of the three deep ones are as follow :—

NORTH TO SOUTH.

N. trench, outer end, to central line	. . . .	3510·2
,, ,, axial length	. .	2130·2
,, ,, inner end, to central line	. . . . . .	1380·0
S. trench, ,, ,, ,,	. . . . . .	1390·7
,, ,, axial length	. .	2093·7
,, ,, outer end, to central line	. . . . . .	3430·4
E.N.E. trench, outer end of axis N. of central line .	. . .	848·3
,, ,, axis cuts N. trench axis N. of central line	. . .	68·5

EAST TO WEST.

N. trench axis, outer end to base	. . . .	1085·5
,, ,, ,, inner ,, ,,	. . . . . .	1080·6
S. trench axis, inner end to base	. . . . . .	1125·4
,, ,, ,, outer ,, ,,	. . . . . .	1122·9
,, ,, ,, E. of N. trench axis, at centre	. . . .	49·7
E.N.E. trench, outer end of axis to base	. . . .	4213·2
,, ,, axial length from N. trench axis	. . . .	3231·1
,, ,, ,, ,, from actual bed of basalt	. . .	2112·6
,, ,, ,, ,, from straight edge	. . . .	2124·7

The slighter trenches are three in number :—

NORTH TO SOUTH.

N.N.E. trench axis cuts N. trench axis N. of central line	. . .	116·0
Trench by N.E. socket, end of axis from N. side of casing	. . .	643·3
,, ,, on the axis, from N. side of casing	. .	1630·8
Trench by trial passages, ends of axis N. of central line	. . .	{ 1563·3 / 1274·4 }

EAST TO WEST.

N.N.E. trench, axis cuts pavement, from N.E. corner	. . .	647·2
Trench by N.E. socket, end of axis from E. side of casing	. . .	203·2
,, ,, on the axis, from E. side of casing	. .	434·1
Trench by trial passages, ends of axis E. of Pyramid base	. .	{ 3161·6 / 3167·6 }

* The broken blocks of basalt, which border a track down the hill side E. of the Pyramid, are almost certainly from this pavement; they are of exactly the same stone, and have many worked faces remaining like those of the pavement. Their placing is quite rude, and looks as if done by some barbarian destroyers.

The subterranean passages are in one group :—

NORTH TO SOUTH.

Trial passages axis, N. of central line, at the station marks .   .   . $\begin{cases} 2233 \cdot 6 \\ 1220 \cdot 8 \end{cases}$

EAST TO WEST.

Trial passages axis, E. of central line, at the station marks .   .   . $\begin{cases} 3446 \cdot 7 \\ 3441 \cdot 2 \end{cases}$

Hence it seems that the axial length of the E.N.E. trench outside the basalt paving is intended to be the same as the axial length of the North and South trenches.

The angles of the axes of these trenches are as follow :—

	To E. Face of Pyramid.	To true North.
N. trench	+ 7' 53"	+ 3' 56"
S. trench	+ 4' 9"	+ 12
E.N.E. trench	+ 76° 2' 26"	+ 75° 58' 23"
N.N.E. trench	+ 24° 25' 34"	+ 24° 21' 37"
Trench by N.E. socket . .	+ 13° 9' 38"	+ 13° 5' 41"
Trench by trial passages .	− 1° 11'	− 1° 15'
Trial passages	+ 18' 40"	+ 14' 43"

Thus the angles between the trenches are: S. trench to E.N.E. trench, 104° 1' 43" (or 2 × 52° 0' 52") ; and E.N.E. to N.N.E. trench, 51° 36' 52.'

With regard to the details of these rock cuttings, the forms of the ends of the N. and S. trenches were plotted from accurate offsets (see Pl. iii.) ; and there is little of exact detail in the cutting to be stated. The axes at the ends were estimated by means of the plans here given, but on double this scale ; and the rock is so roughly cut in most parts that nothing nearer than an inch need be considered. The position of the inner end of the N. trench is not very exactly fixed, an omission in measurement affecting it, mainly from N. to S. In this trench I excavated to 110 below the present surface of the sand, or about 220 below the rock surface, without finding any bottom. The S. trench is more regular than the N. trench ; at the outer end its width is 205 to 206, and at the inner end 134·2 : it has a curious ledge around the inner end at 25 below the top surface. At the outer end the rock is cut, clearly to receive stones, and some plaster remains there ; also some stones remain fitted in the rock on the W. side of this trench. Built stones also occur in the N., E.N.E., and N.N.E. trenches. From the inner end of the S. trench, a narrow groove is cut in the rock, leading into the rock-cut bed of the basalt pavement ; this groove was filled for a short way near the end of the trench by stone mortared in. It was evidently in process of being cut, as the hollows in the sides of it were the regular course of rock-cutting. The rock beside the trenches is dressed flat, particularly on the E. of the

N. trench, and the W. of the S. trench, where the built stones occur. There is a short sort of trench, on the E. side of the S. trench (not in plan); it is about 25 wide, 70 long, and 50 deep, with a rounded bottom; the length E. and W.

The E.N.E. trench is very different to the others; it has a broad ledge at the outer end, and this ledge runs along the sides of the trench, dipping downwards until it reaches the bottom towards the inner end : the bottom sloping upwards to the surface at the inner end. There are stones let into this ledge, and mortared in place, and marks of many other stones with mortared beds, all intended apparently to make good the ledge as a smooth bed for some construction to lie upon. The bottom of this trench I traced all over, by excavations across and along it; looking from the outer end, there first came two ledges—the lower one merely a remainder of uncut rock, with grooves left for quarrying it—then the bottom was found about 200 inches below ground level; from this it sloped down at about 20° for about 200 inches; then ran flat for 300 or 400; and then sloped up for 300 or 400; then rose vertically, for some way; and then, from about 120 below ground level, it went up a uniform slope to near the surface, where it was lost at the inner end under high heaps of chips. At the outer end the width near the top is 152·8, and at 25 down 148·2; the lower space between the sides of the ledge widens rapidly to the middle, from the end where it is 43·0 wide above and 35·0 below. Towards the inner end the rock is very well cut; it has a row of very rough holes, about 6 diam., in the dressed rock along the N. edge of the trench, near the inner end. This dressed side of the trench ends sharply, turning to N. at 1603·6 from outer end of the trench axis; the width here is 170·1, or 172·3 at a small step back in S. side, a little E. of this point. The trench had not been clear for a long time, as many rudely-buried common mummies were cut through in clearing it; they were lying only just beneath the sand and rubbish in the bottom.

The N.N.E. trench was traced by excavations along the whole length of 2,840 inches, up to where it is covered by the enclosure wall of the kiosk. It is fairly straight, varying from the mean axis 2·1, on an average of five points fixed along it. The depth varies from 14 to 20 inches below the general surface. It is 38, 40, 39·2, and 36 in width, from the outer end up to a point 740 along it from the basalt pavement; here it contracts roughly and irregularly, and reaches a narrow part 18·2 wide at 644 from the pavement. The sides are built about here, and deeply covered with broken stones. Hence it runs on, till, close to the edge of the basalt pavement, it branches in two, and narrows yet more; one line runs W., and another turning nearly due S., emerges on the pavement edge at 629·8 to 633·4 from the N.E. corner of the pavement, being there only 3·6 wide. From this remarkable forking, it

H

is evident that the trench cannot have been made with any ideas of sighting along it, or of its marking out a direction or azimuth; and, starting as it does, from the basalt pavement (or from any building which stood there), and running with a steady fall to the nearest point of the cliff edge, it seems exactly as if intended for a drain; the more so as there is plainly a good deal of water-wearing at a point where it falls sharply, at its enlargement. The forking of the inner end is not cut in the rock, but in a large block of limestone.

The trench by the N.E. socket is just like the N.N.E. trench in its cutting and size; and it also narrows at the inner end, though only for about 20 inches length. It has a steady fall like the N.N.E. trench; falling from the S. end 5·5 at 50, 8·5 at 100, 14·3 at 190, 21·0 at 300, and 27·0 at 400 inches. The inner end is turned parallel to the Pyramid, the sides curving slightly to fit it.

The rock cuttings by it are evidently the half-finished remains of a general dressing down of the rock; the hollows are from 3 to 6 inches deep, and so very irregular that they do not need any description beside the plan (Pl. ii.).

The trench beside the trial passages is slight, being but 6 deep at N. and 17 at S.; it is 29·0 wide at N., 26·5 in middle, and 27·9 at S. Its length is 289, with square ends. The sides are vertical at the N., narrowing 3·5 to bottom at S.; ends shortening 3·0 to bottom. The bottom dips slightly to the S., the levels from the N. running 0, — 1·7, — 2·2, — 3·2, and — 5·8.

30. The trial passages (see Pl. iii.) are a wholly different class of works to the preceding, being a model of the Great Pyramid passages, shortened in length, but of full size in width and height. Their mean dimensions—and mean differences from those dimensions—as against the similar parts of the Great Pyramid, are:—

26° 32'	mean difference	·24'	Pyramid passage angle 26° 27'	mean diff.	·4'
41·46	„	·09	„ „ widths 41·53	„	·07
47·37	„	·13	„ „ heights 47·24	„	·05
23·60	„	·08	„ ramp heights 23·86	„	·32
81·2	„	·6	„ gallery widths 82·42	„	·44
28·63	„	·54	„ well widths 28·2	„	·3

The details of the measurements of each part are all entered on the section (Pl. iii.). The vertical shaft here is only analogous in size, and not in position, to the well in the Pyramid gallery; and it is the only feature which is not an exact copy of the Great Pyramid passages, *as far as we know them.* The resemblance in all other respects is striking, even around the beginning of the Queen's Chamber passage, and at the contraction to hold the plug-blocks in the ascending passage of the Pyramid (see section 38). The upper part of the vertical shaft is filled with hardened stone chips; but on clearing the ground over it, I found the square mouth on the surface. The whole of these passages are very smoothly and truly cut, the mean differences in the dimensions being but little more than in the finely finished Pyramid masonry. The part similar to the gallery is the worst executed part ; and in no place are the corners worked quite sharp, generally being left with radius about ·15. The N. end is cut in steps for fitting masonry on to it ; and I was told that it was as recently as 1877 that the built part of it was broken away by Arabs, and it appeared to have been recently disturbed ; in Vyse's section, however, the roof is of the present length, so the removal must have been from the floor. By theodolite observations the plane of the passage is straight and vertical within 5' or less.

31. Having thus finished the statement of the outside of the Pyramid and the works surrounding it, the next subject is the connection of the outside and inside of the building.

To determine the exact place of the passages and chambers in relation to the whole Pyramid, a station of the triangulation was fixed in a hollow just on the end of the entrance passage floor ; and this was thoroughly connected with three main stations. Levelling was also carried up from the casing and pavement below, to this station, and to the courses near it. Thus the inside, as far as Mamun's Hole, is completely connected with the outside ; and in the ascending passages beyond that, there is only 2' of azimuth in doubt.

32. The original length of the entrance passage has not hitherto been known, except by a rough allowance for the lost casing. But after seeing the entrances of the Third Pyramid, the South Pyramid of Dahshur, and the Pyramid of Medum, all of which retain their casing, there seemed scarcely a question but that the rule was for the doorway of a Pyramid to occupy the height of exactly one or two courses on the outside. That the casing courses were on the same levels as the present core courses, is not to be doubted, as they are so in the other Pyramids which retain their casing, and at the foot of the Great Pyramid.* The next step is to see if there is a course equal to the vertical height of the doorway ; and, if so, where such a course occurs. Now the vertical height of the doorway on the sloping face of the Pyramid (or difference of level of its top and base) would be 37·95 if the passage mouth was the same height as the present end, or 37·78 if the passage was exactly the same as the very carefully wrought courses of the King's Chamber, with which it is

---

* The awkward restoration of the casing that Prof. Smyth adopted (Life and Work, iii., Pl. 3) was forced on him by his mistaken assumption of the pavement level 20 inches under the truth (L. and W. ii. 137); hence by Vyse's casing stone measures he made the casing break joint with the core, in defiance of Vyse's explicit drawing of its position ; and was obliged to reduce the pavement to 5 or 10 inches, in place of the 21 inches recorded by Vyse. The drawing of "backing stones," at the foot of Pl. 1., vol. iii., L. and W., is equally at fault ; the casing stones which remain in the middle of the side, ending directly against the core masonry ; and the core at the corners only leaving 34 inches for the casing thickness. No backing stones exist behind the casing of the Third Pyramid or the cased Dahshur Pyramid.

clearly intended to be identical. On looking to the diagram of courses (Pl. viii.) it is seen that at the 19th course is a sudden increase of thickness, none being so large for 11 courses before it and 14 after it. And this specially enlarged course is of exactly the required height of the doorway, its measures running thus :—

By levelling at entrance 37·67, by measuring ⎫ mean. ⎪ 37·95 or ⎫ doorway
courses 37·8 ; by N.E. 38·1, S.E. 37·6, ⎬ 37·94 ⎪ 37·78 ⎬ height.
N.W. 37·5, S.W. 39·1.   ⎭ ± ·17 ⎪   ⎭

Here the agreement is so exact that it is far within the small uncertainties of the two dimensions. Hence, if the passage emerged at the 19th course it would exactly occupy its height (see Pl. xi.).* Besides this, it will be observed that there are two unusually small courses next over this, being the smallest that occur till reaching the 77th course. The explanation of these is clear, if the doorway came out in the 19th course ; an unusually thick lintel course was needed, so two thinner courses were put in, that they might be united for obtaining extra thickness, as is done over the King's Chamber doorway. These two courses are also occasionally united in the core masonry.

The crucial test then is, supposing the passage prolonged outwards till it intersects this course, how will its end, and the face of the casing, stand to the casing stones at the foot of the Pyramid? The answer has been already given in the list of determinations of the casing angle. It requires an angle of slope of 51° 53′ 20″ ± 1′ ; and this is so close to the angle shown by other remains that it conclusively clenches the result to which we are led by the exact equality of the abnormal course height with the doorway height.

The data for calculating the result are : (1) levels of the 19th course by entrance 668·30 and 705·97 ; (2) floor of passage at station mark, level 611·2 ; (3) which is inside the edge of the base of the casing horizontally, 638·4 ; (4) entrance passage angle at mouth 26° 29′ ± 1′ ; (5) entrance passage height 47·26.

33. By a similar method the air channels give a determination of the angle of the faces. It is true that the channels did not occupy a whole course like the entrance ; but as they are uniformly cut out as an inverted trough in the under side of a block which is laid on a broad bed, it is almost certain that they similarly continued to the outside, through the one—or perhaps two—stones now stripped off; and also that their floors thus started at a course level (see Pl. xi.).† If this, then, were the case (as the N. channel cannot by its posi-

---

* It should be explained that this is called the 20th course by Prof. Smyth, owing to his error about the 1st course and pavement level. His measure of it is 38 inches, and the two French measures give it as 37 and 38 inches.

† In the section of the S. air channel mouth published by Prof. Smyth, certainly "the joints are not put in from any measure," nor is any other feature of it. The passage, its bed, and top, are all about half of their true size, and the form of it is unlike anything that has been there, at least since Vyse's time.

tion have come out in any but the 103rd course on the face, and the S. channel in any but the 104th), they would show that the casing rose on the N. face at 51° 51′ 30″, and on the S. face at 51° 57′ 30″, as before stated. The various data are entered on the diagram of the channel mouths. The levels were fixed by measuring several courses above and below the present mouths, and thus connecting them to the course levelling at the corners of the Pyramid. With regard to the main part of these air channels, the details are given further on in the measures of the King's Chamber (section 56); and it is disappointing that they vary so much in azimuth and altitude, that they are useless for connecting the measures of the inside and outside of the Pyramid.

34. The sloping blocks over the entrance to the Pyramid, and the space below them, were examined (partly by means of a ladder), and measured; but the details are not worth producing here, as the work of them is so rough. The large blocks are as follows, in general size :—

	E. upper.	W. upper.	E. lower.	W. lower.
Length on top	[185]	[194]	$151 + x$	167·7
Length below	$117\frac{1}{2}$	121	$84 + x$	107·6
Breadth	80·0 to $91\frac{1}{2}$	88·3	82·6	81·6
Height of mid-line	[114]		91	
Lean of face	20′ to 2° *in*	2° 20′ *in*	20′ to 30′ *out*	25′ to 30′ *in*
Angle on top	35° 40′ to 39° 50′	mean 40°	38° 45′ to 50′	39° 30′
„ on base	38° 45′ to 50′	39° 30′	39° 20′ to 50′	39° 30′ to 55′
„ on butment	49° 50′ to 50° 10′	50° 40′	hidden	50° 30′

The measures in brackets are deduced from the angles and other measures. These blocks are much like a slice of the side of a casing stone in their angle; but their breadth and length are about half as large again as any of the casing stones. Their mean angle from 12 measures is 50° 28′ ± 5′. The thickness of these blocks is only 33 inches, and there are no others exactly behind them, as I could see the horizontal joints of the stones running on behind them for some inches. On the faces of these blocks are many traces of the mortaring which joined to the sloping blocks next in front of them. These were placed some 70 inches lower at the top, and were not so deep vertically. By the fragment left on the E. side, the faces of these blocks were vertical. In front of these came the third pair, similar, but leaning some $7\frac{1}{2}$° or 8° inwards on the face, judging by a remaining fragment. Probably a fourth and fifth pair were also placed here (see Pl. ix.); and the abutment of the fifth pair shows an angle of $70\frac{1}{2}$° or 73° in place of 50°. The successive lowering of the tops, leaning the faces in, and flattening the angle of slope of the stones as they approach the outside, being apparently to prevent their coming too close to the casing. These sloping blocks were probably not all stripped away, as at present, until recently, as there is a graffito, dated 1476 (half destroyed by the mock-antique Prussian inscription) on the face of the remaining block where it is now inaccessible, but just above where the next pair of blocks were placed. The sloping blocks are of remarkably soft fine-grained limestone, about the best that I have seen, much like that of the roofing of the chamber in Pepi's Pyramid; and it is peculiar for weathering very quickly to the brown tint, proper to the fine Mokattam l mestone, darkening completely in about twenty years, to judge by the modern-dated graffiti.

CHAPTER VII.

THE INSIDE OF THE GREAT PYRAMID.

35. HAVING, then, fixed the original position of the doorway of the Pyramid, we may state that it was at 668·2 ± ·1 above, the pavement of the Pyramid ; 524·1 ± ·3 horizontally inside (or S. of) the N. edge of the Pyramid casing ; and its middle 287·0 ± ·8 E. of the centre* of the Pyramid ; or 3723·6 from E. side, and 4297·6 from W. side, at its level ; the probable error being that of fixing the length of the sides. Thus we have the following positions in the entrance passage, reducing all to the true beginning of the floor :—

		W. Floor.	W. Wall Base.	W. Wall Top.	W. Roof.	E. Roof.	E. Wall Top.
Doorway, original . . .		0 ± ·3	0 ± ·3				
End of "basement sheet"		124·2					
Station mark		127·90					
	1	178·75					
	2	226·46					
1			276·63				
3		285·29					
2			331·79				
4		340·56					
2				348·10			
5		406·04					
3			414·21				
6		465·46					
4			474·02				
Scored line			481·59				
5			516·26				
7		531·67					
6			551·66				
8		584·15					
7			606·87				

(left margin, rotated: *Prof. Smyth's joint numbers.*)

* Whenever any point is described as E. of the centre of the Pyramid, it is uniformly meant that it is that amount E. of a vertical plane, parallel to the mean of the Pyramid's E. and W. sides, and which passes through the centre of the Pyramid. Similarly of similar descriptions N., S., and W.

	W. Floor.	W. Wall Base.	W. Wall Top.	W. Roof.	E. Roof.	E. Wall Top.
8		651·91				
9		686·98				
10	700·28					
11	736·28					
10		763·70				
12	776·39					
11		806·14				
13	827·16					
12		865·32				
14	878·58					
13		891·79				
15	915·09					
14		926·69				
16	963·61					
15		967·14				
16		996·27				
17	1003.69					
18	1028·59					
17		1056·78				
19	1063·82					
18		1106·13				
Floor Ascending Passage	1110·64					
20	1127·71					
19		1136·06				
21	1174·22					1163.6
20		1177·14	1177·7			
				1188·1		
					1192·4	1207·1
			1232·1			
					1243·7	1262·3
					1296·1	
			1318·5 Rock.	1340.1 Rock.		
						1347·5 Rock.
					1350·7 Rock.	

The above measures were taken by rods from 124·2 to 285·29 (the rods jointing together with butt ends), by steel tape from 276·63 to 1177·14, and by rods from 1163·6 to the rock; all duly corrected for temperature. On comparing them with Professor Smyth's measures, it will be found that his measures make the passage length about an inch shorter on an average; this is fairly accounted for (1) by his being all piece-meal measures added together, (2) by the rude method of making scratches with a screw-driver to mark the lengths of rod on the stone (L. and W. ii., 46), and (3) by there being "always a certain amount of risk as to the measuring rod slipping on the inclined floor" (L. and W. ii., 35). All these errors would make the reading of the length shorter than it should be ; and all were avoided by the use of a steel tape lying on the side of the floor. Nevertheless, I tested again, by rod measure, some of the points where the difference of Professor Smyth's measures were greatest from the steel tape, and they come out thus :—

Between Joints.	By Steel Tape.	Again by Rods.	By Prof. Smyth.
5 to 6 on Floor . . .	59·42	59·45	59·2
7 on Wall to 8 on Floor	22·72	22·72	22·2
14 „ 15 „	11·60	11·58	10·9
14 „ 16 „	36·92	36·93	37·6
15 „ 16 „	3·53	3·47	2·9

These will practically show what errors may creep in, by not using a continuous measure like a steel tape. The object of measuring the joints, as well as the total length, by steel tape, is sufficiently illustrated by this comparison.

One source of error may arise from following the coarsely-scratched prolongations of the anciently drawn lines, and of the ascending passage floor and roof. These have been made by modern measurers ; and they were always rejected, and a more accurate method employed.

The measures from the steel tape onwards, by rods, down to the end of the built passage, where it rests on the rock, are not of the same accuracy as the others ; the broken parts of the passage sides, and the awkwardness of measuring over the large block of granite, without any flat surface even to hold the rods against, prevented my taking more care over a point where accuracy is probably not of importance.

For the total length of the entrance passage, down to the subterranean rock-cut part, only a rough measurement by the 140-inch poles was made, owing to the encumbered condition of it. The poles were laid on the rubbish over the floor, and where any great difference of position was required, the ends were plumbed one over the other, and the result is probably only true within two or three inches. The points noted down the course of the passage, reckoning from the original entrance (*i.e.*, the beginning of the rock on the E. side of the roof being 1350·7), are the following :—

	E.	W.
Beginning of inserted stones, filling a fissure . . .	1,569	1,555
Joint in these stones	1,595	None.
End of these inserted stones	1,629	1,595
Sides of passage much scaled, 1 or 2 inches off, beyond here	2,750	
Fissure in rock	{ 3,086 to 3,116	{ 3,066 to 3,096
Mouth of passage to gallery		{ 3,825 to 3,856
End of sloping roof (4,137 Vyse, corrected for casing) .	4,143	

I

36. The azimuth and straightness of the passage were carefully measured. The azimuth down the built part was taken by reference to the triangulation, which in its turn was fixed by six observations of Polaris at elongation, from a favourable station (G). The azimuth to the bottom of the rock-cut passage was observed independently, by five observations of Polaris at elongation. The observations of the straightness throughout gives a check by combining these two methods, and they are thus found to agree within 19″, or just the sum of their probable errors, equal to only ·09 inch lineally on the azimuth of the built part. The results are :—

	Azimuth.	Altitude.
Mean axis of whole length	— 3′ 44″ ± 10″	26° 31′ 23″ ± 5″?
Mean axis of built part alone	— 5′ 49″ ± 7″	
Same, by offsets from 3′ 44″ axis	— 5′ 28″ ± 12″	26° 26′ 42″ ± 20″ ?
(Same by Prof. Smyth, two days . — 4′ 27″ and — 5′ 34″		26° 26′ 43″ ± 60″)

The observations of the straightness of the walls, floor, and roof of the passage, when all reduced to offsets from its mean axis of the whole length stand thus :—

Distance from original entrance.	From — 3′ 44″ azim.			From 26° 31′ 23″ alt.		
	W.	Mid.	E.	Roof.	Mid.	Floor.
460	21·1	·3 W.	20·5	23·2	— ·4	— 24·1
710	20·9	·2 W.	20·6	23·4	— ·2	— 23·9
990	20·7	0	20·8	24·1	+ ·4	— 23·3
1,110	...		...	...	...	— 23·4
1,291	21·1?	·1 E.	21·3	...	...	...
1,505	20·5	·2 E.	21·0	23·8	...	...
1,741	20·4	·4 E.	21·1	23·6	— ·1	— 23·9
2,069	20·8	·2 E.	21·1	23·4	— ·4	— 24·2
2,481	21·6	·3 W.	20·9	23·4	...	...
2,971	21·0	0	21·0	...	...	...
3,711	21·3	·4 W.	20·5	24·3	0	— 24·3
4,113 ?	21·3	·4 W.	20·5	23·6	— ·6?	— 24·9 ?
4,140	...	·	20·8	23·9	...	...
Mean error . .		·23			·30	

(Floor at 1,110 interpolated from clinometer curve.)

But the passage in the built part, and indeed for some 40 feet below that, is far straighter in azimuth than the lower part; taking this upper ⅔ths of it alone, it has a mean axis of — 5′ 49″ ± 7″ in azimuth, and varies thus :—

	W.	Mid.	E.
At 460	20·86	·06 W.	20·77
710	20·78	0	20·77
990	20·70	·05 E.	20·80
1,291	21·23	0	21·22
1,505	20·75	0	20·75
1,741	20·76	·01 W.	20·74
Mean Error . .		·02	

These offsets only being read to $\frac{1}{20}$ inch (the $\frac{1}{100}$ths merely resulting from computation) it is remarkable that the errors of the mid-line of the passage are so minute ; and it shows that in this particular we have not yet gone within the builder's accuracy ; readings to $\frac{1}{100}$th inch or to $1''$ on the longer distances, are now required.

The absolute position, then, of the middle of the S. end of the entrance passage floor will be, in level, 668·2—(4140 × sin. 26° 31′ 23″) – ·8 difference of floor offsets, = − 1181 ± 1 ? ; in distance from N. base of pyramid 524·1 + 3704·3 = 4228 ± 2 ? or 306 N. from mid-plane ; and in distance E. from the mid-plane 287·0—[sin. (3′ 55″ – 3′ 44″) × 3704] – ·4 difference of offsets =286·4 ± 1·0.

37. The Subterranean chambers and passages are all cut roughly in the rock. The entrance passage has a flat end, square with its axis (within at least 1°), and out of this end a smaller horizontal passage proceeds, leaving a margin of the flat end along the top and two sides. This margin is 4·5 wide at E., 3·2 at W., and 5·4 to 6·0 from E. to W. along the top. The dimensions and distances are as follow, from the S. end of the floor of the entrance passage (as deduced from the roof, which is better preserved) ; and the axial positions and levels are by theodolite observations :—

	Distance from End of E. P. Floor.	Distance from Mid. Plane of Pyramid.	Width E. to W. Top.	Base.	Mid. from Entrance Axis, continued.	Mid. E. from Mid. Line of Pyramid.	Height. E.	W.	Level above End of E. P. floor.	Level below Pyramid Pavement.
Beginning of Horizontal Passage ...	0	306 N.	40·8		·4 W.	286·4	48·5		0	−1181 floor
	20	...	32·9		1·0 W.	285·8	...		Top+ 38·3	−1143 roof
Fissure ...	76 W. 91 E.	...	...		...	...	...		...	...
In Passage ...	121	...	32·3	32·4	...	...	...		...	...
N. Door of Side Chamber .	218	88 N.	31·6	32·7	...	...	...		...	...
S. ,, ,, ,, ...	291	15 N.	31·9	33·0	...	...	...		...	...
N. Door of Large Chamber	346*	40 S.	32·0	33·3	·5 W.	286·3	35·5	36·0	Top+ 38·9	−1142 roof
S. ,, ,, ,, ...	672	366 s.	29·5	29·5	1·9 W.	284·9	31+2†		Top- 6·6	−1188 roof
In S. Passage ...	760	...	29·6	27·3	...	...	...		...	...
,, ,, ...	900	...	26·7	26·7	...	...	26·3	26·0	...	...
,, ,, ...	1040	...	28·1	29·0	...	...	28·6	27·0	...	...
,, ,, ...	1180	...	30·1	30·0	...	...	29·5	29·3	...	...
,, ,, End ...	1318	1012 S.		26·0	9·7 W.	277·1	...		Top- 2·6	−1184 roof
Large chamber, E. wall 325·9 ; at 100 from W. wall 329·6? ; N. wall 553·5 ; S. wall 554·1							..		Top+125·3‡	−1056 roof
Side chamber W. wall 69½ to 70½ ; N. wall 70·3 ; S. wall 72·3							..		{ Top + 40 to + 48	−1137 roof

The large chamber walls are therefore distant from the Pyramid central axis, 302·9 E. at N. wall ; 299·6 E. at S. wall ; 250·6 W. at N. wall ; 254·5 W. at S. wall ; 40 S. and 366 S. The central axis thus not passing through the chamber, but 40 inches inside the rock of the N. side.

* E. side of door-sill is at 351, and W. side 347, the wall not being fully dressed down there.

† This doorway rounds off at the top, rising 1½ inches in the 10 inches.

‡ The top is + 124·3 at N. doorway, 125·4 to 127·6 at S. doorway ; the roof being cut away higher, just in the corner.

The side chamber is an enlargement of the passage, westward and upward, as are all the chambers of the Pyramid ; it is very rough and uneven, and encumbered now with large blocks of stone.   The large chamber is most clearly unfinished, both in the dressing of the walls, and more especially in the excavation for the floor.   The walls have an average irregularity estimated at ±·7, and projecting lumps of rock are left untouched in some parts.   The roof is more irregular, estimated average variation ± 3.   The floor is most irregular, at the W. end it rises at the highest to only 10 inches from the roof ; and over all the western half of the chamber it is irregularly trenched with the cuttings made by workmen to dislodge blocks of the rock.   It is, in fact, an interesting specimen of quarrying, but unfortunately now completely choked up, by Perring having stowed away there all the pieces of limestone taken out of his shaft in the floor.   After dislodging several blocks, I crawled in over the knobs and ridges of rock, until jammed tight from chest to back in one place ; and thence I pushed about one 140-inch rod, by means of the other, so as to measure the length up to the Western end.   To measure along the W. side is impossible, without clearing away a large quantity of stones ; and as there is no place to stack them safely without their going down the shaft, I could only measure the width at 100 from the W. end, perhaps somewhat askew.   The lower—eastern— part of the floor, 140 below the roof, which is comparatively flat, is, nevertheless, very irregular and roughly trenched, quite unfinished.   The best worked floor surface is just around the square shaft, 198 below the roof, and about 40 below the main part of the floor, which is 155 below roof on a knob of rock beside the shaft.   The square shaft is not parallel to the chamber, but is placed nearly. diagonally.*   Its distances to the walls are, N.W. corner 135 to N. wall ; N.E. corner 60 to E. wall ; S.E. corner 90 to S. wall.   Its sides are, N.E. 68 to 75 ? S.E. 82½ ; S.W. 80 ; N.W. 70 above, 79 below (the N. corner being rounded above) ; N. to S. diagonal 100.   The S.E. and S.W. sides stop at 67 deep, or 265 below roof, or 1,321 under pavement ; leaving a ledge about 20 inches wide, a second or deeper part of the shaft goes downwards, the N.E. and N.W. sides being continuous with those of the upper part ; it is, in fact, a smaller shaft descending out of the N. corner of the larger.   The sides of the smaller shaft are, N.E. 57 ? S.E. 53 ? S.W. 60, N.W. 56.   The original depth of the smaller shaft I could not see, it was apparently about 40 inches according to Vyse, when Perring sunk his round shaft down in the bottom of the ancient square shaft.   This hole in the dimly-lighted chamber, about 30 feet deep (with water in it after heavy rains have rushed down the entrance passage), and with a very irregular and wide opening, makes measurement about here somewhat unpleasant. I avoided filling the shaft with the earth removed from the passage, or with the stones which Perring excavated from it, in case anyone should afterwards wish

* Like the shaft of the tomb chamber of Ti at Sakkara ; an unusual plan.

to excavate farther at the bottom. The southern passage is very rough, apparently merely a first drift-way, only just large enough to work in, intended to be afterwards enlarged, and smoothed; its sides wind 6 or 8 inches in and out.

38. The Ascending passage from the entrance passage is somewhat troublesome to measure, owing to the large plugs of granite that fill some 15 feet of its lower part; and also to the irregular way in which much of its floor is broken up.

For connecting it with the entrance passage, we must first settle the most probable value of its angle, in order to carry on the projection of its floor; and to complete it over the plugging and breakage, which prevent direct measurement. The angle of the whole passage will be discussed further on; it will suffice to say here that the mean angle is 26° 2' 30"; and there is therefore a presumption that the plugged part is about the same angle, and not the $26\frac{1}{2}^\circ$ of the entrance passage. This is confirmed by direct plumb-line measure of the angle of the plug-blocks at their lower end, giving 26° 7' ($\pm$ 2'?); and noting that the end is square with the portion of passage beyond it to within 5'. Also the actual angle of the plug-blocks may be computed from Prof. Smyth's sloping measures, combined with my levelling between the floors of the passages, and plumbing up to the lower end of the plugs.* This gives 26° 12½' for the angle of the lower 300 inches of the passage; and 5' of variation would require a difference of ·4 inch vertical on ·9 sloping. Hence the other data confirm this so far, that it had better be adopted as the angle through the plugged part; until some one shall improve on Prof. Smyth's sloping measure, or on my levelling.

The junction of the passages was not projected over the broken part uncertainly, as had been done before; but a plumb-line was hung from the W. side of the Ascending passage roof, in front of the plug-blocks; and measures vertical, perpendicular, and sloping, were taken to the plugs, the fragments of the ascending, and the top and bottom of the entrance passage. Thus the whole was knit together to a true vertical line, the place of which was fixed on the entrance floor. From the mean of these measures, and 26° 12½' as the ascending angle, with 26° 21' as the descending angle at that spot (by Prof. Smyth), the Ascending passage roof starts vertically over 1110·90 on the sloping floor of the

---

* The elements in question are (1) Prof. Smyth's plumb-line 48·5 on slope below his zero in Ascending passage; and (2) 180·5 on slope of entrance passage, below beginning of Ascending roof. (3) My level in A.P., 71·3 on slope above C.P.S.'s zero in A.P. (4) My level in E.P. 1015·0 on slope below C.P.S.'s E.P. zero. (5) Difference of my A.P. and E.P. level marks 156·2 vertically. (6) My plumb-line on E.P. floor 1027·3 on slope below C.P.S.'s E.P. zero. (7) Height on my plumb to floor of A.P. 37·0. (8) height of plug-blocks 47·3, and angle of end 26° 7'. (9) Angle of E.P. at junction 26° 21'. From these measures we get 125·1 tan. θ +142·9 sin. θ = 124·7; $\therefore$ θ = 26° 12½'.

entrance, reckoning from the casing face ; and the floor cuts the entrance floor at 1110·64 from the same, both probably ±·1.

Further, the lower end of the plug-block is 74·19 from the intersection of the floors ; and the upper end 50·76 from the intersection of the roofs. Having thus fixed the beginning of the Ascending passage, by the point where its floor produced onwards intersects the floor of the entrance passage, we can proceed up the Ascending passage from this as a starting point. The distance past the plug-blocks being determined as above described, and that from the plug-blocks to the S. end of the passage, by steel tape measure on the E. side of the floor ; then, the tape being corrected for temperature and tension, the results are thus, on the sloping floor :—

		Floor, E. side.	Base of E. wall.
Junction of passage floors		0	0
Beginning of actual floor		∴ 59·8	...
Base of plug-blocks		74·2	...
Top of plug-blocks, present		252·7	...
,, ,, ,, ancient		277 ?	...

Joint numbers. Smyth's.	Dixon's.	Floor, E. side.	Base of E. wall.
1	27	298·2	298·2
(Petrie's levelling mark		324·0)	...
2	26	about 333·6	333·6
...	25	...	374·9
6	23	496·6	496·6
7	22	552·3	552·3
...	21	...	593·3
8	...	604·4	...
...	20	...	637·9
...	19	...	690·3
10	18	716·1	716·1
11	17	749·0	748·9
12	...	799·1	...
...	16	...	812·1
...	14	...	848·1
13	...	854·2	...
15	13	922·4	922·2
16	12	955·0	955·3
...	11	...	1006·9
17	...	1008·0	...
...	10	...	1044·9
19	...	1080·3	...
...	9	...	1095·0
20	8	1130·0	1129·9
21	7	1161·5	1161·5
22	...	1202·4	...
...	6	...	1214·2
23	...	1255·4	...

Smyth's.	Joint numbers. Dixon's.	Floor, E. side.	Base of E. wall.
...	5	...	1273·2
25	4	1337·9	1337·9
26	...	1368·6	...
...	3	...	1377·7
27	...	1427·1	...
28	...	1488·7	...
...	2	...	1515·5
Gallery, plumb from wall over door		1546·5	...
29 Floor joint		1546·8	...
Wall joint ⎱ 1 And edge over door ⎰		...	1547·0

On comparing these measures with Prof. Smyth's, it will be seen that he makes the passage about 3 inches shorter; and that this difference mainly occurs in the lower part, where the floor is much broken. Several lengths were therefore measured as tests, just as in the entrance passage, and the results are :—

	1st measure by tape.	2nd measure by tape.	Prof. Smyth, by one rod.
Mark (1) to mark (2)	50·0	50·1	
Mark (1) to 22 (Dixon)	56·3	56·3	
22 Dixon to 21 Dixon	40·9 ⎱ 52·1	41·0 ⎱ 52·1	49·7
21 Dixon to 8 Smyth	11·2 ⎰	11·1 ⎰	
8 Smyth to 20 Dixon	33·3	33·5	
20 Dixon to mark (3)	8·3	8·2	
		by rods.	
11 Smyth to 12 Smyth	50·1	50·2	50·2
12 Smyth to 16 Dixon	13·0 ⎱	13·3 ⎱	
16 Dixon to 14 Dixon	36·0 ⎰ 55·1	36·1 ⎰ 55·1	55·3
14 Dixon to 13 Smyth	6·1 ⎰	5·7 ⎰	
13 Smyth to 15 Smyth	68·2	68·4	67·7

The close agreement of these two series of measures, particularly in those parts twice measured by tape, will show (as in the entrance passage) that the error is certainly in the rod measures, and due to the same causes as the error in the entrance passage, *i.e.*, slipping, irregular placing on broken floor, and the marking off of each length.

The result therefore is that from the intersections of entrance and ascending. passage floors, to the floor joint at the E. side of the grand gallery doorway, is 1546·8 on the slope.*

The granite plugs are kept back from slipping down by the narrowing of the lower end of the passage, to which contraction they fit. Thus at the lower, or N. end, the plug is but 38·2 wide in place of 41·6 at the upper end: the height, however, is unaltered, being at lower end 47·30 E., 47·15 mid, 47·26 W.; and at upper, or S. end 47·3. In the trial passages the breadth is contracted

* On the W. side this joint is 1·2 N. of the side joint of doorway.

from 41·6 to 38·0 and 37·5 like this, but the height is also contracted there from 47·3 to 42·3. These plug-blocks are cut out of boulder stones of red granite, and have not the faces cut sufficiently to remove the rounded outer surfaces at the corners : also the faces next each other are never very flat, being wavy about ±·3. These particulars I was able to see, by putting my head in between the rounded edges of the 2nd and 3rd blocks from the top, which are not in contact; the 2nd having jammed tight 4 inches above the 3rd. The present top one is not the original end ; it is roughly broken, and there is a bit of granite still cemented to the floor some way farther South of it. From appearances there I estimated that originally the plug was 24 inches beyond its present end.

It has been a favourite idea with some, that two horizontal joints in the passage roof just south of the plugs, were the beginning of a concealed passage: I therefore carefully examined them. They are 60·5 (or 60·1 second measure) apart vertically, and therefore quite different to the passages of the Pyramid, which are 47 perpendicularly or 52 vertically. Further, there is no possibility of the blocking up of a passage existing there, as the stone of the roof is continuous, all in one with the sides ; the three roof-blocks between the two horizontal joints are all girdle-blocks, either wholly round the passage, or partially so ; and the block N. of these is a long one, over 125 inches from E. to W., and continuous into both walls. These vertical girdle-blocks are a most curious feature of this passage (first observed and measured by Mr. Waynman Dixon, C.E.), and occur at intervals of 10 cubits (206·3 to 208·9 inches) in the passage measuring along the slope. All the stones that can be examined round the plugs are partial girdle-blocks, evidently to prevent the plugs forcing the masonry apart, by being wedged into the contracted passage. Many of the stones about the blocks in Mamun's Hole are over 10 or 11 feet long ; the ends are invisible, but probably they are about 15 feet over all.

39. For the angle of the passage, and its straightness, it will be well to consider it all in one with the gallery floor, as they were gauged together all in one length. The angle of slope I did not observe, as I considered that that had been settled by Prof. Smyth ; but the azimuth was observed, by a chain of three theodolites, round from the entrance passage. The straightness was observed by offsets to floor and side all along it, read from a telescope at the upper end of the plug-blocks. When I came to plot the results, I found that there were no measures taken at the point where Prof. Smyth's theodolite was set up. The sloping floor is nowhere, having been entirely cut away at the beginning of the gallery ; and the top of the ramp (to which the theodolite had been referred) was not offsetted by me, nor was its slope measured by Prof. Smyth's clinometer for 300 inches from the place. Hence we cannot say exactly what direct relation the theodolite bore to the passage ; but we can obtain the angle of slope very satisfactorily, by taking the angles observed to signal at bottom of ascend-

ing passage, and to signal at top of gallery, and then (knowing the distances of these signals) calculate the angle of slope from signal to signal. This, when corrected for lower signal being ·3 too high, gives 26° 12′ 50″ for mean angle of both passage and gallery together. Hence, from my offsets to the places of these signals, the absolute angle, and the variations from it, can be obtained for either part independently. Thus we have the form and direction of the ascending passage, reckoning from the beginning of its floor on the entrance passage floor, with its variations, as follows :—

From beginning	From −4′ ± 3′ azimuth.			From 26° 2′ 30″ altitude.		
	W.	mid.	E.	roof.	mid.	E. floor.
69	...	...	...	23·1	−·5	24·1
260	20·8	0	20·7	23·6	0	23·6
520	...	...	21·6	...	...	23·5
650	...	...	20·9	...	...	22·4
700	...	...	20·7	...	...	...
840	...	...	21·4	...	...	23·3
1,045	...	...	21·3	...	...	23·7
1,220	...	...	21·9	...	...	24·1
1,365	...	...	21·2	...	...	23·9
1,540	21·0	0	21·1	23·9	+·1	23·6

The surfaces are so much decayed and exfoliated, that it is only just at the ends that two original faces can be found opposite to one another ; hence the width and height cannot be measured, and the offsets can only be stated to one surface.

From this altitude, the sloping length of the passage being 1546·8, the horizontal length will be 1389·5, and the vertical height 679·7, both being corrected for difference in the offsets of the ends. The determination of the azimuth has, unhappily, a large probable error, ± 3′ (owing to bad foundation for the theodolite in Mamun's Hole) ; and its direction, − 4′, is so close to that of the Pyramid side, that it may be assumed parallel to that ± 3′. This, on the passage length, = 1·2 inches for the probable error of the place of the upper end of the passage, in E. to W. direction in the Pyramid.

These, added to previous amounts, give for the absolute place of the floor end at the latitude of the E. wall of the gallery (172·9 + 679·7) = 852·6 ± 3. level above pavement ; (1517·8 + 1389·5) = 2907·3 ± ·6 horizontally from N. edge of Pyramid, or 1626·8 ± ·8 northwards from centre ; and 287 ± 1·5 for middle of passage eastward from centre of Pyramid.

40. The horizontal passage leading to the Queen's Chamber is the next part to be considered. This was measured with steel tape all along, and the levels of it taken with theodolite. The results for its length and levels are thus, reckoning from the mean door of the gallery at 1546·8 from beginning of ascending passage :—

K

	Distance from door.	Northward from Pyramid centre.	Floor level.	∴ Roof level.
Mean doorway on floor ...	0	1626·8±8	852·6±·3	...
On flat floor	52	1575	858·4	...
Floor joint, No. 8, Smyth	312·0	1314·8	857·4	903·8
„ „ No. 16, „	623·0	1003·8	856·1	902·3
„ „ No. 21, „	870·2	756·6	...	...
On floor	1000	627	856·2	902·4
Floor joint, No. 25, Smyth	1177·7	449·1	...	...
Step in floor	1307·0	319·8	{ 854·6 / 834·9	901·0
		(All these are ±·8)	*(All these are ±·3)*	
Chamber { top of door ...	1523·9	102·9	...	...
N. wall { side of door ...	1524·8	102·0	...	...
Floor joint, No. 30, Smyth	1527·0	99·8	...	...
Niche, N. side	1620·7	6·1	834·4	...
Niche, first lapping ...	...	...	...	901·3
Chamber, E. apex ...	1626·5	·3	...	1080·1

The azimuth of this passage was not measured, but the beginning of it is 287±1·5 E. of the middle of the Pyramid; then for the axis of it at the end we may say the same, or 287±3, since the gallery above it only differs about two inches from that quantity. In the above measures of length there is a steadily accumulating difference of about 1 in 300 between Prof. Smyth's measures and these, for which it seems difficult to account; but as in the other passages, I have always found on retesting the measures, that such differences are due to errors in the cumulative single rod measures, and not in my steel tape (which was always verified at the starting point after measuring), it seems unlikely that the steel tape should be in error here. Hence I should adopt these measures without alteration.

41. In the Queen's Chamber it seems, from the foregoing statement, that the ridge of the roof is exactly in the mid-place of the Pyramid, equidistant from N. and S. sides; it only varies from this plane by a less amount than the probable error of the determination.

The size of the chamber (after allowing suitably in each part for the incrustation of salt) is on an average 205·85 wide, and 226·47 long, 184·47 high on N. and S. walls, and 245·1 high to the top of the roof ridge on E. and W. walls. The variations of the horizontal quantities in detail are as follows, from the mean dimensions.

Above Floor.	From below Apex, E. Wall.			From below Apex, W. Wall.			Below Ridge of Roof.		
	To N. Wall.	(Sum.)	To S. Wall.	To S. Wall.	(Sum.)	To N. Wall.	W. Wall.	to	E. Wall.
Mean of all	102·92	205·68	102·76	102·67	206·02	103·35		226·47	
240	...	...	...	...	...	...	−·46	225.51	−·50
210	...	...	...	...	...	...	−·31	225·79	−·37
180	+·16	205·67	−·17	−·14	broken	...	−·24	226·12	−·11
156	+·06	205·60	−·14	...	...	...	...	...	...
127	+·10	205·72	−·06	−·16	206·15	+·29	0	226·37	−·10
99	+·02	205·79	+·09	...	...	...	...	...	...
76	...	...	...	−·09	205·68	−·25	+·24	...	...
67	−·32	205·63	+·27	...	...	...	+·27	226·91	+·17
8	...	...	...	+·37	206·29	−·06	...	...	...
0	...	...	...	...	...	...	+·45	227·47	+·55

For example, to take the first entries, at 180 inches over the floor, on the E. wall, the N. wall is (102·92 +·16) = 103·08 from a vertical line below the apex of the roof; and the S. wall is (102·76−·17) = 102·59 from the same apex line : the sum of these quantities, or the total width, being 205·67. Thus the mean distances of the N. and S. walls from the apex on the E. and W. walls is given at the top of each column ; and beneath that the small variations from those mean vertical wall faces. In the last division are given the distances of the E. and W. walls apart, below their apices ; both the mean dimension, the variations from it, and the total at each point. It will be observed that the E. and W. walls have both a uniform tilt inwards ; if we allow 14′ for this as an average, the mean from a straight line inclined that amount is ·057 on E. and ·025 on W. ; a remarkably small amount of error, comparable to the extremely fine work and close joints of the stones themselves. Also the ridge of the roof is not exactly over the middle of the chamber at either end. Beside the above resulting length of the middle of the chamber on the floor, separate measures were taken on the two walls ; these give N. 227·41, middle (from above) 227·47, S. 227·61 ; mean of all 227·50 for floor length.

42. In the matter of height, the courses vary a good deal ; and far more care was spent on the closeness, than on the regularity of the joints. For a starting point in measurement, the general floor is hopelessly irregular, consisting plainly of rough core masonry ; and furthermore, it has been built over with similar rough masonry, which was afterwards stripped down to insert the chamber walls. This is proved by there being no fewer than eight edges of sunken spaces upon it, made (according to the universal habit of pyramid builders) to let in the inequalities of the upper course into the surface of the course below it. These sunken edges are well seen in other parts of the core masonry, and their

meaning here is unequivocal. But all round the chamber, and the lower part of the passage leading to it, is a footing of fine stone, at the rough floor level; this projects 1 to 4 inches from the base of the walls, apparently as if intended as a support for flooring blocks, which have never been introduced. It is to this footing or ledge that we must refer as the starting point; though what floor was ever intended to have been inserted (like the floor of the King's Chamber, which is inserted between its walls) we cannot now say. Certainly, a floor at the level of the higher part of the passage, would not reconcile everything; as that higher floor is also not a finished surface, but has sundry large round holes in it, like those in the chamber floor and elsewhere; intended, apparently, for use in process of building. Starting, however, from this footing at the base of the walls, the mean elevation of each course above the floor is as follows, with the variation + or − from the mean scale, at eleven points around the chamber :—

Mean of Corners.	N.W. Corner.		N.E. Corner.		E. Side, Mid.	Niche.	S.E. Corner.		S. W. Corner.		W. Side. Mid.
	W.	N.	N.	E.			E.	S.	S.	W.	
245·1	...	...	...	...	{N.+1·0 / S.− ·1}	...	...	...	...	...	{S. −·5 / N.−·6}
214·35	...	...	...	...	+2·05	...	...	...	...	...	−2·05
184·47	−·37		−·18		− ·47	−·47	−·01		+·55		− ·67
179·09	+·67	...	...	−·73	...	...	−·39	...	...	+·45	...
156·07	+·23	−·05	+·67	−·09	+ ·33	+·29	+·01	−·35	−·49	−·01	− ·17
127·13	−·23	−·11	−·03	+·12	+ ·17	+·28	+·50	+·31	−·41	−·20	− ·33
99·13	+·01	−·17	−·13	+·05	− ·03	+·05	+·32	−·11	−·09	+·08	− ·13
67·44	+·28	+·06	−·23	0	+ ·09	−·12	+·06	−·22	−·05	+·09	− ·05
34·13	+·01	−·24	door	0	+ ·17	−·01	+·22	+·02	+3·08	+3·38	− ·19
0		−·18	+·20		− ·2	+·42	encumbered				− ·26

The mean course thicknesses, and their mean differences being—from the base upwards—thus :—34·13 m.d. ·19, 33·31 m.d. ·18, 31·69 m.d. ·14, 28·00 m.d. ·21, 28·94 m.d. ·27, 28·40 m.d. ·48 to top of N. and S. walls. In the first column above, 245·1 is the apex of the E. and W. walls, where the sloping roof stones end at their junction; and the differences entered here, N. and S., are due to the N. and S. slabs not ending at the same level, one having fallen a little below the other in building; the highest shows, therefore, probably the intended point, and this is 1080·1 above the pavement. 214·35, in the first column, refers to the topmost joint on the E. and W. walls. 184·47 is the top of the N. and S. walls, and a joint on the E. and W. walls. 179·09 is a joint that occurs at each side of the E. and W. walls, but which does not run far, being soon shifted upward to the 184 level. 156·07, 127·13, 99·13, are all joint levels around the chamber. 67·44 is a joint level, signalized by the top of the doorway and of the channel mouths in N. and S. walls. 34·13 is a course around the chamber. And o is the fine stone footing of the walls, which is about the level of the variable and rough floor of the chamber. It must be remembered that the above figures only give differences from a mean scale, and do not profess to be levels ; the columns, in fact, being only rigidly connected at the two sides of any one corner, which hence have no dividing line between them in the table. Assuming, however, that the above series of heights of E. and W. walls are pretty closely adjusted to the heights in the corners next to each, we have for the sloping roof block, the following figures, calculating from the above quantities :—

	E. end, N. side.	W. end, N. side.	E. end, S. side.	W. end, S. side.
Sloping length	120·00	119·96	119·12	118·59
Angle	30° 48'	30° 14'	30° 33'	30° 10

These roof blocks are seen—where Howard Vyse excavated beneath one at the N.W. corner—to go back 121·6 on slope, behind the wall face ; this, coupled with the thickness of these blocks (which is certain, by similar examples elsewhere, to be considerable) throws the centre of gravity of each of the slabs well behind the wall face,* so that they could be placed in position without pressing one on another. Hence there is never any arch thrust so long as the blocks are intact ; they act solely as cantilevers, with the capability of yielding arched support in case they should be broken.

The projection on the western side of the doorway, mentioned by Professor Smyth, is really a surplus left on both sides of the corner ; in order to protect the stone in transit and in course of building. This undressed part in the chamber, is cut away down to the true surface at the top and at the middle joint, in order to show the workman exactly to where it needed to be dressed in finishing it off. The excess in the chamber begins 1·3 below joint at top of doorway, and thence projects 1·4, with a width of 5·5 ; it is dressed away for 1·05 at the middle joint, and then continues sloping away rather thinner down to the floor. The projection into the passage is 1·5 maximum at base, usually ·8 ; and it is 5·5 maximum width, or usually 4·5.

43. The niche in the eastern wall of this chamber, from its supposed connection with a standard of measure, was very closely examined. Its original depth back was certainly only 41 inches at every part from the bottom upwards. The surface that might be supposed to belong to the side of a deeper part, is only that of a joint of masonry, one stone of which has been broken up and removed ; this is evident as there is mortar sticking to it, and as it is pick-dressed, quite different to the fine surfaces of the niche sides ; beside this, it is not flush with the side, or any of the overlappings of the niche ; and moreover, all down the niche sides are the traces of the edge of the back, at 41 from the front, where it has been broken away.

*As at Sakkara, in the Pyramid of Pepi.

The general form of the niche was a recess 41 inches (2 cubits) deep back; 62 inches (3 cubits) wide at base, and diminishing its width by four successive overlappings of the sides (at each wall course), each of ¼ cubit wide, until at 156 high it was only 20 (1 cubit) wide, and was finally roofed across at 184 high. Thus, of the 3 cubits width of the base, one cubit was absorbed on each side by the overlappings, leaving one cubit width at the top. This cubit is the regular cubit of 20·6 inches, and there is no evidence of a cubit of 25 inches here. The exact dimensions of every part are as follow, giving the mean dimensions, and the variations of each part, + or −, from the mean. All corrected for the salt exudation on the two lower laps, as estimated at each point; there is no salt on the upper three laps :—

Level above Floor.	Height of Laps of Sides.					From plumb-line below apex of roof,			Width				Depth from back to front.	Excentricity from sides of chamber.
	Mean of All.	Front.		Back.		to N. side.	to Mid.	to S. side.	Mean.	Front.	Mid.	Back.		
		N.	S.	N.	S.									
183·80						15·20S.	25·08	34·95S.					40·72	25·32
170·	27·70	−·02	−·10	+·02	+·10				20·30	−·55	−·02	+·23		
										−·29	+·11	+·33		
156·10										−·17	+·15	+·26		
142·	28·94	+·08	−·06	+·16	−·22	10·21S.	25·21	40·22S.	30·43	−·42	−·08	+·23	41·06	25·39
										−·25	−·11	+·25		
127·16										−·02	+·06	+·35		
113·	28·23 (mid)	−·01	+·01	−·01	+·02	4·55S.	25·28	46·02S.	41·83	−·36	−·13	+·07	41·20	25·44
										−·20	+·05	+·19		
98·93										−·10	+·17	+·31		
83·	31·79	−·08	+·24	−·04 (mid)	−·14	·88N.	25·16	51·02S.	52·74	−·66	−·04	+·19	41·05	25·20
										−·46	+·10	+·34		
67·14						5·41N.	25·31	56.03S.		−·12	+·23	+·36	41·10	25·10
33·70	67·14	−·22	+·23						61·74	−·30	−·10	+·21	41·32	
										−·28	0	+·26		
0										−·32	+·19	+·31		
Means		·08	·13	·06	·12		25·19		41·41	−·30	+·04	+·26	41·07	25·29

44. The channels leading from this chamber were measured by the goniometer already described (*h*, section 10); they are exactly like the air channels in the King's Chamber in their appearance, but were covered over the mouth by a plate of stone, left not cut through in the chamber wall; no outer end has yet been found for either of them, though searched for by Mr. Waynman Dixon, C.E., who first discovered them, and also by myself on the N. face of the Pyramid.

The N. channel is 8·6 high, and about 8 wide in the chamber wall, running horizontally for 76 inches, and then turning upwards. The S. channel is 8·8 high, and runs 80·0 to its turn upwards. The mean angles, measured between the horizontal part and the ascending slope of the channels, are thus :—

	N. Channel.				S. Channel.		
W.	Mid.	E.	Mean.	W.	Mid.	E.	Mean.
37° 33′	37° 25′	37° 25′	37° 28′	38° 28′	38° 20′	38° 35′	38° 28′

each statement being the mean of two observations, which never differed more than 6′.

Hence, if these channels were continued to the outside of the Pyramid, their floors would end on the Pyramid faces at 2641·3 above the base, and 2460·8 from the centre of the Pyramid on the N. face ; and at 2679·1 above the base, and 2431·2 from the centre on the S. face. I observed something like the mouth of a hole in the 85th course on the S. face, scanning it with a telescope from below ; but I was hindered from examining it closely.

45. Returning now to the gallery from which we diverged to the Queen's Chamber, the length of the gallery was measured like the other passages, with the steel tape, but not many joints were measured, and those were on the E. ramp, on which the tape was laid at 6 inches from the edge. The offsets to the floor and E. ramp were also read, in continuation of the series of the ascending passage, as explained before (section 39). The results are as follow, starting from the N. wall of the gallery, at 1546·8 from beginning of ascending passage.

		Distance on Slope.	Variations from Mean Axis of + 1′ 20″ azimuth.			Variations from Mean Axis of 26° 16′ 40″ altitude.	
			W.	Mid.	E.	Ramp Top.	Floor.
N. wall . . .		o	...	...	...	[1·6	22·3]
	At	30	20·9	·1 E.	21·2	...	...
First joint, vertical .		44·6	...	...	...	...	...
	At	150	20·7	·2 W.	20·3	...	...
Joint at "cut off" vertical		223·2	...	...	...	...	...
Face of " cut off " .		223·7	...	...	...	...	...
Second " cut off " .		263·8	...	...	...	...	...
Joint . . .		264·1	20·9	o	20·9	2·0	22·9
	At	400	21·0	·2 E.	21·4	2·3	23·1
	At	700	20·8	·4 E.	21·6	2·6	23·6
Joint . . .		912·4	...	...	...	...	...
	At	1,000	21·1	o	21·0	1·5	23·4
Joint, broken to next		1087·0	...	...	...	...	...
Joint . . .		1186·5	...	...	...	...	...
	At	1,300	21·5	·3 W.	20·8	2·3	23·3
Joint . . .		1454·6	...	...	...	...	...
	At	1,600	21·2	·1 E.	21·4	2·1	22·2
Ramp End . .		1815·5	21·3	o	21·2	1·8	22·1
S. wall, in same line		1883·6	...	...	...	...	...

In the variations in altitude, the height of the axis above the ramp top is stated, as well as its height over the floor. The axis, though different in azimuth and altitude from that of the ascending passage, is reckoned to start from the end of it ; hence the offsets are a continuous series, though measured from a line which is bent on passing from the passage to the gallery. The first-stated floor offset here (in brackets) is not what the continuation of the floor of the ascending passage actually is at the point; but it is the virtual floor of the gallery, *i.e.*, where it would come if the trend of the rest of the gallery was continued, and also (judging by the altitude observations of Prof. Smyth) where it would come if continued parallel to the ramp top.

By successive rod measures, Prof. Smyth made the gallery ·8 shorter than it appears by this continuous measure ; but the continuous measure is certainly better in principle and also in practice, as we have seen in the other passages. The steel tape of 1,200 inches required to be shifted in order to measure from one end to the other of the gallery, and three points were common to both tape lengths ; the distances between these points were 305·5 by first, 305 6 by second measure, and 480·2 by both first and second measures, showing the same accuracy in this as in the taping of the other passages. The difference between Prof. Smyth's measures and the taping occurs almost entirely from the N. wall to the cut out in the floor, and is probably due to want of straightness and squareness in one or other of those surfaces.

Hence the floor of the gallery intersects the S. wall at 1689·0 ± ·5 above the pavement ; at 61·7 ± ·8 S. of the Pyramid centre ; and its middle is 284·4 ± 2·8 E. of the Pyramid centre ; reckoning the measures of length and angle continuously through from the plug-blocks upwards, so as to avoid all uncertainties of connection at the beginning of the gallery, and duly correcting for difference in offsets.

46. The holes cut in the ramps or benches, along the sides of the gallery (see section of them in Pl. ix.), the blocks inserted in the wall over each, and the rough chopping out of a groove across each block—all these features are as yet inexplicable. One remarkable point is that the holes are alternately long and short, on both sides of the gallery ; the mean of the long holes is 23·32, with an average variation of ·73, and the mean of the short holes is 20·51, with average variation ·40. Thus the horizontal length of a long hole is equal to the sloping length of a short hole, both being one cubit. This relation is true within less than half their average variations.

The roof of the gallery and its walls are not well known, owing to the difficulty of reaching them. By means of ladders, that I made jointing together, I was able to thoroughly examine both ends and parts of the sides of the gallery. The roof stones are set each at a steeper slope than the passage, in order that the lower edge of each stone should hitch like a paul into a ratchet-cut in the top of the walls; hence no stone can press on the one below it, so as to cause a cumulative pressure all down the roof ; and each stone is separately upheld by the side walls across which it lies. The depth of two of these ratchet-cuts, at the S. end, I measured as 1·0 and 1·9 to 2·0 ; and the angles of the two slabs there 28° 0′ to 28° 18′, and 27° 56′ to 28° 30′, mean 28° 11′; which on a mean slab 52·2 from N. to S., would differ 1·74 inches from the passage slope. The edge of the southernmost slab is 14·5 from the S. wall; the next slab is 47·4 from N. to S.

The verticality of the ends of the gallery was measured from a plumb-line; and the horizontal distances of the top and bottom of each of the laps of stone from the ends of the roof are thus :—

Laps.		N. End.	Lean out.	S. End.	Lean in.	High on S. End.	Lap on W side.
8		o (?)		o		33·6	
7	top	3·0	o	2·9	−·08	33·7	2·3
	base	3·0		2·82			
			h				
6	top	6·2	+·2	5·80	o	33·0	3·1
	base	6·0		5·80			
			s				
5	top	9·1	+·6	9·00	o	34·0	3·0
	base	8·5		9·00			
			h				
4	top	11·9	−·2	12·08	+·10	33·8	2·9
	base	12·1		12·18			
			h				
3	top	15·1	+·1	15·08	+·10		
	base	15·0		15·18			
			s				
2	top	19·7	+·1	18·10	+·45		
	base	19·5		18·55			
1	top	19·6	+·4	21·5	−·25		
	base	19·2	+1·2	21·7	+·32		
				21·25			

The letters h and s in the column of the N. end show the under edge of the lap of stone to be either horizontal or sloping; on the S. end it is always horizontal. The width of the top of the gallery is 40·9 at N., and 41·3 at S. end. The remarkable groove in the lower part of the third lap, along the whole length of the sides, was measured thus, perpendicularly :—

	N.W.	N.E.	S.W.	S.E.	mean.
Groove upwards	11·7	11·8	11·2	11·0	11·4
from lap edge	to 5·4	5·7	5·1	5·1	5·3

−6·1

At the S.W. it is cut to a depth of ·8 inch, at the S.E. to ·6 (?); the upper edge of it is often ill-defined and sloping. According to Prof. Smyth the mean

L

height of this lap above the gallery floor is 166·2 ± ·8 vertically ; hence the groove is at 172·1 to 179·0 vertically over the floor, and its lower edge is therefore at half the height of the gallery, that varying from 167 to 172. The pickmarks in the groove on the S. end of the W. side are horizontal, and not along the groove, showing that it was cut out after the walls were built, which agrees with its rough appearance. It belongs to the same curious class of rough alterations as the blocks inserted in the sides of the gallery and the rude grooves cut away across them.

At the top of the N. end is a large forced hole, cut by Vyse in 1837, and still quite fresh-looking. The whole of the top lap of stone is so entirely cut away there that I could not decide to where it had come, and only suppose it to project 3 inches, like the others.

From this the length of the roof of the gallery is 1688·9 – 40·45 = 1648·4 horizontal, or 1838·6 sloping.

By plumb-line measure at the S. end, the roof on the E. side is inside the floor edge (or overhangs) 20·50, and on the W. side 20·40. On the S. end (eliminating the lean) the projection is 20·9, and on N. 20·4 ; mean of all, 20·55, for the sum of the seven projections of the laps, or one cubit, the laps being then one palm each in breadth. Thus the laps overhang the ramps along the gallery sides, and the space between the ramps (2 cubits), is equal to the space between the walls at the top.

The remarkable shaft, or " well," that leads away from the lower end of the gallery down to the subterranean passage, was fully measured about its mouth ; but it appears to be so rough and so evidently utilitarian (for the exit of workmen) that it is not worth while to publish more complete measures than those of Prof. Smyth. As, however, the position of its mouth has been supposed to have a meaning, it should be stated that the opening is from 21·8 to 49·0 horizontally from N. wall of gallery on floor, 21·8 to 48·7 near its top; and 21·9 to 48·9 by the sloping distance reduced. Thus the middle of it is at 35·40 35·25, or 35·37 by different methods. The part of the shaft that passes through a rock fissure filled with gravel (often called the " grotto ") has been steined with 10 courses of small stones, varying from 7¼ to 8 inches in height.

At the upper end of the gallery, we have already stated the S. wall to be 61·7 ± ·8 S. of the Pyramid centre ; and hence the face of the great step at the head of the gallery (which descends behind both floor and ramps) is (61·7 – 61·3) = ·4 ± ·8 S. of the Pyramid centre. It may, therefore, be taken as intended that the face of this step, and the transition from sloping to horizontal surfaces, signalizes the transit from the Northern to the Southern half of the Pyramid. This same mid-plane of the Pyramid being also signalized by the mid-plane of the Queen's Chamber, which is measured as ·3 ± ·8 N. of the Pyramid centre.

The ramps along the sides, where they join this great step, are very irregular. Their top surfaces slope away downwards toward the side walls; thus the E. ramp top varies from 13·20 to 12·18 below the step from E. to W., and the W. ramp top from 12·82 to 12·2 (?) from W. to E. At present, moreover, the ends of the ramps are parted away from the face of the step by ·30 on E. and ·44 on W., an amount which has been duly subtracted from my length measures of the gallery. Beside this, the top of the step itself, though, straight, is far from level, the W. side being about 1·0 higher than the E. side. And the sloping floor seems to be also out of level by an equal amount in the opposite direction; since on the half width of the step (*i.e.*, between the ramps) the height of the step face is 34·92 or 35·0 on E., and 35·80 or 35·85 on W. The length of the step from N. to S. is: on E. side 61·0, and on W. 61·5. All these measurements are very carefully taken with elimination of wear, fractures, and shifting of the stones at the joints. Hence, at the line along which I measured, 6 inches from the edge of the ramp, the step will be 61·1 long; and this at the angle 26° 12′ 50″ (by which the end of the gallery was calculated from the plug-blocks) will be 30·08 vertically, for the virtual * above the actual floor end. Then the top of the step will (by above measures) be here 34·88 above actual floor end, and the step dips about ·64 to the S. wall at this part; so the top of the step at the S. wall is 34·88 − ·64 − 30·08 = 4·16 (say ± ·2) above the virtual floor end at the line of taping. And as the virtual floor end is at 1689·0 ± ·5, the step surface at the E. side of the S. doorway is 1693·2 ± ·6 over the pavement.

47. The Antechamber and its passages were measured both by steel tape and rods, in one length, from the step to the King's Chamber; and the joints and floor levels are as follow:—

	Along Floor on E. side.	Southward from centre of Pyramid ± ·9.	Level over virtual end of gallery ± ·2.	Level over pavement. ± ·6.
Face of step . .	− 61·32	·4	4·7 E. 5·6 W.	1693·7 to 1694·6
S. wall of gallery .	0	61·7	4·2 E.	1693·2
N. end of Antechamber	52·02	113·7		
Joint, granite begins .	64·90	126·6	{ 3·6 { 3·9	1692·6 1692·9
Granite of wall begins	75·26	137·0		
Edge of wall groove .	91·79	153·5		
Joint of floor . .	112·15	173·8	{ 3·7 { 3·2	1692·7 1692·2
Edge of wall groove .	113·48	175·2		
„ „ „ .	119·26	181·0		

* The virtual floor end is where the general floor slope, if carried on through the step, would intersect the plane of the S. wall.

	Along Floor on E. side.	Southward from centre of Pyramid ± ·9.	Level over virtual end of gallery ± ·2.	Level over pavement. ± ·6.
Joint of wall . .	134·17	195·9		
S. end of Antechamber	168·10	229·8		
Joint of floor . .	198·41	260·1	{ 2·9 / 2·8	1691·9 / 1691·8
Base of King's Ch. wall	268·9	330·6	— ·5	1688·5
End of passage floor	269·04	330·7	3·0	1692·0
Raised floor, King's Ch.	269·17	330·9	3·8	1692·8

These measures vary somewhat from those of Professor Smyth in 1865 ; and, comparing the greatest differences, they stand thus :—

	Steel tape, 1882.	Rods, 1880.	Rods, 1865.
N. end Antechamber to joint S. of it	12·88	12·88	13·6
Next joint to S. end Antechamber .	55·95	55·73 and 55·80	55·5

So here, as elsewhere, the measures in 1880–2 by steel tape and rods, entirely independent of each other, agree fairly together, and suggest that the 1865 rod measures were somewhat in error. This is due generally to the latter starting from different points on different occasions, and to their different series being insufficiently locked together. Hence I adopt the steel tape measures as the most satisfactory.

48. Taking the Antechamber alone, we may say that its dimensions above the granite wainscot of the sides, are as follow :—

Height above floor.	Length, N. to S.				Breadth, E. to W.			
	2 from W.	Middle.	12 from E.	E. side.	2 from N.	40 from N.	76 from N.	2 from S.
147	116·85	116·22	116·05	115·65	64·80	64·48	64·96	64·76
129	117·00	116·18	116·03	115·37	64·72	64·98	65·26	65·25
114	117·00	116·11	115·73	114·07	65·06	65·00	65·48	65·21
95	116·55		115·91					
70	116·58		115·93					
45	115·91		116·12					

Diagonals N.W. to S.E. { 133·15   at 2 from ceiling   133·14 } N.E. to S.W.
                        { 133·07   over wainscot   132·98 }

The height was measured as follows :—

	Near N. wall.	14 from N.	59 from N.	61 from N.	S. wall.
At E. side . .	149·47	149·09	149·17	149·62	149·63
Middle . . .	149·53	...	...	149·64	149·64
At W. side . .	149·32	149·01	149·10	149·65	149·57
Mean . . .	149·44	149·05	149·13	149·64	149·61
Above gallery end .	153·04	152·95	152·83	152·84	152·61

The mean length is thus 116·30 (by the two series from top to base), breadth 65·00, and height 149·35 ; or the ceiling over the virtual end of the gallery floor, 152·85 ± ·2, and 1841·8 ± ·6 over the pavement.

49. Coming now to details of the walls, the rough and coarse workmanship is astonishing, in comparison with the exquisite masonry of the casing and entrance of the Pyramid ; and the main object in giving the following details is to show how badly pyramid masons could work. The great variation in the foregoing measures illustrates this.

The N. wall is all rough picked work, with ·2 variation commonly ; there is a great irregular flaw, and a piece broken out of the stone about the level of the top of the leaf, as much as 1 inch deep. The E. wall has the granite by the side of the leaf wavy and winding, and bulbous at the base, projecting 1·4. On the wainscot block at the S. end of this wall, which is all in one with the S. end of the chamber, are two conjoined deep scores or scrapes nearly vertical, much like the beginning of a regular groove ; their distance from the S. wall is 3·6 to 7·2 at 90, and 2·6 to 6·4 at 52 from floor, where they end ; they are ·48 deep at maximum. The S. wall has all up the E. side of it, over the wainscot, a projection, just equal in width to the wainscot, and varying in thickness from ·31 at top to 1·7 half-way down, and thence fading off down to the top of the wainscot. On the W. side of the S. wall the granite has been daubed over for 2 to 6 inches in breadth, with a thin coat of cement ; this, at 1 inch from the side is ·35 thick ; also at 13 from the W. side is a slight sinking of the granite, from ·34 to ·60 in depth, all quite ill-defined. The W. wall has the top of the granite wainscot uneven, rising toward the front, and there sinking suddenly ·35 at 1·4 from the front edge. The southern of the three semicircular hollows on the top of this wainscot (see Pl. xii.)* has the granite defective at the back of it, and is backed with rough limestone there. The southernmost stone over the wainscot is dressed very flat and true, but rough, + or — ·03. The next block has a raised edge to it on the S. side (figured by Prof. Smyth), and along the base of it, which consists of granite left rough, not dressed away in finishing ; about 4 inches wide, and ·4 projection along the lower edge of the block ; and 2 wide and 1·2 maximum projection at the side. The other edges of this block were marked out by saw-cuts in the granite, about ·2 deep, to guide the workmen in dressing the face.

The various courses and stones of the chamber were measured, but the only points of interest are the following.

The south wall has four vertical grooves all up it, which have been hitherto supposed to have extended down to the top of the passage to the King's Chamber. This was not the case, however ; for, though much broken away, it is still clear that they became shallower as they neared the bottom, and probably

---

* The forms of the curves are plotted from offsets taken at every inch along them.

ended leaving an unbroken flat surface over the doorway. Their depths (as well as the forms of their sides) show this, as follows :—

Height above door.	E. groove.	2nd	3rd	W. groove.
at 10	2·8	Much	Slight	2·8 at 8
at 7	2·5	broken.	curve.	2·5 at 7
at 5	1.75			2·0 at 5½

50. The granite leaf which stretches across the chamber, resting in grooves cut in the granite wainscots, must be somewhat less in width than the breadth between the grooves, *i.e.*, 48·46 to 48·76. Its other dimensions were carefully ascertained, as much theoretic importance had been attached to them ; though to anyone looking at the object itself, the roughness and irregularity of it would put any accuracy of workmanship out of the question. The thickness of the two stones that form it was gauged by means of plumb-lines at 33 points ; it varies from 15·16 to 16·20, but the details are scarcely worth printing. This leaf is not simply a flat slab of granite, but on both its upper and lower parts it has a projection on its N. side, about 1 inch thick, where it is included in the side grooves. The edge of this projection down the W. side has been marked out by a saw cut ; and the whole of the granite on the inner side of this cut has been dressed away all over the face of the leaf, leaving only one patch or boss of the original surface of the block.

This boss, of which so much has been made by theorists, is merely a very rough projection, like innumerable others that may be seen ; left originally for the purpose of lifting the blocks. When a building was finished these bosses were knocked away (I picked up a loose one among waste heaps at Gizeh) and the part was dressed down and polished like the rest of the stone. It is only in unimportant parts that they are left entire. This boss on the leaf is very ill-defined, being anything between 4·7 and 5·2 wide, and between 3·3 and 3·5 high on its outer face ; at its junction with the block it is still less defined, and might be reckoned anything between 7·2 and 8·2 wide, and 5·6 to 6·6 high. It projects ·94 to 1·10 from the block, according to the irregularities of the rough hammer dressing. Anything more absurdly unsuited for a standard of measure it would be difficult to conceive. I write these remarks with a sharp plaster cast of it before me that I took in 1881. Traces of another boss remain on the W. wall of the Antechamber, above the wainscot ; here there has been a boss 12 inches wide and 9 high, which has been knocked away, and the surface rough dressed, though the rest of the face of the stone is ground down elsewhere. The block has been turned in building, so that the flat under-edge of the boss is toward the N. Remains of another boss may be seen on a block in the passage to the King's Chamber ; remains of 15 or 16 others in the King's Chamber ; 5 others complete in the spaces above that ; and many on the casing of the Third Pyramid and elsewhere (see Pl. xii.). The E. to W. breadth of the leaf between its side ledges in the grooves, varies from 40·6 to 41·2 at different heights up the middles of the ledges; but furthermore, the edges are not square, and we may say that 40 to 42 will about represent its irregularity. Yet this was another so-called "standard of measure" of the theorists. The top of the upper block of the leaf is a mere natural surface of the granite boulder out of which it was cut, utterly rough and irregular; and not materially broken away as it dips down deeply into the grooves, and is there plastered over. It varies from 51·24 to 59·0, and perhaps more, below the ceiling. Yet the cubic volume of this block was eagerly worked out by the theorists.

51. The King's Chamber was more completely measured than any other part of the Pyramid; the distances of the walls apart, their verticality in each corner, the course heights, and the levels were completely observed; and the results are given in Plate xiii., in which all variations from the mean amounts are shown on their actual size. The principle of *concentrated errors* enables the eye to grasp at once the character of the variations in workmanship, in a way that no table of figures could show it.

For example, the N. wall is on an average 412·59 inches long (see bottom of Pl. xiii.); but the "face of West end" (see left hand of plate) is at the top ·18 outside the mean vertical line, and the "face of East end" is ·42 inside the mean vertical; hence at the top the length is actually (·42 – ·18) shorter than the mean, *i.e.*, it is 412·35. The line of the ceiling on the W. edge of the N. wall will be seen to be ·18 over the mean level of the course, marked "5" at each side of the sheet; and the ceiling line at the E. edge is as much as 1·00 over the same mean level; hence the ceiling slopes ·82 on its length along the N. side. Referring now to the floor or to the 1st course, where the mean levels are marked by continuous straight lines all across the diagram, it will be seen how far the variable lines of the "Actual First course" or "Actual Floor" fluctuate up and down, in relation to their mean level; the first course, beginning at the N.W., is at ·23 over its mean level (marked 1 at the edge), and runs upward until it is 1·03 over its mean level at the N.E., then down to below mean level at the S.E., then still further down along the S. wall, turning a little up to the S.W. corner, and then rapidly rising to above its mean level again at the N.W. corner, whence we started. Only the first course and floor were directly levelled all round; the upper courses were connected by vertical measures in each corner, hence their fluctuations along the sides were not measured, and they are only marked by broken lines. On looking down, say, the "Face of West-end," from joint 5 to 4, it is seen that the line bends out, showing the stone to be slightly hollowed;* but on the average it is about square with the course line; and any error seen in squareness of angle in the diagram, represents only $\frac{1}{60}$ of

---

* The middle of the course was only thus offsetted on the top course; the other courses were read on at the top and base of each, to give their errors of cutting and of placing.

the actual angular error, or 5° equals 6′. Then, below that, it is seen that the line from joint 4 to 3 begins very slightly outside the line from joint 5 to 4 ; showing that the stone of the 4th course is set back by that amount, owing to error in placing it. Similarly the squareness of faces, and truth of setting of the stones, is shown for all the other courses in each corner. In fact, a paper model, showing all the errors on the actual scale, might be made by cutting out four sides, following the outlines of the faces of the walls as here marked, and bending each side to make it fit to the irregular edge of its adjacent side.

This diagram will represent with quite sufficient accuracy, without numerical tables, the small errors of this chamber ; especially as it must be remembered that this shows its actual state, and not precisely its original form. On every side the joints of the stones have separated, and the whole chamber is shaken larger. By examining the joints all round the 2nd course, the sum of the estimated openings is, 3 joints opened on N. side, total =·19; 1 joint on E. =·14; 5 joints on S. =·41 ; 2 joints on W. =·38. And these quantities must be deducted from the measures, in order to get the true original lengths of the chamber. I also observed, in measuring the top near the W., that the width from N. to S. is lengthened ·3 by a crack at the S. side.

These openings or cracks are but the milder signs of the great injury that the whole chamber has sustained, probably by an earthquake, when *every* roof beam was broken across near the South side ; and since which the whole of the granite ceiling (weighing some 400 tons), is upheld solely by sticking and thrusting. Not only has this wreck overtaken the chamber itself, but in every one of the spaces above it are the massive roof-beams either cracked across or torn out of the wall, more or less, at the South side ; and the great Eastern and Western walls of limestone, between, and independent of which, the whole of these construction chambers are built, have sunk bodily. All these motions are yet but small—only a matter of an inch or two—but enough to wreck the theoretical strength and stability of these chambers, and to make their downfall a mere question of time and earthquakes.

52. Applying, then, these corrections of the opened joints to the lengths of the lower course—and also, as being the most likely correction, to the upper parts as well—we have the following values for the original lengths of the chamber, and for the error of squareness of the present corner angles.

	N.	N.E.	E.	S.E.	S.	S.W.	W.	N.W.
Top	412·14	+ 4"	206·30	− 35"	411·88	+1′ 35"	206·04	− 1′ 4"
Mean	412·40	− 2′ 57"	206·29	+2′ 20"	412·11	−1′ 2"	205·97	+1′ 39"
Base	412·78	− 4′ 54"	206·43	+4′ 40"	412·53	−4′ 5"	206·16	+4′ 19"

Now it will be observed that though the lengths can be corrected by the sum of the openings, the angles cannot be so corrected, as we do not know which angle the change of length has affected.   Hence the present angles are entered above, with the reservation that the sides having altered about 1 in 1,000 of their length, the original angles may have easily been 3' or 4' different ; and, therefore, all that we can say about the angles is, that the builders were probably not 5' in error, and very possibly less than that ; also that the errors change sign from base to top, so that each course must be a true right angle at some level up it.

Probably the base of the chamber was the part most carefully adjusted and set out ; and hence the original value of the cubit used can be most accurately recovered from that part.   The four sides there yield a mean value of 20·632± ·004, and this is certainly the best determination of the cubit that we can hope for from the Great Pyramid.

The top course of both the E. and W. walls consists of a single stone ; on the N. and S. walls the joints of it were measured thus :—N. wall, E. end o, joints 62·1, 248·8 ; S. wall, E. end o, joint 189·2.

The average variation of the thickness of the courses from their mean is ·051, the mean being 47·045 between similar joints, or including the top course, which was necessarily measured in a different way, 47·040 ± ·013.

53. The roof of the chamber is formed of nine granite beams, of the following breadths, the two side beams partly resting on the ends of the chamber :—

	Along N. Side.		Along S. Side.		Skew.	Difference of End Widths.
	Stones.	Total.	Stones.	Total.		
E.		o − x		o − x		
	22·4 + x		17·8 + x			
		22·4		17·8	−4·6	
	45·5		45·8			+ ·3
		67·9		63·6	−4·3	
	52·5		53·0			+ ·5
		120·4		116·6	−3·8	
	49·1		51·0			+1·9
		169·5		167·6	−1·9	
	53·9		55·4			+1·5
		223·4		223·0	− ·4	
	44·8		45·8			+1·0
		268·2		268·8	+ ·6	
	58·1		59·3			+1·2
		326·3		328·1	+1·8	
	62·7		60·8			−1·9
		389·0		388·9	− ·1	
W.	23·3 + x		23·4 + x			
		412·3 + x		412·3 + x		

The column of "skew" shows the difference in the position of the joints on the opposite sides of the chamber; and the "difference of end widths" the variation between the two ends of the same beam. From this table it seems probable that the roofing in of the chamber was begun at the W. end, as the skew of the beams increases up to the E. end; and also as the largest beams, which would be most likely to be first used, are at the W. end. The numbering of the slabs in the top space above the King's Chamber also begins at the W. end. Vyse, however, states that these "chambers of construction" were begun at the E. end.

These roofing-beams are not of "polished granite," as they have been described; on the contrary, they have rough-dressed surfaces, very fair and true so far as they go, but without any pretence to polish. Round the S.E. corner, for about five feet on each side, the joint is all daubed up with cement laid on by fingers. The crack across the Eastern roof-beam has been also daubed with cement, looking, therefore, as if it had cracked *before* the chamber was finished. At the S.W. corner, plaster is freely spread over the granite, covering about a square foot altogether.

54. The floor of the chamber, as is well known, is quite disconnected from the walls, and stands somewhat above the base of the lowest course. It is very irregular in its level, not only absolutely, but even in relation to the courses; its depth below the first course joint varying 2·29, from 42·94 to 40·65. This variation has been attributed to the sinking caused by excavation beneath it, but this is not the case; it has been only undermined at the W. end beneath the coffer,* and yet the floor over this undermined part is 1½ inches *higher* in relation to the first course, than it is at the S.E. corner; and along the S. side where it has not been mined it varies 1⅓ inches in relation to the first course. In these cases I refer to the first course line, as that was the builder's conception of level in the chamber, to which they would certainly refer; but if we refer instead to absolute level, the anomalies are as great and the argument is unaffected.

It appears, then, that the floor never was plane or regular; and that, in this respect, it shared the character of the very variable floor of the passage that led to the chamber, no two stones of which are on the same level. The passage floor, even out to the great step in the gallery, is also inserted between the walls, like the floor of the chamber.

55. Among peculiarities of work still remaining, are the traces of 15 bosses or lugs on the faces of the granite blocks, all on the lower course. Those best seen are two on the fourth block of the N. wall, counting from the door; they have been about 12 inches wide and the same high, 14 inches apart, and their flat bottom edges 3 inches from the base of the block (see Pl. xii.). They may be very plainly seen by holding a candle close to the wall below them; this

---

* I know the hole well, having been down into it more than once.

shows up the grinding around them, and the slight projection and very much less perfect grinding of the sites of the bosses.   There is a remarkable diagonal drafted line across the immense block of granite over the doorway ; it appears not to run quite to the lower corner on the E. side ; but this is doubtless due to the amount by which the block is built into the E. wall, thus cutting off the end of the diagonal line.   This sunken band across the stone appears to have been a true drafted straight line cut in process of working, in order to avoid any twist or wind in the dressing of the face ; this method being needful as the block was too large to test by the true planes otherwise used (see section 135).

The position of the King's Chamber in the Pyramid is defined thus : N. wall at base 330·6 ± ·8 S. of centre of Pyramid ; S. wall 537·0 ± ·8 from centre ; E. wall (284·4 ± 20·7) = 305·1 ± 3·0 E. of centre ; W. wall 107·7 ± 3·0 W. of centre.   Base of walls 1686·3 to 1688·5 ± ·6 above pavement ; actual floor 1691·4 to 1693·7 ± ·6 above pavement ; ceiling 1921·6 to 1923·7 ± ·6 above pavement.

56. The air channels leading from this chamber have been already mentioned (see section 24) and reference has been made to Pl. xi. for the positions of their outer ends.   The angles of them had not yet been accurately measured, and therefore I carefully observed them by a sliding signal and a theodolite. The angles on the floors of them at different distances from the theodolite station at the present outer ends are thus :—

N. Channel.			S. Channel.			
At 84 to 180	32°	4′ 45″	At 0 to 120	45°	25′	6″
180 to 300	31°	37′ 15″	120 to 240	45°	30′	7″
300 to 372	30°	43′ 15″	240 to 360	45°	25′	57″
			360 to 480	45°	25′	14″
Mean	31°	33′	480 to 600	45°	15′	19″
			600 to 720	45°	7′	42″
			720 to 840	44°	26′	18″
			Mean	45°	13′	40″

For example, on the floor of the N. channel, the angle on the part from 180 to 300 inches from the mouth averages 31° 37′ 15″ ; this is, of course, quite apart from whatever the dip may be from the passage mouth to those points ; and it is reduced from the actually observed quantities.   The above list of angles are just equivalent to observations by a clinometer, sliding to different parts of the passage.   It is striking that the slope of both passages continuously increases up to the outside (except just at the mouth of the S. channel) ; hence these quantities, which only extend over a part of either passage, cannot give the true mean slope ; probably on the whole length the means would not be greater angles than 31° and 44½° respectively.

The N. channel has been forced open as a working passage for some way inwards, only leaving the floor and W. side perfect.   The channel is now blocked, just below the end of the enlarged part, and on working a rod 4½ feet into the sand, it ran against limestone.   The sand in the hole has blown in during gales, which sweep up sand like mist.   The remains of the original channel show it to have varied from 8·9 to 9·2 (mean 9·0) in width, and to have been 8·72 and 8·74 in height.

The S. channel is blocked by sand at 76 feet down.   It is not straight in the clear length, curving more than its own width to the east; and the sides often shift a few tenths of an inch in passing from one stone to another.   These details were seen by examining it with a telescope on Feb. 8, and by photographing it on Nov. 2, 1881; these being the days on which the sun shines down it at noon.   Its width at the top is 8·35 and 8·65, and its height 8·7 to 8·9.

57. The coffer in the King's Chamber is of the usual form of the earliest Egyptian sarcophagi, an approximately flat-sided box of red granite.   It has the usual under-cut groove to hold the edge of a lid along the inside of the N., E., and S. sides; the W. side being cut away as low as the groove for the lid to slide over it; and having three pin-holes cut in it for the pins to fall into out of similar holes in the lid, when the lid was put on.   It is not finely wrought, and cannot in this respect rival the coffer in the Second Pyramid.   On the outer sides the lines of sawing may be plainly seen: horizontal on the N., a small patch horizontal on the E., vertical on the S., and nearly horizontal on the W.; showing that the masons did not hesitate at cutting a slice of granite 90 inches long, and that the jewelled bronze saw must have been probably about 9 feet long.   On the N. end is a place, near the W. side, where the saw was run too deep into the granite, and was backed out again by the masons; but this fresh start they made was still too deep, and two inches lower they backed out a second time, having altogether cut out more than $\frac{1}{10}$-inch deeper than they intended.   On the E. inside is a portion of a tube drill hole remaining, where they tilted the drill over into the side by not working it vertically.   They tried hard to polish away all that part, and took off about $\frac{1}{10}$-inch thickness all round it; but still they had to leave the side of the hole $\frac{1}{10}$ deep, 3 long, and 1·3 wide; the bottom of it is 8 or 9 below the original top of the coffer.   They made a similar error on the N. inside, but of a much less extent.   There are traces of horizontal grinding lines on the W. inside.   Reference should be made to section 129 for the subject of stone-working in general.

58. The coffer was very thoroughly measured, offsets being taken to 388 points on the outside, to 281 points inside, or 669 in all; besides taking 281 caliper measures.

Before raising it from the floor to measure the bottom, its place as it stood on the chamber floor, tilted up at the S. end by a large pebble under it, was observed thus :—

	N.E. to N. Wall.	N.W. to N.	N.W. to W.	S.W. to W.	S.W. to S.	S.E. to S.
Top	... 47·70	48·90	53·34	56·50	67·92	[68·60]
Base	... 48·35	50·06	53·32	56·54	67·62	68·06

S.E. to S. wall in brackets, was taken at 10 below top, owing to breakage above that.

On raising the coffer no trace of lines was to be found to mark its place on the floor, nor any lines on the floor or bottom of the coffer.

The flint pebble that had been put under the coffer is important. If any person wished at present to prop the coffer up, there are multitudes of stone chips in the Pyramid ready to hand. Therefore fetching a pebble from the outside seems to show that the coffer was first lifted at a time when no breakages had been made in the Pyramid, and there were no chips lying about. This suggests that there was some means of access to the upper chambers, which was always available by removing loose blocks without any forcing. If the stones at the top of the shaft leading from the subterranean part to the gallery had been cemented in place, they must have been smashed to break through them, or if there were granite portcullises in the Antechamber, they must also have been destroyed; and it is not likely that any person would take the trouble to fetch a large flint pebble into the innermost part of the Pyramid, if there were stone chips lying in his path.

59. The measurements of the coffer surfaces by means of offsets from arbitrary lines, have all been reduced in both tilt and skew, and are stated as offsets or variations + and − (*i.e.*, in excess or deficiency of stone) from a set of mean planes. These mean planes, then, are supposed to lie half in and half out of the stone, being in the mean position and direction of the face. The mean planes adopted for the E. and W. sides, both in and out, are all parallel; hence variations from these planes represent errors of flatness of the surfaces, and also errors of parallelism of the quasi-parallel surfaces. The mean planes adopted for the N. and S. ends, both in and out, are similarly all parallel. The mean planes adopted for the bottom, both in and out, and the top, are also parallel These mean planes of the E. and W. sides, and of the N. and S. ends, are all square with the planes adopted for the bottom and top. There is no exception from parallelism in the system of comparison planes; and but one exception from squareness, in that the N. and S. planes are not adopted square with the E. and W. planes. · There was such difference from squareness in the work, that to make the planes square with each other, would have altered the offsets so much as to disguise the small curvatures of the faces; and adopting the planes slightly out of square, makes no difference in taking out quantities of length, surface, or bulk, from the tables of offsets.

The mean planes to which the coffer surfaces are referred here, and from which the actual surfaces differ by an equal amount $+$ and $-$, yield the following dimensions : —

N. end thick	5·67	E. side thick	5·87	Inner depth	34·42
Inside length	78·06	Inside width	26·81	Base thick	6·89
S. end thick	5·89	W. side thick	5·82		
				Outer height	41·31
Outside length	89·62	Outside width	38·50		
				Ledge depth	1·70

The vertical planes all square with the horizontal; but N. and S. planes cut E. and W. planes at 89° 47′ at N.E. and S.W. corners, and at 90°13′ at N.W. and S.E. corners.

For convenience of reference the whole coffer was divided by imaginary lines or planes, 6 inches apart in each direction, and represented by rows of chalk spots during the actual measurements. Thus at the S. end the first vertical plane across the coffer from E. to W. is A, through the midst of that end; the second plane is B, which passes 3 inches clear of the end; then C; and so on to O, which is 3 inches clear of the N. end; and P the last line, through the midst of the N. end. Then at the W. side the first plane is a, the second β, an inch clear of the side, then γ, δ, ϵ, ζ, an inch clear of the E. side, and η through the E. side. Then vertically the plane b is 4 inches above the inside bottom, and c, d, e, f, are at six-inch intervals; occasionally, in the most perfect parts, another line, g, could be measured on the outside, just at the top. The inside plane, a, was taken at only 3 inches below b, or 1 inch over the bottom; but the outside plane, a, was taken the full six inches below b, i.e., 4 or 5 inches above the outside bottom. In taking means in the inside the offsets to a are only allowed half weight, as they belong to a much shorter space than the others; they ought, theoretically, to have even less weight, but as the inner planes gather in rapidly, just at the bottom below a, this half weight probably gives the truest results.

Having, then, adopted the above mean planes for the sides, and divided them for reference at every six inches, we can state all the variations of the actual surfaces as being either $+$ (*i.e.*, an excess of stone beyond the plane) or $-$ (*i.e.*, a deficiency of stone), either inside or outside the coffer.

These variations are as follow, stated in hundredths of an inch :—

		A	B	C	D	E	F	G	H	J	K	L	M	N	O	P
		South end.													North end.	
Top.	g	...	...	...	...	+2	...	...	...	...	...	...	− 1	− 3	...	...
	f	+10	+ 8	+ 8	+4	+3	−4	+ 1	+ 1	0	− 1	− 3	− 1	0	+ 1	− 1
West	e	+12	+ 7	+14	+5	+1	−1	− 5	− 6	− 8	−10	−12	− 8	− 5	+ 3	+ 5
outside.	d	+14	+ 8	+12	+9	+1	−7	−13	−14	−16	−14	−15	−12	− 8	+ 1	+ 1
	c	+17	+10	+10	+9	+6	−2	− 8	−11	−13	−13	−13	−10	− 6	0	+ 3
	b	+20	+10	+ 9	+9	+2	−4	− 9	−10	−14	−12	−11	− 7	0	+ 8	+12
Base.	a	+21	+10	+ 9	0	−6	−8	− 9	− 8	− 6	− 2	+ 2	+10	+17	+26	+31

South end. ... **North end.**

Top. East outside. Base.

		A	B	C	D	E	F	G	H	J	K	L	M	N	O	P
g	much	...		...	...	...	...	...	...	...	+5	+8	+9	+9	...	
f	broken			...	−7	−5	−4	−3	0	+1	+2	+4	+7	+7	+7	+9
e	away			−8	−6	−5	−3	−2	0	0	+2	+2	+5	+5	+4	+7
d		−13	−11	−7	−5	−4	−3	0	+1	+1	+3	+2	+5	+5	+5	+8
c		−12	−11	−8	−7	−5	−3	−2	+1	+1	+2	+2	+6	+6	+5	+8
b		−12	−12	−8	−7	−4	−4	−1	+1	+1	+2	+3	+7	+7	+7	+8
a		− 9	− 9	−7	−4	0	+1	+1	+2	+3	+4	+5	+8	+8	+5	+6

West side. ... **East side**

Top. North outside. Base.

	α	β	γ	δ	ε	ζ	η
g	...	+39	+35	...	...	+21	...
f	+35	+31	+29	+21	+21	+20	+18
e	+16	+ 9	+ 3	− 2	+ 1	+ 7	+13
d	+13	− 2	−14	−21	−15	− 6	+ 2
c	+ 5	+ 2	−10	−17	− 9	− 2	+ 3
b	− 3	− 3	− 3	− 9	− 8	− 4	+ 2
a	− 6	−12	−20	−36	−27	− 4	+13

West side. ... **East side.**

Top. South outside. Base.

	α	β	γ	δ	ε	ζ	η
g	...	...	...	...	...	...	...
f	−12	− 7	+ 1	+ 2	+7	+24	+34
e	−12	−12	− 9	− 4	+3	+22	+34
d	−21	−24	−16	−11	−2	+22	+37
c	−25	−27	−21	−15	+1	+22	+43
b	−27	−30	−20	−14	−4	+26	+47
a	−22	−32	−16	−13	−2	+29	+54

South end. ... **North end.**

West. Bottom outside. East.

		A	B	C	D	E	F	G	H	J	K	L	M	N	O	P
α		...	...	+15	+15	+17	+13	+12	+16	+11	+ 5	+ 1	− 7	+ 9	+ 4	...
β		...	...	+20	+15	+16	+ 9	+14	+ 4	+ 6	− 1	−11	− 3	+ 4	− 1	...
γ		...	...	+22	+22	+19	+ 8	+ 8	− 2	+ 1	− 4	− 9	−18	− 4	− 8	...
δ		...	+10	+17	+21	+17	+ 3	− 3	− 4	− 6	−11	−16	−15	− 9	−12	...
ε		...	+ 9	+17	+12	+ 9	+ 1	− 8	− 1	−11	−13	−25	−12	−10	−15	...
ζ		...	+13	+ 7	+12	+ 4	− 2	− 6	− 7	−12	− 8	−17	−12	−20	...	...
η		...	− 8	+ 8	+ 5	+ 4	− 7	− 5	− 8	−13	−12	−10	−14	−15	...	...

South end. ... **North end**

Top. West inside. Base.

		B	C	D	E	F	G	H	J	K	L	M	N	O
f		+ 3	+ 5	+1	+ 5	+10	+11	+12	+14	+16	+15	+13	+12	+12
e		− 1	+ 1	−3	+ 3	+ 4	+ 4	+ 3	+ 5	+10	+12	+10	+ 9	+ 8
d		+ 1	− 1	0	+ 1	+ 3	0	− 5	− 5	− 1	+ 8	− 1	+10	+12
c		− 1	− 2	−2	0	− 1	−11	−17	−16	−12	− 2	− 4	+10	+ 7
b		+ 4	− 1	−3	− 2	−11	−22	−28	−27	−18	− 7	− 7	−10	+ 4
a		+19	+14	+8	− 5	−19	−27	−33	−34	−24	− 7	− 8	+ 7	+ 6

South end. ... **North end.**

		B	C	D	E	F	G	H	J	K	L	M	N	O
Top.	f	− 5	+ 1	+ 2	+ 7	+ 7	+ 7	+ 4	+ 2	+ 2	+ 3	−12	− 1	+ 1
	e	− 5	+ 1	+ 2	+ 4	+ 6	+ 7	+ 2	+ 4	+ 4	+ 4	+ 2	− 1	− 1
East inside.	d	− 4	+ 2	+ 4	+ 4	+ 3	− 1	− 6	− 5	− 4	+ 1	0	0	− 2
	c	− 6	+ 1	+ 3	+ 3	+ 5	+ 1	− 7	−11	−11	− 3	− 3	− 1	0
	b	− 6	+ 1	+ 1	+ 2	+ 6	+10	− 2	−12	−16	− 9	− 5	− 2	− 1
Base.	a	0	+ 3	+ 2	+ 1	+ 5	+10	− 2	−10	− 8	+ 3	+ 6	+ 5	+ 4

West side. ... **East side.** | **West side.** ... **East side.**

		β	γ	δ	ε	ζ		β	γ	δ	ε	ζ
Top.	f	0	− 7	+ 1	+ 2	+ 4	.Top. { f	+ 3	0	− 1	− 2	−10
	e	0	− 8	− 3	− 6	− 8	e	− 5	− 5	− 4	− 5	− 9
North inside.	d	0	− 2	0	− 1	− 5	South inside. { d	− 4	− 3	− 1	− 1	− 5
	c	− 3	− 3	− 1	+ 1	− 1	c	+ 1	0	+ 2	+ 2	− 4
	b	+ 1.	+ 1	− 1	− 1	+ 2	b	− 5	+ 1	+ 4	+ 4	+ 2
Base.	a	+20	+16	+18	+10	0	Base. { a	+11	+13	+24	+23	+17

South end. ... **North end.**

		B	C	D	E	F	G	H	J	K	L	M	N	O
West.	β	− 1	− 3	+ 5	.0	− 4	+ 1	+ 8	+ 5	+ 1	+10	+ 9	+11	+ 4
Bottom inside.	γ	− 8	− 5	− 3	−18	− 5	0	− 2	+ 1	− 5	− 2	+ 5	+ 1	0
	δ	− 5	− 6	− 4	− 1	+ 2	+ 2	+ 2	0	− 2	0	+ 1	− 2	+ 7
	ε	+12	− 9	+ 9	− 6	+ 6	−13	− 2	− 1	− 2	+ 1	0	−15	−12
East.	ζ	+ 2	+ 5	+ 3	+ 2	+ 5	+19?	+ 2	+ 1	+11?	− 4	+ 1	− 5	0

South end. ... **North end.**

		A	B	C	D	E	F	G	H	J	K	L	M	N	O	P	
West.	α			[o]	[+1]	[+4]	[+2]	[+4]	[+5]	[+4]	[+7]	[+6]	[+6]	[+5]	[+8]	[+8]	...
	β		[−2]	...			...			...			...			[−1]	
Top.	γ		...	(Offsets in brackets are from points on the cut out ledge, raised 1·70											[o]	
	δ		...	inches, which is the mean level of the ledge below adjacent points											[+1]	
	ζ		...	of the remaining top; thus restoring the top as nearly as may be...											[−3]	−1
East.	η		...	...	...	...	...	...	...	[−4]	[−4]	[−1]	[o]	[+4]	[o]	[−8]	−3

from the ledge. The actual top only remains at six points)

actual top ... −4 −4 0 +1 −3

If, for example, the length of the E. side of the coffer is wanted, from the foregoing tables, at the level of d, half way up; on referring to " North outside " and " South outside " it will be seen that at d on East side the coffer is in excess of the mean length by +·02 on N. and +·37 on S.; adding these to the mean length (89·62+·02+·37)=90·01 is the result for the E. outside of the coffer half way up. Similarly at 8 inches under the top on the same side, at f it is (89·62+·18+·34)=90·14 in length; or at 4 inches above the bottom (which is about the lowest point uninjured) it is at a (89·62+·13+·54)=90·29 in length. Or if the inside width is wanted, half way up the N. end, at d; referring to " West inside " and " East inside," at North end, d level, it is seen to be the mean inner width, 26·81, −·12 on W., +·02 on E.=26·71; the signs being, of course, *reversed* in adding *internal* offsets *together*. Similarly at the middle of the length of the coffer (H, d) the internal width is 26·81 + ·06 + ·05 = 26·92

If the thickness of the middle of the bottom is wanted, referring to "Bottom outside" and "Bottom inside," at H, δ, it is seen that the mean thickness, 6·89 is changed by − ·04 and +·02, and it is therefore 6·87 thick at that point. Or if the thickness of the middle of the N. end is wanted at d and δ, referring to "North outside" and "North inside," it is seen to be $(5·67 - ·21 + 0) = 5·46$; or the middle of the N. end at the top is $(5·67 + ·21 + ·01) = 5·89$. Thus the dimensions internal or external, or the thickness of any part, can be easily extracted from the tables by merely adding the corresponding offsets to the mean dimension.

60. The thicknesses of the sides, however, are involved in the measurement of the cubic bulk of the coffer, and therefore need to be very accurately known, in order to test the theories on the subject. And by the above method the thickness is dependent on the combination of many separate measures, and is, therefore, subject to an accumulation of small errors. To avoid this uncertainty, the sides were independently calipered; observing at every six inches, on the same spots on which the offsets were read. And it is to these caliperings which follow that I would mainly trust for determining the solid bulk of the coffer. The thickness is stated in hundredths of an inch.

		South end. B	C	D	E	F	G	H	J	K	L	M	North end. N	O
Top.	f	598	599	587	593	597	604	593	597	599	597	600	599	598
Thick-	e	592	597	583	579	586	584	580	579	582	585	590	590	597
ness of	d	595	591	594	590	578	568	561	561	570	577	581	589	597
West	c	596	589	592	588	576	561	555	553	559	571	579	591	596
side.	b	600	590	592	582	561	548	541	542	553	571	587	594	593
Base.	a	617	613	602	582	576	557	548	576	586	602	607	619	610
Means		598	595	591	586	579	572	564	570	573	581	590	595	598

		South end. B	C	D	E	F	G	H	J	K	L	M	North end. N	O
Top.	f	...	...	...	592	594	594	594	594	596	597	582	600	597
Thick-	e	...	583	587	589	593	594	593	597	595	596	596	594	595
ness of	d	575	585	588	589	597	587	586	586	591	594	597	596	596
East	c	571	581	587	587	592	590	584	583	581	589	593	596	596
side.	b	572	583	586	590	591	597	591	579	577	586	591	595	596
Base.	a	591	587	592	591	598	603	597	601	601	597	602	599	613
Means		575	585	588	590	594	593	590	589	589	593	592	596	597

		West side. β	γ	δ	East side. ϵ	ζ				West side. β	γ	δ	East side. ϵ	ζ
Top.	f	596	583	589	589	595		Top.	f	591	595	...	...	...
Thick-	e	574	561	564	560	571		Thick-	e	579	585	588	593	...
ness of	d	569	548	549	552	559		ness of	d	567	575	572	587	600
North	c	564	553	551	560	567		South	c	564	573	575	588	604
end.	b	567	561	553	563	572		end.	b	562	570	576	587	609
Base.	a	580	578	563	561	570		Base.	a	584	595	601	615	638
Means		574	563	561	564	573		Means		574	581	584	594	609

N

From these caliperings the mean thickness of each of the sides, as compared with the results of the offsets, are thus :—

		By Calipers.	By Offsets.	Difference.
Thickness of	N.	5·67	5·67	0
	E.	5·90	5·87	− ·03
	S.	5·88	5·89	+ ·01
	W.	5·84	5·82	− ·02

Hence there appears to be a constant error of − ·01 on an average, making the result of the thickness by the offsets to be less than the truth. This may be due to a tendency to read the offsets too large, or else possibly to a slight skewing of the calipers, as 3° skew would make this difference on 6 inches.

To compare in detail the results by calipers and offsets, over a small space, let us take the thickness of the N. end, along the lines *c* and *d*, which are near the mid height :—

		β	γ	δ	ϵ	ζ
At *d*	by offsets .	5·65	5·51	5·46	5·51	5·56
	by calipers .	5·69	5·48	5·49	5·52	5·59
At *c*	by offsets .	5·66	5·54	5·49	5·59	5·64
	by calipers .	5·64	5·53	5·51	5·60	5·67

Thus the mean difference between the thicknesses as ascertained by the two methods is ·022, with a constant difference in one direction of ·012 on an average. The spots observed on in the two methods were not always exactly identical; and so some difference may be due to waves of short length in the surface of the stone.

In stating the offsets on the top, the mean plane adopted is not the simple mean of all the offsets, but the mean of diagonally opposite pairs of offsets, so far as they can be taken. This is necessary in order to obtain a true result, as otherwise (the top being broken away all at one corner) any great tilt that it may have had, in relation to the base planes, would vitiate the result.

61. From the foregoing data the cubic quantities may be calculated of a simple rectilineal box, omitting all notice of the attachments for the lid, employing the mean planes :—

Contents = 72,030 ; solid bulk = 70,500 ; volume over all, 142,530 cubic inches. Or by the caliper results, instead of the mean planes, the bulk is $\frac{1}{580}$ more, and the contents probably about $\frac{1}{1000}$ less ; hence the quantities would be—

Contents = 71,960 ; solid bulk = 70,630 ; volume over all, 142,590.
These quantities have a probable error of only about 60 cubic inches on contents and volume, and 100 inches on the bulk. The bulk of the bottom is = 23,830 ; and hence one side and end is on an average = 23,335. Bulk of bottom × 3 is then = 71,490 ; and $\frac{3}{2}$ × bulk of sides and ends = 70,000, subject to about 100 cubic inches probable error.

62. The spaces, or " chambers of construction," as they have been called, which lie one over the other above the King's Chamber, are entered from a small passage which starts in the E. wall of the gallery, close under the roof. This is apparently an original passage, and leads into the lower chamber ; the other four spaces above that can only be entered by the forced ascent cut by Col. Howard Vyse. This latter passage is not so easy to go up as it might be, as it is nearly all in one continuous height, so that a slip at the top chamber means a fall of thirty feet ; and as there are no foot-holes, and the shaft is wide, and narrows upwards, an Arab guide of Dr. Grant's refused to venture up it, alleging that he had a wife and family to think of. Ali Gabri, however, was quite equal to the business, and held a rope ladder to help me, which he and I together held for Dr. Grant.

The mouth of the passage out of the top of the gallery is 26·3 wide horizontally at top, 26·2 at base, the S. side of it being formed by the topmost lap of the S. end of the gallery. The top and base of the mouth follow the slope of the gallery, the top being the top of the gallery, and the base the bottom of the topmost overlapping ; thus the mouth is 29·4 high, square with the gallery. The rough passage is 28½ wide, 32 inches high, and over 20 feet long.

All these chambers over the King's Chamber are floored with horizontal beams of granite, rough dressed on the under sides which form the ceilings, but wholly unwrought above. These successive floors are blocked apart along the N. and S. sides, by blocks of granite in the lower, and of limestone in the upper chambers, the blocks being two or three feet high, and forming the N. and S. sides of the chambers. On the E. and W. are two immense limestone walls wholly outside of, and independent of, all the granite floors and supporting blocks. Between these great walls all the chambers stand, unbonded, and capable of yielding freely to settlement. This is exactly the construction of the Pyramid of Pepi at Sakkara, where the end walls E. and W. of the sepulchral chamber are wholly clear of the sides, and also clear of the sloping roof-beams, which are laid three layers thick ; thus these end walls extend with smooth surfaces far beyond the chamber, and even beyond all the walls and roofing of it, into the general masonry of the Pyramid.

The actual dimensions of these chambers are as follow :—

	N.	E.	S.	W.
Top	462 to 470	...	468·4	247
4th	481	196	467	198
3rd	479 (?)	...	472	198
2nd	...	204·65	471·8	...
1st	460·8	205·8	464·6	205·9
(King's	412·8	206·4	412·5	206·1)

But these dimensions are merely of the rough masonry; and some lengths could not be measured owing to the encumbrance of blocks of stone and rubbish left in the chambers from Vyse's excavations.

63. In the first chamber the S. wall has fallen outwards, dragging past some of the roof-beams, and breaking other beams at the S.E. corner. The E. and W. end walls have sunk, carrying down with them the plaster which had been daubed into the top angle, and which cracked freely off the granite roofing. On the E. end one block is dressed flat, but all the others are rough quarried.

In the second chamber are some bosses on the N. and S. wall stones; and several of the stones of the N. wall are smoothed, and one polished like those in the King's Chamber, seeming as if some spare blocks had been used up here. The S.E. corner shows cracks in the roof ·52 wide. The masons' lines, drawn in red and black, are very remarkable in this and the upper chambers, as they show, to some extent, the methods of working. Some of the lines in this chamber, drawn in red on the S. wall blocks of granite, are over some of the plastering, but under other parts of the plaster. These lines, therefore, were drawn during the building, and while the plaster was being laid on, and slopped like whitewash into the joints. The red lines are always ill-defined and broad, about ¼ to 1½ inch; but, to give better definition, finer black lines were often used, either over the red or alone, about $\frac{1}{10}$ inch wide. On the S. wall, starting from a drafted edge on the W. wall, 4 inches wide, there is a vertical mason's-line at 22·3, a very bad joint at 51·5, another line at 70·5, another at 435·8, and the E. wall at 471·8. Thus the two end lines are 413·5 apart, evidently intended for the length of the King's Chamber below them, and define the required limits of this upper space. On the E. wall is a vertical mid-line drawn, with a cross line and some signs; from this mid-line to a line at the S. end is 101·8, and to a line at the N. end of the wall is 102·85; total, 204·65, intended for King's Chamber width. There is a large cartouche of Khnumu-Khufu, nearly all broken away by Vyse's forced entrance; but this and other hieroglyphs need not be noticed here, as they have been already published, while the details of the masons' marks and lines of measurement have been neglected.

In the third chamber, the N. and S. sides are of granite as before; but they rest on pieces of limestone, put in to fill up hollows, and bring them up to level: this showing, apparently, that the stock of granite supporting blocks had begun to run short at this stage of the building, and that any sort of pieces were used up, being eked out by limestone, which in the upper chambers supplied their places altogether. The flooring beams are very unequal in depth. and hence the sides of many of them are exposed, and show us the masons' marks. On the 1st beam from the E. end is a mid-line on the W. face at 98 from the S. On the 4th beam is a mid-line on the E. face, 102·8 to N., and 101 to S. On the 6th beam is a mid-line on W. face, 100 to N. and 101·5 to S.; these N. and S. ends being merely the rough sides of the chamber. There are two bosses on the S. side of the chamber. The chamber sides are much slopped over with liquid plaster. On the N. side is a vertical line on the western granite block, over the edge of a limestone block beneath it, apparently to show the builders where to place it. From the W. end of the chamber this line is at 10 inches, joints at 210 and 246, a red line at 260, chamber end at 479 (?), and end of granite blocks at 503.

In the fourth chamber the supporting blocks along the N. and S. sides are all of limestone, and are much cracked and flaked up by top pressure. The great end walls, between which all these chambers stand, have here sunk as much as 3 inches in relation to the floors and sides ; as is shown by the ledges of plaster sticking to them, which have originally fitted into the edges of the ceiling. The roof-beam by the forced entrance has been plastered over, then coloured red, and after that accidentally splashed with some thin plastering. Along the N. wall, from the E. end of the floor as 0, there is a line at 37·8, another at 58·5, another at 450·6, and the W. end at 481 : thus the extreme lines are 412·8 apart, with a supplemental line at 20·7 from one of them. This last was probably put on in case the end line should be effaced in building, so that the workmen would not need to remeasure the whole length. One stone, 65 inches long, has a mark on it of " 3 cubits." On the S. wall, from the E. end=0, there is a line at 32·6, another at 384·7, another at 446·5, and the W. end at 467 ; here the extreme lines are 413·9 apart, with a supplemental line 61·8 (or 3 × 20·6) from one end. Along both sides of the chamber is a red line all the way, varying from 20·6 to 20·2 below the ceiling ; with the vertical lines just described crossing it near each end. Remembering the Egyptian habit of building limestone courses in the rough, and marking a line to show to where they were to be trimmed down level, this line seems to have been put on to regulate the trimming down of these lime-stone sides ; either as a supplemental line, like those one cubit from the true marks on the granite beams, or else placed a cubit lower than the trimming level, in order that it should not be effaced in the cutting. On the E. floor-beam is a line 98·6 from the S. end. On the third beam is a line 100 to N. and 96·2 to S. end. On the 4th beam a line 98·3 to N., and 100·6 to S. end. On the sixth beam a horizontal line running all along it, with a mid-line 98·0 to N. and 98·1 to S. end ; and a supplemental line at 20·3 to 20·6 from S. end. On the other side of the beam a line is at 98·1 to N. and 96 to S. end. The rough tops of the floor-beams of this chamber show most interestingly the method of quarrying them ; exactly as may be seen on the rough tops of the granite roofing inside the Third Pyramid. On the top of each stone is a hollow or sinking running along one edge ; and branching from this, at right angles across the stone, are grooves 20 to 25 inches apart, about 4 wide, and 1½ deep. These seem to show that in cutting out a block of granite, a long groove was cut in the quarry to determine the trend or strike of the cleavage ; and then, from this, holes were roughly jumped about 4 inches diameter and 2 feet apart, to determine the dip of the cleavage plane. This method avoids any danger of skew fractures, and it has the true solidity and certainty of old Egyptian work.

In the fifth or top chamber, the width is quite undefined ; and we can only say that between the points where the sloping roof-slabs appear is 247 inches. The roof-slabs have separated at the apex 1·55 at E. end, and 1·0 at W. end. The end walls are very rough, being merely the masonry of the core. On the second floor-beam are two horizontal lines 20·6 to 20·7 apart, with three vertical lines across them, 103·1 and 103·5 apart. They have triangles drawn in black on both the vertical and horizontal lines, the triangle on the horizontal being 12·5 from the end vertical line, and therefore not apparently at any exact distance along it. On the fourth beam from the E. is a horizontal line on its W. side, with four vertical lines : these are a mid-line, others at 102·6 and 102·6 from it, and a supplemental line 20·0 from one of these. On the E. side of the same is a horizontal and three vertical lines ; the two end ones 206·3 apart, and a supplemental line 21·0 from one end. Both of these horizontal lines have a small black triangle, with one side on the line. The third beam from the E. has four verticals, with a triangle beyond the last. These are 103·3 and 103·25 from a mid-line, with a supplemental line 20·95 from one end. The E. beam has five verticals, 103·0 and 102·7 from the mid-line, with supplemental lines at 20·7 and 19·4 from the ends ; it has also a horizontal line, with a large red triangle on the lower side of it, and a smaller black triangle inside the red. On the S. side is a line 29·3 from the W. end, apparently one terminal of the 412-inch length. The roofing-beams are all numbered, beginning at the W. end of the N. side, going along to the E., turning to the S. side, and so back to the W. end. The numbers visible on the under-sides of the beams are 4, 18, 21, and 23 ; probably the numbers of the others are on the sides now covered.

From all these details of the lines, it seems that the roofing-blocks had usually a mid-line and two end lines marked on their sides as a guide in placing them ; and, in case of obliteration, extra lines were provided, generally a cubit (20·6) from each end, but sometimes at other points. The horizontal lines were probably to guide the workman in cutting the straight under-sides of the beams ; and it would be desirable to measure through some cracks to find their distances from the ceiling side. The flooring of the top chamber has large holes worked in it, evidently to hold the butt ends of beams which supported the sloping roof-blocks during the building.

64. General summary of the positions inside the Great Pyramid :

	Horizontally.			Vertically.
	From N. Base.	From Centre.	E. from Centre.	Above Pavement.
Beginning of entrance	524·1± ·3	N. 4010·0± ·3	mid. 287·0± ·8	+ 668·2± ·1
S. end of entrance passage	4228· ±2·	N. 306· ±2·	mid. 286·4±1·	− 1181· ±1·
S. end of N. subterranean passage	4574· ±2·	S. 40· ±2·	mid. 286·3±1·	− 1178· ±1·
Subterranean Chamber, centre ...	4737· ±2·	S. 203· ±2·	mid. 25·9±2·	− 1056· ±2· roof
N. end of S. subterranean passage	4900· ± 2·	S. 366· ±2·	mid. 284·9±1·	− 1219· ±1·5
S. end ,, ,, ,,	5546· ±3·	S. 1012· ±3·	mid. 277·1	− 1213· ±2·
Beginning Ascending ,,	1517·8± ·3	N. 3016·3± ·3	mid. 286·6± ·8	+ 179·9± ·2
End of ,, ,,	2907·3± ·8	N. 1626·8± ·8	mid. 287· ±1·5	+ 852·6± ·3
Queen's Chamber, N.E. corner ...	4402·1± ·8	N. 102·0± ·8	side 308· ±3·	+ 834·4± ·4
,, ,, mid. W. roof...	4533·8± ·8	N. ·3± ·8	side 72· ±3·	+1078·7± ·6 roof
Gallery, virtual S. end, floor	4595·8± ·9	S. 61·7± ·9	mid. 284·4±3·	+1689·0± ·5
Gallery, top of step face............	4534·5± ·9	S. ·4± ·9	mid. 284·4±3·	+1694·1± ·7
Antechamber, N. end, floor	4647·8± ·9	S. 113·7± ·9	same ?	+1692·6± ·6
,, S. ,, roof	4763·9± ·9	S 229·8± ·9	same ?	+1841·5± ·6 roof
King's Chamber, floor	4865·0± ·9	S. 330·9± ·9	mid. same ?	+1692·8± ·6
,, ,, N.E. wall base	4864·7± ·9	S. 330·6± ·9	side 305·0±3·	+1688·5± ·6
,, ,, roof..............				+1921·6± ·6
				to 1923·7± ·6

CHAPTER VIII.

THE OUTSIDE OF THE SECOND PYRAMID.

65. THE casing of the Second Pyramid is different in its arrangement from that of the Great Pyramid, as already mentioned (section 15). The lowest two courses* of the casing are of granite, very well preserved where it is not altogether removed. In order to avoid the risk of working an acute angle for the lower edge of the bottom course, the builders made the face drop down for some depth vertically from the edge of the slope, building the pavement against the vertical face (see Pl. xii.). Thus no edge of the block was sharper than a right angle, and the two outer edges top and bottom were considerably over a right angle, and therefore not liable to injury. But by so arranging it they required the vertical foot of the casing to be as high as the pavement thickness, or else to be raised ; and as the pavement must not be too thin, for fear of cracking, and also as they did not wish to be limited to the exact amount of surplus that formed the vertical foot ; they therefore cut the rock to support the casing-blocks at a higher level than that for the pavement bed. The result is that though both casing and pavement may be destroyed, there still remains a raised square of rock, standing some inches above the surrounding surface, and marking out the original extent of the Pyramid. An arrangement which was thus far more permanent than that of the Great Pyramid, where the casing and pavement, if once removed, leave behind no evidence of their site. The nature of this arrangement can be easily examined at the W. end of the S. side, where a block of casing remains, slightly shifted at one side, but otherwise *in situ;* it rests on the raised square of rock, and has the S.W. corner of the raised square within a few yards of it, showing the relationship very plainly.

Accordingly I did not waste labour by needing to search for actual casing stones under the high rubbish heaps, in the midst of the sides ; at which points, moreover, the casing would not define the direction of each side. I merely required to uncover this raised square of rock, at places near the ends of each side, and I also obtained the corners at the N.E., S.E., S.W. At the N.W. the whole rock is dressed flat, the pavement having been the same thickness as the

---

* I have seen but one course ; Vyse reports finding two courses.

casing foot, but the raised square is found a short way from this corner along each side.

66. Having, then, found and fixed twelve points of the sides, the actual corners of the square were adopted as being probably the most accurately executed points, to define the intended size; and they (with the points near the N.W. corner) yield a square of the following size :—

	Length.	Difference from mean.	Azimuth.	Diff. from mean.
N. side	8471·9	− 3·0 inches	− 5′ 31″	− 5″
E. „	8475·2	+ ·3	− 6′ 13″	− 47″
S. „	8476·9	+ 2·0	− 5′ 40″	− 14″
W. „	8475·5	+ ·6	− 4′ 21″	+ 65″
Mean	8474·9	1·5	− 5′ 26″	33″

The various other points of the square of rock that were fixed, differ from the above square but little.

At 425 N. of S.E. corner, the edge is 2·6 inside the square.
At 720 W. of „   „   „   ·2   „
At 367 E. of S.W.   „   „   „   ·7   „
At 330 E. of „   „   „   ·2   „

Thus there is a mean variation of ·9 inch from the adopted square.

But beside this there is the casing still remaining on the upper part of the Pyramid; and the lowest corner of this casing at each edge of the Pyramid was observed on in the main triangulation by the 10-inch theodolite. Hence there is another check on the raised square. Taking, then, the differences between the corners observed on, and the diagonals of the raised square, these differences of the casing are thus :—

N.E. + 1·7 ; S.E. + ·6 ; S.W. + ·3 ; N.W. + ·3 ; mean + ·7 inch.

From this it is seen that the builders skewed round the planes of the casing as they went upward; the twist being + 1′ 40″ on the mean of the sides; so that it is absolutely − 3′ 50″ from true orientation at the upper part. But it must be remembered that these differences include the errors of recognising the same point of a stone, by natural markings without any definite signal or station, and viewed from different directions at about ¼ mile distance.

The collateral evidence, then, confirms the position of the square, as first stated.

67. For the angle of slope of the faces, the direct measures by goniometer and level on the granite *in situ* gave 53° 12′ ± 2′, but by measurement from plumb line 53° 2′; the block has been slightly shifted, but the top surface only varies 1′ from level, being high on the outer edge. By goniometer measures of

O

24 blocks, both of granite and limestone, lying around the Pyramid, the mean is 53° 14′ ± 5′ ; and though this involves the assumption of horizontal courses, if this be taken as the angle of slope, yet it agrees so closely with the casing *in situ,* that probably 53° 10′ ± 4′ will be the best statement.

Hence the height will be 5,664 ± 13 inches.

68. The lowest course of casing was of granite, and is 41·52 ± ·05 high, vertically, from the top to the base of its slope, and its vertical face below that 11 high, as measured at the S.W. The raised square of rock at the S.W. under this casing, is only 1·3 to 1·9 above the pavement bed ; at the S.W. corner it is 9·8 high ; at the S.E. corner, 2·3 to 2·8 high ; and at the N.E. 0 to 4½ high. All along the edge of it are holes, rudely rectangular, beginning in the pavement bed, and sloping deeper down into the raised square, where they end vertically. Their average size is 10 inches along the rock edge, the sloping bottom beginning 10 inches outwards from the rock edge, and running 5 inches into it, with a depth there of about 4 inches ; distance between one hole and another 12 inches. These holes are evidently intended to allow space for the ends of crowbars or beams used in placing the casing in position.

The upper part of the Pyramid was cased with Mokattam limestone, of a rather different quality to that of the Great Pyramid ; it is grayer, harder, more splintery, and of not such a regular and certain fracture.

Where some foundation stones had been removed, low down under the S.E. socket, a coin of Sultan Hasan, 1347–1361, was found in clearing the sand in 1881. As the mosque of this Sultan is said to have been built with stones from the Pyramids, this coin rather suggests that some stones were removed for that purpose from the base of the Second Pyramid. The casing in general, however, was said to be still in its place in the time of Palerma, 1581, and of Albinus, 1591 ; though in Sandy's view, 1611, only the present cap of casing is shown.

The lower part of the Pyramid core, all round, is of rock ; unmoved, but hewn into shape ; higher on the W. and lower on the E. side. Above this lie two or three courses of huge blocks of Gizeh rock, much larger than those brought from the Mokattam quarries on the E. bank.

The heights of the lower courses, and position of the rock, and rock blocks, are as follow :—

N.E.	S.E.	S.W.		N.W.	
458·0	457·0	457·5		458·0	
438·0	437·0	437·5		437·0	
416·0	416·0	416·5		417·0	
381·0	381·0	381·5		381·0	
340·0	340·0	340·0		340·0	
291·5	295·0	293·0		292·0	
242·5	245·0	242·5	rock blocks	250·5	rock blocks
...	213·0	207·5	„ „	220·0	„ „

N.E.	S.E.	S.W.	N.W
193·5	...	...	210·0 ledge
...	179·0	179·5 rock blocks	170·0 rock top
159·0 rock blocks	162·0 rock blocks	...	...
...	143·0 „ „	142·5 rock top	133·0
136·0 „ „	...	132·5	127·0 ledge
74·5 rock top	78·5 rock top	86·5	85·0
62·5	...	41·5	37·5
o pavement	o	o	o
− 14·5 raised square	− 11·0 raised square	−10·5 raised square	
− 18 (?)paving bed	...	−20 paving bed	− 23·5 paving bed
	− 52·5 rock	...	...

These series of measurements were not levelled together, but are only adjusted, so that they represent the builder's intention, though not his errors of level. It is seen that though the courses are not very regular in thickness, yet the 10th course at 20 cubits level (416) runs all round; and the 5th course is at 10 cubits level (207·5) on S.W., and at the ledge (*i.e.*, casing back) at N.W. The first course is 2 cubits high (41·5) where seen at S.W.

69. The pavement around the Pyramid was sunk slightly in the rock, and the edges of its bed were found near the N.W. corner. They were 528·8 and 527·9 distant from Pyramid base on the N., and 530·9 on the W. side. This is just about the same as the most usual breadth of the Great Pyramid pavement bed. Vyse reports finding 432 inches breadth of paving still in existence.

70. The whole site of the Pyramid is artificially levelled; it is cut into the sloping rock of the hill-side, deeply on the W., and less along the N.; it is built up at the N.E. to support the pavement, by a platform of immense blocks; and at the S.E. the rock falls rapidly away and has probably also been built over, in order to level it up for the pavement.

The great shelf or area (see Pl. iv.), thus cut out on the hill-side to hold the Pyramid, has approximately vertical sides along the W. and N. But these sides are not equidistant from the Pyramid; the top edge of the W. side being 1,105 distant from the N.W., and 1,083 from the S.W. corners of the Pyramid; while the N. side is 2,255 from the N.W. corner, and 2,312 from near the middle of the Pyramid side. The directions are not parallel to the Pyramid, the W. side lying − 8′ from the Pyramid azimuth, and the N. side − 56′.

Within this lowered area are rows of grooves and cross grooves cut in the rock, which is thus divided up into squares. These are the remains of the trenches by which the workmen cut out the whole of this space; the reasons for their being so are (1) they are considerably askew to the finished work, and irregular in size, and have therefore not been made for any structural purpose; (2) they are simply grooves and cross grooves, so that they could not be the beginning of any erection or rock chamber; and (3) the grooves are exactly like others, on the rock surface outside the lowered area, just N. of these, and in other places ; which others are clearly remains of unfinished dressing down of the rock.

The sizes of these squares are rather variable ; the average distances of similar parts being 132·3, with a mean difference of 5·7 ; and this is divided into 20·2 for the groove, and 112·1 for the block between the grooves. These are by measures from E. to W. ; the average breadths from N. to S. are 20+109=129 ; evidently intended for the same, but only measureable on 4 or 5 squares, instead of 18 from E. to W.

Outside of the lowered area are other grooves on the rock N. of it, the most distinct and continuous of which varies from 350 at W. end to 390 (at 4,400 E. of that) from the edge of the area.

71. Around the N., W., and S. sides of the Pyramid and its area is a large peribolus wall. This wall differs in its character on each side, and does not seem to have been planned with any uniformity. On the N. side it is a wide substructure of very large blocks, rather rudely hewn, and bearing cubit marks and numbers on the backs. The N. face (which was the only one left exposed) is 2,733 from the edge of the area, nearly opposite the middle of the Pyramid, and 2,808 from the area at the N.W. corner. This substructure is 300 ± 3 inches wide near the E. end, and 344 at the W. end ; but it is difficult to recognise its original alignment as so much of it has been removed or buried. On the top of this is a crest of wall, the N. face of which is + 15′ different from the Pyramid azimuth ; it is of less width than the substructure, being 108· near the E. and 206· near the W. end ; but it is probable that this really refers to different lines of construction. A higher part of it at the W. end appears to recede 8 inches on the S. side, and a footing, formed by a lower course, projects 18 inches. On the whole, it appears that each course was set a little backward ; and without largely uncovering it, it would be hard to make certain what its original width was before it was dilapidated. It is altogether about 13,300 long, or rather over ¼ mile. Its original height cannot be easily settled ; probably 20 feet would be below the mark. On the S. side this wall is much less finished, and has been banked up to the top of the broad part by a vast heap of chips, which have been kept in position by building retaining walls in them. Two of these retaining walls that I partly uncovered, were of rough broken stone, neatly put together, and mud plastered on the S. faces. They had a considerable batter, and the tops of their S. faces were at 137 and 299 from the S. face of the great wall. Among the stones I observed pieces of basalt and granite waste ; these probably came from cutting the basalt pavement E. of the Great Pyramid, and from trimming the granite of the King's Chamber, or the lowest course of the Second Pyramid.

Exactly from the end of this great wall, there turns off a much narrower wall which runs parallel with the W. side of the Pyramid. This W. wall is 70 wide at the top, with a moderate batter of about 1 in 10. It is built of rough scraps and blocks of limestone, neatly fitted together with a smooth face ; and was probably 6 or 8 feet high when complete. The intention seems to have been to place it as far from the edge of the area as is the N. wall ; the outer face of the N. wall being 2,733 to 2,808 from the area, and the outside of the W. wall 2,795 from the N.W. corner of the area, to 2,923 from the area at the S.W. corner of the Pyramid. The azimuth of this W. wall is + 38' from the Pyramid azimuth, and it runs on till it joins the wall of the Third Pyramid.

The true peribolus wall of the Second Pyramid, on the S. side, is only a short piece, 500 feet long, which appears to have been incomplete when the Third Pyramid walls were begun ; since it was merged into the latter by an elbow wall, instead of being uniformly finished. It is a fine piece of work as far as it goes, and was apparently intended to be at the same distance from the Pyramid as is the great North wall. It is 5,166 at its outer side, from the S.E. corner of the Pyramid ; and the outer face of the N. wall is 5,043 from near the N.E. corner of the Pyramid. Thus the N. and S. walls were equidistant from the Pyramid ; but the N. and W. walls were equidistant from the edge of the area. The azimuth of the inner face of the S. wall is −9' from Pyramid azimuth. The wall is broad in the lower part ; with a narrower crest upon the top of it, which is 131 wide at the E. end, narrowing upwards to 113 in breadth.

72. Beyond the western peribolus wall there lie the large barracks of the workmen. These have been hitherto considered merely as lines of stone rubbish, or masons' waste heaps ; and though Vyse cut through one part, he merely says that the ridges "were found to be composed of stones and sand, and their origin was not discovered" (vol. ii. p. 88). But on looking closely at them I observed the sharply defined edges of walls ; and as soon as these were begun to be cleared, the ruined tops of the walls were seen, the spaces being filled with blown sand. The wall first cleared was traced continuously for some 80 feet ; and at last the arrangement in all parts was found to consist solely of long galleries. In the plan of Lepsius there is a variation apparently at the easternmost walls, where something like a chamber is shown : nothing of the kind is visible on the surface, and on cutting along the northern ends and middles of all these galleries, nothing but uniform walls were found. Also nearly the whole length of the first gallery from the peribolus was cleared, showing a continuous wall right along the site where the separate buildings are marked in the "Denkmäler."

These galleries are built of rough pieces of limestone (somewhat like the W. peribolus wall), bedded in mud, and faced with hard mud, or mud and lime ; the floors of the galleries are also of hard mud. The walls are all united at one end into one head wall, which runs 14' skew of the Pyramid on the W. ; and the open ends of the walls are finished with wider pilasters, or *antae*, of hewn stone. The length of the galleries headed by the W. wall were measured as 1,062 at the S. end of the row, and 1,058 at the N. end; and the gallery next the peribolus wall is 1,033 inches long. The enlarged ends of hewn stone are 62 to 75 inches long; so the total length of the galleries is 1,124, 1,127, and 1,108 in different parts. The walls average 51·5 thick at the top, with a batter of 1 in 10; and their centres are 164·6 apart, leaving a clear width of 113·1 for the gallery. The hewn stone ends of the walls are 80 wide, thus leaving an entrance of 85 inches wide. These measures are on the northern walls; those of the western range are farther apart, their centres averaging 176 apart, and the ends 77 to 87 wide, leaving entrances 90 to 100 wide. There are in all 91 galleries; which make an aggregate of over a mile and a half of gallery length, 9½ feet wide, and 7 feet high.

For what purpose, then, can such a vast amount of accommodation have been provided? Not certainly for priests' dwellings, since it is too extensive, too rough in work, and in the very opposite direction to the temples. Hardly either for storehouses, since it is so much out of the way, and too large for any likely amount of stores. It seems, therefore, only attributable to the workmen's barracks. The work is just suitable for such a purpose; strong and useful, and with about as much elaboration as an Egyptian would put into work that had to last in daily use for one or two generations. The extent of the galleries is also very reasonable. Supposing the men had a fair allowance of room (more than in some works at present) the whole barrack would hold about 4,000 men; and such would not be an unlikely number for the permanent staff of masons and their attendants employed on a pyramid. There is no probability of the walls being later than the Second Pyramid, because (1) they are arranged square with it; (2) at a part of the hill which would be out of the way for any other work; and (3) they are built of exactly the same style as the adjoining western peribolus wall and the retaining walls.

Most of the excavating that I did here was only on the tops of the walls, to show their position; but part of the westernmost of the N. series of galleries was cleared out to within a foot or two of the bottom; and then, while I watched them, two men turned over all the remaining sand, down to the floor, keeping a clear strip of floor between the shifted and unshifted sand. Several yards' length were thus cleared, and I closely looked at each shovelful of sand as it was thrown. Many scraps of pottery were found, much like the style of the pottery of the Great Pyramid masons; but nothing else artificial appeared. I had not time to make further clearances here; but the barrenness of a spot only $\frac{1}{500}$ of the whole extent of the galleries, should not discourage further work in a place so likely to yield good results. During the general clearing of the walls, many fragments of statues were found, in diorite and alabaster, of the fourth dynasty style : and among a large quantity of quartzite scraps lying on the surface, I found part of a life-size head, of an unusual type. Unaccountable blocks of granite were often found, lying loose in the sand ; they are smoothed all over, about 30 lbs. weight, and of pillowy forms, with rounded faces and slight edges. They never showed any wear, and so could hardly be corn-rubbers ; and yet they were too smooth and not flat enough to be intended for a building.

CHAPTER IX.

THE INSIDE OF THE SECOND PYRAMID.

73. THE doorway of the Second Pyramid is lost, along with the casing; and the granite blocks of the passage end irregularly. The position of the passage was fixed from a station mark near it; its axis is 490·3 E. of the middle of the N. face. Its azimuth was already observed by Prof. Smyth, as — 5′ 37″; which is almost exactly the mean azimuth of the sides, as by my triangulation they are — 5′ 26″, with a mean difference of 33″. Hence, if the horizontal passage is the same azimuth as the sloping, the chamber lies altogether E. of the Pyramid centre by about 47 inches. This is much the same arrangement as in the Great Pyramid.

The entrance passage is entirely of rough dressed granite, none of it polished; like the work of the King's Chamber ceiling and the Antechamber, and not like the King's Chamber walls in the Great Pyramid. The flaws in it are made good with plaster, much of which is to be seen on the first roof-stone, and all along the side of the roof, sometimes half-way across it. This was laid on with a board or trowel, and afterwards painted red, like the plastering in the Granite Temple.

This passage was measured thus, in height and breadth :—

	E.	W.	Top.	Base.
At mouth	47·33	47·32	41·62	41·21
Half-way down	47·31	47·13	41·08	41·17
Near end	47·44	47·23	41·34	41·33
Means	Height 47·29±·03		Width 41·29±·05	

The greater irregularity in the width than in the height of the passage, shows the builders to have been less careful than the masons; since the height depends on gauging the side blocks to a uniform height, whereas the width only depends on their position.

74. At the bottom of the slope, the roof has a half-round drum or roll across it (see Pl. xii.), like the "roller" over all the tomb doors. From this the passage goes southward horizontally (see Pl. vii.). From the end of the sloping roof to the other side of the roll is 11·7 on E., 11·6 on W.; or, to the portcullis groove

40·92. The portcullis is a slab of granite working in vertical grooves in the granite sides of the passage; the width of the passage being 41·38 there, the grooves are 9·68 deep on E. and 10·05 on W., making 61·11 in all; the width by a single measurement being 61·14 in front, or N., and 61·35 at back, or S. The width of the grooves is 15·77 E., and 15·19 W., and the stone slab of the portcullis is about ½-inch thinner. Thus it is almost the same as the granite leaf in the Great Pyramid, which is 15·14 to 16·28 thick. The granite walling and roofing ends at 41·4 to 43·0 behind the portcullis. The portcullis was fiercely attacked by Perring, who tried to break it up, with the vain idea of finding a passage leading out of the top of its groove; but it resisted all his efforts, and it is now propped up high enough to crawl under it, by rough pieces of limestone in each groove. All the lower part of the entrance passage is obstructed with stones, left there by the Arabs when removing building materials from the interior. At the end of the granite the walls are of good limestone with finely-picked faces, like the walls of the gallery in the Great Pyramid; and the passage roof immediately rises 23·0, so that it measures thus :—

	E.	W.	Top.	Base.
Near portcullis .	70·76	70·38	41·56	41·78
Beyond gaps in floor	71·53	71·36	41·65	41·55
Near chamber . .	71·27	71·10	41·70	41·30
Means . .	Height 71·06±·13		Width 41·59±·04	

The height on the W. side, near the chamber, is taken to irregular plastering on the roof. The fine picked walls near the portcullis, soon merge along the horizontal passage into very rough picked work cut in the rock, and plastered over; farther on there is more masonry, but all plastered; and after that the rock continues on to the chamber. The intention in the 71 inch height seems to be to make it half as high again as the ordinary passage: 71·06 × ⅔ = 47·38±·09; and the other passage is 47·29±·03.

75. The great chamber is entirely cut in the rock, excepting the pointed gable roof, which is built of limestone beams, like that of the Queen's Chamber in the Great Pyramid. Stone has been let into the walls to make good defects; and the whole surface was stuccoed. The floor is partly of rock and partly paved; the paving is of fine limestone 9 to 14 inches thick, except around the coffer at the W. end, where it is of deep granite blocks. The coffer is of the usual form, like that in the Great Pyramid, but was let into the floor up to the level of its sliding lid. The floor was lamentably torn up by Perring in search of other chambers, and the stones are now piled up all over the E. wall. The chamber is,

195·8 on E., 195·9 on W.; 557·9 on N., 557·4 on S.;
206·4 high at N.W.; 206·3 and 206·5 (?) at S.W.

Vyse gives 38 inches for the gable roof rise (though measuring the height from the wall base instead of the floor), and this gives 244·4 for the height of the ends. The doorway is on the N. wall at 104·3 to 144·9 from the E. wall. On both N. and S. walls there is a vertical red line drawn, on the N. at 198·3 from E., and on the S. at 198·6 from E. These red lines on both walls run up to ·5 or ·1 on the W. side of a blind hole in the rock, which looks like the beginning of an air-channel; and there is a square of the same size marked adjoining the line some way below the hole, as if it had been at first intended to cut the hole lower down. These holes and squares were measured thus :—

| | | Hole. | | | | | Square. | | | | Base of Hole. | |
	E.	W.	Top.	Base.	Deep.	E.	W.	Top.	Base.		To Ceiling.	To Square.
N. .	11·5	11·2	8·8	9·1	11·5	12·2	11·8	8·7	9·0		53·6	62·8
S. .	10·5	10·2	7·4	8·1	13·4	11·6	11·5	8·7?	9·0		55·2	62·1

The backs of the holes are quite irregular and unfinished.

The coffer is on the outside 43·1 at N., and 42·9 at S. end, distant from W. wall; increased now by ·5 in shifting it. To the N. wall it is 42·5, and to the S. wall 50·0.

76. The coffer is well polished, not only inside but all over the outside; even though it was nearly all bedded into the floor, with blocks plastered against it. The bottom is left rough, and shows that it was sawn and after-wards dressed down to the intended height; but in sawing it the saw was run too deep and then backed out; it was, therefore, not dressed down all over the bottom, the worst part of the sawing being cut ·20 deeper than the dressed part. This is the only error of workmanship in the whole of it; it is polished all over the sides in and out, and is not left with the saw lines visible on it like the Great Pyramid coffer. The finish is about the same as on the walls of the King's Chamber, and the horizontal polishing lines can be seen inside the N. end.

The lid is lying on the floor of the chamber, unbroken; it was slid on to the coffer, and held by a projection on its base, which fitted into undercut grooves along the N., E., and S. sides of the coffer, the W. side being cut away to the depth of the groove. The grooves in the coffer are not parallel, but are wider apart at the W., so that the lid should have no chance of jamming in being put on. When finally slid into place, two pins (probably of bronze) dropped down out of holes in the lid, into corresponding holes in the W. side of the coffer.

The designers were evidently afraid, however, of the coffer being turned over, so as to let the pins drop back into the lid; they therefore sunk the coffer into the floor. To make it still safer they put resin in the pin-holes, where it may still be seen; then the pins, being ready heated, were put into the holes in the lid, which was quickly closed ; thus the pins sank ½ inch to 1 inch, melting their way into the resin, and probably forcing it up their sides. This process made sure that there could be no way of getting the lid off without breaking it, and the design answered perfectly ; the lid never was drawn off, On one side of the groove in the coffer may be seen a little scrap of cement· this shows that the lid was cemented on in the grooves, and that it never was slid back, or it must have rubbed off such a fragile scrap. This cementing on of the lid was also of use to prevent any shake ; so that the labour of wrenching it off, and bruising the undercutting to pieces by wriggling and jogging it up and down, must have been enormous. This seems, however, to have been the way of forcing it, as the undercutting is much broken, and the cement in the groove, and the melted-in pins, make it impossible to suppose any other mode of removing the lid. There is a good deal of crystallized salt on the inside of the coffer.

77. The size of the coffer was measured thus :—

		E.	Mid.	W.		Mean.	Mean error.
Outer length	Top	103·62	103·64	103·69		103·68	·04
	Mid.	103·73	Inaccessible.			±·02	
	Base	103·72	„				
		N.	⅓ along.	⅔ along.	S.		
Outer width	Top	41·96	41·97	41·96	41·99	41·970	·015
	Mid.	41·95	Inaccessible.		42·00	±·006	
	Base	All inaccessible.					
Outer height	E.	38·12	38·12	37·98	38·07	38·12	
	W.	All inaccessible.				intended.	
Sides thick at the top	E.	7·65	7·66	7·59	7·61	7·645	·03
	W.	7·62	7·64	7·70	7·69	±·01	
		E.	Mid.	W.			
Inner length	Top	84·63	84·68	84·63		84·73	·07
	Mid.	84·74	84·80	84·91		±·02	
	Base	84·69	84·76	84·80			
		N.	⅓ along.	⅔ along.	S.		
Inner width	Top	26·66	26·68	26·73	26·67	26·69	·04
	Mid.	26·73	26·74	26·79	26·76	±·01	
	Base	26·70 ?	26·71	26·70	26·73		
Inner depth	East	29·51	29·58	29·62	29·57	29·59	·03
	Mid.	29·59			29·58	±·01	
	West	29·68			29·61		
		N.	Mid.	S.			
Ledge depth	East	1·72	1·76	1·60		1·70	·04
	West	1·73		1·69		±·02	

Ledge wide, 1·20 to 2·30 on N., 1·08 to 1·90 on S.

Lid, 103·73 on W., 42·03 on S. Thickness, 9·89 W.S.W., 8·20 S.S.W., 8·22 S. 8·24 S.E.

The mean error of the dimensions is thus only ·04 inch. The two pin-holes in the top of the W. side are cut with a tube drill, and average 1·07 diameter ; their sides are thus :—

N. hole...... 5·40 to 6·42 from N. inner end.   3·76 to 4·84 from W. outside.
S. hole...... 5·74 to 6·85 from S.   „   „   3·86 to 4·92   „   „   „

On the outside bottom the height is constant all over the dressed part, being 38·12 ; and it only diminishes at the part where the saw ran too deep, and where it has not been at all farther reduced by dressing.

This coffer being 42·0 inches wide, can never have been taken through the passages, as the upper passage is only 41·3 wide, and the lower is 41·2 and 41·6. Hence it must have been put into the chamber before the roofing was laid over it, and so before the Pyramid was built upon that.

78. Beside the coffer chamber there is one lower in the rock, which has a rock passage leading to it, descending northwards out of the floor of the horizontal passage (see Pl. vii.). This passage runs down for some way ; then goes horizontal, has an enlargement on the E. side, and a sloping passage to a chamber on the W. side ; and then re-ascends ; and (if cleared out) would come out on the pavement in front of the N. face. The descending part is all plastered with a flat tool. The lower chamber is also plastered, and is cut very roughly in some parts ; on the roof even 6 inches too much having been taken off, and then plastered up ; this great deficiency is, however, the same on both sides of the roof, and it looks as if some different form had been begun, and then abandoned. This chamber is

411·9 on N.   411·2 on S.   123·1 on E.   123·6 on W.

The door in the E. side is 41·2 wide ; and 40·9 from N., 41·0 from S. side. The short sloping passage into the chamber is 41·0 wide at top, where it branches from the other passage, which is 41·2 and 41·6 wide. The recess opposite the passage into the chamber is 123·8 long in front (W.), 122·0 at back (E.), and 68·2 wide on N., 67·8 on S., beside the width of the passage, which makes a total of 109·4 N., and 109·4 S. The use of such a recess opposite the passage, which turns off at right angles, is plainly seen in the small pyramids to be for turning a coffin so as to pass it into the chamber. This shows that it was intended to introduce a coffin into the lower chamber, about 40 × 105 long. There is good reason to regard this chamber as a second place of interment ; and it might well have been used quite apart from the other chamber and passages, by blocking the communication between them, and reaching this by the opening in the pavement. The passage to the pavement is blocked up with limestone ; which was partly removed, but not opened through, by Vyse.

This passage was closed by a granite portcullis, and it is important to observe how this was introduced. The block of granite was taken along the passage from the southward on edge, and the wall was cut away on one side in a slope, so as to just allow of the block being turned flat across the passage by slewing it round in a complex way. The block was then pushed up into the groove cut in the rock for it, and the cutting in the side required to get it in was filled up by masonry at the back of the block. Thus, to any one forcing an entrance, nothing but rock and the granite slab would meet them. The skill required to turn over and lift such a block, in such a confined space, is far more striking than the moving of much larger masses in the open air, where any number of men could work on them. By measuring the bulk, it appears that this portcullis was nearly two tons in weight, and would require 40 to 60 men to lift it ; the space, however, would not allow of more than a tenth of that number working at it; and this proves that some very efficient method was used for wielding such masses, quite apart from mere abundance of manual force.

CHAPTER X.

THE OUTSIDE OF THE THIRD PYRAMID.

79. THE Third Pyramid has never been quite finished. Its granite casing blocks are left in probably the same condition that they were sent from Assouan, with their outer faces in the rough,* but smoothly dressed down on the joint surfaces. These surfaces of contact are flat dressed, with a slightly projecting line of polished stone round the edges of the faces ; thus the stones would be in contact along the outer surfaces of the joints, though there was cement between the stones on the face in general. This line of polish is well defined on its outer edge, the stone being quite rough outside it, and sinking away sharply from it. This is important for estimating the intended plane of finish. The limestone casing which covered the upper part of the Pyramid was finished off like that of the other Pyramids ; as may be seen by the worked faces, in the heaps of chips left by the Arab destroyers. But the pavement seems most probably never to have been placed around the Pyramid ; Perring found nothing but a substructure of rough megalithic blocks, with wide joints, and concluded that it was to be covered with finer work. On uncovering the granite casing, not only did I find no paving there, but the casing foot is quite in the rough, so that no pavement could be fitted to it ; and none underlies it, as the granite rests on rough limestone.

The question then is, whether the casing was to be finished like that of the Second Pyramid, with a vertical foot, and the square-cut paving fitted against it ; or whether any other plan was to be followed ? The evidence seems rather in favour of a formation like that of the Second Pyramid. First, the lower course is thicker than any other, being 4 to 8 inches thicker than those

* One writer has described them as " rusticated," as if the roughness was a prepared feature ; and another has attributed all the rounded irregularity of the stones to their weathering away since they were built. To say nothing, however, of innumerable cut holes in the outer surface, left for lifting the blocks, no weathering would add to a stone a part above its original face (see Pl. xii.). I had the pleasure of showing these details to an Engineer officer, experienced in Indian granite works, and he perfectly concurred as to the method of leaving an excess of stone on the face, to prevent injury to the block in transit.

just above it. Secondly, the evidence of the stones in the rough shows that their slope could not be continued down to their base : at the N.N.E. the face of the bottom course is somewhat smoothed, though not finally dressed, and it ends with a rounded fall at 8 inches above the rough pavement, the granite descending also 9 inches below the limestone. At the E.N.E. the line of finish of the side joint runs straight at 51° down the side of the block, but ends abruptly at an irregular outer surface some inches above the base. Similar rough terminations of the intended slope are seen at the E.S.E. and S.S.E.; the abrupt end being 6 to 18 inches above the limestone outside of the casing. Thus, in four out of five places where the casing foot is known, it is certain that the finished surface was not intended to run down in a slope to the rough limestone outside of it. It is most likely, therefore, that the face was intended, when finished, to end in a vertical foot ; and this would be covered by the pavement to be afterwards added.

What, then, is to be reckoned as the size of the true base of the Pyramid ? Not the present edges of the granite, for they are utterly rough. And not the ends of the fine-dressed edges of the joints, for they end at various levels. But looking to the fact that all the courses of granite are intended to be equal, and a rather short two cubits each, it seems most suitable to take a mean of all the granite courses (since the upper are not thinner than the lower ones), and reckon the intended base of the Pyramid at one mean course height (40.3 ± 1.5) below the first joint. Remembering also that the Second Pyramid courses average two cubits each near the base, and the bottom course was just two cubits above the pavement.

80. At this level, then, the various data of the intended surfaces give the following size for the base, reducing those data that are on higher levels by the angle 51° 0' :—

	Length.	Difference from Mean.	Angle.	Difference from Mean.
N.	...	...	+ 16′ 48″	+ 2′ 45″
E.	4149·2	−4·4	+ 12′ 23″	− 1′ 40″
S.	4157·8	+4·2	+ 12′ 57″	− 1′ 6″
W.	4153·9	+ ·3	...	...
Mean .	4153·6	3·0	+ 14′ 3″	1′ 50″

The N. end of the W. side could not be reached, after several attempts ; and hence the lack of knowing the length of the N. or azimuth of the W. side.

The above results are from the best data of each part, but there are other points which are useful as checks. The actual points used are : at N.N.W., finished line on top of 4th course ; at N.N.E., close joint of face on 1st course ; at E.N.E., line of finish along the side of casing, at adopted base level ; at E.S.E., foot of rough casing, which is further in than even the joint surface requires ; at S.S.E., finished line on top of 3rd course ; at S.S.W., close joint on face of 1st course; at W.S.W., finished line on top of 4th course. The check measures are the following three: at the N. side, courses by the entrance projected down at 51° 0′, fall ·8 beyond the side stated; on the E. end of the S. side the rough foot of the casing which was to be dressed down projects 4·3 beyond the side stated; and at the W. end of the S. side the line of finish on the 4th course, projected at 51° 0′, falls ·9 beyond the side stated.

It must be remembered that if any different base level should be supposed to have been intended, it will make no difference in the above azimuths, nor in the differences between the sides.

81. For the angle of the Pyramid, the data are rather divergent; and not only do different methods vary in result, but the measures of similar stones vary far beyond the errors of measuring the angle or judging of the surfaces.

By 7 measures on finished granite, *in situ* ... ... 50° 57′±28′
By 1st and 4th courses, *in situ*, at S.S.W. ... ... 50° 42′± 7′
By 6 single blocks of granite, shifted ... ... 51° 0′± 9′
By 9 pieces of limestone casing (brought to England) ... 51° 58′±15′

Considering the various sources of error: that the dressed granite *in situ* is very irregular; that the 1st course joint at S.S.W. may easily be estimated too far out; and that we have no guarantee in the moved granite blocks, or the limestone from the upper part, that the courses were horizontal (on the contrary, one granite block has two different joint surfaces, 1° 40′ different); the best conclusion seems to be 51° 0′ ± 10′. But from a consideration of the granite courses (see below), the angle would be 51° 10′ 30″ ± 1′ 20″; and this might well be adopted, as being close to the very uncertain result from the measured angles.

Hence the height of the Pyramid would have been 2564±15; or 2580·8±2· by the granite courses.

82. The courses were measured to rather more than half-way up the N.E. corner, beside measures of the lower courses taken at each corner. The series at the N.E. is as follows, reducing to the base level above adopted, 40·3 below the first joint:—

40	1383·5		35	1214·1		30	1077·9		25	943·5
		33·4			22·8			25·6		
39	1350·1		34	1191·3		29	1052·3		24	916·8
		31·5			35·7			29·3		
38	1318·6		33	1155·6		28	1023·0		23	890·6
		33·9			21·0			20·6		
37	1284·7		32	1134·6		27	1002·4		22	860·4
		33·8			32·2			35·4		
36	1250·9		31	1102·4		26	967·0		21	831·8
		36·8			24·5			23·5		

The difference columns (between successive courses) also include: after course 25, 26·7; after course 24, 26·2; after course 23, 30·2; after course 22, 28·6; after course 21, 33·0.

Limestone.			Granite.								
20	798·8			15	606·4		10	401·0		5	197·7
		39·9				42·6			41·9			36·8
19	758·9			14	563·8		9	359·1		4	160·9
		33·9				39·9			42·7			38·6
18	725·0			13	523·9		8	316·4		3	122·3
		35·6				42·8			40·3			40·8
17	689·4			12	481·1		7	276·1		2	81·5
		44·2				38·7			42·4			41·2
16	645·2			11	442·4		6	233·7		1	40·3
		38·8				41·4			36·0			40·3

The full height of the bottom course is : N.E., 45·5 ; S.E., 55·3 ; S.W. 43·7. The granite is here marked as ceasing at 645·2, *i.e.*, including the lower 16 courses. The reasons for this are : (1) the highest remaining fragments of granite (mere back ends of casing stones) are at the same level on each of the sides ; hence, the granite must have come as high, and probably did not go higher, as all the pieces are on the same course ; (2) there is a thicker course next over this, as if some great change took place there, and a fresh start was made ; the 17th course is thicker than any other course of the whole Pyramid, and is followed by a course thinner than any that underlie it ; (3) Diodorus states that the casing was of black stone up to the 15th course, and like the other Pyramids above that level. Now, by the stumps of the stones the granite must have come to the 16th, and probably the lowest course was covered with sand in his day ; but it is unlikely (unless we credit him with loose errors like modern guide books *) that the casing went much higher. Hence the strong suggestions (1) and (2) are confirmed by (3), and may well be accepted.

This being settled, it is worth notice that the granite just covered one quarter of the height of the Pyramid, the total height being $4 \times 641 \pm 4$. Conversely this may be taken as giving a determination of the original total height, perhaps more accurately than by the varying angles of the casing, thus :—

645·2 ($\pm$·5 (?) for uncertainty of paving) $\times 4 = 2580·8 \pm 2$·
And this yields an angle of $51° \ 10' \ 30'' \pm 1' \ 20''$.

The mean planes of the edges of the core masonry are far more irregular than those of the Great Pyramid. At the base level adopted they are 4,082 on E., 4,077 on S., and 4,109 on W., averaging 4,089 apart ; and their mean distance

* In one of the most scientific of guide books it is said that the Third Pyramid cannot be ascended (it is easier than the Great Pyramid) ; and that it was " covered with *slabs* of *polished* granite, and the upper part with *rough stones !* " or, making matters worse still, " in the case of the Third Pyramid the *whole* surface was to be, as it were, *veneered with slabs* of granite ! " showing that the writer had never realised the proportions of a casing stone. But descriptions of the Pyramids are usually replete with extraordinary mistakes—" granite " for " limestone," " height " for " width," &c.

from the casing plane varies from 14 to 46, averaging 33. The core has no uniform skew to the casing, as in the Great Pyramid. The thickness of the top of separate granite casing stones is from 35 to 46, averaging 41.

The casing, though partly attacked in the 12th and 13th centuries, does not seem to have been removed in the time of Belon (1548), or of Villamont (1589), who describe it as perfect, and without steps.

83. The peribolus walls around the Third Pyramid (see Pl. v.) are all built of unhewn stone, neatly laid with mud mortar, like the walls of the barrack galleries of the Second Pyramid. They are, however, irregular in their position, some being nearly square and parallel with the Pyramid, and the others on the South being very different. They were all fixed in the survey by triangulation, with more accuracy than the wall-surface can be defined.

The N. wall joins the portion of a wall, S. of the Second Pyramid, by an elbow, and runs thence westwards at $-14'$ from true W. Beyond its corner, where it turns to the S., a fainter enclosure wall begins, running due W. The spaces along these walls are proportional to each other; from the corner of the

small enclosure, E, to that of the larger, D ...	...	6,275 }	$\div 4 = 1,559$
or by the Southern side, F to G	...	6,196 }	
Corner, D, to junction of Second Pyramid peribolus, B		7,689	$\div 5 = 1,538$
Peribolus B to junction of cross-wall, A ...		7,813	$\div 5 = 1,563$

The mean of these is 1,553, which is perhaps 75 cubits of 20·71 inches.

Not only does the peribolus of the Second Pyramid appear to be thus connected in its position, but the wall at the head of the galleries, if prolonged, would pass but 29 inches within the W. side of the Third Pyramid; and therefore these seem to be intended for the same line. And this connection is confirmed by the equality of the two divisions of this line :—

Outside of last gallery to S. side of Third Pyramid peribolus...	3,258
or inside „ „ „ „ ...	3,304
S. side of peribolus to N.W. corner of Third Pyramid ...	3,309
Also, W. side of gallery wall, C, to E. side Second P. peribolus	3,308

The mean of the latter three is 3,307, which is, perhaps, 160 cubits of 20·67 inches.

The length of the W. enclosure, 9,599 N. to S., is subdivided by a very faint ridge, in which no wall could be found. But this ridge runs straight towards the centre of the Pyramid, and it appears to be roughly about the breadth of the Pyramid, or 200 cubits, from the S. wall. Referring to the Pyramid side produced out westwards, as being the best-defined line of division for this, the N. side of the Pyramid is $(3,309 + 92 (?)) = 3,401$ from the outside of the N. peribolus; and as this is intentionally in line with the N. wall of the W. enclosure, therefore the S. wall of that enclosure is $(9,599 - 3,401) = 6,198$ S.

of the N. face of the Pyramid by intention—*i.e.*, as laid off by the builders.*
Now this is exactly the breadth of this enclosure (6,196 to 6,275), and is equal to
300 cubits of 20·66. Hence the design of this W. enclosure is a square of 300
cubits, W. of the peribolus wall and S. of North face of the Pyramid, while its
N. wall is advanced to the line of the N. peribolus wall. The W. wall of the
enclosure is nearly straight, two points fixed on it lying 3 and 12 inches outside
a line joining the corners.

The total length of the W. wall of the peribolus, 14,049 from corner to
corner (D to J), does not seem to have any simple relation to other parts; and
the only connection observed in it is that the distance of the S.W. corner (J)
from the S. wall of the enclosure (F) is equal to the distance of the W. peribolus
from the side of the Pyramid. The measures are :—

S.W. corner (J) to S. wall of enclosure (F) ...	...	4,450
W. wall peribolus, from W. side Pyramid ...	...	4,450
Or N.W. corner peribolus to line of galleries (C)	...	4,451
S.W. corner (J) to branch wall (at K)	8,897 = 2 × 4,448	

This length is necessarily (375 − 160) cubits by the previous relations; and the
mean 4,450, equals 215 cubits of 20·70.

So it would seem that these walls had not been planned all in one design,
but added on by different schemes; referring more or less to the Pyramid,
and using round numbers of cubits in general, but getting more complex
quantities by addition or subtraction of simple lengths. The irregularity of the
S. peribolus wall exactly agrees to this view, as it is impossible to suppose its
skew and bowing line to have been laid out along with the very regular lines of
the other parts.

The end of the S. wall runs through the side of a large mound, and
disappears, so that it could not be exactly fixed. The end of the branch wall
likewise runs through the side of a mound, and then ceases. These mounds
would have been cut through, had time allowed. The temple on the E. side of
this Pyramid appears to have been the most perfect that was visible at Gizeh in
1755; and Fourmont mentions four pillars as then standing in it. It has now
lost all its casing (used by the Mamelukes for houses at Gizeh), and merely the
core blocks remain, weathered away in some parts so as to have fallen over.
The marks where the walls have been cut, to fit in the backs of lining blocks,
show that it was cased (probably with granite) like the temple of the Second
Pyramid and the Granite Temple.

The causeway is just the width of the entrance passage walls; it is built of

---

* To understand a scheme it is necessary to take measurements, as far as possible, in the
same order that the builders took them—*i.e.*, including their mistakes in each step of the laying
out; and so see, not what errors there are from a mathematically rigid plan, but what errors
there are in each part as it was planned.

large blocks, and raised, probably, 20 or 30 feet above the plain, though the sides are now much hidden by sand. It ran down the hill for about 800 feet from the temple ; but it had no connection with the other causeway, situated half a mile further E. in the plain below, though they are often confounded together. The lower causeway is not in the line of the upper, nor parallel to it ; and it only ran up to the quarries in the limestone hill, which is such a striking feature in the neighbourhood.

There was a considerable village of Græco-Roman age around the Third Pyramid. A great amount of crude brick and pottery lies on the S.E. ; crude brick is also found on the causeway, and is mentioned by Vyse as found on the pavement at the N. side.

CHAPTER XI.

THE INSIDE OF THE THIRD PYRAMID.

84. THE entrance is in the fourth course, or from 165·3 to 202·1 vertically above the base; it is in the middle of the face, unlike that of either of the larger Pyramids. The centre of it is 2078·9 from the E. side of the Pyramid; and though we do not know the exact length of the N. face, yet this is precisely half the length of the S. face.

The azimuth of the passage is + 13′ 16″, which is just between the varying azimuths of the Pyramid sides.

The granite just around the doorway has been dressed down to pretty nearly its final surface, but there is no trace of decoration or inscription.* The edges of the doorway are much broken away, so that no remains of any means of closing it can be traced.

The entrance passage is built of granite, until it enters the rock, in which it is afterwards cut; and all the chambers of this Pyramid are entirely hewn in the rock.

85. Just beyond the foot of the slope of the passage, it opens into the first chamber. This is symmetrical on each side of the passage, and the sides measure thus :—

N. 125·5   S. 124·2   E. 153·7   W. 153·9

The ends are divided in equal thirds, by the doorway and the two side spaces, like the lower chamber of the Second Pyramid.

| N.E. | 41·9 | 42·0 | 41·6 | N.W. |
| S.E. | 40·8 | 41·1 | 42·3 | S.W. |

Both the sides and the ends are decorated with the panel ornament (Pl. xii.) so universal in the earliest tombs, but not used before in a pyramid. The mean dimensions of this panelling are marked on the diagram. The granite lintel of the south door of this chamber is lying on the floor. It has a half-round drum,

---

* The name of Menkaura, recorded by Diodorus as being on the N. side of this Pyramid, was probably cut in the bold characters of the early kingdom upon the limestone above the granite, easily visible, but safe from idle mischief.

or roll, sculptured on it (like that in the Second Pyramid, Pl. xii.), and the width between the square ends, which rested on the jambs, varies from 41·23 to 41·35; the ends are 10·7 to 10·9 wide, making 62·78 to 62·99 length over all. The breadth of the block is 18·4, and its depth 15·0 inches. The granite jambs are 18·1 broad. In the passage beyond this chamber are the sites of apparently three sliding portcullises, situated at 63·9 to 75·0, 108·1 to 121·4, and 149·3 to 161·5 beyond the doorway. Beyond this last portcullis the passage rises from its previous height of 49·0; with a half-round drum and raised band above that; and at the entry into the second chamber the passage is 71·1 high, like the passage of the Second Pyramid.

This passage has evidently been excavated from the South outwards; whenever the excavators ran wrong (and they did so several times) the false cut goes deeper towards the N., and then ends abruptly when the error was seen. Also the direction of the pickmark points to its outward working. How the men got inside the rock to begin with, is plain from a second passage which runs above this; and which opens into the second chamber blankly, without any means of getting to the chamber floor, except by a ladder or other help. This upper passage runs through the rock up to the masonry, and was cut from the North inwards.

86. The full dimensions of this second chamber are:

N. 560·2, S. 559·5, E. 151·6, ⅓ along 152·0, ⅔ along 152·6, W. 152·5.

But the length of it is divided into two parts, by projecting pilasters cut in the rock; these separate it into an eastern space of 416·3 N., and 415·9 S.; pilaster of 41·7 N., and 41·4 S.; and a western space of 102·2 on both N. and S. The pilasters project 13·1 N.W., 12·6 N.E., 11·7 S.E., and 13·0 S.W. The doorway enters on the N. side of the chamber at 103·7 to 145·1 from E. wall. It is 71·1 high; and above it at 117·7 to 172·1 over the floor opens the upper passage, which is at 105·2 to 144·2 from the E. wall. The ceiling here is 191·8 over the floor. Thus the [1] east part, [2] pilaster, and [3] west part, are nearly equal respectively to the [1] west of the door, [2] door, and [3] east of the door; and these are also nearly the same as the similar divisions of the Second Pyramid chamber.

This second chamber is not, however, the chamber that contained the coffer, though it has a recess apparently intended to hold a coffer. Out of the middle of its floor a sloping passage descends westwards, turns horizontal, and then comes into the E. side of the granite-lined sepulchral chamber. The floor of this passage begins at 203·2 from E. side of second chamber; and the passage is 35·4 to 35·6 wide, and 35·6 high. There are some remarkable holes cut in the walls, apparently to hold the ends of rollers, over which ropes were run in lowering the coffer; these holes were not cut by Perring, as he engraves them in his plates.

87. The granite chamber is hewn in the rock with a flat ceiling like the

other chambers. The granite lining and floor of it is built in; and in order to introduce the roof-blocks a hole is cut from the end of the second chamber, into the top of the lower chamber. The roofing is not by beams, as in the King's Chamber, nor by cantilevers, as in the Queen's Chamber of the Great Pyramid; but by sloping blocks resting one against the other with a thrust, the essential principle of an arch. The under-sides of these blocks are cut into a barrel or hemi-cylindrical roof, like passages in tombs of the early period. This cavity above the roof, entered from the second chamber, was originally closed; but the masonry has been forced out, and now the tops of the roofing slabs can be easily seen. These have been quarried by means of a groove, and holes drilled at intervals to determine the cleavage plane; as was the roofing of the spaces over the King's Chamber. The introduction of these massive blocks through such a small space, and the placing them in such a confined position, is a good piece of work.

This granite chamber is not at all as regular in form as it is in appearance. The walls measure thus :—

E. 260·75. W. 258·83.

N. 104·06, near N. 103·85, mid. 103·80, by door 103·7, over door, 103·50, S. 103·25.

Height $\begin{cases} \text{N.W. } 105\cdot8, \text{ N.E. } 105\cdot7, \text{ S.E. } 105\cdot4, \text{ S.W. } 105\cdot9 ; \\ \text{N. mid. } 134\cdot6, \text{ mid. } 134\cdot6, \text{ S. mid. } 135\cdot5. \end{cases}$

The doorway is 54·52 wide, and one side of it in the plane of the S. wall. The courses at the door (S.E. corner) are :

27·6 on floor, 26·5 next, 26·7 top of door, 24·2 over door ; total 105·2.

88. Beside the first, second, and granite chambers, there is a loculus chamber : this is entered by a flight of steps turning out of the passage to the granite chamber. These steps are by far the earliest known in any building or excavation : they are six in number, and their breadths are from 10·5 to 12 inches, averaging 11·3. This loculus chamber was doubtless intended to contain coffins, judging by the sizes of the recesses. The chamber is on

N. 74·0, S. 77·0, E. 211, W. 205·1 ; 78·2 high on N., 80·0 in mid., 78·2 on S.

The doorway is in the S. wall at 38·0 to 73·9 from the E. side. In the E. wall are four loculi, and in the N. wall two, of the following shapes :—

		From S. wall.	Width.	Height.	Depth.
In E. wall		10·0 to 42·7	32·7	59·5	102½
		65·1 to 98·9	33·8	56·8	101
		120·2 to 153·6	33·4	55·3	101½
		176·0 to 208·	32·0	55·3	97
		From E. wall.			
In N. wall		0 to 27·5	27·5	(about	101
		48·3 to 74·0	25·7	55)	102

The floors of the loculi are level with the floor of the chamber, and their tops average 22·1 below the ceiling. Their inner ends are not fully worked to the width of the openings, as they are left rather in the rough.

89. Reverting now to the original entrance passage (above the present entrance), by which the chambers were first begun, it is 39.3 wide and 51·0 high at the chamber. It runs horizontally for some distance northwards, and then slopes up at the usual passage angle (27° 34′ Vyse); and it is 40·6 wide, and 49·0 high, square with the passage floor. It runs through the rock, and then through some masonry; and ends at last at about the level of the present entrance, but far behind—or south of—that, in the masonry of the Pyramid. Over the end of it is a large block, roughly 11¼ × 8½ × 7 feet, or about 50 tons weight; used exactly as the lintel blocks over the entrance passages in the smaller Pyramids.

From all these details it seems plain that the Third Pyramid was first begun no larger than some of the small Pyramids on the same hill. That it had a passage descending as usual, with a large lintel block over it; and running horizontally in the rock, into a rock-cut chamber, whose roof was 74·1 above the passage floor. That after this was made, the builders, for some reason, determined on enlarging the Pyramid before it was cased, and on deepening the chamber. They accordingly cut a fresh passage, from the new floor level of the chamber, working this passage from the inside outward. They not only deepened the chamber, but also cut the sloping passage to the lower, granite-lined, coffer chamber; for the granite lining could not be put in until the second chamber had been deepened to its present extent; so the granite chamber must be part of the second design, or is perhaps in itself a third design. The old entrance passage was then built over on the outside, and the greater part of its height blocked up. The blocking that remains is clearly ancient, as it consists of large blocks wedged in by chips, and worn by passing over the tops. On one block is a saw cut, 6 inches deep in part, running vertically on the face; this cut must therefore have been made by the Pyramid builders, before they used the block for filling the passage.

CHAPTER XII.

THE LESSER PYRAMIDS OF GIZEH.

90. OF the smaller Pyramids I had not time to uncover the bases, nor to open those now closed. Only two of them remain open at present, the northern and middle ones by the Great Pyramid.

The northern one by the Great Pyramid (marked 7 by Vyse) has the azimuth of its passage axis $- 14' \ 40'' \pm 20''$; but the passage narrows to the bottom, being 41·5 at 520 up it, and only 40·0 at bottom ; hence the azimuth of the sides of the passage is about $- 9'$ on E. and $- 20'$ on W., so that we may say $- 15' \pm 2'$, considering the possibility of the axis being better adjusted than either side.

The entrance passage, from the end of its sloping part, proceeds horizontally, cut in the rock for 111·4 measured on roof ; the edge of the roof is bevelled 17·5, however, so that the really flat roof is only 94. The passage then opens into a chamber, whose floor slopes down to the S. This sloping floor ends in a flat part, along the S. side of the chamber, 38·3 wide ; from the W. end of which starts another sloping passage leading down westwards into the coffer chamber. The upper chamber is :

On N., 69·7 ; on S., 69·9 ; on W., 167·9.

The sloping floor is $(167·9 - 38·3) = 129·6$ wide horizontally ; 48·6 below ceiling at N., and 115·8 (W.) to 116·0 (E.) below the ceiling at S. end. The angle, therefore, between it and the flat ceiling is about $27° \ 29'$. The floor is much damaged by the tearing out of various blocks which had been inserted to make good flaws in rock.

The most remarkable feature in this chamber (which is entirely rock-hewn) is the cutting made to get the coffer passed through it into the lower chamber, this last being entered by a passage turned at right angles to the entrance passage. In order to turn the coffer, a recess was needed in the E. wall, opposite the mouth of the passage to the lower chamber. This recess ends at the S. wall, and is 77·3 long on the E. wall, but slopes at its N. end, so as to be only 68·1 long on its back. It is cut 20·7 into the wall, and its roof is 45 to 48 below the ceiling, so that it is 68 to 71 high. It has never been filled up with

R

masonry. The coffer cannot have been over 38 wide,* as it had to go down the lower passage; and the maximum length that could be turned by using this recess, is 88. So probably the coffer was about 37 × 84, allowing for a little free space. The recess would also allow the roofing-beams of the lining of the lower chamber to be passed down; a beam 10·3 wide (½ cubit) and 126 long could be turned without needing to take a cubic diagonal. If the beam was 20·6 (1 cubit) deep, as seems probable, then, by taking full advantage of the cubic diagonal, it might be 139 long; this would be amply sufficient for the roofing, leaving 10 inches for a bearing at each end.

Not only is there this recess, but at the S.E. corner, in the floor of the recess, is a circular hole over 15 deep and 7·3 diameter. The centre of this hole is at 19·2 from S. wall, and 5·1 from back of recess; it has a vertical groove in the recess back exactly behind it, 8·6 wide and 3·5 deep, which runs up the wall for 15, sloping off to 20 inches above the floor. The use of this circular hole seems to be for holding a stout post, around which ropes could be passed to control the coffer when sliding it down the lower passage, the groove behind it being to allow for the thickness of the rope. The centre of the hole is 19·2 from S. wall, and the middle of the passage is 19·15 from the same; hence the hole is exactly in line with the passage axis.

The roof of the lower passage begins at 78·5 below the ceiling of the upper chamber; and the passage is 49·6 high vertically (or 41·3 perpendicular) and 38·3 wide. The passage floor really begins its slope in the chamber, on the flat strip of floor along the S. side, at 18·8 from the W. wall. The sloping length of the passage is 160·1. On the N. side it is lined with two courses of stone 17·8 thick, and the top one 13·45 high.

The lower chamber differs from all other parts of the inside in being lined with fine Mokattam limestone. The dimensions are—

In rock . N., 201·4; S., 202·1 (?); E., 165·7; W., 166·3.
In lining. N., 139·8 (?); S., 140.5;   (?)   W., 118 (?)

Only portions of the lining remain, and the floor is deeply cumbered with blocks of lining, and probably also of roofing. The lining has a ledge left on it 2·6 to 4·5 wide along the E. and W. sides—or it may be said to recede and become thinner—at 25·0 below rock roof on E., and 25·1 to 25·8 on W. This probably was where the long sides of the roofing-beams rested, overlapping the wall-lining; their length must have been from N. to S., as that is the shortest way of the chamber; and as they could not support an end over the doorway, which is the full height of the chamber wall. Over the doorway a dovetail stone is very neatly inserted to make good a flaw.

* It might have been 40 wide (as the entrance), and the lining on one side of the lower passage may have been inserted afterwards, but this would not materially affect its turning.

The lining blocks which remain are of the following thicknesses :—S.E., 30·8.; W.N.W., 31·0 ; N.N.W., 25·1 to 26·5. The doorway sides are 36·3 from .N. rock, or 10 (?) from N. lining ; and 92·7 from S. rock, or about 61 from S. lining.

91. The middle one of the small Pyramids by the Great Pyramid (No. 8, Vyse) is almost exactly similar in arrangement to the preceding. The azimuth of its passage axis is − 3′ 20″±10″ ; but the difference in the width of the ends make the sides − 1′ 20″ on E., and − 5′ 20″ on W. Probably − 3′±1′ is the truest statement.

The sloping passage ends in a horizontal passage 112 long and 38·4 wide, which leads into the upper chamber. The chamber ceiling is 13·2 above the passage top, and is all flat. The floor slopes down southward, to a flat strip along the S. wall ; and dips down within the chamber, to begin the floor of the lower passage, which turns out of the W. wall. The chamber is not square, from the E. side of the entrance to the E. wall being askew ; this E. side of it is really an enlarged form of the recess for turning the coffer and roofing-beams.

The chamber, then, is on N. 63·7+66·6 along diagonal slope to E. wall ; 71·2 on E. wall ; 118·0 on S. ; 110·6 on W. The N. side consists of 38·4 doorway, and 25·3 wall on W. of it, =63·7.

The slope-ended recess, or eastern enlargement of the chamber, would allow a coffer 113 long to be taken in ; more likely it was 95 or 100 long ; the width being limited to 38·4 by the entrance passage. The necessary roofing-beams, for lining the lower chamber, could also be passed down.

The upper chamber is 93 high, from the flat strip of floor on the S. of it ; but the floors are all so encumbered, and so rotten, that no precise height can be taken.

The sloping roof of the lower passage begins 58·4 below the chamber roof ; and is 103·8 long horizontally.

The lower chamber is lined, like that in the other Pyramid, with fine limestone. Its size is

In rock	...	209·5 N.	212·8 S.	209·8 E.	209·0 W.
In lining	...	(?)	(?)	(?)	121·6 W.

The N. side of the rock has been cut away too deeply over most of it ; but the chamber length is shown, by the lining remaining, to have been about 121·6. As the largest beams that could be brought in (of 20·6 × 10·3 section) would be 164 long, there would be probably 15 inches of bearing at each end, and 10 inches allowed for free turning in bringing them in.

There are red lines on the rock walls, showing where the planes of the inside of the lining were to come. These lines are on the S. wall at 28·8 from E. and 29·2 from W. ; on the W. wall at 21·7 from S. ; and on the

E. wall at 20·9 from S. The corresponding casing actually measuring 28·2 and 27·9, for the 29·2 lines; and 21·0 for the 21·7 and 20·9 lines; the small differences being due to irregularities in the rock cutting.

There are no traces of the cementing-in of the lining above 32·8 or 33·0 from the roof (except on the N. side); and this probably shows at about what level the walls ended, and the roofing-beams were put on. The doorway roof ends at 28·2 (N.) to 28·8 (S.) below the rock roof; and probably the ceiling-beams would be flush with that. The sides of the doorway are of polished rock, evidently never lined; they come at 136·3 from the N. rock wall, and 34·9 from the S. rock wall; the passage being 38·6 wide.

A part of the casing of the southernmost of the Pyramids by the Great Pyramid (No. 9, Vyse) was accidentally uncovered by the Arabs digging for nitrous earth; and I measured it as follows :—52° 10′, 52° 28′ (both good measures), 52° 0′, 52° 25′, 51° 0′ (bad). Giving the good double, and the bad half, weight of the others, the mean is 52° 11′±8′.

CHAPTER XIII.

THE POSITIONS AND ORIENTATIONS OF THE PYRAMIDS.

92. THE relative positions of the three larger Pyramids to one another were completely fixed in the triangulation, which included them all. The following are their distances apart, as measured on parallels inclined $-5'$ to true N.—*i.e.*, at the mean azimuth of the First and Second Pyramids; and also the distances, and the angles from these parallels, of the direct lines from one Pyramid to another :—

			N.	E.	Direct.
Centre of First to centre of Second Pyramid	...	13 931·6 and 13	165·8=19	168·4 at 43° 22′ 52″
„ „ „ Third „	...	·29 102·0 and 22	616·0=36	857·7 at 37° 51′ 6″
„ Second „ „ „	...	15 170·4 and 9	450·2=17	873·2 at 34° 10′ 11″

There does not appear to be any exact relation between their centres, or between the corners ; and from the nature and appearance of the ground, and the irregularity of the peribolus walls, it would not seem likely that any connection had been planned.

93. The orientation of the Great Pyramid is about 4′ West of North ; a difference very perceptible, and so much larger than the errors of setting out the form (which average 12″), that such a divergence might be wondered at. When, however, it is seen that the passage, which was probably set out by a different observation, nearly agrees in this divergence, it seems unlikely to be a mere mistake. And when, further, the Second Pyramid sides, and also its passages, all diverge similarly to the W. of North, the presumption of some change in the position of the North point itself, seems strongly indicated. The Third and lesser Pyramids are so inferior in work, that they ought not to interfere with the determination from the accurate remains ; they would, however, scarcely affect the mean deviation if included with the better data. The azimuths of the two large Pyramids are thus :—

Great Pyramid, casing sides	.	.	.	.	$-3'\ 43''\pm\ 6''$
„ „ core „	.	.	.	.	$-5'\ 16''\pm 10''$
Second „ casing „	.	.	.	.	$-5'\ 26''\pm 16''$
„ „ passage (Smyth)	.	.	.	.	$-5'\ 37''\pm 10''(?)$
Great „ „	.	.	.	.	$-5'\ 49''\pm\ 7''$

In considering these results, the difference of the casing and core azimuths of the Great Pyramid shows that probably a re-determination of the N. was made after the core was finished; and it must be remembered that the orientation would be far more difficult to fix after, than during, the construction; as a high face of masonry, for a plumb-line, would not be available. The passages of the Great and Second Pyramids are the most valuable elements; as, being so nearly at the polar altitude, a very short plumb-line would transfer the observations to the fixed plane. Considering, then, that the Great Pyramid core agrees with the passages far closer than does the casing, the inference seems to be that the casing was fixed by a re-determination of N., by the men who finished the building. These men had not the facilities of the earlier workers; and are shown, by the inferiority of the later work in the Pyramid, to have been far less careful. Hence the casing may probably be left out of consideration, in view of the close agreement of the four other determinations, one of which—the passage—was laid out by the most skilful workmen of the Great Pyramid, with their utmost regularity, the mean variation of the built part being but $\frac{1}{30}$ inch.

The simple mean of the last four data is $-5'\ 32''\pm 6''$; their divergences being just what would be expected from their intrinsic probable errors. The passages are, however, probably far the most accurate lines in their execution; and as the Second Pyramid is inferior in its workmanship, $-5'\ 45''\pm 5''$ might be well taken as the result from them alone. On the whole, considering the various values of the data, $-5'\ 40''\pm 10''$ may be taken as a safe statement of the suggested place of the pole, at the epoch of the Pyramid builders.

94. There are, however, two checks on the supposition of such a change in the pole: the observations of any change in later times, and the existence of an adequate cause for the change. Now, the best latitude observations at Greenwich, those on Polaris—least affected by erroneous refractions—appear to show a latitude of $51°\ 28'\ 38.58''$ during 7 years, 1840–7; $38.30''$ during 10 years, 1851–61; $38.22''$ during 3 years, 1862–5; and $38.30''$ during 8 years, 1868–76;* or on an average a decrease of ·28″ latitude in 28 years, or 1·0″ per century. But Maskelyne's discussion in the last century yielded 39·7″, for mean epoch 1761. This implies a decrease of 1·38″ per century, agreeing as closely as could be expected with the change in recent observations.

Hence, in 4,000 to 6,000 years—the age of the Pyramids by different chronologers—the change of Greenwich latitude would amount to just about 1′. Thus, as far as observation can lead us, it seems to show a shift of the earth's axis in longitude 0° to a fifth of the extent shown in longitude 121° by the Pyramid orientations; and therefore a change of the same order, and not improbable in its extent.

* See diagram in Mr. Christie's paper: Mem. Ast. Soc., xlv.

As to the adequacy of a cause for such a change, it is hopeless, in our ignorance of the exact amount and velocity of the ocean currents at different depths, for us to strike a balance of them, and see how much motion is outstanding to affect the axis of rotation. But we can at least see what sort of proportion the required effective current would bear to the whole of the currents. Assuming a change of place of the axis amounting to 1' in 1,000 years, it seems that a ring of water circulating around the earth, across the Poles, at 1 mile per hour, and only 4 square miles in section, would suffice to cause such a change. This is an amount of unbalanced, or outstanding, current which is quite imperceptible in the balancing effects of the various ocean currents; and therefore amply accounted for by existing and known causes, even apart from atmospheric currents.

Thus the apparent change in the axis of rotation shown by the orientation of the Pyramids, is of the same order as a change actually observed. It is also far within the changes likely to be produced by known causes, and the uniform deviation is otherwise unaccountable in its origin. Hence it appears that it may legitimately be accepted as a determination of a factor which is of the highest interest, and which is most difficult to observe in any ordinary period.*

* Careful re-determinations of the meridians fixed in the beginning of the Ordnance Survey might be of value ; as (according to the Pyramids) a change of 5″ might be expected in their azimuths.

CHAPTER XIV.

THE GRANITE TEMPLE, AND OTHER REMAINS.

95. THE Granite Temple stands near the Sphinx, at the foot of the hill of Gizeh ; and is directly connected with the Second Pyramid, by means of a causeway which leads from its entrance, straight up to the entrance of the temple of that Pyramid.

This causeway was a grand work, about 15 feet wide and over quarter of a mile long.   The rock has been uniformly cut down to a sloping bed, on which has been laid apparently two layers of fine white limestone.   The rock looks at first as if it were all masonry, owing to every stone that was placed on it having been more or less let into its surface, just like the building of the Pyramid courses one on the other.   All the paving has been torn up, and only a few blocks are left lying about : these have a shallow drain cut in them, apparently on the upper side of the lower layer of paving.   This causeway was only discovered two or three years ago ; though Professor Smyth, as far back as 1865, had mentioned that the entrance of the Granite Temple pointed to the Second Pyramid, and had thence argued for a connection between them.

The direction selected for this causeway is not due E. from the temple of the Second Pyramid ; and it is therefore not square with the Pyramids, nor with the Granite Temple, which is similarly oriented.   For this divergence from the nearly universal orientation of other constructions here, there seems good reason in the fact of a very suitable ridge of rock running in this direction, with a sharp fall away on each side of it.   Hence, unless an enormous mass of masonry had been built up, to fill a valley that runs due E. of the Second Pyramid, there was no means of making the causeway square with the other constructions.   This causeway may have been regarded as a Via Sacra ; for on both sides of it the rock is closely perforated with the large shafts of rock tombs, over which chapels were probably built, bordering the causeway.

The two temples which this causeway connects—the upper one, in front of the Second Pyramid, and the lower one, or Granite Temple—are closely alike in their character ; and the temple of the Third Pyramid seems to have been similar to them.   Both of them were built with a core of megalithic blocks of limestone, ranging in their weight to over a hundred tons each ; and these were cased over by massive blocks of granite or of alabaster. The upper temple has been far more destroyed than the lower; only a few blocks of its polished granite remain, and its ruins are half buried in heaps of chips of alabaster,* limestone, and granite. It had a sloping ascent, like the lower temple, probably to a court over the roof of its chambers; and innumerable fragments of polished diorite statues, beside alabaster vases and inscribed ornaments, are mixed together in the rubbish, evidently derived from the destruction of statues like those of Khafra, which were found dashed into the well in the lower temple.

96. The lower temple, or Granite Temple, which has also been called the Temple of the Sphinx, was apparently a free-standing building, like the upper temple. This is not the view of some who have seen it, and who suppose that it is a rock-excavated work, lined with granite, at least in the lower parts, for the upper half is manifestly built. But Mariette (Rev. Pol. et Lit. 6 Dec., 1879) expressly says that it is all built; and he describes the outer surfaces as being smooth, and "ornamented with long grooves, vertical and horizontal, skilfully crossed," which seems to imply a design like the lattice-work pattern of the early tombs. As far as the outside can be now seen, to about fifteen feet above the base, it is built of megalithic blocks; and in the inside a rough chamber, to which an entrance has been forced, shows the hidden construction; and here it is all built of immense blocks of limestone, resting on a bed of rock at the base level of the temple. Again, just outside it, on the N.E., is an enclosure of crude brick and rough stone, lately cleared, and there the rock is at about the level of the base of the temple. It seems most probable, therefore, that it is entirely built; though possibly heaped round with stones and sand on the outside, like the tombs on the S. of the Great Pyramid, and at Medum. Until the outside shall be cleared, and the construction put beyond doubt, the evidence points to this resembling the upper temple in every respect.

The arrangement of the Granite Temple will be seen from the plan, Pl. vi. The causeway from the upper temple runs down the hill, in a straight line, into the passage which slopes down into the great hall. The pillars in this hall are all monoliths of dark red granite, like that of the walls; they are 41 inches (2 cubits) square, and 174·2 high, weighing, therefore, about 13 tons each. The two larger pillars, placed at the junction of the two parts of the hall, to support three beams each, are 58 inches wide, and weigh over 18 tons each. All these pillars support beams of granite, which are likewise 41 inches square in the double colonnade, and 47·8 to 48·4 deep in the single colonnade, where their span is greater. The shorter spans are 128, and the longer 145 inches; so that the beams are not as heavy as the columns, the two sizes being $9\frac{1}{2}$ and $12\frac{1}{2}$ tons.

* This is carbonate of lime, in crystalline nodular sheets; and is called Oriental alabaster, by the wide use of that word for both sulphate and carbonate.

Six of these beams, or a third of the whole, are now missing. The Arabs say that they were found lying dislodged in the temple; and that Mariette, when clearing up the place to exhibit (at the festivities of the opening of the Suez Canal) had them blasted to pieces by soldiers. This seemed scarcely credible, although very similar stories are reported of that Conservator of Antiquities; but among the quantities of broken granite, which is built into a rude wall to keep back the sand, I found many pieces with polished surfaces like the beams in question, and with distinct blast-holes cut in them, quite different in character to the holes drilled anciently. This ugly story, therefore, seems confirmed.

Besides this great hall, with the colonnades 222·4 inches high, there is another hall to the east of it, which has been much higher; and from each end of the eastern hall is a doorway, one now blocked up, the other leading to a chamber. Out of the great hall a doorway, in the N.W. corner, leads to a set of six loculi; these are formed in three deep recesses, each separated in two by a shelf of granite. These recesses still have their roofs on, and are dark except for the light from the doorway, and from a ventilator. The lower part of the walls of each recess is formed of granite, resting on the rock floor; this is 61·6 to 61·7 high. Above this is the granite shelf, 28 thick, which extends the whole length of the recess. In the southern recess this shelf is nearly all of one block 176 × over 72 × 28. Upon this shelf, over the lower recesses, are placed two walls of alabaster, dividing the upper three loculi; both walls are irregularly a few inches southward of the lower walls. The extraordinary length of these loculi—over 19 feet—seems strange; especially as the turn to the side loculi would prevent any coffin larger than 30 × 76 inches being taken in unless it were tipped about to get the benefit of the cubic diagonal. The doorway is only 80·45 high, so that nothing over 80 inches long could be taken in on end.

On the S. side of the short passage leading to these loculi, a stone has been removed from the wall, and by climbing in, a curious irregular chamber is reached, evidently never intended to be seen. It is entirely in the rough, the N. and part of the W. side being merely the backs of the granite blocks of the hall and passage; these are irregular, in and out, but nevertheless very well dressed, flat and true in most parts. The rest of this chamber is of rough core masonry, just like the core of the upper temple, and the floor is of rock, with a step down across it (broken line in plan) about the middle of the chamber. The base of the S.W. corner of the chamber is entirely in one block, the lower or sunken part of the rock floor being levelled up by a base plane cut in the block, and the S. and W. sides being two vertical planes in the same block, so that it forms a hollow corner all in one piece. On the S.E. the chamber is bounded by a rough wall of stone scraps built in when it was recently opened. In the chamber were found, it is said, several common mummies; perhaps of late date, like those I found in the E.N.E. rock trench.

The history of the opening of this secret chamber seems to have been that in destroying the temple, for the sake of building stones, the pillagers began at the S.E. and S.W. corners ; here they pulled stones away until they opened into this chamber, and then, finding a granite wall on one side of it, they dragged out the smallest block, and so broke through into the passage. A clearance of the outside of the temple is needed, however, to settle this as well as other questions.

Another covered chamber also exists, branching from the entrance passage ; this is built of alabaster and granite. Opposite the entrance to it is a doorway, leading to an inclined passage, which was the ascent up to the former roof of the great hall. This passage is of alabaster, and the upper doorway of granite.

The whole of the area above the great hall appears to have been at one level, and to have formed a large uncovered court, surrounded by high walls. That it was not subdivided into chambers would appear from the character of the facing of the wall, which remains in one corner over the six loculi. This wall is of fine limestone, and not of granite or alabaster, which were used in covered parts of the building ; and it has a considerable batter, unlike the walls of the halls or chambers below, and only resembling the external walls of tombs. Each feature shows, therefore, that it was open to the sky. As no temples more complete than this are known, except those built one to three thousand years later, it is unsafe to argue by analogy ; but still there is no case, I believe, of a second story to a temple ; and smaller temples over the large one (as at Dendera) are of the character of additions built in a court on the roof, and not upper stories as parts of a whole design.

The ventilators are a peculiar feature of the building, though somewhat like those to be seen in the tombs. They were formed by sloping slits along the top edge of the walls, a few inches wide, and usually 41 inches long. Only one remains perfect, that opening out of the chamber of loculi ; this slit opens into a rectangular shaft, which rises to some way above the roof, and there opens with a square mouth of alabaster on the face of the upper court wall. The mouth is on the same side of the shaft as the slit ; and hence the only light entering is reflected from the side of the shaft. The slits cut for these ventilators exist all along the Western part of the great hall, and are marked on the walls in the plan.

The Eastern hall appears to have been formerly much higher, probably as high as the smaller chamber on the N. of it, which rises several feet above it. The signs of this are the absence of ventilating slits along the present tops of its walls, and the two large recesses at each end of it, which are now less than half their original height. What these recesses originally were like may be seen by a similar recess in the small chamber at the N. end. Here is a large recess in the W. wall, quite rectangular, and free from any ornament, like all the other parts; it is roofed across by a deep lintel, the whole being of the same red granite as the rest of the walls.

What may have been the use of these recesses, is an inquiry which seems to be solved by the other question, as to where were the original sites of the diorite statues, so many of which were found thrown into the well in the Eastern hall. These statues must have had some appropriate place in this hall, and no sign appears of any pedestals upon which they could have stood. We might look, then, on such niches or recesses in the walls as the original sites of the great diorite figure of Khafra, of his lesser statues, and of the equally valuable (though sadly neglected) cynocephalus apes of Tahuti, carved in gray granite and green basalt, which now lie scattered about the building. These recesses at the end of the Eastern hall are 80·9 (S.) and 85·5 (N.) in width; that in the north chamber is not accessible.

97. The workmanship of the building in general, though fine looking, is not at all equal to that of the Great Pyramid. The granite blocks are fitted together anyhow, so long as their joints are horizontal, and somewhat upright; and in some cases even a re-entering angle is cut in one stone to receive the corner of another. The walls are also far from vertical, or square with each other in plan. The Eastern hall is longer on the present top than at the bottom by 7·2 on E. and 9·7 on W. side, the difference being nearly all due to a very perceptible batter of the S. end. It is also wider at the top than the bottom, by 4·1 on N. end and 2·9 on S. end. The orientation of it is fairly close; for, judging by the noonday gun of Cairo, it is $+16'$ or $-12'$ from true N. by two different days' observations. The irregularity of the walls discouraged me from using polestar observations for it, the difference of width of the ends being equal to 10' on the length. All the dimensions marked on the plan are as measured at the base, except the Western part of the great hall, which is much buried in the sand.

The building is peculiar in the fitting of the corners; not only are the courses bedded alternately one over the other up a corner, as in the Great Pyramid, but each course goes an inch or two round the corner; the angle being actually cut out in each stone. This may be very probably explained by what we see in the granite casing of the Third Pyramid; there the face was left rough, to be dressed down after building. If, then, the faces of these blocks were left with a small excess on them, and dressed down afterwards, that would make each block turn the corner in the way described.

All the doorways seem to have been fitted with double valve doors: the doorway to the loculi is the best to examine. There the pivot-holes cut in the granite lintel by a jewelled tube drill are plainly to be seen; with the stump of the core left by the drill, still sticking in the southern hole. On the floor beneath these there is, not another hole, but a highly polished piece of black basalt, quite flat, and free from scratches. It is difficult to see what was the use of such a stone, or how the doors were worked.

98. This Granite Temple, then, appears to have been a mass of masonry, probably cased externally with fine limestone ; and measuring about 140 feet in each direction, and 40 feet high. This contained a hall about 60 feet long, 12 wide, and 30 feet or more in height, with a large recess at each end containing a statue. These recesses were high up above the doors which led into lesser chambers, also containing statues, and from which outer doorways may have led. Beside this hall there was the great hall, entered by a doorway over 8 feet wide and 14 feet high, and dimly lighted by its ventilators ; one part of this was 81 feet long, 22 wide, and 19 feet high, the roof supported by six massive pillars ; while the remainder was 55 feet long, 33 wide, and $18\frac{1}{2}$ high, with its roof supported by ten of the same monolithic pillars. There were also six loculi, each 19 feet long, in one of the side chambers. Over all this was the open-air court on the top, reached by a sloping passage of alabaster, and cased with fine white limestone ; its area about 80 feet by 100 feet, and the walls around it over 15 feet high. From the great ceiled halls of dark red granite—with their ranks of square monoliths, and vistas as much as 100 feet in length, all dimly seen by the light reflected through the openings along the roof—the main passage led out in one straight line, up the wide dazzling white causeway, for more than a quarter of a mile ; thus entering the similar temple that stood before Khafra's Pyramid, richly furnished with statues, bowls, and vases engraved with his royal name and titles.

99. The date of the Granite Temple has been so positively asserted to be earlier than the fourth dynasty, that it may seem rash to dispute the point. Recent discoveries, however, strongly show that it was really not built before the reign of Khafra, in the fourth dynasty.

The main argument for its earlier date is the mention of the " Temple of the Sphinx," in the celebrated tablet discovered at Gizeh. But I found that the building to which this tablet belonged was of the twenty-first dynasty ; and, as will be seen in the " Historical Notes " (section 118), this tablet is either a refurbished and altered copy of an older inscription, or more probably an entire invention. In no case, however, would it be certain that the Granite Temple was the identical temple of the Sphinx, rather than the temple of Isis, or that of Osiris, which are also mentioned ; and there may easily have been other temples in the neighbourhood, whose foundations are as unknown now as the whole Granite Temple was a generation ago. The whole reasoning turns on the supposition that a building which is near the Sphinx, though not known to be in any way connected with it, is yet necessarily identical with a temple of the Sphinx, mentioned on a tablet which has internal evidences of being untrustworthy, and which was written about a couple of thousand years after the time mentioned upon it.

The argument, on the other hand, for the Granite Temple being of the fourth dynasty, is drawn from its own construction, and is, therefore, contemporary evidence. The great causeway from the temple runs askew to the orientation of the temple and Pyramids ; and the adequate reason for this is the presence of a ridge of rock running along in that direction. But the entrance passage, which is built all in one mass with the temple, and is certainly contemporary with it, is also skewed exactly as the causeway. This shows that the causeway cannot have been designed after the temple, since there must be a strong reason for building one part of an oriented structure askew to the rest of it. If the causeway, then, is as old as the temple, what could be the meaning of running a causeway up to a bare hill-top, if no temple or Pyramid existed there ? more especially as all other causeways and approaches run east instead of west. The only adequate reason for this arrangement is the pre-existence of the Second Pyramid and its upper temple, before the causeway and lower temple. The same conclusion is arrived at when we consider the other Pyramid causeways, and see that the causeway of the temple was (in the cases of the Great and Third Pyramids) doubtless the causeway by which the materials were brought during the building. If the Granite Temple existed before the causeway, and so blocked the end of it, there would be no way of taking the stones up for building the Second Pyramid. The lower end of the causeway must have opened freely on to the plain, until the completion of the Pyramid and upper temple.

Thus the arrangements of the buildings themselves point clearly to the following order of design. First, the Pyramid of Khafra ; second, the temple built symmetrically in front of that Pyramid ; third, the causeway, leading askew from that temple down a ridge of rock ; and fourth, the Granite Temple at the foot of the causeway, with its entrance passage skewed into line with the causeway, though the rest of the temple was oriented, like everything else in the neighbourhood.

The fact that the only dateable remains found in the Granite Temple were statues of Khafra also shows that it is of his period ; since the idea of his appropriating an earlier building is very unlikely.

Such, then, is the contemporary evidence on the age of this building, given by the causeway and passage.

100. There are, at Gizeh, remains of various other great buildings of the Pyramid period, as well as the Granite Temple (or rather the lower Granite temple of Khafra) and the upper temple by the Second Pyramid.

On the east side of the Great Pyramid a large building existed, of which but little can be found to show its nature. The great basalt paving, about 90 feet by 180 feet, has been described already (section 28), and a great platform of this sort must have been part of some large work. The superstructure, now destroyed, appears to have been lined with granite, like the temples of Khafra ; many large pieces of polished granite are to be seen lying on the S. side of the basalt paving ; and on the E. side, in the inner end of the E.N.E. trench, is a block with two adjacent faces, and a third worked surface on it is precisely like that of the holes for the pivot blocks of the doors in the Granite Temple. Again, when excavating on the basalt pavement, at the middle of it, I found several large hewn blocks of granite, mixed up with the blocks of basalt which lie all torn up there. By the basalt paving I also picked up several flat pieces of diorite ; some polished, and others rough-dressed as for cementing in a building. To understand somewhat more of the nature of this part, the whole site of the basalt paving and around it should be cleared of sand and chips, and all pieces of granite and diorite carefully noted down.

The great rock-cut trenches on the E. of the Great Pyramid have every appearance of having been lined with fine stone ; not only in each of them are blocks inserted with plaster, and other plaster remaining, but the surfaces are very irregular, and certainly not final ; and in most parts the characteristic recessing is to be seen, cut out to hold the irregular backs of the lining blocks, as they were fitted one by one, exactly as in both of the granite-lined temples of Khafra. This recessing can never occur from any cause, except the actual fitting in of the irregularities of the individual blocks of lining ; and it must always show, not only that a lining was intended, but that it was also fitted in. Again, the irregular, but flat, ledges on many parts (such as around the inner end of the S. trench, and along the sides of the E.N.E. trench) are exactly what would be made for fitting blocks of lining. Now the width of the inner end of the S. trench is only 134 inches, and that of the E.N.E. trench 170, and its outer end 150 ; and lining blocks can hardly be reckoned at less than 30 inches thick, considering the height was 20 feet ; hence these trenches must have been narrowed to long vertical slits or crevasses about 5 or 6 feet wide, 20 feet deep, and 160 feet long, lined with costly polished stone.

Of the smaller trenches, the N.N.E. is partly built, and was almost certainly, by its form, position, and wear, a drain to carry off the washing of the basalt pavement, or possibly for some sacrificial arrangement ; the other slight trench, at the N.E. corner of the Pyramid, has a uniform fall, as if for a drain.

101. On the E. side of the Great Pyramid, among the rubbish near the smaller Pyramids, were found two pieces of the casing of a Pyramid, each unique. One is a piece of a basalt casing stone, with three worked faces, *i.e.*, two outer faces of a Pyramid, and the horizontal joint below them ; being, in fact, a bottom corner of a ridge casing stone. The fragment is about 7 inches high on the faces, and 5 inches wide along the base. The joint surface is beautifully worked, by pick-dressing slightly ground ; being seldom over $\frac{1}{60}$ inch from a true plane, and generally much less. The angle of slope must have been 51° 9' ± 5',

as determined by the angle of meeting of the faces ; but the joint dipped down 1° 18', so that the angle of the block is 52° 27'. From this it seems probable that one of the smaller Pyramids had arris lines of basalt down each corner, to prevent wear and weathering ; the general casing of all of these Pyramids was eertainly limestone ; as I picked up pieces (with the angle of slope) by each of them.

The other remarkable piece of casing is a bottom corner, with an upright joint, of a diorite casing stone. The idea, even of arris lines being cased with a stone so valuable and difficult to work, is almost incredible ; but this chip, some four inches long on the face, and one inch on the joint, cut to the regular angle (*i.e.*, 52° 30' ± 10'), seems to admit of no other explanation.

It therefore appears as if the small Pyramids of the family of Khufu were adorned with the protection of edges of the hardest and toughest stones, which embraced the faces of polished white limestone ; an architectural effect quite new to our ideas.

102. The use of diorite at Gizeh is worthy of study ; it is far from a common stone, and was generally reserved for statues, no building stones of it being known *in situ*. Hence, wherever it is found it is both unmistakable and important. Of wrought and finished diorite, I found opposite the N. face of the Great Pyramid two pieces ; each with three faces meeting at right angles, two faces rough dressed and cemented, and the other face fine ground. These must have belonged to some building work in diorite ; and probably belonging to the same were two angle pieces with both faces polished, and two plane chips, both polished. Beside these, in the same place, were many pieces of diorite with slight saw cuts in them, ½ to 2 inches deep, and hammer-dressed surfaces ; and also innumerable chips of diorite lying about. All these pieces are solely found lying on the surface, and never within the sloping stratification of the ancient Pyramid masons' rubbish. They seem exactly as if some small construction, or object, in diorite, had been smashed up in one spot ; but there are no foundations or traces of a building on the bare rock, for hundreds of feet on either side of it. The site of these fragments is exactly opposite the entrance to the Great Pyramid. Now, Greaves (in 1638) mentions a tradition that the niche in the Queen's Chamber was the place for an idol; and it would be a very suitable recess to hold a great diorite statue like that of Khafra, which probably stood in a recess in the Granite Temple. If, then, such a statue and its pedestal had been broken up, and carried out of the Pyramid, and finally chipped to pieces at the edge of the hill,—with the same intensity of hatred that is shown in the destruction of the other statues at the temple of the Second Pyramid, at Abu Roash, at Sakkara, and elsewhere,—this would account for the corners of built blocks found here, which might be parts of the pedestal ; for the rough pieces, which might be the backs of the blocks ; for the various pieces of polished diorite ; for

the quantity of diorite chips; and for some pieces of diorite statues, and other dressed fragments, found a couple of hundred feet to the westward. There is no place so likely for the diorite to be brought from, as from the Great Pyramid; since this site is the part of the hill edge nearest to the entrance, but not near to any other place. Unhappily, there has been such a large amount of quarrying and replacing in the Queen's Chamber, and so much rubbish from there has been distributed elsewhere, that it is vain to look for any diorite chips still remaining there.

Beside the diorite on the above site, I found many fragments of polished statues, and probably thrones, among the rubbish overlying the tombs on the E. of the Great Pyramid; and also specimens illustrating tube-drilling, ordinary sawing, and circular sawing in diorite. For an account of these, see the "Mechanical Methods."

Beyond the tombs south of the Great Pyramid, I found a piece of a statue; but this most likely came from the great site for such pieces, the temple of the Second Pyramid. There, in the rubbish, any quantity of chips of statues, bowls, and other objects in diorite, may be found. Bits of statues large and small, fingers, toes, drapery, and hieroglyphs are readily to be picked up.

Behind this Pyramid, in excavating the workmen's barracks, I turned up several pieces of statues, both in diorite and alabaster; these had been less worn than is usual with such fragments, and all retained traces of their colouring; black for hair, and green for dress, on the alabaster; and uniform white plastering on the diorite. Beside these I found a small piece of diorite, hammer-dressed in curve, opposite the door of the Second Pyramid, on the rubbish.

The exact position of all wrought fragments of diorite, should be carefully noted when they are found; as by this means many suggestions may be obtained as to objects that are now entirely destroyed.

T

CHAPTER XV.

TOMBS AT GIZEH.

103. ALTHOUGH plans were made in 1880–81, of all the accessible tombs of Gizeh, it is hardly desirable to add them to the bulk of the present volume, especially as they have not much bearing on the Pyramids and temples. But the determination of the typical angle of the built tombs is interesting, not only in itself, but also in connection with the Mastaba-Pyramids of Sakkara and Medum (see section 110).

The rows of tomb-chapels (in Arabic *mastaba*) built on the surface of the rock at Gizeh, are nearly all constructed with the same angle. To determine the amount and variations of this, I measured the following tombs, which I selected as being mostly well wrought and in good condition. The numbers given are those of Lepsius.

No. 45	mean of	9	measures,		74°4′	±40′
No. 49	„	2	„		74°55′	1°20
No. 37	„	9	„		75°15′	25
Between	(„	7	„	N. and S.	75°34′	5
Nos. 37 and 40) (	„	6	„	E. and W.	80°57′	15)
No. 14	„	12	„		75°36′	25
No. 44, N. part,	„	15	„		76° 0′	5
No. 18	„	13	„		76°30′	1°30′
No. 17	„	7	„		78° 3′	1°

Properly weighting these data (inversely as the squares of their probable errors) the mean is 75°52′±10′; and No. 44, which is by far the finest work of all, is 76° 0′ ± 5′. Now 75° 57′ 50″ is the angle produced by a rise of 4 on a base of 1; hence the rule for the mastaba-angle seems to have been to set back the face 1 cubit in every 4 cubits of height. The slope of 80°57′±15′ on E. and W. of one mastaba is probably designed on the same principle; as a rise of 6 on 1 yields a slope of 80° 32′ 15″.

104. The very remarkable tomb known as Campbell's tomb, requires some notice here, as it has been associated with the name of Khufu by some writers. For a detailed plan and measurements reference should be made to Col. Vyse's volumes; but we may state the general form of it as a large square pit in the

rock, 26 by 30 feet, and 53 feet deep; outside this there is a trench, running all round it at 9 to 22 feet distant; this is 5 feet wide and 73 feet deep. Bars of rock are left at intervals across this trench. Altogether about 10,000 tons of limestone have been excavated here.

The gold ring found here, bearing the cartouche of Khufu, only belonged to a priest of that king in late times, and the king's name on it is only introduced incidentally in the inscription, which does not profess to be of early period. But there is, nevertheless, ground for believing this excavation to be the remains of a tomb of the Pyramid period.

When this pit was cleared out by Vyse, he found a tomb built in the bottom of it; but this cannot have been the original interment, for the following reasons. On the sides of the pit may be seen the characteristic marks where the backs of lining blocks have been fitted into the rock (see section 100); and on the surface round the pit and the trench are numerous traces of the fitting of stones, and of plastering, and even some remaining stones let into the rock. Hence this pit has been lined with fine stone, and a pavement or a building has existed above it at the ground level. This lining would so far reduce the size of the pit, from 315 width to probably about 206 inches, that it could be roofed either with beams or with sloping blocks. But the object of such a deep pit seems strange, as it would form a chamber 50 feet high. Perhaps the great rock-pit of the Pyramid at Abu Roash explains this; as Vyse says that in his day, there were signs that it had been filled up with successive spaced roofs, like those over the King's Chamber.

The remaining indications then show that this pit is merely the rough shell of a fine-stone chamber, probably roofed with successive ceilings for its greater security, and having some pavement, or probably a great mastaba chapel, on the surface above it. The access to it was perhaps down the square shaft in the rock, which still remains. It is certain, then, that the tomb of the twenty-sixth dynasty, built of small stones in the bottom of the great pit, after all the lining had been removed, and when it was again a mere shell, cannot have been the original interment. And from the character of the design, and its execution, there can be but little hesitation in referring the original work to the fourth dynasty. Though it may not have been the tomb of Khufu himself, as some have suggested, yet the trench around it may at high Nile have readily held water, insulating the central pit; and it may thus be the origin of the description of Khufu's tomb, given by Herodotus. For the details of the levels connected with the question, and also plans and measures, see Prof. Smyth's account in Edinburgh Ast. Obs., vol. xiii., page 101.

CHAPTER XVI.

NOTES ON OTHER PYRAMIDS.

105. SOME of the other pyramids that I have examined have such important bearings on those of Gizeh, that it will not be out of place to give some notes here upon their construction, though they have been mostly described by Vyse and Perring, to whose account this must only be considered supplementary.

Beginning at the north, the first Pyramid is at Abu Roash, five miles N. of Gizeh. It is situated on the top of a striking hill of white limestone, a culminating point of the Libyan Desert, which is seen from far in the Nile Valley. This hill is deeply scored by watercourses which wind through it ; and its Nile face rises at a steep slope of 35°. The wild and desolate valleys of it were used for interment by the ancient Egyptians ; as outside a cave, now partly fallen in, I found fragments of bronze, and of a very large, thin, translucent alabaster bowl. On this hill there are apparently the remains of two Pyramids, but of one of them nothing much can be stated without excavations. Of the other, the general appearance is a large pit cut in the rock, with a passage leading down to it ; about ten courses of limestone around it, and a great quantity of broken stones heaped about it, making a mass some 300 feet square and 40 feet high. Beyond this are heaps of granite chips lying in a line all round the Pyramid, and most abundant just in front of the entrance. Leading away northward from the Pyramid is a causeway, nearly a mile long, and in some parts 40 feet high, running down to the plain.

The rock-cut pit and passage were originally lined with fine Mokattam limestone, which, it is said, was stripped out in the time of Mohammed Ali by a mudir. Since Vyse's time some more masonry is gone ; and this Pyramid (perhaps the most ancient in existence) is being quarried during high Nile at the rate of 300 camel-loads a day, I was told.

The pit is now about 30 feet N. to S., by 70 feet E. to W., and about 30 feet nigh, besides the depth of a large quantity of broken stone in it, beneath which Vyse found the pavement. The passage is about 18 feet wide. The sides have a batter of about 1 in 30. The entrance passages of Pyramids are in no case over about 40 inches wide ; if such was the case here, then the lining must have been 7 feet thick. Now, looking at the rock-pit, this would imply a chamber about 16 feet by 56 feet (or probably 17 feet, *i.e.,* 10 cubits, in width), the length of it being, perhaps, divided in separate chambers ; and what makes this the more likely is that, by this thickness of lining, the sloping roof-beams would lie on it and act as cantilevers without any thrust, just as they do at Gizeh and Sakkara. Perring considered that there were traces of superposed ceilings and spaces, like those over the King's Chamber at Gizeh ; and such a covering seems very likely. Roughly observed, by the noon-day gun of Cairo the rock-cut passage is only 20′ W. of N. ; this, at least, shows it to be as well oriented as could be expected in a mere rock cutting which was to be afterwards lined.

An important question about this Pyramid is, whether it was ever finished. It has been often written of by Vyse and others as being unfinished ; and the rude stone hammers met with here have been classed as implements left by the workmen. We now know, however, that jewelled saws and drills were the tools used by Pyramid builders ; and the rough stone hammers are of exactly the types belonging to the rude remains of Ptolemaic times. These, therefore, more probably tell of destruction rather than of construction. The great heaps of granite all round the Pyramid show that it has been cased with granite ; and as it is always believed that no casing was put on a Pyramid until the core was entirely finished, this is evidence of the completion of the Pyramid. The far larger heaps of granite in front of the entrance, show that it has been lined in part with granite. Now, all these heaps, like the hammers, tell of destruction, for throughout them broken pieces of worked surfaces of granite may be seen, some with two planes meeting; and also many blocks which have cleavage holes in them, are too large to be masons' waste, and too small for casing blocks, but exactly such as would result from cutting up the casing. The large amount of masonry carried away is shown by the depth of 6 or 8 feet of chips lying on the top of the remaining courses ; so that the objection that there is not sufficient bulk here for the Pyramid to have been complete, is put to rest at all respects by the remains of what has been destroyed.

Whether the body of the king was actually placed in the Pyramid or no, is a point of less consequence compared with the fact of finding pieces of granite coffer, and of diorite statue. The pieces of the granite coffer, which I observed in the rubbish which had been carried out of the inside, are some of them curved ; belonging, therefore, to a modified box-coffin, partially suited to the figure. One curved piece of coffer is 8·1 thick, and a plane piece is 10·2 thick. Besides this I found fragments of the diorite statue, including several pieces of the figure, and one piece of the throne. This throne had borne an inscription arranged exactly like that on Khafra's large statue, and of the same scale ; the fragment found reads, ". . . . nub (Ramen . . . .)," showing that the king's name was MEN . . . . RA (see Pl. xii). Altogether, eight pieces of the polished surface and quantities of unwrought chips, were picked up ; and beside these I also found chips of basalt (one wrought), and several scraps of Mokattâm limestone. Everything here has been smashed with great care ; the wrought granite had been mainly burnt and powdered ; and the surfaces of the statue were bruised to pieces before it was broken up ; the block with the piece of cartouche on it had been used as a hammer, having a groove cut round it to hold a cord by which it was swung. Exploration here would be most desirable, to recover more of these remains, considering how much was found without any aid in a couple of casual visits. For the remarks on the builder, see the Historical Notes, section 112.

There is a large quantity of broken pottery on the N.E of this Pyramid, and well-wrought flint flakes mixed with it. This, from its character, I concluded to be of late period ; and this opinion was confirmed by finding a green bead accidentally baked in one pot, which proved it to belong to the later dynasties.

106. The recently opened Pyramid of Pepi of the sixth dynasty, at Sakkara, is very interesting as showing many details of construction. The first description of it that was published was one that I sent to Dr. Birch, and which was communicated by him to the Society of Biblical Archæology, in April, 1881, with seven plates of inscription which I copied one day.* As the description then given did not contain all the measurements that were taken, I repeat them here. The chamber is of the form of the Queen's Chamber in the Great Pyramid ; the beams of the gable roof rest $\frac{3}{5}$ on the side wall, and projects $\frac{2}{5}$ over the chamber ; thus they were completely cantilevers, and were quite free from arch thrust until they were broken. The roof is not merely formed of one set of these deep beams on edge, but of three successive layers of beams, or complete roofs, one over another in contact. Yet the destroyers have forced a way through all the beams, and broken them up, so that many of them are upheld by merely the thrust of the fragments against each other. Like the spaces over the King's Chamber in the Great Pyramid, the E. and W. walls of this chamber are wholly independent of the N. and S. sides and of the roofing-beams, the great end walls extending into the masonry of the Pyramid past the building of the rest of the chamber.

The chamber is 123 wide (=6 × 20·5), and 307·6 long (= 15 × 20·51) ; the roof being composed of five beams (therefore of 3 cubits each), which divide it thus from the E. end 0, 62?, 122·2, 182·9, 244·7, 307·6. The vertical lines of the inscription on the W. wall are spaced thus, beginning at the S. end each successive ten columns occupies 21·3, 21·4, 21·3, 21.3, 21·8 and seven columns 15·2.

---

* Unfortunately the lithographer confounded hawks and eagles, which were carefully separated in the MS.

The roof-beams being 85 long over half the chamber, shows their angle to be about 43½° ; and they extended 93 inches horizontally over the wall, or 128 of their total length of 213 on the under-side. These 30 beams of limestone therefore weigh over 30 tons each.

The coffer itself is of black basalt, of the plain box-shape; slightly curved, with about 2 inches swell in the sides, to fit the body. The lid slid on from the W.; and to support it a sort of side-board of masonry appears to have been built up between the W. wall and the coffer, from off which the lid could be slid over the coffer. The coffer has only one band of inscription, which is along the E. side; this is only the name Ra-meri and usual brief titles. The form of the box is remarkably massive, the sides being over a foot thick, and the bottom 20 inches, although it was only 2 feet wide inside. The dimensions are :—

Outside	106·5 long	48·6 wide	44·7 high.
Inside	82 ?	24·3	24·8 ± ·2

The bottom was measured, in perhaps a rather different part to the depths above, as 20·3 thick ; this might make the inside width and depth equal. The ledge for the lid is 1·9 below top, and 1·3 extreme width ; the lower side of it being cut with a deep groove along its back, so that the surface in which the lid would rest is convex. This was probably done to prevent scraps lodging in the groove, and jamming the lid in its sliding. The bottom of the coffer is crusted with resin ; but this may have been melted out of the mummy wrappers when the coffer was raised on stones, and a fire burnt under it, as appears to have been the case during its destruction. It has been broken up by cutting rows of grooves in it, and banging it to pieces ; one end being even broken off through the 12 inches thickness of the sides. On the E. inside are two nearly vertical grooves, leaning towards the S. at the top ; their places measured from the N. end are at 23·6 to 25·0, and 26·2 to 27·6.

Beside this coffer there is a square box of granite sunk in the floor ; it is 28·1 × 27·9 across the inside, and the sides are 6·2 thick; thus outside it would be 40·4. There is a covering slab, quite flat, and without pin holes or fastenings, 41·2 square and 9·0 thick.

The chamber is at present half full of chips of the N. and S. walls, which had been industriously destroyed in early times ; and of the large quantity of the fragments taken out in the recent opening of the Pyramid, it will be impossible to restore the inscription now, as the inscribed parts were never collected or examined, but lay with the rubbish and were carried off by Arabs and travellers. Thus much of an extensive text of the early period has been lost. The heaps still remaining in the Pyramid should be carefully sorted, and from the large pieces of inscription which are among them a good deal might be put together. The E. and W. walls are perfect ; but only the W. is yet visible, of which I copied more than half. The hieroglyphs are beautifully cut in the fine white limestone and are painted bright green.

The general bulk of this Pyramid is of very poor work; merely retaining walls of rough broken stones, filled up with loose rubble shot in. This appears to be the usual construction under the sixth dynasty. On a block of the W. wall of the chamber, where it was covered over by the roof-beams, is a painted slab. It is of the style of tomb decoration, with figures variously engaged, and brief inscriptions. But it is very rough, and has been built in as a common building stone and slopped over with mortar. It therefore seems probable that we have here the first example yet known of a learner's work; great quantities of such must have been done by an artist, before he could be entrusted with the execution of the bold clear drawing for decorating a tomb.

107. The Great Pyramid of Dahshur is of fine work, about equal to that of the second Pyramid of Gizeh; and it was cased with fine white Mokattam limestone like that on the Great Pyramid of Gizeh. The entrance passage of limestone has never been polished, but is about equal in work to the fine hammer-dressing of the granite passage of the Second Pyramid. The passage is 41·3 wide, and 47·5 high; the fine stone of the floor is two courses deep, but does not go very far under the sides. The first chamber has 11 overlappings, like those of the Great Pyramid gallery, and the work of it is much like that; it measures:

N. 143·9, S. 142·8, E. 328·5, W. 330·0, N. door 41·2, S. door 41·1.

Height to first overlapping is 87·0 N., and 87·2 S., above the tops of the doorways (whose floor is invisible owing to encumbrance); from the first to the second lap is 35·5, thence to third lap 32·0; width of first lap is 5·4 to 6·0. The whole height of 87· is filled by a single block over each door; these single blocks extend 115·2 on the N., and 113·6 on the S. wall, besides a part of each hidden in the side wall. The passage to the second chamber is 124·6 long; and the second chamber 103·0 wide, with a doorway 41·2 wide. The dimensions were evidently in the usual cubits; $329·7 \div 16 = 20·61$, $143·4 \div 7 = 20·49$, $124·6 \div 6 = 20·73$, $103·0 \div 5 = 20·60$, 41·1 to $41·2 \div 2 = 20·6$. In the chamber are many ox-bones; some in bitumen, and therefore probably ancient. The passage is much polished, as by continual passing, and some animal has a lair in the inner chamber; I did not disturb it, being unarmed and miles from any help; and a pair of hyænas with a family might have proved awkward acquaintances.

108. The Southern or Blunted Pyramid of Dahshur, is in many respects the most interesting of any existing, as the greater part of its casing still remains; it is so out of the way, that the tide of Arab pillage (which only stripped the Gizeh Pyramids in the last few centuries) has only lately reached it; and much of the destruction has been done in the present century, and even a few years ago. It is also remarkable for containing two hieroglyphic scribbles of visitors, the only examples of such known in the Pyramids; and a curious Greek drawing,

of a beast of the pug-dog type. It is cased with yellowish Mokattam limestone, of the same quality as that of the Second Pyramid of Gizeh. This is broken away just round the bottom in most parts, also all over the top, and over a large part of the W. and S. sides ; the S.W. corner being so much ruined that it can be very easily ascended. The courses at the top are 20 to 21 inches high ; a reputed cartouche of King Unas on one block is merely a royal bee. The casing blocks are very deep from back to front, about 80 inches ; though only 20 inches high, and about 60 wide. They are more like layers bevelled off at the edges than a coating of " slabs of stone," as such casing has been described. The joints are not quite horizontal, but dip inward a little ; they are very good and close.

109. The most valuable part of the remaining casing is that of the door-way, as it shows the arrangement for closing the Pyramid (see Pl. xi.). On either side of the passage is a hole in the wall ; now very rounded and cavernous, owing to weathering ; but apparently about 3 or 4 inches in diameter, and 5 or 6 deep, originally. These two holes are just opposite one to the other, the centres being about 13 inside the Pyramid, and 6 above the passage roof.* From the point above these holes, the roof slopes upward more steeply to the outside, being cut away ; the joint of the passage side, however, continues in a straight line. This formation of the passage seems exactly adapted for a stone door working on a horizontal hinge ; the holes being for the bronze bearings of the pivot, and the cut-out of the roof being to allow the top edge of the door to rise when turning it on its hinge.

Some way within this point is a vertical hole in the roof, 6·2 to 8·2 from the W. side, or 33·5 to 35·5 from the E. side of the passage ; and from this hole inwards the roof is cut away horizontally for about 32 inches. It is plain that this is intended for a door, probably of wood by the smallness of the pivot, and working on a vertical hinge. The cut-out in the roof shows this by its length, which agrees with the width of the door required ; and also by its only extending over the eastern part of the roof, up to the pivot ; while W. of that, the 6 inches behind the door when opened, the roof slopes down as elsewhere. Unhappily, the floor is all torn up for 195 inches from the outside ; a layer of 19 or 20 inches being missing from 36 to 195 inches, and a thicker amount of 25 inches from 36 to the outside. Hence the lower pivot hole and other details are missing. At about 130 inches down the passage are two holes on each side, one near the top and one near the bottom ; they are about two inches wide and one deep, flat on the N. and curved on the S. Probably they were for some fittings.

The form of the outer stone door may be roughly estimated by the requirements and limitations of the case. A plain flat slab is what would probably first occur to the observer ; but such a slab, which must be 20 inches

* The sides of the holes are 11 to 15½ on E., 11 to 16·2 on W. ; the tops and bottoms are 4 to 8½ on E. ; 2 to 8 on W.

U

thick by the position of the pivots, would need a pull varying from 700 to 1,500 lbs. to lift it up, which could hardly be applied in such a position; also it would leave a gap 13 inches wide at the top edge when shut.   Considering the various data, we may conclude that the door must have been thinned at the lower edge to permit of a person getting in without needing to tilt it so much as to require a great amount cut away at the top edge, and probably the mass would be extended to the S. of the pivot, so as to bring the centre of gravity more nearly under the pivot, and thus make the door easier to open. Thus the conditions almost limit the form of the door to that shown in open shade on the diagram (Pl. xi.); the closed position of it being outlined by dots. The pull required to open such a door by the lower edge would vary from 2½ cwt. at the beginning, to 5 cwt. when fully open; and it could be easily kept open by a rod put across the mouth of the passage at A.   Thus, when lifted, there would be an opening about 15 inches high and 41 wide, for 4½ feet long under the block, which would leave access to the lock of the wooden door inside. For the further discussion of this, and the confirmatory passages of Strabo and an Arabic author, see the Architectural Ideas, section 126.

The passage of this Pyramid is lower than any that I have measured, being :—

Near the mouth ...	...	41·7	wide	41·7 high
Above the dislocation	...	41·9	„	42·8 „
Below	...	41·35	„	43·1 „

The dislocation is at a remarkable place, where the roof and floor in their outward course suddenly turn up in a curve to a point 11·1 above the true line, and then dropping sharply, they begin again only 1·1 above the true line, and fully regain the old direction in 23 inches distance.   This formation is not due to a settlement, for (1) a settlement of 11 inches in such solid masonry, not far from the ground, is impossible, the more so as it would need a uniform settlement of the whole of the lower part of the passage, which should quickly cease at one point, and soon after continue at an equal amount; and (2) because the roof on the upper side of the dislocation is cut away in a slope for 23 inches, 1·1 being removed at the maximum.   This shows that the builders were well aware of this formation in their time; and yet that they did not wish to smooth it all out, as if it were an accident or settlement, though nothing would have been easier for them than to have removed all trace of it.   This part, like the rest of this Pyramid, needs far more examination.

The general work of this Pyramid is about equal to that of the Larger Pyramid of Dahshur, and like that of the Gizeh Pyramids; it is entirely of a superior class to that of the sixth dynasty Pyramids of Sakkara.

110. The Pyramids which have been described above are all true Pyramids;

though they are often confounded all in one class with the Mastaba-Pyramids *
of Medum † and Sakkara (the Step-Pyramid), which are really of a different
class, distinct in their system and construction. The Mastaba-angle of about
76°, or a rise of 4 on a base of 1, has been already described (section 103), and
the usual Pyramid angle of about 52° is well known. The two are wholly
distinct, and the examples of them do not merge one into the other. And it
may further be stated that there are no true Step-Pyramids. Those commonly
so called (at Gizeh, for instance,) are merely in process of destruction, showing
the successive working platforms of the building, which rise far steeper than the
Mastaba-angle ; and of one of the most step-like of all (the middle small one by
the Great Pyramid), sloping casing may still be picked up around it, and found
in situ under the rubbish. There are only two of the so-called Pyramids that
were not cased in a slope without re-entering angles ; these are the two Mastaba-
Pyramids of Sakkara and Medum, which really consist of superposed Mastabas,
with the characteristic angle of 76°.‡

The tower-like appearance of the Medum Pyramid is only due to the
lower steps having been broken away. Not only may the places where the
steps joined the existing surface be seen, but the lower part of each step-face
may be found standing in the rubbish at the base (see F. F. in Pl. vii., drawn
from a photograph). The roughened part of the face, where the step joined it,
has been supposed to be for affixing some decoration or moulding ; but (beside
the fact that such ornament is unknown in Pyramid architecture) the start of
the top of the step may be seen in some parts projecting out from the face.
The lower parts of the sloping faces which are still to be seen in the rubbish
(well figured in Denkmäler) are also conclusive evidence of faces having
existed outside of the present tower form ; these faces must have ended their rise
and been joined to the tower horizontally, at some level ; and the probable equality
of the steps would require them to join the body at just the places where the
roughened lines of junction are still visible. An historical proof of the existence
of the steps formed by these lower faces is given by Abu Abdallah Muhammed,
quoted by Makrisi (circ. 1400 A.D.), § who mentions a Pyramid built in *five*
terraces, and called " Meidoun." It is true that he says it is the highest of the
Pyramids, which it is far from being ; but, from its situation in a plain, as a

* *Mastaba* is the native Arabic name (adopted by antiquarians) for the sloping sided tombs,
of about 76° angle, and 10 to 20 feet height.

† This name has always been variable. In the third dynasty it is *Metun ;* Mariette, from
some hieroglyphic source, spells it *Metum* or *Meri-tum ;* Abu Abdallah Muhammed (*ante*,
1400 A.D.) writes *Meidoun ;* modern Arabs say *Medum.*

‡ The Pyramid of Riga, near Abusir, is stated by Vyse to have had a slope of 75° 20′ on
the upper part, and of 50° below that ; if so, it was a Pyramid on the top of a Mastaba ; but
more excavation and critical examination of it is needed.

§ See Vyse, ii. 354.

modern author writes, " It is most imposing, more so than Gizeh, more so than Sakkara ;" and the name is conclusive as to which Pyramid he intended. The five terraces visible about six centuries ago would be the five upper ones, showing that the lowest was ruined, or buried in a heap of rubbish, at that time. Both of these Mastaba-Pyramids are also peculiar as having been repeatedly enlarged.   In no case have successive enlargements been found in a true Pyramid ;* but both of these structures have been several times finished, each time with a close-jointed, polished casing of the finest white limestone ; and then, after each completion, it has been again enlarged by another coat of rough masonry and another fine casing outside of the former casing.   This explains how readily the Medum Pyramid was stripped into a towering form ; there were the older polished casings inside it ; as soon as the later coats were stripped off, the older surface was revealed again.

The Step-Pyramid of Sakkara is of poorer work, but on just the same principle as that of Medum ; and in this case the additions have been very one-sided, since on the South two finished fine casings may be seen far inside it, only about a third of the distance from the present middle to the W. side (see F. F., Pl. vii.).   On the South may also be seen, at the E. end, two polished casings, one about 8 feet inside the present rough stripped outside, and another 10½ feet inside of that casing.   These two casings are not quite at the same slope, showing that the exact angle of it is not important, as the additions were not uniformly thick all over one side : hence the difference of a couple of degrees, between this Pyramid and the best Mastaba-angle, is not astonishing.

The Step-Pyramid, or Mastaba-Pyramid, of Sakkara is of an oblong plan ; unlike any Pyramid, but similar to the Mastabas.   The Mastaba-el-Farun at Sakkara is an intermediate form, being as large as the base of a Pyramid, but as oblong and low in its proportion as a Mastaba.   Now that the name of King Unas has been found in one of the Pyramids, it is evident that his name occurring in the Mastaba-el-Farun merely shows that he built it ; probably as a base for an obelisk, such as is often seen in early inscriptions representing a monument or temple to Ra.

* Even the Third Pyramid of Gizeh, the size of which has been increased from that of the first design, has not been enlarged over a finished casing, but merely modified in the course of its building.

CHAPTER XVII.

HISTORICAL NOTES.

111. IN considering the arrangements of the early monuments, the questions of the invariability of the climate, and the state of the ground when they were built, become of interest. Was the sand as encroaching then as now? And did the builders anticipate the half-buried state of many monuments?

In considering these questions we must first glance at the general course of Egyptian climate. The country has undoubtedly been gradually drying up. The prodigious water-worn ravines in the cliffs of the Nile valley show this; and there are remarkable evidences of the Nile having been habitually some 50 feet above its present level, thus filling up the whole valley at all times of the year. At many points of the Nile valley, particularly at Tehneh, the cliffs are all water-worn in holes, exactly in the manner of solution under water; while above this action, over about 50 feet level, the cliffs are worn by aerial denudation in a wholly different manner: also the lower part projects forward as a foot, in front of the upper part, the action by water being apparently much slower than that in air, and tending to prevent aerial denudation afterwards.

Besides this, at the foot of the cliffs, particularly at Beni Hassan, wherever the scour of the current was less, or ravines debouched into the main valley, large banks of *débris* have been formed, showing the former power and height of the stream. That it was fed by local rains throughout its course is seen by the deep gorges in the cliffs, often a mile long, and ending in dried-up waterfalls. In the history of the Faium the same drying up is seen; that district appears to have been originally a large lake, which has been gradually reduced, partly artificially, until it is now not a tenth of its former size.

It therefore appears certain that the general change has been one of desiccation; and the inquiry to be made is, if there be any evidence to show whether this change has been continuing in historic times.

Rain was certainly known in Lower Egypt in the Pyramid times, though there is but one evidence of it in the monuments; the water-spout carved in stone, leading from the roof of one of the tombs of the fifth dynasty at Gizeh, is a proof that such a feature was known, and perhaps in common use on the mud-brick houses. Nevertheless, the rain can hardly have been much commoner then than now, or more signs of its action on the tombs would remain. In Greek times the rain appears to have been just as rare as it is now, or even rarer, in Upper Egypt. Herodotus says that the last that fell at Thebes was two centuries before his time, under Psamtik, and then only in drops. Now, last year, Mr. Tristram Ellis, while at Negadeh, just below Thebes, expected rain one day, but he was told that none had been seen there for 45 years. So there does not appear to have been appreciable climatic change in the Thebaid during the last two thousand years. The pits in the Tombs of the Kings, sometimes supposed to have been intended to arrest any storm-flooding, may as likely have been to arrest or hinder intruders; or may be sepulchral pits abandoned, owing to the changes and amplifications of the plans. Again, it may be observed that neither rain, nor any sign of rain, is shown in the paintings of the tombs; no wide hats, no umbrellas, no dripping cattle, are ever represented. Mud-brick tombs, covered with stucco, still remain from the third or fourth dynasty, when they were built without any apparent fear of their dissolution.

On the whole, the rain-fall does not appear to have perceptibly changed during historic times.

The Nile, though so much higher in pre-historic or geologic times, as just mentioned, does not seem to have sunk at all, in Middle or Lower Egypt, in historic times; though above the cataracts it has fallen some twenty or thirty feet. Below the cataracts, on the contrary, it has actually risen, owing to silting up; for many of the deepest tomb-shafts at Gizeh have now several feet of water in them at high Nile, and can only be entered just before the inundation. Also the thickness of mud over the remains both at Memphis and Karnak shows not only the great amount of deposit, but also how much the river must have risen for it to lay down mud so many feet above the old level of deposit.

The rise due to silting up proceeds, then, much faster than any slight diminution of the river which may take place.

The amount of the sand, then, cannot be affected by any variation in moisture; and on looking back it seems very doubtful if there has been any change in it. The sand over the Serapeum might be supposed to have increased, as it has buried the Sphinxes there. But these are of Greek work, and were only erected shortly before the time of Strabo; and he, nevertheless, mentions them as being nearly buried in his day, though doubtless some attempt was made then to keep them cleared. Before this, in the dream of Tahutmes IV., the Sphinx at Gizeh appears to have been buried very much as at present. And on looking to the remains of the early dynasties at Gizeh and elsewhere, their buried state seems rather to be due to artificial changes accumulating the sand than to any great increase in the general amount of sand.

The usual way in which the sand is moved is by a few high winds in the course of the year. These tear over the ground, as opaque as a London fog, bearing just as much sand as their whirling will support; and as soon as any obstacle checks their velocity the surplus of sand is dropped, and thus accumulates. Now the tombs are either rock-hewn, in which case a face of rock is artificially scarped for the fronts, or else they are built on the surface. In either case an eddy is formed in the wind, and this will cause quantities of sand to be thrown down during a sand storm. Again, the erection of the Pyramids would be sufficient to interrupt the steady blow of the wind by causing numerous oblique currents, and would so produce an increase of wind-borne sand in the neighbourhood. Whatever cause checks the velocity of the wind is sure to lead the sand to accumulate; the Arabs know this well, and plant frail rows of reeds (even spaced apart) around their gardens bordering the desert; these make the wind drop the sand, so as to form a bank outside them, and thus keep the enclosures clear.

The general conclusion as to the climate, then, seems to be that there has been no appreciable change in rain-fall, river-flow, or sand-blow during historic times.

112. The builder of the Pyramid of Abu Roash and his epoch have hitherto been quite unknown; there being merely a presumption that it is one of the earliest Pyramids, because it is the most northerly. Now that we have obtained part of the builder's name on the fragment of diorite throne that I found there, we have some clue to the age. No name is known on the monumental lists like Men......ra, beside the three kings Men-ka-u-ra of the fourth, Men-ka-ra of the sixth, and Ra-mentu-hotep of the eleventh dynasty. But M. Maspero has informed me that there were other kings named Men-ka-ra, or Men-ka-u-ra, in the second dynasty; and Bunsen, in his fourth volume, edits Eratosthenes as giving Menkheres II. in succession to Menkaura of the fourth dynasty.

When we consider the claims of these kings, some are disallowed by reason of external circumstances. The Pyramid of Menkaura of the fourth dynasty is well known already at Gizeh; and the workmanship of the Pyramid at Abu Roash excludes it from the period of the rubble Pyramids of the sixth dynasty at Sakkara, and of the mud-brick Pyramids of the eleventh and twelfth dynasties at Thebes and Howara. Thus it is almost certain that we must look either to some king of the second or third dynasties not found in the lists, or to a second Menkaura, successor to Menkaura of the fourth dynasty.

The work of this Pyramid suggests that of the fourth dynasty. The Pyramid of Khufu at Gizeh had no granite outside it; that of Khafra had one or two courses of granite; that of Menkaura had nearly half its surface covered with granite casing; thus there is a progressive use of granite by these successive kings; and at Abu Roash the Pyramid was entirely cased with granite, and therefore next in order of work after that of Menkaura of Gizeh. And this is all the stronger evidence, because no other examples of granite casing on a Pyramid are known.* Again, the diorite statue at Abu Roash was apparently like that of Khafra in size, material, and inscription (section 105), which also tends to fix this Pyramid to the fourth dynasty. Hence, until more remains shall be found at Abu Roash, and more is known of the other reputed Menkaura kings, it may be considered that this Pyramid was built next after the three Pyramids of Gizeh, though making a slight reservation in favour of the earlier dynasties.

113. The builder of the Great Pyramid of Gizeh is well known. Khufu (Grecianized as Kheopa† and Soufis,‡ and Anglo-Grecianized as Cheops) is named both by historians and by his cartouches, which are found as quarry-marks on the building stones. But another name is found on the blocks in the Pyramid, side by side with those bearing the name of Khufu. This other name is the same as that of Khufu, with the prefix of two hieroglyphs, a jug and a ram ; and it is variously rendered Khnumu-Khufu, Nh-Shufu, and Shu-Shufu. The most destructive theory about this king is that he is identical with Khufu, and that the ram is merely a symbol of the god Shu, and put as " the deter-minative in this place of the first syllable of the name." But against this hypo-thesis it must be observed (1) that the pronunciation was Khufu, and not Shufu, in the early times; (2) that the first hieroglyph, the jug, is thus unexplained ; and (3) that there is no similar prefix of a determinative to a king's name, in any other instance out of the hundreds of names, and thousands of variants, known.§

On the monuments bearing the name of Khnumu Khufu at Gizeh, and at Wady Maghara, there also occurs, with different titles, the name of Khufu himself. That the names should thus be found together is very likely, if they were co-regents, as their joint occurrence in the Pyramid would lead us to expect.

The choice, then, lies between the simple idea of a co-regency, such as we know often existed ; or else, on the other hand, adopting a late pronunciation, ignoring one character of the name, inventing the application of prefixed determinatives in cartouches, and supposing that the king's name would be put in duplicate on public monuments with and without a determinative. These requirements are contradicted by the well-known usage found on all other remains.

114. Beside Khumu-Khufu, there is the name of another king which

---

* Excepting some on the anomalous little Pyramid at Riga, of the fifth dynasty.
† Herodotus. ‡ Manetho.
§ Sent is sometimes named by a fish, a determinative without hieroglyphics ; and An sometimes has a fish as a determinative *in* the name ; but there is no case of a determinative prefixed.

belongs to this period, and which is equally rare, though more often mentioned by modern writers. This is Ra-tat-ef (or Doudew-Ra of the French), who is placed in the monumental lists next after Khufu, and whose name is only found in those lists, compounded in names of places, and as being worshipped with Khufu and Khafra at a late period. That he did not succeed Menkaura, as the name Ratoises in Manetho might indicate, is shown by the concurrence of the monumental lists, and by Aseskaf being both successor and adopted son to Menkaura. Here, then, are two names, Khnumu-Khufu and Ra-tat-f, apparently contemporary, and yet never found placed together. It seems not improbable, then, that these are the two names of one king ; that Ra-tat-f was the personal name of the co-regent of Khufu, the name given to his lands, and by which he was worshipped in later times ; and that Khumu-Khufu, or " he who is united with Khufu " (*v.* Ebers on Khnum), was the name of the co-regent when he was joined with Khufu in the government. It must be remembered that the duplication of names is always difficult to prove ; and it is only by a single point of evidence in each case that the identity of such well-known kings as Kaka and Nofer-ar-ka-ra, of An and Ra-en-user, or of Assa and Tat-ka-ra, has been inferred.

115. Khafra* has, on the strength of the historians, been considered by most writers as the builder of the Second Pyramid ; but there was, till lately, no monumental evidence on this point. About three years ago, however, the great causeway was discovered which led from the lower granite temple, where the statues of Khafra were found, to the upper temple by the Second Pyramid. A closer connection of Khafra with this upper temple, I was happy enough to find while there ; from the heaps of chips in the temple, I obtained (without excavating) a piece of white magnesite, steel-hard, with part of the cartouche and standard of Khafra, exquisitely cut ; and also a piece of alabaster with the cartouche alone. Besides this, the base of a diorite statue that I found here, is of just the same gauge as a piece of the base and feet of a small diorite statue that I picked up at Sakkara, inscribed ". . . . nofer nuter, neb khaui . . . ." and which is therefore almost certainly of Khafra. The finding of these cartouche fragments gives the clearest monumental proof that has yet been obtained of the Second Pyramid belonging to Khafra. It may be mentioned here that I also picked up at Gizeh a piece of diorite bowl inscribed ". . nofru"; perhaps, therefore, of Senofru ; and another piece with the standard of Khufu.

116. The attribution of the Third Pyramid to Men-ka-u-ra, the successor of Khafra, is disputed ; and the reasons for doubting his sole ownership appear to be as follows. First, that the Pyramid has certainly been altered from its first

* Here, again, Herodotus retains the final vowel, though adding a nasal in Khefrena.

design in the inside, and also, perhaps, on the outside ; secondly, that there appear to have been two coffers in it; thirdly, that Diodorus says that Menkaura died before it was finished ; and, fourthly, that Manetho attributes it to Nitakerti, the queen in whom the sixth dynasty became extinct, and who is supposed to be identical with the Men-ka-ra of the lists of Abydos.

The change of design in this Pyramid does not seem, however, to have been due to a later reign ; but to have occurred, like some after-thoughts in the Great Pyramid, while it was in course of construction. It has been already pointed out (section 89) in the description of this Pyramid, that no part of the panelled chamber, of the lower (granite) chamber, or of the present floor of the upper chamber, can belong to a first design, of which the upper and disused passage was a part. Hence, if an earlier burial had existed before the finishing of the Pyramid, the coffer must have stood in the upper chamber, the only one then existing, and have been shifted about during the internal deepening of that and the excavation of the other chambers, and finally reset in a fresh place, if the coffer socket in the upper chamber be attributed to an earlier coffer ; a proceeding that is not likely on the part of a ruler who violated the sepulchre, and appropriated it. Also it would be difficult to see the object of so altering and enlarging an existing Pyramid ; as such a Pyramid would supply but $\frac{1}{8}$th of the whole mass required, and its excavations would be still more trifling compared with the existing chambers. There would be, therefore, no adequate reason for such an appropriation. Besides this, the plan of the Pyramid is shown to have been enlarged while it was in course of construction, and not in a later reign, by there being no finished casing to be found at the upper end of the blind passage, the place where any earlier casing would be discoverable, if it had ever been put on. The masonry about that part has been forced in various directions, in search of any continuation of the passage ; and hence, if any older finished casing existed, like that of the inner coats of the Mastaba-Pyramids, it would certainly have been found.

Next, looking at the historical side of the question, this Pyramid (as all writers are agreed) cannot be earlier than the Pyramids of Khufu and Khafra, by reason of its inferiority of position ; the poorer site was accepted for it, in a way that clearly stamps it as being later. The question then lies thus : is the basalt coffer that was found in the lowest chamber, that of the first builder or of any later occupant ? Undoubtedly of the latest occupant, if there were two ; since it was far more carefully concealed, and more finely enshrined, than any coffer could have been in the upper chamber. Now the lid of the basalt coffer of the lower chamber was found lying in the upper chamber ; and along with it the lid of a wooden coffin, bearing the well-known inscription of Menkaura. And therefore the basalt coffer is always accepted, and rightly so, as that of Menkaura of the fourth, and not of Menkara of the sixth dynasty. Thus, by the spelling, the latest occupant of the Pyramid was the same king that we have already seen must be the earliest builder of it ; so that any double origin, or later appropriation of it is thus contradicted.

The evidence from the character of the work is entirely in favour of its being of the fourth, and not of the sixth dynasty. The panel ornament both in the first chamber and on the coffer (which is like that of tombs of the fourth),—the absence of any stone-cut inscriptions, such as cover the walls of the pyramids of the sixth dynasty,—the use of granite for the lower casing, and for the lining of a passage and chamber,—the position of the Pyramid in relation to the others,—the peribolus of the Pyramid of Khafra being unfinished when the Third Pyramid peribolus was being built,—and the absence of any remains of the sixth dynasty in the neighbourhood,—all these characteristic features point clearly to the dynasty, and even to the reign, of Menkaura successor to Khafra.

The socket cut in the floor of the upper chamber, which Perring thought might be for a second coffer, was also suggested by him to be for holding a blind coffer to deceive explorers. It may very possibly have been intended to hold the basalt coffer, for which afterwards another finer and more secret chamber was prepared ; or it may very possibly have held the base of a diorite or basalt statue of Menkaura. In any case no coffer, or fragments of one belonging to this place, was to be found.

The evidence of Manetho is not quite certain in the mere extracts that we possess ; he only mentions that Nitakerti built " the Third Pyramid," without saying where it was ; and it is only a presumption that it refers to the same group as " the largest Pyramid," which he mentions 20 reigns earlier. It might have referred in the full original text to one of the Sakkara groups, where we should naturally look for works of the sixth dynasty.

Diodorus Siculus, though saying that Menkaura died before the Pyramid was finished, yet expressly states that he was a son of Khufu. The unfinished state of the granite casing, and absence of pavement, exactly accord with the premature death of the king.

Thus the four reasons for doubting the earlier date of this Pyramid are reversed or neutralized on examining the details ; excepting the testimony of Manetho. The choice then lies between—on the one hand, Manetho being misunderstood, or in error by confounding Menkaura and Menkara ; or, on the other hand, ignoring the spelling of the names,—the character of the construction and decoration,—the situation of the Pyramid,—the connections of the peribolus, —the date of the neighbouring tombs,—and the testimony of Herodotus and Diodorus.

117. Regarding the age of the brick Pyramids, it is well known that such were built in the eleventh dynasty by the Antef kings at Thebes ; and probably in the twelfth dynasty by Amenemhat III. at Howara, by the side of the labyrinth in

which that king's name is found.   This shows that as a class they belong to the times after the stone Pyramids, and thus gives a general clue to age of those at Dahshur.   Unhappily, Perring only found the end of a cartouche in his digging there, with " . . . . . kau " upon it.   This mere fragment, however, is of value, as there is no king in the lists whose name ends in kau until the eighth dynasty ; excepting Ramenkau, whose Pyramid is the Third of Gizeh, and Hormenkau, whose Pyramid is believed to be at Sakkara, by the slab bearing his figure being found there in the Serapeum.   It is not till the end of the eighth dynasty, when there occurs three names ending in kau, that we meet then with any name that can be applied to the S. brick Pyramid of Dahshur.   The style of work of the frag-ments found along with the cartouche is also clearly of about this date ; they are not in the style of any dynasty before the seventh, nor in that of the twelfth or later periods ; but they most resemble a tomb of the eleventh dynasty at Kom Ahmar (lat. 28° 5′). Hence, by the fragment of the name,—by the character of the work, —and by the material used,—there seems little doubt but that the brick Pyra-mids of Dahshur belong to the dark and troubled period between the sixth and eleventh dynasties ; and that they may probably be assigned to the end of the eighth dynasty.

118. The celebrated tablet containing a reference to the Sphinx requires some notice here of its age and history.   While I was Gizeh, the official excavations by the authorities disclosed some fresh parts of the temple in which this tablet was found ; it lies close to the E. side of the Pyramid, No. 9 of Vyse, the southern of the small Pyramids by the Great Pyramid.   Most happily the exca-vations disclosed a scene of the king offering to Osiris ; and, though much decayed, the cartouche was legible, and was in every hieroglyph that of Petukhanu of the twenty-first dynasty : he is represented wearing the crown of Lower Egypt. This, then, gives the date of the temple ; and the character of all the work agrees well to this epoch.

Now the question of the critical value of the little tablet that mentions the Sphinx, turns on the choice of three hypotheses.   1st. That it is the original tablet of the age of Khufu, preserved through at least 1500 years (or, according to Mariette, double that time), and built into the temple of Petukhanu.   2nd. That it is a copy of such a tablet, more or less exact.   3rd. That it is an unhistorical inscription written for the decoration and honouring of the temple of this usurping dynasty.   And it should be noted that it does not profess to be con-temporary with Khufu, or even to be a copy of an early record.   The style of the engraving is quite unlike the work of the Old Kingdom ; in place of the finely rounded and delicate forms in low relief, and the bold, handsome execution, of the time of Khufu, this insignificant-looking tablet is cut in scratchy intaglio, worse than any of the poorest tomb-decorations of the early times, and looking like nothing but a degradation of the work of the decadence of the twentieth dynasty. Most authorities now agree that it cannot be contemporary with Khufu.   Is it then an exact copy of any earlier tablet? This can only be judged by its matter, and on looking at the figures represented on it, it will be seen that they are such as are not found on early monuments; they comprise Osiris, Isis and Horus, Isis Selk, Khem, Bast? the human-headed uræus, and the sacred bark. Of these, scarcely one can be found on any monument, public or private, of the Old Kingdom; not all of these figures could be matched under the twelfth dynasty; even the monuments of the eighteenth and perhaps nineteenth dynasties do not often show such an assemblage together; and it would be an entire novelty to find such a company on any stele that Khufu could have seen. In the inscription itself, moreover, Osiris is repeatedly called "Neb Rustau," or, "lord of the abodes of the dead" (Brugsch): this title is one that does not occur in any of the dozen of inscribed tombs of the Old Kingdom that are visible at Gizeh; but it is found repeatedly in this temple, built by Petukhanu in the twenty-first dynasty, from which this tablet came. Also, though Pyramids are often mentioned in early inscriptions, Isis is never connected with any of them, and her name is hardly ever found in Pyramid times; so that the title of "Patroness of the Pyramid" seems (like "Mother of the Gods," also found there on the tablet) to be as late an invention as "Neb Rustau."

Thus, by all that can be so clearly seen of the well-marked styles and characteristics of the different periods of Egyptian art and religion, and by the titles here used, this tablet is relegated to the third hypothesis, and stands as an invented inscription designed for the decoration of the temple. This relieves us from an apparent anachronism, as no trace of a Sphinx in statuary, tablets, or inscription, is to be found until the Hyksos period; and such a form was not common until after that. It would seem, therefore, to be an Asiatic idea, akin to the human-headed lions, bulls, and dragons of Assyria and Babylonia. In any case, the allusions to the Sphinx in this tablet were merely topographical, and might be struck out or inserted without altering the sense of it; hence, even if it were a refurbished copy of an older inscription, it would not be of critical value in relation to the age of the Sphinx unless its rigorous accuracy and freedom from additions could be proved.

119. Though the age of the foundation of buildings is always examined, yet the date of their destruction is often of greater historical importance. The many erasures of the names of Set, of Amen, of Hatasu, and others, show very important changes, and the mode in which many of the remains have been destroyed is also very suggestive. The Pyramid of Pepi shows one of the most striking examples of spiteful violence that may be found. Such destruction is commonly attributed to the Persians, or the Hyksos; but the details seem to show violence of an earlier date. In the passage of this Pyramid, the name Ra-meri is chopped out in almost every place, without the rest of the inscription being attacked. This shows a personal spite, beyond the mere destructiveness of an invader, and which can hardly be accounted

for even by the Hyksos conquest. Again, not content with tearing the body out of its wrappings, the massive and tough basalt coffer was raised on stones, lines of cleaving-holes cut in it, a fire burnt beneath it, and, with the utmost violence, it was split asunder ; yet the religious inscriptions on the wall beside it are uninjured. Such care in destruction is more than would be produced by a general hatred to a conquered race.

Again, at Gizeh, the diorite statues in the lower granite temple have been dashed down from their niches, and thrown into the well; but in the upper granite temple, by the Second Pyramid, the destruction is far more laborious and elaborate ; the statues are broken into small chips ; a single toe, or half a hieroglyph, is almost as much as can be found in one piece; the diorite and alabaster vessels are broken in shivers ; and an imperfect cartouche is the greatest prize obtainable from the ruins.

Again, at Abu Roash, the king's diorite statue was not only broken up, but the surfaces were bruised to powder, and a block of the tough diorite was grooved round by chipping, so as to hold a rope by which it could be swung to and fro, until even the ends of it were shivered, and it was finally cracked in two. The granite coffer was burnt, and mostly ground to powder ; while stray chips of basalt show that some other object existed which is quite unknown.

All this vehemence of destruction, this patient, hard-working vengeance, can scarcely be attributed to an age, or a people, which only knew of the kings as historical names. It is to the dark period of the seventh to the eleventh dynasties that we must rather look for the destroyers of the Old Kingdom monuments. The fourth, fifth, and sixth dynasties were one continuous and peaceful succession ; and when that was broken up, apparently by civil war and rival dynasties, it would be highly probable that such personal spite, and intelligent wrath, would be shown by embittered revolutionists. A modern parallel to this vengeance was seen in the careful and painstaking clearance of the bodies of the French kings out of Saint-Denis, and the fate allotted to their monuments, in 1790; the latter were only saved from annihilation by the strenuous claim of Lenoir and others on behalf of the museum.*

In later times there are some curious details of destruction at Karnak. The great fallen obelisk of Queen Hatasu has her name unerased on the top of it; but the name of the god Amen is erased. This shows that Khuenaten took means of erasing the name of Amen in places in which Tahutmes III. did not care to hunt down the name of Hatasu. Her name and portraits in the innermost chamber of her temple at Deir el Bahari were also not effaced ; though in every other part they were cut away. On the standing obelisk of

* See the *Procès-verbal* in " Monographie de l'Eglise de Saint-Denis," par le Bon. De Guilhermy. 1848.

Hatasu at Karnak neither Amen nor Hatasu are erased. This suggests that the fallen obelisk may have been overthrown by Khuenaten, perhaps to destroy the name of Amen; and as it lies upon a high mound of fragments of the works of his predecessors, Tahutmes I. and Amenhotep III., it is not at all impossible that such was the case. It is, in fact, so curiously perched, exactly along the top of this mound of rubbish, as to suggest that the mound was placed to receive it, and perhaps it was broken by careless letting down. To Khuenaten, also, may well be due the careful abolition of the great temple of Amenhotep III. at Thebes, of which but two colossi remain erect.

It may seem a strange idea that there should have been ruins lying about, while the Great Hall was being built close to them, by Seti I. and Ramessu II.; but it is certain that such was the case. In the pylon of Horemheb stones may be found with defaced cartouches of Khuenaten on their inner sides; and the columns of the eastern temple of Ramessu II. are clearly built of ruined polygonal pillars of Tahutmes I., plastered over, and roughly fitted together. So, probably, ever since the dilapidation of the first temple of Usertasen, Karnak has always shown an increasing amount of ruins, often worked up into later buildings, which in their turn were ruined; the destruction being partly due to fanaticism, and partly to later builders, who would worship their predecessors while destroying their works; somewhat in the spirit of Caracalla, who deified Geta, saying, " Let him be a god, provided he is not alive."

120. The accuracy of the descriptions of the Greek travellers deserves notice, as they are often much more accurate in their facts than modern writers. Herodotus* states the base of the Great Pyramid to be 8 plethra, or 800 feet, and it is actually 747 Greek feet; so that he is as accurate as he professes to be, within about half a plethron. The height he states to be equal to the base; and the diagonal height of the corner (which would certainly be the way of measuring it, and was the later Egyptian mode of reckoning) is $\frac{19}{20}$ of the base, or quite as close as the statement professes. The name of the builder is given almost unaltered, Kheopa for Khufu. In describing the Second Pyramid, he states it to be 40 feet less in height than the Great Pyramid; the difference is not quite so great, but the historian's error is only $\frac{1}{27}$ of the whole height. He is quite correct in saying that the foundations were of Ethiopian stone, *i.e.*, red granite. Of the Third Pyramid, the statement, apparently so precise, that the base was 280 feet seems in error. It is over 340 Greek feet, and such a difference could hardly be a mere oversight. It is just possible that this measure refers to the base of the limestone part, which

---

* The accuracy with which Herodotus states what he saw, and relates what he heard; the criticism he often applies to his materials; and the care with which he distinguishes how much belief he gives to each report;—all this should prevent our ever discrediting his words unless compelled to do so.

was about 275 of such feet as go 800 in the Great Pyramid base. Of the Third
Pyramid casing, he says that "half of it consists of Ethiopian stone"; and
actually about $\frac{7}{16}$ of the casing was of granite. The Rhodopis story seems akin
to the ruddy Nitokris of Manetho ; and there is a curious possibility of the whole
description of Nitokris having been transferred from the Pyramid itself to the
ruler who built it.

Diodorus Siculus states the distance of the Pyramids from the Nile with
greater accuracy than we can now settle the ancient position of the river-bank.
The base of the Great Pyramid he gives as 7 plethra, or 700 Greek feet, as
against 747 such feet in reality ; hence he is accurate to less than half a
plethron. The height, he says, is more than 6 plethra ; the arris height is
actually just over 7 plethra, when complete. He mentions the fine preservation
of the stone, and that the original jointing was uninjured by time, showing that
the fine joints attracted his attention. The Second Pyramid he only roughly
describes as a stadium wide ; but this is not far wrong, as it is $1\frac{1}{8}$ stadia. The
Third Pyramid he underrates as 300 feet long, whereas it is 340 Greek feet ; if
however, he originally wrote 3 plethra, he would be correct to less than half a
plethron, as he is in the Great Pyramid size. It is noticeable that he slightly
underrates all the Pyramids, his statements being respectively ·94, ·87, and ·88
of the truth. He states that the sides up to the 15th course were of black
stone ; actually it seems probable that the dark red granite ended at the
16th course : and he says that the upper part was cased with the same stone
as the other Pyramids, which is plainly true to any one who sees the angular
fragments lying thickly around it. Though Vyse was disappointed at not
finding the name of Menkaura inscribed over the doorway, yet Diodorus only
says that it was on the N. side of the Pyramid ; hence it was probably on the
fine limestone above the granite.

Strabo's account is less careful in the dimensions, merely giving roughly a
stadium for the height and base of each of the larger Pyramids, and saying that
one is a little larger than the other. As these dimensions vary from ·85 to 1·25
stadia, he is, at least, quite as accurate as he professes to be. He gives the
invaluable description of the Great Pyramid doorway, which (as will be seen in
sect. 126) so exactly accords with the only remaining doorway of a pyramid.
He also mentions the Third Pyramid being cased nearly up to the middle with
black stone from Ethiopia.

Pliny gives a more exact measurement than any other ancient author,
stating the Great Pyramid base as 883 feet. This would require a foot of
10·2705 inches ; and this is just half of the cubit of 20·541, or a rather short form
of the Egyptian cubit. Taking the mean cubit, we cannot tax him with a
greater error than $\frac{1}{280}$ of the whole, which is quite as close as some of the most
credible measures taken in this century.

Thus we see that there is in these historians an honesty and correctness in their descriptions, and a fulfilment of the amount of accuracy which they profess, which it would have been well for many—perhaps for most—modern writers to have imitated.

The clear and unexaggerated account of the passages of the Great Pyramid given by Edrisi, in 1236 A.D., deserves notice for its superiority to the greater number of Arabic accounts.

CHAPTER XVIII.

ARCHITECTURAL IDEAS OF THE PYRAMID BUILDERS.

121. IN this chapter the more general principles, common to all the pyramids, will be considered ; leaving the points which are peculiar to the Great Pyramid, to be discussed in the History of the Great Pyramid and its design.

The characteristic Mastaba-angle, and the nature of Mastaba-Pyramids and true Pyramids, have been already stated (section 103). The design of the various slopes that are met with, appears to be always a simple relation of the vertical and horizontal distance. It is important to settle this, as it bears strongly on the whole planning of each building. And though the vertical and horizontal distances would seem to be the natural elements for setting out a slope, yet proof of this is necessary ; for Ahmes, in his mathematical papyrus, defines pyramids by their sloping height up the arris edge, and their diagonal of the base beneath that line. Such a method of measurement would naturally be adopted, when the knowledge of the design was lost, as the arris height could be easiest measured ; but it is very unlikely as a specification of design.

The angles of the various Pyramids, and so-called Pyramids, are as follow :—

Building.	Observer.	Observation.	±	Theoretical Angle.			Difference.	
Mastaba, between 37 & 40, Gizeh	(Petrie)	80° 57'	15'	80° 32' 15'' rise of 6 on	1		25' ±	15'
Mastaba 44 Gizeh (the best)	,,	76° 0'	5'	75° 57' 50'' ,,	4 on	1	2' ±	5
Mastabas, mean of all, Gizeh	,,	75° 52'	10'	75° 57' 50'' ,,	4 on	1	4' ±	10
Mastaba-Pyramid, Medum	(Vyse)	74° 10'	1°?	75° 57' 50'' ,,	4 on	1	1° 47' ± 1°?	
,, ,, Sakkara	,,	73° 30'*	2°?	75° 57' 50'' ,,	4 on	1	2° 27' ± 2°?	
Kursi Farun Beyahmu	,,	63° 30'		63° 26' 6'' ,,	2 on	1	4'	
South brick Pyramid Dahshur	,,	57° 20' 2''		57° 15' 54'' ,,	14 on	9	4'	
South stone ,, base, ,,	,,	54° 14' 46''		54° 9' 46'' ,,	18 on	13	5'	
Second ,, Gizeh	(Petrie)	53° 10'	4'	53° 7' 48'' ,,	4 on	3	2' ±	4'
Ninth ,, ,,	,,	52° 11'	8'	52° 7' 30'' ,,	9 on	7	4' ±	8'
Great ,, ,,	,,	51° 52'	2' {	51° 50' 35'' ;,	14 on	11	1' ±	2'
			{	51° 51' 14'' ,,	4 on	π	46'' ±	2'
North brick ,, Dahshur	(Vyse)	51° 20' 25''		51° 20' 25'' ,,	5 on	4	0'	
Third ,, Gizeh	(Petrie)	51° 10'	10'	51° 20' 25'' ,,	5 on	4	10' ±	10'
Small ,, Dahshur	(Vyse)	50° 11' 41''		50° 11' 40'' ,,	6 on	5	1''	
North stone ,, ,,	,,	43° 36' 11''		43° 36' 10'' ,,	20 on	21	1''	
South ,, ,, top ,,	,,	42° 59' 26''		43° 1' 31'' ,,	14 on	15	2'	

By photographs of the inner casings they vary from 69° to 85° ; averaging 70°12.'

The angles determined by Perring for Colonel Vyse cannot be considered very satisfactory for comparison with theories, as they seem in one case to be distinctly in error (in the Second Pyramid angle) ; and some of the observations are so extremely near to theoretical angles, that they seem to have been modified by the observer. But taking those Pyramids of which I measured the angles repeatedly in many ways, the variations from the slopes which would result from integral amounts, is usually about half the probable error ; and the variation only equals the probable error in the Third Pyramid, which is least accurately built. From these close coincidences it seems clear that the rule for slopes in designing, was to set back the face an integral number of cubits, on a height of an integral number. The use of angles of 4 on 3 (which has hypothenuse 5), and 20 on 21 (which has hypothenuse 29), seems to suggest that the square of the hypothenuse being equal to the squares of the two sides may have been known ; particularly as we shall see that the use of squared quantities is strongly indicated in the Great Pyramid.

122. No discussion of the sizes of the Pyramids can lead us to the ideas involved in their design, unless it is first settled whether they were each completely planned at their beginnings, or each carried forward as far as the life of the builder permitted. This last idea, which may be called the " theory of accretion," would show that the size of each Pyramid was solely due to a series of accidental events ; and that no foreseen design can be expected in the external dimensions, or in their relations to the inside. As several names have been associated with this theory, it will be best to avoid them all ; and treat it on its own merits impersonally, like all other theories mentioned in this work

We will first, then, consider the questions that have been put forward on Pyramid building, and the applicability of the theory of accretion to each of them, and after that notice some of the other points bearing on this theory.

(1) How does it happen that the Pyramids are of such different sizes? The theory of accretion answers that each king continued building his Pyramid until his death, and hence the Pyramids differ in size because the reigns differed in length. When, however, we see that the lengths of the reigns are not in proportion to the bulk of the respective Pyramids, this apparent explanation merely resolves itself into saying, that because two quantities vary they must be connected. On comparing the lengths of the reigns with the sizes of those Pyramids whose builders we know, the disproportion is such that Khufu, for instance, must have built the Great Pyramid 15 times as fast as Raenuser built the Middle Pyramid of Abusir ; or else Raenuser built for only $\frac{1}{15}$th of his reign ; either alternative prevents any conclusion being drawn as to inequalities in time producing inequalities in the sizes of the Pyramids.

(2) How could later kings be content with smaller Pyramids after **Khufu** and **Khafra** had built the two largest? This question the accretion theory

cannot explain; for many of the later kings lived nearly as long as Khufu and Khafra (one even much longer), without producing anything comparable in size. When we look at the mournful declension in the designs of Pyramid building, from the beauty of the fourth down to the rubble and mud of the sixth dynasty, the falling off in size as well as quality is merely part of the same failure.

(3) How is the fact to be accounted for that an unfinished Pyramid is never met with? In the same work in which this question is asked, it is said of one of the Abusir Pyramids, that it " seems never to have been completed ;" and of the South Stone Pyramid of Dahshur, "The whole pyramid was probably intended to have the same slope as the apex, but the lower part was never completed." This question is only another form of No. 5.

(4) How could Khufu have known that his reign would be long enough to enable him to carry out such a vast design? However this may be, he certainly worked far more quickly than any other king, and the arrangement of the interior of his Pyramid, as we shall see below, proves that it was all, or nearly all, designed at first.

(5) If a builder of a great pyramid had died early, how could his successor have finished the work, and built his own pyramid at the same time? First, we have no proof that a successor did not appropriate the work to himself, or share it with the founder ; and, secondly, no other kings worked at a half, or perhaps a tenth, of the rate that Khufu and Khafra worked, or with anything like the same fineness ; and hence any king might easily have had two pyramids on hand at once, his father's and his own.

The accretion theory, then, though not actually condemned by the application of these questions which are adduced in its support, is at least far from being the " one entirely satisfactory answer " to them, as it has been claimed to be. And the supposed proof of it, from the successive coats of the Mastaba-Pyramids of Medum and Sakkara, is, in the first place, brought from works that are not true Pyramids ; and, in the second place, shows that the buildings quoted were completely finished and cased many times over, probably by successive kings, and not merely accreted in the rough, until the final casing was applied. A confirmation claimed for this theory is " the ascertained fact that the more nearly the interior of the pyramid is approached, the more careful does the construction become, while the outer crusts are more and more roughly and hastily executed." This is certainly not true in many, perhaps most, cases. The Pyramids of Sakkara, as far as they have been opened, show quite as fine work in the outer casing as anywhere else ; and the rubble of the inside is equally bad throughout. The Great Pyramid of Gizeh shows far finer work in the outermost parts of the passage, casing, and pavement, than in most, or perhaps all, of the inside, and the Second Pyramid is similar. In a great part of the pyramids we

know nothing of the comparative excellence of the work of different parts, comparing fine work with fine work, and core with core masonry.

123. Now, if the accretion theory were true, it ought to be of the greatest
value when applied to the largest Pyramids ; for these are the most difficult to
account for, and their extraordinary size is the main feature appealed to in
support of the theory.

Let it then be critically applied to the Great Pyramid of Gizeh, the largest
known (see Pl. vii.). First, it must be noticed that the centre of the Pyramid
cannot have been much shifted by accretion on one side of it, as all the chambers
are near the middle ; and if any shift of its axis were due to this, the accretion
must have been on the N. side, as two chambers are S. of the middle. Trying,
therefore, how small a Pyramid might have been begun, let it be taken at A : if
a Pyramid existed of this size, it would be completely anomalous, and unlike
anything known ; it would have (1) a horizontal passage, (2) opening near the
top of it ; (3) a chamber close to the top of the Pyramid ; and (4) an entrance
to the lower chamber far outside the Pyramid. Each of these peculiarities condemn it as impossible. The next larger size that would not leave chambers
half exposed on the outside of the building, would be at B. With this size there
would be the anomalies of (1) two entrances on one face ; (2) one sloping upwards ; (3) a great hall and a chamber close to the outside, and near the top of
the Pyramid. Each of these points condemn such a design as un-Egyptian, and
unlike any other known pyramid, no matter how small. The least size, then,
that could possibly be supposed to be the first design would be at C, as it is
clear that any lesser design would leave impossible anomalies in the arrangements. Thus it is plain that the accretion theory breaks down in its application
to any size under 600 feet for the Great Pyramid ; and if we are thus compelled
by its arrangements to acknowledge a primary design of a base of 600 feet
(which is larger than nineteen-twentieths of the other pyramids), what need is
there of a theory of accretion to account for its being 750 feet ?

Next let this theory be applied to the Second Pyramid of Gizeh, which is
only exceeded in size by that we have discussed above (see Pl. vii.). Here the
chamber is practically central, and the axis of the Pyramid cannot therefore
have been much shifted by one-sided accretion. Supposing that it was designed
of any size less than A, there would then be the anomalous features of (1) an
entrance on the ground level ; and (2) a secondary entrance far out from the
Pyramid. These features are unknown in any other pyramid, large or small,
and the need of them thus condemns, as practically impossible, any design of
less size than about 500 feet. Here then the accretion theory breaks down, as
in the Great Pyramid design.

124. The summing up on this theory then is, that every argument brought
forward in its support is either inconclusive, or false in examples ; and that on

applying it critically to the two cases in which it is most needed, and which have been mainly adduced to support it, it is completely contradicted by the essential formation of the pyramids. If we are then forced to accept the fact of gigantic primary designs for the largest pyramids, where is there any need of a theory to account for the far smaller designs, of very inferior workmanship, seen in the other pyramids? That some of the lesser and ruder pyramids (as the Third of Gizeh, which is ninth in order of size) may have been enlarged, is not unlikely; but such enlargement was an accident of increased ambition, and not a general law of construction; and it has nothing to do with the great designs, so magnificently carried out in the largest pyramids.

125. A theory which has obtained much belief, is that of the passages of each pyramid having been plugged up after the interment of the builder. But though this is often alluded to by some writers as even an undisputed fact, yet the evidence for it is not forthcoming. No doubt special parts were plugged up so as to conceal the openings of passages; and some disused passages might be blocked, more or less entirely; but, generally speaking, there is no evidence of a plugging of the entire passages.

In the Great Pyramid the entrance passage is often spoken of as having been plugged up; and the holes in the floor are adduced in proof, as showing where the destroyers got under the blocks to force them out. But these holes have been cut by a person standing in the clear passage below them, and picking at the stone from the southward; as is clearly seen on examining the cutting marks. Also the floor, being not only the most awkward part to work upon, but also the hardest stone, would certainly not be attacked to loosen any plugs; but the sides or roof would rather be chosen. Again, the holes are not deep enough to hold a man, though five or six feet long; and they only reach as far as Mamun's Hole, and not down to the subterranean parts. Moreover, if plug-blocks had been dragged out, or broken up in the passage, the walls and roof would inevitably have been bruised or broken where each block was attacked; whereas, there is no trace of such injury visible; and the triangular stone covering the plug-blocks in the roof would have been broken loose before Arabic times. Besides these points, in the upper corners of the passage may be seen remains of the plaster, rubbed by the fingers into the angle; and this would have been displaced if any blocks that were cemented in had been dragged out.

There is, of course, no question but that the lower end of the ascending passage is plugged up with granite blocks, but it is very doubtful if there ever was much more plugging than is there at present. It is clear that the Arabs, on forcing the way by Mamun's Hole, ran along the side of the granite plugs, until they reached a higher point in the passage, where, owing to some reason, they could get into the passage more easily. And if the rest of the passage had been plugged, they would either have forced their way in the softer limestone alongside of the plugs, as they had already done; or else, if the plugs were removable they would have filled up the awkward hollow of Mamun's Hole with them, to avoid the labour of carrying them all out of the Pyramid. But there is not one known, out of the large number of such blocks that ought to be found if the whole passage had been plugged up.

The mouth of the passage to the Queen's Chamber was certainly blocked; but no one has supposed that the whole of that passage, or that the gallery, was blocked.

Thus there is an absence of any trace of blocking of the passages, beyond the closing of the mouths of two passages, merely to prevent their being detected.

In the Second Pyramid the flaws in the passage are plastered up—sometimes over a large surface—and then tinted red; if, then, any blocks had been drawn out, this plastering would have been scraped, and at least the colouring rubbed off. On the sides of the passage are also projecting scraps of plaster ·1 to ·15 thick; and in the top corner of the E. side are some scraps ¾-inch thick; these would have been rubbed off in removing any plugging. The evidence here, then, is decidedly against the main passage having been plugged. The lower passage from the pavement, as being a duplicate passage not required, was plugged up, like the duplicate and disused passage in the Third Pyramid.

In the Pyramids of Dahshur, the passages have been filled with desert pebbles, sand, and masons' chips; a filling which could not come in by accident, and would not be put in by design except by the builders. This, therefore, was a filling up to prevent casual access to the inside; but such as could be readily taken out if it was required to be opened. It shows that no stone plugging, or building up, was put in the entrance passage; although a duplicate passage in one of these Pyramids was plugged by blocks.

In the Pyramid of Pepi, and in another at Sakkara, the passages are lined with long and delicate inscriptions; which, at least in that of Pepi, do not show any mortar in the hollows. Indeed, it would not be likely that an inscription should be put where it was to be built over afterwards with plug-blocks.

Not only, then, is the evidence inconclusive that the main passages of the Pyramids were ever plugged throughout their length, but, on the contrary, there are incidental proofs that no general plugging was ever introduced or extracted.

126. The possibility of the Pyramids having had movable doors has been quite overlooked in modern times, owing to the general belief that the passages were plugged up. Of course, if a passage was filled up solid there could not have been any door to it; but as we have seen that there is no evidence of

such plugging, doors may have existed. And as we shall further see that there is very substantial evidence of the former existence of doors, we have, therefore, equally valid proofs of the non-existence of any plugging.

The traces of a stone flap door, or turning block, in the mouth of the South Pyramid of Dahshur, have been already described (section 109), as well as the signs of a wooden door behind that. Such a formation of the passage mouth is unmistakable in its purpose ; but after drawing conclusions from that doorway, it was a most satisfactory proof of the generality of such doors, to observe the following passage from Strabo on the Great Pyramid. "The Greater (Pyramid), a little way up one side, has a stone that may be taken out (εξαιρεσιμον, *exemptilem*), which being raised up (ἀρθεντος, *sublato*) there is a sloping passage to the foundations." This sentence is most singularly descriptive of opening a flap door ; first, the stone is taken out, or lifted outwards from the face ; and then, being thus raised up, the passage is opened. The two different words exactly express the change in the apparent motion, first outwards and then upwards ; and they show remarkable accuracy and precision in their use. Besides this description, there is another statement that the Pyramids of Gizeh had doors, in an Arabic MS., quoted by Vyse ; this was written in 850 A.D., and, therefore, only twenty or thirty years after Mamun had forced his way into the Great Pyramid, and thus re-discovered the real entrance.

The mechanical proofs of the existence of a door to the Great Pyramid are of some weight, though only circumstantial, and not direct evidence like that of the above authors. No one can doubt that the entrance must have been closed, and closed so as not to attract attention at the time when the Arabs made their forced passage, about a hundred feet long, through the solid masonry. Moreover, it is certain that the entrance was not covered then by rubbish : (1) because the Arabic hole is some way below it, and the ground-level at the time of the forcing is seen plainly in the rubbish heap ; (2) because the rubbish heap, which is even now much below the original doorway, is composed of broken casing, and the casing was not yet broken up at the time of forcing the passage. Therefore the doorway must have been so finely closed that the various accidental chippings and weathering on all the general surface of the casing completely masked any wear or cracks that there might be around the entrance ; and so invisible was the door then, that, standing on the heap from which they forced their hole, the Arabs could not see anything to excite their suspicion on the surface only 35 feet above them ; they, therefore, plunged into the task of tearing out the stone piecemeal, in hopes of meeting with something in the inside. Yet we know from Strabo that the Romans had free access to the passage, though he says that it was kept a secret in his time. No extractable plug or block, weighing necessarily some tons, would have been replaced by every visitor until the Arab times, especially without there being any shelf or place to rest it on while it was removed.*

The restoration of a door shown in Pl. xi., would agree to these various historical requirements, and be in harmony with the arrangement at Dahshur ; such a block would only need a pull of $2\frac{1}{2}$ cwt. on first taking it outwards, and 4 cwt. to lift it upwards to its final position ; it would leave no external opening ; it would also allow just half of the passage to be quite clear ; and from the passage being halved in its height by two courses at the beginning, such an opening is the most likely. Though the general form is thus indicated, the details are of course conjectural.

To sum up. A self-replacing door, which left no external mark, is absolutely required by the fact of the Arabs having forced a passage. Only a flap door, or a diagonal-sliding portcullis slab, can satisfy this requirement. A flap door is unequivocally shown to have been used at Dahshur. And Strabo's description of the entrance agrees with such a door, and with no other. Such is the evidence for the closing of the Pyramids by doors ; equally proving also the absence of any plugging up of the entrance passages.

127. Reference has often been made in previous pages, to the varying character of the work of the Pyramids ; both for its own interest, and for its historical value. Some connected remarks are therefore desirable, on the different architectural ideas of the builders, in their general style of construction : and an attempt is here made to range the principal pyramids in the order of their excellence of workmanship.

The Great Pyramid at Gizeh (of Khufu, fourth dynasty) unquestionably takes the lead, in accuracy and in beauty of work, as well as in size. Not only is the fine work of it in the pavement, casing (section 26) King's (section 52) and Queen's Chambers (section 41), quite unexcelled ; but the general character of the core masonry is better than that of any other pyramid in its solidity and regularity.

The small Pyramids by the (Great Pyramid of Khufu's family, fourth dynasty) are of very good work in their passages, and in the remains of their chambers ; they are also good in the core masonry (excepting one that has crumbled), and were well cased with fine limestone. Considering the internal work, and the apparent use of hard-stone edging of diorite and basalt in the quoins (section 101), these Pyramids may rank next to the Great Pyramid.

The Third Pyramid (of Menkaura, fourth dynasty), though not so accurate in its interior as some of the others, may nevertheless come next, by reason of

---

* Exactly the same reasoning applies to the Second Pyramid. Diodorus Siculus mentions the foot-holes up to its entrance, and Herodotus correctly describes the form of its passages ; and yet the Arabs forced a large passage in it, in entire ignorance of the real entrance, which must, therefore, have had a door like the Great Pyramid.

the excellence of its core masonry. In this it equals the Great Pyramid, and is far better than any other.

The rank of the Pyramid of Abu Roash (of Menkaura, fourth dynasty ?) is doubtful, owing to its ruined state. The design of the vast rock chamber, afterwards so massively lined, is very bold : its core masonry might rank almost as high as that of the following Pyramids ; and the use of a very large amount of intractable red granite, both internally and externally, raises it character.

The Second Pyramid at Gizeh (of Khafra, fourth dynasty), would rank next to the Great Pyramid by its accuracy of work, both inside and outside ; and even before the Great Pyramid in the work of its coffer. But the lamentably bad stone of its general core masonry, the rounded and carelessly shaped blocks, and the inferior quality of its casing stone, prevents its taking the second place.

The North Pyramid at Dahshur is about equal in general masonry to the Second of Gizeh ; but inferior in the accuracy of its internal work. It is most of all like the Great Pyramid of Gizeh in its style of work, the fineness and whiteness of its casing, and the design of the overlapping roofs ; but it is inferior to that Pyramid in every detail.

The South—or blunted—Pyramid at Dahshur is of good work ; very good in the lower part of the core, but poorer in the upper parts, both in quality and working of the stones. There, is however, some very good work in the joints of the casing of it ; flaws in the stone have been cut out, and filled in with sound pieces. It is only inferior to the preceding in the quality of the casing. The general impression received, from the work and design of these two large Pyramids of Dahshur, is that they are more archaic than the Great Pyramid of Gizeh ; and the builders seem to be feeling their way, rather than falling off in copying existing models.

The Mastabat-el-Farun (of Unas, fifth dynasty) at Sakkara can scarcely be judged, without seeing either the casing or the inside ; but by the general masonry, and the large size of the blocks used, it should rank close to the preceding buildings.

The Mastaba-Pyramid at Medum is of good work ; the joints of its casing are fine and close, and the joint-surfaces are well dressed. The core masonry is passable ; but it is inferior to those already mentioned in the size of the stones of all parts.

The Pyramids at Abusir (of Sahura and Raenuser, fifth dynasty) may, perhaps, take about this rank ; for though good in their fine masonry, the general bulk of the core is poor, and begins to show the system of retaining walls filled in with rubble.

The Mastaba-Pyramid at Sakkara (or Great Step-Pyramid) is built of bad and small stones, often crumbling to dust : its casings are fairly good, though of small stones; but as they vary in angle, no accuracy seems to have been aimed at.

The other Pyramids of Sakkara (of end of fifth, and of sixth dynasty) as far as their construction is visible, appear to be all of the same type. They are made up of rude retaining walls, not even built continuously, but merely piecemeal ; these walls are of rough broken small stones laid in mud ; and they are filled in with loose stones, without even any mud. The outer casing was, however, of very good work, and consisted of large stones of fine quality ; and the interiors are equally good. It was in the unseen mass of the masonry that deterioration took place.

The mud-brick Pyramids might, perhaps, stand before the generality of the rubble Pyramids just mentioned ; as some skill is needed in the production of sound bricks of large size, that will bear at the present day being bowled down from top to bottom of the Pyramid, by the official excavators, without breaking. The casing of these Brick Pyramids was also of excellent white Mokattam limestone, where it has been seen.

Having thus pointed out a few of the reasons for assigning the above order of excellence to the Pyramids, it may be observed that (as far as is yet known absolutely) there is but slight exception to the rule of continuous decadence. The Third Pyramid of Gizeh is ranked next above the Second, and the Mastabat-el-Farun next above the Pyramids of Abusir ; but otherwise the degeneration of design and work, so particularly seen in the hidden parts, follow the order of time. It is not likely that this is entirely the case if we knew the name of the builder of each Pyramid, but it is at least a general clue of value. And whether the Mastaba-Pyramids and those of Dahshur may prove to be the oldest examples or no, still, it would be almost impossible to assign a rubble Pyramid—so clearly a deteriorated type—to the age of the sound masonry of the fourth dynasty.

128. The use of plaster by the Egyptians is remarkable ; and their skill in cementing joints is hard to understand. How, in the casing of the Great Pyramid, they could fill with cement a vertical joint about 5×7 feet in area, and only averaging $\frac{1}{50}$ inch thick is a mystery ; more especially as the joint could not be thinned by rubbing, owing to its being a vertical joint, and the block weighing about 16 tons. Yet this was the usual work over 13 acres of surface, with tens of thousands of casing stones, none less than a ton in weight.

The Egyptian notions about the use of plaster and stucco were very free ; they never hesitated to use plaster in making good small defects in any place. In the monolith pillars of the Granite Temple, the flaws are filled by plaster, which is coloured red ; the same is done on the roof of the King's Chamber, and the granite passage of the Second Pyramid. On limestone also plaster was freely used, especially in the faulty parts of the rock in the tombs. Often the rock has weathered away in powder, leaving the plaster with its hieroglyphs as sharp and fresh as when first laid on ; this is well seen in the tomb of Khafra-ankh (" Tomb of Numbers "), and in tombs in the cutting round the Second Pyramid. Probably the continual use of plaster, to make good defects in building, was a habit which arose from the necessity of using it for flaws in the rock in the large number of excavated tombs ; these are of the earliest time, the use of fine stone linings to the rock being a later method, not common till the fifth dynasty.

It is not usually known that the statues carved in diorite and alabaster were painted. Yet such seems certainly to have been the case. The fragments of diorite statues, that I found W. of the Second Pyramid, where all stuccoed on the outside, with a firm hard white coat ; and the fragments of alabaster statues had bright green paint on the dress, and black on the plaited wig. Though it has long been known that the limestone statues were generally painted, and that those of granite were partially coloured ; yet the concealing of the translucent alabaster, and of the polished and variegated diorite, by a coat which might merely hide limestone or plaster, seems to have escaped notice hitherto. This custom shows that the qualities of the stone were regarded more for preciousness than for beauty.

CHAPTER XIX.

THE MECHANICAL METHODS OF THE PYRAMID BUILDERS.

129. The methods employed by the Egyptians in cutting the hard stones which they so frequently worked, have long remained in doubt. Various suggestions have been made, some very impracticable; but no actual proofs of the tools employed, or the manner of using them, has been obtained. From the examples of work which I was able to collect at Gizeh, and from various fixed objects of which I took casts, the questions so often asked seem now to be solved.

The typical method of working hard stones,—such as granite, diorite, basalt, &c.,—was by means of bronze tools; these were set with cutting points, far harder than the quartz which was operated on. The material of these cutting points is yet undetermined; but only five substances are possible: beryl, topaz, chrysoberyl, corundum or sapphire, and diamond. The character of the work would certainly seem to point to diamond as being the cutting jewel; and only the considerations of its rarity in general, and its absence from Egypt, interfere with this conclusion, and render the tough uncrystallized corundum the more likely material.

Many nations, both savage and civilized, are in the habit of cutting hard materials by means of a soft substance (as copper, wood, horn, &c.), with a hard powder supplied to it; the powder sticks in the basis employed, and this being scraped over the stone to be cut, so wears it away. It is therefore very readily assumed by many persons (as I myself did at first) that this method must necessarily have been also used by the Egyptians; and that it would suffice to produce all the examples now collected. Such, however, is far from being the case; though no doubt in alabaster, and other soft stones, this method was used.

That the Egyptians were acquainted with a cutting jewel far harder than quartz, and that they used this jewel as a sharp-pointed graver, is put beyond doubt by the diorite bowls with inscriptions of the fourth dynasty, of which I found fragments at Gizeh. These hieroglyphs are incised, with a very free-cutting point; they are not scraped nor ground out, but are ploughed through the diorite, with rough edges to the line. As the lines are only $\frac{1}{150}$ inch wide (the figures being about ·2 long), it is evident that the cutting point must have been much harder than quartz; and tough enough not to splinter when so fine an edge was being employed, probably only $\frac{1}{200}$ inch wide. Parallel lines are graved only $\frac{1}{30}$ inch apart from centre to centre.

We therefore need have no hesitation in allowing that the graving out of lines in hard stones by jewel points, was a well-known art. And when we find on the surfaces of the saw-cuts in diorite, grooves as deep as $\frac{1}{100}$ inch, it appears far more likely that such were produced by fixed jewel points in the saw, than by any fortuitous rubbing about of a loose powder. And when, further, it is seen that these deep grooves are almost always regular and uniform in depth, and equidistant, their production by the successive cuts of the jewel-teeth of a saw appears to be beyond question. The best examples of equidistance are the specimens of basalt No. 4 (Pl. xiv.), and of diorite No. 12 ; in these the fluctuations are no more than such as always occur in the use of a saw by hand-power, whether worked in wood or in soft stone.

On the granite core, broken from a drill-hole (No. 7), other features appear, which also can only be explained by the use of fixed jewel points. Firstly, the grooves which run around it form a regular spiral, with no more interruption or waviness than is necessarily produced by the variations in the component crystals ; this spiral is truly symmetrical with the axis of the core. In one part a groove can be traced, with scarcely an interruption, for a length of four turns. Secondly, the grooves are as deep in the quartz as in the adjacent felspar, and even rather deeper. If these were in any way produced by loose powder, they would be shallower in the harder substance—quartz ; whereas a fixed jewel point would be compelled to plough to the same depth in all the components ; and further, inasmuch as the quartz stands out slightly beyond the felspar (owing to the latter being worn by general rubbing), the groove was thus left even less in depth on the felspar than on the quartz. Thus, even if specimens with similarly deep grooves could be produced by a loose powder, the special features of this core would still show that fixed cutting points were the means here employed.

That the blades of the saws were of bronze, we know from the green staining on the sides of saw cuts, and on grains of sand left in a saw cut.

The forms of the tools were straight saws, circular saws, tubular drills, and lathes.

130. The straight saws varied from ·03 to ·2 inch thick, according to the work ; the largest were 8 feet or more in length, as the cuts run lengthways on the Great Pyramid coffer, which is 7 feet 6 in. long. The examples of saw cuts figured in Pl. xiv. are as follow. No. 1, from the end of the Great Pyramid coffer of granite, showing where the saw cut was run too deep into the stuff twice over, and backed out again. No. 2, a piece of syenite, picked up at Memphis ; showing cuts on four faces of it, and the breadth of the saw by a cut across the top of it. This probably was a waste piece from cutting out a statue in the rough. No. 3,

a piece of basalt, showing a saw cut run askew, and abandoned, with the sawing
dust and sand left in it ; a fragment from the sawing of the great basalt pavement on the East of the Great Pyramid. No. 4, another piece from the same
pavement, showing regular and well-defined lines. No. 5, a slice of basalt from
the same place, sawn on both sides, and nearly sawn in two. No. 6, a slice of
diorite bearing equidistant and regular grooves of circular arcs, parallel to one
another ; these grooves have been nearly polished out by crossed grinding, but
still are visible. The only feasible explanation of this piece is that it was produced by a circular saw. The main examples of sawing at Gizeh are the blocks
of the great basalt pavement, and the coffers of the Great, Second, and Third
Pyramids,—the latter, unhappily, now lost.

131. Next the Egyptians adapted their sawing principle into a circular,
instead of a rectilinear form, curving the blade round into a tube, which drilled
out a circular groove by its rotation ; thus, by breaking away the cores left in
the middle of such grooves, they were able to hollow out large holes with a
minimum of labour. These tubular drills vary from $\frac{1}{4}$ inch to 5 inches diameter,
and from $\frac{1}{30}$ to $\frac{1}{5}$ inch thick. The smallest hole yet found in granite is 2 inches
diameter, all the lesser holes being in limestone or alabaster, which was probably
worked merely with tube and sand. A peculiar feature of these cores is that
they are always tapered, and the holes are always enlarged towards the top.
In the soft stones cut merely with loose powder, such a result would naturally
be produced simply by the dead weight on the drill head, which forced it into
the stone, not being truly balanced, and so always pulling the drill over to one
side ; as it rotated this would grind off material from both the core and the
hole. But in the granite core, No. 7, such an explanation is insufficient, since
the deep cutting grooves are scored out quite as strongly in the tapered end
as elsewhere ; and if the taper was merely produced by rubbing of powder, they
would have been polished away, and certainly could not be equally deep in
quartz as in felspar. Hence we are driven to the conclusion that auxiliary
cutting points were inserted along the side, as well as around the edge of the
tube drill ; as no granite or diorite cores are known under two inches diameter,
there would be no impossibility in setting such stones, working either through
a hole in the opposite side of the drill, or by setting a stone in a hole cut
through the drill, and leaving it to project both inside and outside the tube.
Then a preponderance of the top weight to any side would tilt the drill so as to
wear down the groove wider and wider, and thus enable the drill and the dust
to be the more easily withdrawn from the groove. The examples of tube
drilling on Pl. xiv. are as follow :—No. 7, core in granite, found at Gizeh.
No. 8, section of cast of a pivot hole in a lintel of the granite temple at Gizeh;
here the core, being of tough hornblende, could not be entirely broken out, and
remains to a length of ·8 inch. No. 9, alabaster mortar, broken in course of

manufacture, showing the core in place ; found at Kom Ahmar (lat. 28° 5′), by Prof. Sayce, who kindly gave it to me to illustrate this subject. No. 10, the smallest core yet known, in alabaster ; found with others at Memphis, by Dr. Grant Bey, who kindly gave me this. No. 11, marble eye for inlaying, with two tube drill-holes, one within the other; showing the thickness of the small drills. No. 12, part of the side of a drill-hole in diorite, from Gizeh, remarkable for the depth and regularity of the grooves in it. No. 13, piece of limestone from Gizeh, showing how closely holes were placed together in removing material by drilling ; the angle of junction shows that the groove of one hole just overlapped the groove of another, without probably touching the core of the adjacent hole ; thus the minimum of labour was required. The examples of tube drilling on a large scale are the great granite coffers, which were hollowed out by cutting rows of tube drill-holes just meeting, and then breaking out the cores and intermediate pieces ; the traces of this work may be seen in the inside of the Great Pyramid coffer, where two drill-holes have been run too deeply into the sides ; and on a fragment of a granite coffer with a similar error of work on it, which I picked up at Gizeh. At El Bersheh (lat. 27° 42′) there is a still larger example, where a platform of limestone rock has been dressed down, by cutting it away with tube drills about 18 inches diameter; the circular grooves occasionally intersecting, prove that it was merely done to remove the rock.

132. The principle of rotating the tool was, for smaller objects, abandoned in favour of rotating the work ; and the lathe appears to have been as familiar an instrument in the fourth dynasty, as it is in modern workshops. The diorite bowls and vases of the Old Kingdom are frequently met with, and show great technical skill. One piece found at Gizeh, No. 14, shows that the method employed was true turning, and not any process of grinding, since the bowl has been knocked off of its centring, recentred imperfectly, and the old turning not quite turned out; thus there are two surfaces belonging to different centrings, and meeting in a cusp. Such an appearance could not be produced by any grinding or rubbing process which pressed on the surface. Another detail is shown by fragment No. 15 ; here the curves of the bowl are spherical, and must have therefore been cut by a tool sweeping an arc from a fixed centre while the bowl rotated. This centre or hinging of the tool was in the axis of the lathe for the general surface of the bowl, right up to the edge of it ; but as a lip was wanted, the centring of the tool was shifted, but with exactly the same radius of its arc, and a fresh cut made to leave a lip to the bowl. That this was certainly not a chance result of hand-work is shown, not only by the exact circularity of the curves, and their equality, but also by the cusp left where they meet. This has not been at all rounded off, as would certainly be the case in hand-work, and it is a clear proof of the rigidly mechanical method of striking the curves.

Hand graving tools were also used for working on the irregular surfaces of statuary ; as may be well seen on the diorite statue of Khafra found at Gizeh, and now at Bulak.

133. The great pressure needed to force the drills and saws so rapidly through the hard stones is very surprising ; probably a load of at least a ton or two was placed on the 4-inch drills cutting in granite. On the granite core, No. 7, the spiral of the cut sinks 1 inch in the circumference of 6 inches, or 1 in 60, a rate of ploughing out of the quartz and felspar which is astonishing. Yet these grooves cannot be due to the mere scratching produced in withdrawing the drill as has been suggested, since there would be about $\frac{1}{10}$ inch thick of dust between the drill and the core at that part ; thus there could be scarcely any pressure applied sideways, and the point of contact of the drill and granite could not travel around the granite however the drill might be turned about. Hence these rapid spiral grooves cannot be ascribed to anything but the descent of the drill into the granite under enormous pressure ; unless, indeed, we suppose a separate rymering tool to have been employed alternately with the drill for enlarging the groove, for which there is no adequate evidence.

134. That no remains of these saws or tubular drills have yet been found is to be expected, since we have not yet found even waste specimens of work to a tenth of the amount that a single tool would produce ; and the tools, instead of being thrown away like the waste, would be most carefully guarded. Again, even of common masons' chisels, there are probably not a dozen known ; and yet they would be far commoner than jewelled tools, and also more likely to be lost, or to be buried with the workman. The great saws and drills of the Pyramid workers would be royal property, and it would, perhaps, cost a man his life if he lost one ; while the bronze would be remelted, and the jewels reset, when the tools became worn, so that no worn out tools would be thrown away.

135. Of the various other details of mechanical work mention is made in different sections of this volume. The red marking of the mason's lines is described in section 63. The use of testing-planes in working surfaces, in section 170. The use of drafted diagonals, in section 55. The character of the fine joints, in section 26. The accuracy of levelling, in section 26. The fitting of the courses one on the other, in section 41. The arrangement of the courses on the ground before building, in section 168. The lugs left for lifting the stones, in sections 50, 55, and 63. The method of raising the stones, in section 169. The labour system employed on the Egyptian monuments, in section 166. And the use of plaster, in section 128. A general statement of all these mechanical questions, with fuller details of some of the specimens and examples of work, will be found in a paper on the " Mechanical Methods of the Egyptians," in the *Anthropological Journal* for 1883.

CHAPTER XX.

VALUES OF THE CUBIT AND DIGIT.

136. THE measurements which have been detailed in the foregoing pages supply materials for an accurate determination of the Egyptian cubit. From such a mass of exact measures, not only may the earliest value of the cubit be ascertained, but also the extent of its variations as employed by different architects.* There is no need to repeat here all the details of each case already given, nor to enter on the principles of the determination of units of measure from ancient remains, which I have fully described in " Inductive Metrology."

For the value of the usual cubit, undoubtedly the most important source is the King's Chamber in the Great Pyramid ; that is the most accurately wrought, the best preserved, and the most exactly measured, of all the data that are known. The cubit in the Great Pyramid varies thus :—

By the base of King's Chamber, corrected for opening of joints	20·632±·004
By the Queen's Chamber, if dimensions squared are in square cubits (section 153)	20·61 ±·02
By the subterranean chamber	20·65 ±·05
By the antechamber	20·58 ±·02
By the ascending and Queen's Chamber passage lengths (section 149)	20·622±·002
By the base length of the Pyramid, if 440 cubits (section 143)	20·611±·002
By the entrance passage width	20·765±·01
By the gallery width	20·605±·032

The passage widths are so short and variable that little value can be placed on them, especially as they depend on the builder's and not on the mason's work. The lengths of the passages are very accurate data, but being only single measures, are of less importance than are chambers, in which a length is often repeated in the working. The chamber dimensions are rather variable, particularly in the Subterranean and Antechamber, and none of the above data are equal in quality to the King's Chamber dimensions. If a strictly weighted

* On the façade of one of the tombs at Beni Hassan there is a scratch left by the workman at every cubit length. The cubit there is a long variety, of 20·7 to 20·8.

mean be taken it yields 20·620±·004 ; but taking the King's Chamber alone, as being the best datum by far, it nevertheless contracts upwards, so that it is hardly justifiable to adopt a larger result than 20·620±·005.

137. In the Second Pyramid the base is very indirectly connected with the cubit, so that it is not probable that reference was made to the cubit, but only to the King's Chamber or passage height which are derived from it. The cubit found varies thus :—

By the tenth course level ...   .   20·82 ±·01
By the first course height ...   .   20·76 ±·03
By the passage widths   ...   .   20·72 ±·01
By the great chamber, dimensions squared being in square cubits   20·640±·005
By the lower chamber, sides in even numbers of cubits   ...   20·573±·017

The course heights and passage widths are less likely to be accurate than the chamber dimensions ; a strictly weighted mean is 20·68±·03 ; but, considering the details, probably 20·64±·03 would be the truest determination of the cubit here.

In the Third Pyramid the work is very rough in comparison with the preceding, and the cubit is correspondingly variable.

By the base   ...   .   20·768±·015
By the course heights of granite   ...   ...   20·162±·017
By the first chamber ...   .   20·65 ±·10
By the second chamber   ...   .   20·70 ±·05
By the granite chamber   ...   .   20·74 ±·2

Here it is evident that the courses are all too thin on an average, though varying from 36·0 up to 42·8, and they are certainly not worth including in a mean. The average of the other elements, duly weighted, is 20·76±·02, or the simple average (as the previous gives scarcely any weight to the chambers) is 20·71±·02, which may be most suitably adopted.

Arranging the examples chronologically, the cubit used was as follows :—

Great Pyramid at Gizeh,   Khufu   ...   20·620±·005
Second   .,   „   Khafra   ...   20·64 ±·03
Granite temple   „   „   ...   20·68 ±·02
Third Pyramid   „   Menkaura   ...   20·71 ±·02
        „   „   peribolus walls   „   ...   20·69 ±·02
Great Pyramid of Dahshur   (?)   ...   20·58 ±·02
Pyramid at Sakkara   Pepi   ...   20·51 ±·02

Fourth to sixth dynasty, mean of all   ...   20·63 ±·02
Average variation in standard   ...   ·06

138. Besides these examples of the cubit as used in various buildings, the other principal unit of early times—the digit—may be obtained from the tombs. A usual feature of the decoration, of both the rock-cut tombs and the built Mas-

tabas, is a list of offerings ; these are usually written in a tabular form, in a number of square spaces like a chessboard.   It was therefore necessary for the workman to set out a series of equal spaces, and to do this he most naturally marked off an even number of whatever small measure he was in the habit of using ; just as an English workman would mark off a number of spaces of three or four inches each, rather than adopt any irregular fractions.   These lists are particularly valuable in giving the unit, for two reasons : first, the designer was usually unfettered by limits, he could make the spaces a little larger or smaller, so as to work in round numbers, and he could mark off the lengths on a smooth wall with great nicety ; and, secondly, the repetition of so many equal spaces gives an admirable means of ascertaining where the workman's errors lay, and also gives such a number of examples that the exact quantity may be very accurately determined.

In the examples of such lists measured by me, the regularity of the spaces deserves notice ; the errors of workmanship, shown by the average variations of the lengths from the mean of the whole, stand thus :—

				In Width.	In Height.
(1)	Tomb No. 15 of Lepsius, Apa	.	.	·013	·024 inch.
(2)	„ „ 68	. . . .	.	·038	·050 „
(3)	„ W. of Great Pyramid, Ka-nofer-a			·074	·038 „
(4)	„ No. 64	. . .	.	·042	·072 „
(5)	„ Under 69	. . .	.	.025	·043 „
(6)	„ Ases-kaf-ankh			·022	·044 „
(7)	„ (Painter's canon)	„		·018	·022 „
(8)	„ „	„		·041	·026 „

Here it is seen that, with one exception, the error of marking the spaces one over the other is greater than that of marking them side by side.   Omitting the tomb of Ka-nofer-a (which was never finished, and is merely in the first blocking out), the mean error in width is ·028, and in height ·040.   Considering that the engraved lines are usually about $\frac{1}{10}$ inch wide, a mean error of $\frac{1}{25}$ or $\frac{1}{35}$ inch on the length of the spaces shows very careful work.

139. Of these engraved lists the first two have a unit of a decimal division of the cubit ; in No. 1 the spaces are $\frac{16}{100}$ of a cubit wide, and $\frac{20}{100}$ high, or $\frac{4}{25}$ and $\frac{5}{25}$; and in No. 2 the spaces are $\frac{14}{100}$ wide, and $\frac{16}{100}$ high, or $\frac{7}{50}$ and $\frac{8}{50}$.   The cubit of No. 1 would be 20·45 $\pm$ ·05, and of No. 2, 20·58 $\pm$ ·08.   This is of course inferior as a cubit standard to the determinations from large buildings ; but it is very valuable as showing the decimal division of this cubit, which is also found in other countries.

140. Of the digit there are three good examples :—

No. 3, squares of 8 digits wide, 9 high, mean digit ·739 $\pm$ ·004
No, 4, „ 4 „ „ 5 „ „ „ ·728 $\pm$ ·001
No. 5, „ 3 „ „ 4 „ „ „ ·722 $\pm$ ·002

Weighted mean .   .   .   . ·727 $\pm$ ·002

The squares of No. 6 may be designed in digits, but they seem to be irregular, being 3·600 ± ·004 wide, and 3·775 ± ·012 high. In the same tomb of Aseskaf-ankh, are two subjects with the artist's canons, drawn over the finished and painted subject. What the purpose of this can have been it is not easy to say ; but the squares in one subject are ·4675 ± 0015 ; and in the other 1·407 ± ·005, or three times ·4690 ; the mean of both is ·468 ± ·001, which is not simply connected with any other quantity of digits or cubits.

141. The values of the cubit and digit, found in use in the cases mentioned in this chapter, agree remarkably closely with what has been already worked out. For the cubit I had deduced (Inductive Metrology, p. 50) from a quantity of material, good, bad, and indifferent, 20·64 ± ·02 as the best result that I could get ; about a dozen of the actual cubit rods that are known yield 20·65 ± ·01 ; and now from the earliest monuments we find that the cubit first used is 20·62, and the mean value from the seven buildings named is 20·63 ± ·02. Here, then, by the earliest monument that is known to give the cubit, by the mean of the cubits in seven early monuments, by the mean of 28 examples of various dates and qualities, and by the mean of a dozen cubit rods, the result is always within $\frac{1}{60}$ inch of 20·63. On the whole we may take 20·62 ± ·01 as the original value, and reckon that it slightly increased on an average by repeated copyings in course of time.

The digit, from about a dozen examples deduced from monuments (Ind. Met., p. 53), I had concluded to be ·7276 ± ·001 ; here, from three clear and certain examples of it, the conclusion is ·727 ± ·002 for its length in the fourth dynasty, practically identical with the mean value before found.

As I have already pointed out (Ind. Met., p. 56), the cubit and digit have no integral relation one to the other ; the connection of 28 digits with the cubit being certainly inexact, and merely adopted to avoid fractions. Now these earliest values of the cubit and digit entirely bear out this view ; 28 of these digits of ·727 is but 20·36 ± ·06, in place of the actual cubit 20·62 ± ·01. Is there then any simple connection between the digit and cubit ? Considering how in the Great Pyramid, the earliest monument in which the cubit is yet found, so much of the design appears to be based on a relation of the squares of linear quantities to one another, or on diagonals of squares, it will not be impossible to entertain the theory of the cubit and digit being reciprocally connected by diagonals. A square cubit has a diagonal of 40 digits, or 20 digits squared has a diagonal of one cubit ; thus a square cubit is the double of a square of 20 digits, so that halves of areas can be readily stated. This relation is true to well within the small uncertainties of our knowledge of the standards ; the diagonal of a square cubit of 20·62 being 40 digits of ·729, and the actual mean digit being ·727 ± ·002. This is certainly the only simple connection that can be traced between the cubit and digit ; and if this be rejected, we must fall back on the supposition of two independent and incommensurable units.

CHAPTER XXI.

THEORIES COMPARED WITH FACTS.

142. NOW that we are furnished, for the first time, with an accurate knowledge of the ancient dimensions of the Pyramids, we can enter on an examination of the theories which have been formed, and test them by the real facts of the case. Hitherto, on even the most important and crucial question, the only resource has been taking the mean of a number of contradictory results ; a resource which has been, in the case of the Great Pyramid, more fallacious than was suspected, owing to a complete misinterpretation of the nature of the points measured.

The question of the value to be assigned to earlier measurements of the Great Pyramid base, and the way in which the accurate observations agree with the present survey, is discussed at the end of this chapter, in section 163.

In mentioning the following theories, it seemed best to avoid any prejudice for or against them, and also to avoid questions of priority, by stating them without any reference to their various sources. A theory should stand on its own merits, irrespective of the reputation of its propounder. There is no need here to explain the bearings of, and reasons for, all these theories; most of them stand self-condemned at once, by the actual facts of the case. Others, framed on the real dimensions, will bear the first and indispensable test of measurement, which is but the lowest class of the evidences of a theory. Some theories which have not appeared before now, need explanation to make them intelligible. The general question of the likelihood of the theories, judging by their connection together, and by analogies elsewhere, is summed up in the Synopsis, section 157 ; and the conclusion formed, of what theories are really probable, is given in section 178.

143. Applying, then, the first, and direct test—that of measurement—to the most prominent subject of theorising—the size of the Great Pyramid— the base was, as we have seen,

Average	9068·8± ·4
By theory, Circuit of 5 stadia (or ½ geographical mile of equator meridian) .	9068·6± ·4
Side 360 cubits of 25·2 (cubit of Egyptians, Assyrians, Jews, &c.) .	9072· ±35·
Side 440 cubits of 20·620 (Egyptian cubit, as in Great Pyramid) .	9073· ± 2·

By theory, Circuit 50,000 digits of ·727 (Egyptian digit) .   .   .   .   .   9087· ±25·
        Side 500 cubits of 18·2405 (Greek cubit, also claimed as Egyptian) . 9120·2
        Side = width of band round the earth containing 10^{11} square feet . 9128·
        Side 452 cubits of 20·2208 ($\frac{1}{80}$ of a second of latitude)   .   . 9139·8
        Side 365·242 cubits of 25·025 (theoretical Polar cubit)   .   . 9140·2
        Circuit 355 units of 5 Egyptian cubits .   .   .   .   . 9155·0
        Side 366·256 cubits of 25·025 (theoretical Polar cubit)   .   . 9165·2
        Side 360 cubits of 25·488 .   .   .   . 9175·7

Most of these theories are manifestly beyond consideration, but on two or three of the best some further notes are desirable. The 440 cubit theory is supported by the fact of the height being 280 cubits; so that the well-known approximation to π, $\frac{22}{7}$, appears here in the form of the height being 7 × 40 cubits, and the semi-circuit 22 × 40 cubits. From other cases (in the interior) of the ratio of radius to circumference, it seems probable that a closer approximation than 7 to 22 was in use; and it is quite likely that the formula employed for π was $\frac{22}{7}$, with a small fractional correction applied to the 22; such is the most convenient practical way of working (if without logarithms), and it is the favourite method of expressing interminable ratios among most ancient nations. In any case all arithmetical statements of this ratio of π are but approximate, and the question is merely one of degree as to the amount of error, in any figures that can be used for it. The 360 cubit theory is simple-looking; but no examples of such a cubit are known in the Pyramids, and it is not prominent among other Egyptian remains. The stadium theory fits remarkably closely to the facts. Beside the stadium of $\frac{1}{10}$ geographical mile on the equatorial meridian, there are several other modes of measurement on the earth's surface, and it should be noted that these agree closely with what the Pyramid circuit would be at the various levels of the sockets. Thus, 5 stadia on

Equatorial meridian	(stadium 7254·9) =	Pyramid circuit	·1 above base.		·0 = pavement.
Mean ,, outside Arctic circle .	(7281·6) =	,,	,,	21·2 ,,	,,	23·0 = S.W. socket.
Mean of a whole meridian . . . .}	(7292·0) =	,,	,,	29·5 ,,	,,	28·5 = N.E. socket.
Mean of all azimuths at the Pyramid. .}					
Mean of all azimuths, everywhere . .	(7296·3) =	,,	,,	32·9 ,,	,,	32·8 = N.W. socket.
Mean of equatorial circle . . .	(7304·5) =	,,	,,	39·4 ,,	,,	39·9 = S.E. socket.

There are many arguments both for and against this theory; and they branch into so many collateral subjects that it would be beyond both the size and the nature of this statement to enter into them here.

144. For the height of the Great Pyramid there are also several theories :—

    The actual height originally was .   .   .   .   .   5776·0±7·0
    By theory, 280 cubits of 20·632±·004 (Egyptian cubit) . 5776·9±1·1
        $\frac{1}{10}$ of Roman mile, 58220±40   .   .   5822· ±4
        Circumference of earth ÷ 270,000   .   .   5832·7
                       { perihelion   .   .   5783
      Sun's distance ÷ 10^9 { mean .   .   .   5886
                       { aphelion   .   .   5989

145. For the angle of the Great Pyramid, of course any theory of the base, combined with any theory of the height, yields a theoretic angle; but the angles actually proposed are the following :—

Angle of casing as measured . . . . . . 51° 52'   ±2'
By theory of 34 slope to 21 base . . . . . 51° 51' 20"
          height : circumference :: radius to circle . 51° 51' 14·3"
          9 height on 10 base diagonally . . . 51° 50' 39·1"
          7 height to 22 circumference . . . 51° 50' 34·0"
          area of face = area of height squared . . 51° 49' 38·3"
          (or sine = cotangent, and many other relations)
          2 height vertical to 3 height diagonal . . 51° 40' 16·2"
          5 height on 4 base . . . . . 51° 20' 25"'

The weight of the Pyramid has been compared with that of the earth; but by the preceding data of size of the Pyramid, and the value already accepted by the theorists for specific gravity of the earth, the

          weight of the Great Pyramid in English tons is 5,923,400
          and the weight of the earth ÷ 1,000 billion is 6,062,000

or a difference of $\frac{1}{42}$ of the whole.

146. The height of the courses has also been theorised on.

The 25th course is at . . . . 885·0
By theory equal to Queen's Chamber level at   . . 858·4
The 50th course is at . . . . 1697·6
By theory equal to the King's Chamber floor level, 1691·4 to 1693·7

The position of the remarkably thick courses, which start out afresh as the beginning of a new diminishing series, at so many points of the Pyramid's height, are shown in Pl. viii.; they do not seem to have any connection with the levels of the interior (see Pl. ix.), nor any relation in the intervening distances or number of courses. It is, however, possible that a relation may be approximately intended between the introduction of the thick courses, and the various levels at which the area of the Pyramid's horizontal section is a simple fraction of the base area. Thus if we divided the base into 5 parts, or its area into 25 squares, there are the following number of such squares in the Pyramid area at different levels :—

			Level above base.	Mean course level.		
	½	square at .	4959·2	4954·3 top of thick course		180
I × I	I	„ .	4620·8	4620·6 top of „ „		164
	2	squares .	4142·3	4138·3 base „ „		144
2 × 2	4	„ .	3465·6	3445·9 to 3472·6 „ „		116
	6	„ .	2946·4	2945·8 base of „ „		98
	7	„ .	2719·6	2711·2 to 2749·6 „ „		90
3 × 3	9	„ .	2310·4	2317·8 base of „ „		74
	10	„ .	2122·9	2112·4 to 2146·9 „ „		67
	14	„ .	1453·6	1460·9 base of „ „		44
4 × 4	16	„ .	1155·8	1137·7 to 1187·2 „ „		35
5 × 5	25	„ .	0	0 base of thickest course		1

These points are marked along the top edge of the diagram (Pl. viii.), by which their coincidence with the courses can be seen by eye. It appears that though nothing exact was intended, yet as if the increased course thickness was started anew when the horizontal area had been reduced to a simple fraction of the base area: nearly all the prominent fresh starts of the courses are in the above list; and the fact that it includes each of the points where the simple length of the side is a direct multiple of $\frac{1}{5}$ of the base, is also in favour of the theory; or, in other terms, a thicker course is started at each fifth of the whole height of the Pyramid.

147. The trenches in the rock on the E. side of the Pyramid have

Angle between S. and E.N.E. trench axes $104° 1' 43'' = 2 \times 52° 0' 52''$

Angle between E.N.E. and N.N.E. axes $51° 36' 52''$

By theory equal to angle of slope of the Pyramid $= 51° 52'$

The distances of the Pyramid pavement, trench axes, and basalt pavement, outwards from the Pyramid base, may have a connection with the interior of the Pyramid. It has been a favourite notion of many writers to regard the sides of the Pyramid as laid open around the base, like the form of a " net " for making a Pyramid model. If then the East side be laid off from its base, the height of the interior levels carried out to the slope of the face, nearly coincide with certain distances on the ground.

In Pyramid.	Level.	On face from base.	On ground from base.	Outside Pyramid.
Gallery doorway	852·6 ∴	1084·0	1080·6 to 1085·5	Axis of N. trench.
Axis of Queen's passage	877·9	1116·1	1122·9 to 1125·4	Axis of S. trench.
Gallery N. top (852·6 + 344·4)	1196·8	1521·5	1521·4	Axis of mouth of N.N.E. trench.
King's { wall base	1688·5	2146·6	2148·0 }	Outer edge of basalt pave-
Chamber { high floor	1693·7	2153·3	2153·0 }	ment.

The idea seems intrinsically not very improbable, and the exactitude of three of the four coincidences is remarkable, being well within the variations of workman-ship, and errors of measure.

Of the many coincidences pointed out about the trenches, we will only stop to notice those that are within the bounds of possibility. The axis of the N. and S. trenches is supposed to be a tangent to a circle equal to the core-base of the Pyramid; the trenches, as we now know, have not the same axis; the S. being a tangent to a circle of a square 115 inside the finished base, and the N. being a tangent to a circle of a square 165 inside. Now, as the casing (on the N. side) averages 108 ± 8 thick at the base, the theory is possibly true of the S. trench. The outer ends of the trenches are said to be opposite to the points where the core-base would be cut by an equal circle; if so, this would require the casing to be 86· wide at the base; at the corner it is about 80 at the base, so this is not far from the truth. The inner ends of the trenches are said to be points lying on the circle equal to the finished base of the Pyramid; the inner end of the N. trench is nearest to that, being 5,782 from the Pyramid centre; the Pyramid height being 5,776 ± 6, or the radius of the base circuit 5,773·4. A line drawn from this same point, the inner end of the N. trench, to the centre of the Pyramid is at 103° 48′ 27″ to the face of the Pyramid ; and it is said to be parallel to the axis of the E.N.E. trench, which is at 103° 57′ 34″, a difference equal to 15 inches in the position of the trench end. On all these theories of the ends of the trenches, it must be remembered, however, that they were lined (section 100); and therefore the finished length was very different to what it is at present.

148. The main theory of the positions of the chambers in the Great Pyramid, depends on the idea of a square equal in area to the vertical section of the Pyramid ; and one-half of this square, subdivided into thirds, is said to show the levels of the Queen's, King's, and top construction chambers ; and divided in half, the level where the entrance passage axis passes the middle of the Pyramid. The side of such a square is 5117·6, and the levels therefore are thus :—

Queen's Chamber passage axis (claimed in theory)	879·3 }	852·9	one-third of half square.
Gallery doorway (fits better)	852·6 }		
King's Chamber floor	1691·4 to 1693·7	1705·8	two-thirds „ „
Entrance passage axis at Pyramid centre	— 1307·	1279·4	half „ „

Thus the King's Chamber and the entrance passage decidedly disagree with this theory ; and the Queen's Chamber passage has to be abandoned, in favour of the N. door of the gallery. There is, however, a rather similar theory, derived from a square inscribed in the vertical section of half of the Pyramid. The levels in that would be :—

Queen's Chamber passage	834·9 and 854·6	846·8	one-third of square.
King's Chamber floor	1691·4 to 1693·7	1693·6	two-thirds „
Around well in subterranean	— 1254·	1270·2	half „

This agrees closely to the best defined level—of the King's Chamber ; but is no better than the other theory on the whole.

Another theory is that the chambers are at intervals of 40 cubits, the height being 280 cubits.

Queen's Chamber	. . . 834·4	825·1	40 cubits } as by
King's Chamber wall	. . . 1688·5	1650·3	80 „ } total
Top of construction chambers	. 2525 ?	2475·4	120 „ } height.
Pyramid apex	. . . 5776	5776	280 „

This theory, therefore, fails worse than the others, the most definite level needing a cubit of 21·1 to fit it.

We will now note some connections which appear between the exact dimensions.

The level of the virtual end of the gallery floor is   .   .   .   . 1689·0 ± ·5
The horizontal length of the gallery floor is   .   .   .   . 1688·9 ± .2
The level of the base of the King's Chamber walls is   . 1686·3 to 1688·5 ± ·6
The level of the King's Chamber floor is .   .   . . 1691·4 to 1693·7 ± ·6
The level of the horizontal area of Pyramid = ½ of base area is   1691·7 ± 1·8
(or vertical area of the Pyramid divided in half ; or
    diagonal of the Pyramid = side of Pyramid at base.)

Here then are three entirely independent quantities, all agreeing within about three inches, or but little more than the range of the probable error of determining them, even omitting the question of errors of workmanship. According to this coincidence, then, the design of the level of the King's Chamber was the halving of the vertical area of the Pyramid ; and we have already seen a very similar idea in the thick courses, which are introduced apparently at levels where the horizontal area of the Pyramid had simple relations to the base, or where the vertical area was simply divided.

For the Queen's Chamber there is no similar theory of sufficient accuracy ; falling back, therefore, on the very general idea of its being at half the level of the King's Chamber above the base, we are met with the question, What level is to be taken for the Queen's Chamber : (1) the N. door of the gallery, (2) the rough floor of the passage, (3) the rough floor of the chamber, (4) the finished ceiling of the passage, or (5) the level of some supposed floor which was intended to be introduced ? Remembering what accuracy is found in the King's Chamber level, and its cognate lengths, this will be best answered by seeing what level is at half the King's Chamber level. This is intended to be at 1688·5 ± ·4, judging by the gallery length ; and half of this is 844·2 ± ·2. No existing level in the Queen's Chamber agrees to this ; so if the chamber was to be at half the height of that above it, it would only be so on the hypothesis of a fine limestone floor to be inserted. Such a floor must be (844·2 − 834·4) = 9·8 inches thick, not dissimilar to the floor in the Second Pyramid. Is there then any confirmation of this hypothesis in the chamber itself ? The heights will be all 9·8 less from the supposed floor, and the height to the top will be 235·3 over this floor level, or exactly the same height as the King's Chamber walls, 235·31 ± ·07. This is the more likely, as the width of this chamber is the same as that of the King's Chamber. This is then the only hypothesis on which the Queen's Chamber can have been intended to be at half the height of the King's Chamber.

The level of the apex of the construction chambers (according to Vyse's measure above the King's Chamber) is about 2,525 ; and this is nearly three times the Queen's Chamber level, or three halves of the King's Chamber level, as was commonly supposed ; the exact amount of that being 2532·7.

For the subterranean chamber levels the same principle, of even fractions of the King's Chamber level, seems not impossible. But the fractions required being less simple, the intention of the coincidence is less ; and the levels below are more likely to result from a combination of other requirements.

| King's Chamber level | × $\frac{5}{8}$ = 1055·3 | 1056 ± 2 level of subtn. chamber roof. |
| ,,   ,,   ,, | × $\frac{7}{10}$ = 1181·9 | 1181 ± 1 level of end of entrance passage. |

149. Coming next to the passages of the Pyramid, the entrance is said to

be 12 cubits of 20·6 east of the middle. This would be 247, whereas it is really 287.

The theory of the inside of the Pyramid, which has lately been published with the greatest emphasis, is that the distances from certain lines drawn in the entrance passage, up to the N. door of the gallery, reckoned in so-called " Pyramid inches," is equal to the number of years from the date of the building of the Great Pyramid to the beginning of our present era, which is claimed to be the era of the Nativity. Granting, then, two preliminary theories : (1) that the Nativity was at the beginning of our era (and not four or five years before, as all chronologers are agreed), and (2) that the epoch of the Great Pyramid was when a Draconis was shining down the entrance passage, at its lower culmination (which is very doubtful, as we shall see below)—granting these points—the facts agree within a wide margin of uncertainty. The epoch of a Draconis is either 2162 or 2176 B.C., according as we take the angle of the built part of the passage or of the whole of it ; and the distance in theoretical Polar-earth inches between the points mentioned is 2173·3. With such a range in the epoch, nothing exact can be claimed for this coincidence ; and the other coincidences brought forward to support it—the date of the Exodus, &c.—are of still less exactitude and value. The 8th of August, 1882, which was to have been some great day on this theory, has passed quietly away, and we may expect the theory to follow it in like manner.

The theory of the date of the Great Pyramid—that it was the epoch when the pole-star was in line with the entrance passage—seems likewise untenable in the light of the facts. There is no fresh evidence to be produced here about it ; so it will suffice to remark that the only chronologer on whose system such a synchronism is possible, omitted ten dynasties, or a third of the whole number known, by a supposed connection, which even his followers now allow to be impossible. Such being the case, the chronology which admits of the fourth dynasty being as late as 2200 B.C., appears to be hopeless ; and with it the theory of the pole-star connection of the entrance passage falls to the ground. The only possible revival of the theory, is by adopting the first appearance of the star at that altitude in 3400 B.C. ; but this omits half the theory (that part relating to the Pleiades) and may be left at present for chronological discussion.

The total original length of the entrance passage floor being 4,143, appears to have been designed as 200 cubits of 20·71 each ; the roof is 4,133, or 200 × 20·66.

The length of the ascending passage is 1546·5 inches ; this is equal to 75 cubits of 20·620 ; and therefore is ⅜ of the length of the entrance passage.

The length of the Queen's Chamber passage seems to have been ruled by the intention of placing the chamber-ridge exactly in the mid-plane of the Pyramid ; but the curiously eccentric niche on the E. wall seems as if intended to mark some distance ; and measuring from the N. wall of the gallery, where the passage virtually begins, to the middle of the niche. is 1651·6, which equals 80 cubits of 20·645, and is, therefore, ⅖ of the length of the entrance passage.

The horizontal length of the gallery at the top is also just about the same amount, being 1648·5, or 80 cubits of 20·606, which may possibly be intentional; this length, however, seems far more likely to be ruled by the horizontal length at the bottom being equal to the level of the King's Chamber, or upper end of the gallery floor, above the base level; and the top being narrowed 1 cubit at each end, as it is at each side, by the over-lappings.

150. The theories of the widths and heights of the passages are all connected, as the passages are all of the same section, or multiples of that. The entrance passage height has had a curiously complex theory attached to it; supposing that the vertical and perpendicular heights are added together, their sum is 100 so-called "Pyramid inches." This at the angle of 26° 31′ would require a perpendicular height of 47·27, the actual height being 47·24±·02. But in considering any theory of the height of this passage, it cannot be separated from the similar passages, or from the most accurately wrought of all such heights, the course height of the King's Chamber. The passages vary from 46·2 to 48·6, and the mean course height is 47·040±·013. So although this theory agrees with one of the passages, it is evidently not the origin of this frequently-recurring height; and it is the more unlikely as there is no authentic example, that will bear examination, of the use or existence of any such measure as a "Pyramid inch," or of a cubit of 25·025 British inches.

Another theory of the passage height is that the diagonals of the passage, in a vertical section across it, are exactly at the angle of the Pyramid outside, *i.e.*, parallel with E. or W. face of the Pyramid. Taking the passage breadth, as best defined by the King's Chamber, at 41·264 (the passages varying from 40·6 to 42·6), the Pyramid angle at 51° 52′±2′, and the passage angle as 26° 27′, the perpendicular height of the passage should be 47·06±·05 by theory; and the King's Chamber course is actually 47·04±·01, a coincidence far closer than the small uncertainties. This, if combined with the following theory, requires a passage slope of 26° 26′±8′.

The most comprehensive theory about the passage height is one which involves many different parts of the Pyramid, and shows them to be all developments of the same form. It is to the King's Chamber that we must go for the explanation, and we see below how that type is carried out :—

	Wide.	High.		
King's Chamber, mean dimensions	206·13	235·2	or 5 × 41·22 and	47·04
Gallery, lower part, vertically	82·42	92·4 to 94·6	2 × 41·21 and	46·2 to 47·3
Passages	40·6 to 42·6	46·2 to 48·6	40·6 to 42·6 and	46·2 to 48·6
Ramps of gallery, vertically	19·3 to 20·4	22·65 to 23·76	½ × 38·6 to 40·8 &	45·3 to 47·5

Here is a system based on one pattern, and uniformly carried out; for though the measure is taken **perpendicularly** to the floor in the passages and King's

Chamber, and vertically in the gallery, yet as we have seen that the horizontal, and not the sloping, length of the gallery was designed, so here the vertical measure is in accordance with that.

To determine the origin of this form, the King's Chamber theories must be referred to. One theory, that of the chamber containing 20 millions of the mythical Pyramid inches cubed, is cleared away by measurement at once. Taking the most favourable of the original dimensions, *i.e.*, at the bottom, it needs a height of 235·69 to make this volume, and the actual height differs half an inch from this, being 235·20±·06. The only other theory of the height of the walls is similar to one of the best theories of the outside of the Pyramid ; it asserts that taking the circuit of the N. or S. walls, that will be equal to the circumference of a circle whose radius is the breadth of the chamber at right angles to those walls, or whose diameter is the length of those walls. Now by the mean original dimensions of the chamber the side walls are 412·25 long, and the ends 206·13, exactly half the amount. Taking, then, either of these as the basis of a diameter or radius of a circle, the wall height, if the sides are the circumference of such circle, will be 235·32±·10, and this only varies from the measured amount within the small range of the probable errors. This theory leaves nothing to be desired, therefore, on the score of accuracy, and its consonance with the theory of the Pyramid form, and (as we shall see) with a theory of the coffer, strongly bears it out.

But it is not the side wall but the end which is the prototype of the passages ; and so this theory would not be directly applicable to the passages. There are, however, some indications that it was in the designer's mind. The vertical section of the part of the gallery between the ramps is the same width as the passages, though only half their height ; hence in each direction it is just $\frac{1}{10}$th of the side wall of the King's Chamber, or the breadth : its circuit :: a diameter : its circumference. This same notion seems to be present at the very entrance of the Pyramid, where the passage height is divided in half by two courses being put instead of one ; thus either the upper or lower half of the passage from the middle joint is $\frac{1}{10}$th of the chamber side as above. The awkwardness of making a passage nearly twice as wide as it is high, might well cause the builders to adopt the end rather than the side of the King's Chamber as a prototype ; just marking that the passage was designed of double height by putting two courses in its sides, and in the gallery making the beginning of the sides only rise to a single height. Thus this family of dimensions, which so frequently recur, seems to have originated.

151. The angle of the passages has two or three different theories attached to it, besides the rough notion that it is merely the angle at which large masses would just slide down the slope. As to this last idea, in the first place it does not seem that any large masses ever were required to slide along it, except three plug-blocks in the ascending passage ; and secondly, it is decidedly over the

practical angle of rest on such smooth stone, as any one will know who has done work on such a slope.

Another theory, which is quite impossible, is that the passages were regulated by the divisions of the square, equal in area to the Pyramid section. It was supposed that the slope from the centre of the Pyramid up to the gallery N. wall, where that was cut by the $\frac{1}{3}$ of equal-area square (or by the Queen's passage axis), was parallel to the entrance passage ; but this gives an angle of 27° 40′. The other theory, of a line from the Pyramid centre, up to where the semicircle struck by the Pyramid's height is cut by the level of the top of the equal area square, requires an angle of 26° 18′ 10″ ; this is not the entrance passage angle, though it might be attributed to the gallery ; but as the equal-area square has just above been seen to be impossible in its application to the chambers, this rather cumbrous application of it is certainly not to be thought of. We have also seen already that the chronological theory of the pole-star pointing of the entrance appears to be historically impossible.

There then remains only the old theory of 1 rise or 2 base, or an angle of 26° 33′ 54″ ; and this is far within the variations of the entrance passage angle, and is very close to the observed angle of the whole passage, which is 26° 31′ 23″ ; so close to it, that two or three inches on the length of 350 feet is the whole difference ; so this theory may at least claim to be far more accurate than any other theory.

152. The subterranean chamber dimensions may be accounted for in two ways, thus :—

Length	553·5 to 554·1	= 27 cubits of 20·50 to 20·52	Squared = 720 square cubits of 20·63 to 20 65
Width	325·9 to 329·6 ?	= 16 ,, 20·37 to 20·60 ?	,, = 250 ,, ,, 20·61 to 20·85 ?
Height	121·2	= 6 ,, 20·2	
	or 163·0	= 8 ,, 20·37	,, = 60 ,, ,, 21·04
	or 198·		,, = 90 ,, ,, 20·87

Here one theory supposes the length to be in whole numbers of cubits, while the other theory supposes the square of each dimension to be in round numbers of square cubits. This latter theory may seem very unlikely at first sight ; but, as will be seen further on, it is applicable to all the chambers, and the only theory that is so applicable. This second theory fits decidedly better to the plan of this chamber than does the first ; but on neither theory are the heights satisfactorily explained, though rather the worse in the first.

153. The most comprehensive theory of the Queen's Chamber is similar to the above ; showing that the squares of the sides are in round numbers of square cubits. This type of theory was first started in connection with this chamber, and was only proposed as showing that the squares of the sides were multiples of a certain modulus squared, without its being perceived that the square modulus was just 20 square cubits. A beautiful corollary of this theory is that the squares of the diagonals, both superficial and cubic, will necessarily be also in round numbers of square cubits ; such a design is, in fact, the only way of rendering every dimension that can be taken in a chamber equally connected

with a unit of measure without any fractions. Taking the mean dimensions, and dividing them by the square roots of the corresponding numbers of square cubits, the cubit required by each is as follows :—

Width .	. 205·85 (max. 206·29)	÷ √100	20·585 (max. 20·629)
Length .	. 226·47 (min. 225·51)	÷ √120	20·674 (min. 20·586)
Wall height .	184.47	÷ √ 80	20·625
Ridge height .	245·1 (min. 244·76)	÷ √140	20·713 (min. 20·686)

Thus, though the mean dimensions do not agree very closely, yet the variations of each will suffice to cover their differences ; except in the case of the height to the roof ridge, the minimum of which is ·66 too large for even the maximum breadth. The applicability of similar theories to other parts, and the absence of any more exact theory of this, gives it some amount of probability.

Another theory is that the chamber contains ten million " Pyramid inches"; the contents by the mean dimensions are 10,013,600 British cubic inches, and this is $\frac{1}{800}$ short of the required quantity, or would need a change of $\frac{1}{8}$ inch in some one mean dimension.

Another theory is that the circuit of the floor is $\frac{1}{3}$ the circuits of the King's Chamber side walls, which we have lately seen to be probably formed from a circle struck with 10 cubits as a radius ; also the diagonal of the chamber end is claimed as a diameter of a circle equal to the floor circuit ; and the passage height is claimed as half of the radius of this same circle. The measures are :—

Mean circuit = 864·64	× 3 = 2593·92	2590·20 circuit of King's Ch. walls.
Circuit ÷ π = 275·22		275·6 minimum diagonal of end.
Circuit ÷ 2 π = 137·61	× ½ = 68·81	66·5 to 69·0 passage height.

None of these relations are close enough to be very probable, and the absence of a satisfactory representation of the radius or diameter of this circuit makes it improbable that it was intended.

The theory of the wall-height being $\frac{1}{50}$ of the Pyramid base is quite beyond possibility, the wall being 183·58 at even the minimum, and $\frac{1}{50}$ of the base being 181·38.

The theory of the wall height : the breadth :: breadth : King's Chamber height is quite possible. 184·47 : 206·02 :: 206·02 : 230·09, so that the breadth required (206·02), though a little over the mean, is well within the variations. Or it might be stated that the product of the breadth of King's and Queen's Chambers is equal to the product of their heights.

The simplest theory of all is that the dimensions were all regulated by even numbers of cubits.

Height of side .	183·58 to 185·0?	÷ 9	20·398 to 20·555.
Breadth .	. 205·67 to 206·29	÷ 10	20·567 to 20·629.
Length .	. 225·51 to 227·47	÷ 11	20·501 to 20·679.
Height of ridge .	244·76 to 245·9	÷ 12	20·397 to 20·492.

But by this theory the maximum height is ·9 too small to agree with the minimum breadth ; and in its applicability it is inferior to the theory of the squares first described.

Taking next the niche, which has been abundantly theorized on, there are two instances claimed to show the so-called " sacred cubit " of 25 " Pyramid inches," or 25·025 British inches. The breadth of the top of the niche is not, however, 25 inches, but only averages 20·3, and it is intended for a regular Egyptian cubit, roughly executed. The excentricity of the niche is nearer to the theoretical quantity, though in all parts it is too large for the theory, the amount being 25·19 (varying 25·08 to 25·31) from below the apex of the roof, or 25·29 (varying 25·10 to 25·44) from the middle of the wall. So here, as elsewhere, the supposed evidences of this cubit vanish on testing them.*

Then the niche height × 10 π is said to be = Pyramid height. This coincidence is close, the niche being 183·80, and the Pyramid height being 10 π × 183·85, but the use of π here is so arbitrary and unsystematic, that this cannot rank as more than a chance coincidence. The "shelf" at the back of the niche, being merely a feature of its destruction, and not original, cannot have any connection with the original design. The niche being intentionally the same height as the N. and S. walls, no theory can be founded on the very small and fluctuating differences between them.

154. In the Antechamber only two or three dimensions have been theorized on. The principle theory is that the length of the granite part of the floor is equal to the height of the E. wainscot of granite, and that the square of this length is equal in area to a circle, the diameter of which is the total length of this chamber. Now, as accurately measured by steel tape along the E. side the granite floor is 103·20, and the E. wainscot varies from 102·18 to 103·35 in height. A square of 103·20 is equal in area to a circle 116·45 diameter, and the length of the chamber varies from 114·07 to 117·00. So no very exact or certain coincidence can be proved from such quantities.

But it is also claimed that there are other coincidences " not less extraordinary, connected with their absolute lengths, when measured in the standards and units of the Great Pyramid's scientific theory, and in no others known." Now since 103·2 is exactly 5 common Egyptian cubits, the negative part of this boast cannot be true. And on testing the positive part of the declaration it proves equally incorrect. For 116·30 × π × ·999 is 365·1, and not 362·1, the number of so-called " sacred cubits " in the Pyramid base. Again, 116·30 × 50 is 5,815, and not 5,776, the number of inches in the Pyramid height. And also 103·2 × 50 is 5,160, and not 5117·6, the side of a square of equal area to the half of the Pyramid's vertical section. Thus the flourishing dictum with which

* There is doubtless a well-known ancient cubit of 25·3 inches; but that is decidedly not as short as 25·0, nor is it found employed in the Great Pyramid.

2 C

these coincidences were published is exactly reversed; the quantities have no such relations to the Pyramid, as are claimed; and 103·2 is simply a length of Egyptian cubits, and 116·3 possibly a derivative of that quantity.

The only satisfactory theory of the chamber is that of the squares of the dimensions being even numbers of square cubits.

Length . . . 116·3 (var. 114·1 to 117·0)	116·7 squared is 32 square cubits.	
Upper breadth . 65·0 (var. 64·48 to 65·48)	65·24 „ 10 „ „	
Lower „ . var. 41·2 to 41·45.	41·26 „ 4 „ „	
Height, E. wainscot 103·01 (var. 102·30 to 103·36)	103·15 „ 25 „ „	
Height over „ 46·32 (var. 45·96 to 47·14)	46·13 „ 5 „ „	

Thus each dimension is fairly accounted for; though not much certainty can be placed on any theory of this chamber, owing to its great irregularities.

The total length of the horizontal passages, beginning with the great step in the gallery, and going through to the King's Chamber, is 330·5; this equals 16 cubits of 20·66. The number somewhat confirms the notion of 32 square cubits in the square of the length of the Antechamber.

About a dozen other theories on the dimensions of this chamber have been proposed, of more or less complexity; but when they are deprived of the support of any deep meaning in the main dimensions, they are not worth time and paper for discussion.

The granite leaf, which has been so much theorized on, is but a rough piece of work; and the "boss" on it is not only the crowning point of the theories, but is the acme of vagueness as well. To seriously discuss a possible standard of 5 "Pyramid inches," in a thing that may be taken as anywhere between 4·7 and 5·2 inches in breadth; or a standard inch in a thickness of stone varying from ·94 to 1·10, would be a waste of time. Enough has been said of the character of this leaf (in describing it, section 50), and of the various other bosses in different parts of the Pyramid, to make a farther notice of the theories about it superfluous.

155. The principal theory of the King's Chamber has been already stated in connection with the passages of which it is the prototype. There were two theories of the origination of its dimensions, which were each apparently very exact (to $\frac{1}{8000}$), but which contradicted each other, and which are now known to be both false. Compared with the real dimensions these are :—

Half-breadth of King's Chamber 103·15	102·33 $\frac{1}{100}$ diam. of circle whose area = Pyramid base.	
Length of „ „ 412·64	408·4 $\frac{1}{20}$ of line from apex to circle of Pyramid base.	

The only connections traceable between the real dimensions of the Pyramid outside, and those of the King's Chamber, are merely by the intermediary of the common Egyptian cubit used alike in laying out both of them.

The connection of the passages with this chamber involves its wall-height; but, besides this, there is the height above the irregular floor; this latter is explained by the theory of the squares of the dimensions.

Width 206·12±·12 squared, is 100 cubits of 20·612±·012
Length 412·24±·12   „   400   „   20·612±·006
Height 230·09±·15   „   125   „   20·580±·014

Thus this theory agrees with the facts within little more than the small range of the probable errors. From the squares of the main dimensions being thus integral numbers, it necessarily follows that the squares of all the diagonals are integers ; and one result, that the height is half of the diagonal of the floor, is very elegant, and may easily have been the origin of the height.

The mean of the heights of the wall, and of the chamber from the floor, is stated to be double the length of the Antechamber ; it is actually double of 116·36, and as the Antechamber varies from 114 to 117, it, of course, includes this and any quantities at all near it.

Another theory involving the height is, that the contents of the chamber are 1,250 cubic "sacred cubits." As yet, every instance of this supposed cubit has melted away on being touched by facts, and in this instance it also disappears : the theory requires a height of 230·48, which is ·39 over the truth, and far beyond the range of probable error.

The simplest theory of the height is, that the floor was raised above the base of the walls a quarter of a cubit ; according to the mean of the measures (of which I took about 32) it is raised 5·11±·12 inches, and the quarter of a cubit is 5·16. It is not a little singular that in this case the same theorist, whose unhappy inversion of facts was noted above, has again dogmatized in exactly the opposite direction to the truth ; he writes of this 5·11, or quarter cubit, that it is "quite an unmeaning fraction when measured in terms of the profane Egyptian cubit," as it pleases him to call the only standard of measure really discoverable in the Great Pyramid.

The only other theory involving the height concerns the coffer. It is said that the lower course of the King's Chamber surrounds a volume equal to 50 times that of the coffer. Now, the coffer's contents are, by different modes of measurement, 72,000±60 cubic inches, and for the first course to comprise 50 times this amount it must be 42·30±·04 inches high ; whereas it is but 41·91±·12, or about $\frac{4}{10}$ inch too small. If, however, refuge be taken in the inexact relation of the contents of the coffer about equalling its solid bulk, the mean of the two amounts requires the course-height to be 41·87, or close to the irregular quantity as measured. The most passable way, then, to put this is to say that the outside of the coffer fills $\frac{1}{25}$ of the volume of the chamber up to the first course.

156. The theories of the coffer itself are almost interminable, and they find ample room for discrepancies between them in the great irregularities of the working of the coffer. The various theories have so much connection with each other, and each have so many consequences which may be

geometrically traced, that it is difficult to select the best phase of each theory.

The most fundamental idea is that the solid bulk of the granite is equal to the hollow contents : this is on the assumption that the grooves for a lid, and the different height of the sides, are ignored, and the vessel treated as having sides approximately uniform in height and thickness in every part. The relative amounts by the two independent methods are

By offsets from planes, contents 72,030, bulk 70,500 cubic inches. Difference 1,530
By calipers   „   71,960   „   70,630 „   „   „   1,330

The difference, then, between the amounts of contents and bulk is, on an average, $\frac{1}{50}$ of the whole ; and, looking at this difference as applied to the least certain of all the dimensions—the thickness of the sides—it amounts to ·11 inch, a quantity very far beyond any possible errors of measurement. It is certain, then, that there is no transcendent accuracy in this particular.

Another, and further, theory is that the volume of the sides is double that of the bottom ; or that the solid is divided into equal thirds, a side and end, another side and end, and the bottom.

	Bottom.	Mean side and end.	Difference.
By mean planes entirely	23,830	23,335	495
By mean planes, cutting at *actual* edge of bottom	23,895	23,303	592
By calipered sides		23,343	552

The differences here average $\frac{1}{45}$ of the whole ; and if the bottom were neglected altogether, and only the sides compared with the contents, there would still remain a difference of 500 cubic inches on the contents.

The theory of 50 times the coffer being contained in the first course of the King's Chamber is already noticed above.

The volume of the coffer has been attributed to the cube of a double Egyptian cubit ; but this theory would need a cubit of 20·803, a value decidedly above what is found in accurate parts of the Pyramid workmanship.

The volume has also been attributed to a sphere of $2\frac{1}{2}$ cubits (or $\frac{1}{4}$ width of the chamber) in diameter ; by the true contents this would need a cubit of 20·644, which is very close to the best determinations.

The main theory of the coffer contents, that such a bulk of water equals in weight 12,500 cubic " Pyramid inches " of earth of mean density, cannot be tested without accurate knowledge of the earth's density. As far as the best results go, the coffer would require the density to be 5·739, and the earth's density is 5·675±·004 (by Baily) ; this is somewhat clouded by other methods giving 5·3 and 6·5, but those other methods, on their own showing, have respectively but $\frac{1}{200}$ and $\frac{1}{22}$ of the weight of Baily's result. If it were desirable to take a strictly weighted mean, of results of such different value, it would come out 5·711.

Theories of lineal dimensions of the coffer have been less brought forward. The principal one is the π proportion of the coffer; the height being stated to be the radius of a circle equal to the circumference. Now this has a strong confirmation in such a proportion existing, on 5 times the scale, in the chamber. There, as we have seen, a radius of 206 inches has a circumference equal to the circuit of the N. or S. walls at right angles to it; and similarly the radius or height of the coffer, 41·2, has a circumference nearly equal to the circuit of the coffer. The height of the coffer is not very certain, owing to so much of the top having been destroyed; but comparing its dimensions with those of the King's Chamber (which, as already shown, agrees to the π proportion) they stand thus :—

Circuit of chamber side wall		1295.1	129·16 (+·3 ? originally) N. and E. sides at base.	
			127·96 S. and W. sides at base.	
Radius of circuit	206·12	÷ 5= 41·224	41·31 (var. 41·14 to 41·50).	

The length of the E. side was originally about ·3 more than the length to the broken parts now remaining, judging by the curvatures of the N. and S. faces. This would make it 90·6 long; and Prof. Smyth prolonging the broken parts by straight edges read it as 90·5.

An old theory now revives, by having a shorter base for the Pyramid; for $\frac{1}{100}$ of the Pyramid base is 90·69; and here the maximum length appears to have been about 90·6, so that the theory of their connection is not at all impossible.

The most consistent theory of the coffer, and one which is fairly applicable to all the dimensions, is that of the lengths squared being in even numbers of square fifths of the cubit, or tenths of the height squared. On the decimal division of the cubit, see section 139. By this theory :—

Outer length squared	= 480 square units, if	90·40	90·6 (?) actual maximum.			
Outer width	„	= 90	„	„	39·14	38·97 (?) „ „ (39·12 Smyth).
Outer height	„	= 100	„	„	41·26	41·14 to 41·50 actual.
Inner length	„	= 360	„	„	78·29	78·23 actual maximum.
Inner width	„	= 42	„	„	26·74	26·81 „ mean.
Inner height	„	= 70	„	„	34·52	34·54 „ maximum.

Though these multiples may seem somewhat unlikely numbers, yet they are simply related to one another throughout. The squares of outer and inner lengths are as 4 : 3; of outer and inner height as 10 : 7; of inner width and height as 3 : 5, &c. And in all cases the required dimensions are allowably within the variations of the work. This theory, though perhaps not very satisfactory, has at least a stronger claim than any other, when we consider the analogous theories of other parts of the building.

Another theory of the coffer outside, is that its circuit is half of the cubic diagonal of the King's Chamber. This cubic diagonal actually is 515·17, and its half is 257·58, against 257·4 (?) for the coffer circuit. But these quantities may both be simply derived from one common source, the cubit; for the cubic diagonal of the chamber is 25 × 20·607, and the circuit of the coffer is 12½ × 20·59. So that unless analogies can be shown elsewhere, the design might be simply in numbers of cubits.

The length, breadth, and height, have also been attributed to fractions of this cubic diagonal, by taking $\frac{1}{40}$ of it. This theory of the height requires, however, 40·46, and the minimum height is 41·14; the bottom not being at all hollowed, as had been supposed. The length and breadth theory only amounts to an additional proposition that these are in the proportion of 7 : 3 ; which is quite within their actual variations.

The outer length has also three other quantities connected with it, which coincide far within the variations ;

Outer length mean.	Cube root of 10 × contents.	Cubic diagonal of mean inside.	¼ cubic diagonal of Queen's Chamber.
89·62	89·62	89·43	89·33

and further, the diameter of a sphere containing 1000 × ⅓ contents (or volume of bottom) is 357·85, nearly the diagonal of the Queen's Chamber, and 4 × 89·46· This and the above value of the cube root of 10 × contents, are connected by the similarity of π and 3·125 or $\frac{100}{32}$, which often leads to coincidences in variable and uncertain quantities.

A π proportion has been seen in the inside ; the circuit of the inner end being equal to a circle inscribed on the outer end ; or else the circuit of the two inner ends have their diameters at right angles to them and joining, forming the inner length.   The quantities are :—

Mean circuit of inner ends } $122 \cdot 46 \div \pi = 38 \cdot 98$ | 39·03 half inner length, mean. | 38·50 outer width, mean.

The diagonal of the inside end of the coffer rises at 52° 5′, by mean measures ; and this has been compared with the angle of the Pyramid itself, 51° 52′.

Several direct connections of the dimensions with the cubit, have been theorized on.   The diagonal of the bottom inside is by mean measures 82·54, or 4 cubits of 20·63, exactly the value shown by the chamber.   The inner diagonal being thus double the outer height, is analogous to the diagonal of the chamber being double of its height.

It is already mentioned that the contents are equal to a sphere of 2½ cubits diameter ; this implying a cubit of 20·64. But this length of 2½ cubits (51·58 inches), or ¼ the chamber breadth, may be connected with other dimensions of the coffer thus :

$51 \cdot 58 \times \frac{4}{5} = 41 \cdot 26$ | 41·31 (var. 41·14 to 41·50) outer height.
$\times \frac{7}{4} = 90 \cdot 26$ | 89·63 (var. 89·18 to 90·6 ?) outer length.
$\times \frac{3}{4} = 38 \cdot 68$ | 38·50 (var. 38·35 to 38·87) outer width.
$\times \frac{3}{2} = 77 \cdot 37$ | 78·06 (var. 77·64 to 78·23) inner length.
$\times \frac{2}{3} = 34 \cdot 39$ | 34·42 (var. 34·36 to 34·54) inner height.

These theories comprise all that have any chance of showing intentional relations ; others are either too diverse from the facts, or of too complex a nature, to have any probability.

157. In considering the probability of these theories having been in the designer's mind, it is (after settling the bare question of fitting the facts) of

the first importance to trace any connections and general plans running through the design. Theories which are dissimilar from those of other parts of the structure, may be judged almost alone; merely from a general sense of the character of the design elsewhere. But where the same motive appears in many different parts, each occurrence of it strongly bears out the others; and it must stand or fall as a whole. It is hardly necessary to say that where there is a choice of two equally concordant theories, the simpler of the two is the more likely to be the true one; but individual prepossession of the reader in some cases will have to turn the balance of his opinion. On the knotty question of the possible intention of two motives combined in one form, or necessarily inter-related, the individual feelings will hold a still stronger place; and the proba-bilities of intention—like many other questions—will be believed or disbelieved, not so much on physical as on metaphysical grounds, and conditions of mind.

There are three great lines of theory throughout the Pyramid, each of which must stand or fall as a whole; they are scarcely contradictory, and may almost subsist together; but it is desirable to point out the group of each, so as to judge of their likelihood of intention. These are (1) the Egyptian cubit theory; (2) the π proportion, or radius and circumference theory; (3) the theory of areas, squares of lengths and diagonals. Without, then, restating what has been already described, we will briefly recall the coincidences which support each of these theories.

(1) By the cubit theory, the—

Outside form of Pyramid is 280 and 440 cubits, confirmed by the π theory.

Breadth of the passages are certainly in cubits.

Lengths of passages, entrance, ascending, and antechamber, and perhaps Queen's and gallery, are in cubits.

Subterranean chamber sides squared are in square cubits.⎫ Many of these
Queen's Chamber sides and height   „   „   ⎪ dimensions are
Antechamber sides and height   ,,   „   ⎬ also simple
King's Chamber sides and height   ,,   „   ⎪ numbers of
Coffer dimensions, in and out,   ,,   „   ⎭ cubits.

(2) To the π theory, the—

Outside proportion of the Pyramid exactly agrees.

(Azimuth trench may indicate points on the π circle of the base).

Passage sections agree, being on one type derived from King's Chamber.

King's Chamber wall dimensions are precisely agreed.

Coffer proportions outside, and perhaps inside, are agreed.

By the theory of areas, the—

Outside proportion of the Pyramid is exactly given.

Large courses occur at proportionate levels.

Level of King's Chamber halves the Pyramid areas.

Subterranean chamber sides squared give areas in square cubits.

Queen's Chamber sides and height squared give areas in square cubits.

Antechamber sides and height squared give areas in square cubits.

King's Chamber sides and height squared give areas in square cubits.

Coffer dimensions, in and out, squared give areas in square cubits.

From this the diagonals of these parts, superficial and cubic, will, if squared, also give areas in square cubits. And by the theories of the diagonals also the—

Level of the King's Chamber is where the Pyramid diagonal equals the base side.

Diagonal of passage section (vertical) rises parallel to the Pyramid face (51° 52′).

Diagonal of inside end of coffer rises parallel to the Pyramid face (51° 52′).

Diagonal of inside bottom of coffer is double its height, or 4 cubits.

Diagonal of floor of King's Chamber is double its height.

These theoretic systems scarcely contradict one another; and, generally speaking, there is nothing in most of these theories which would prevent their being accepted as being parts of the real design. The other theories stated in the previous pages are partly independent of these, and partly contradictory; and they are not strengthened by a unity of design like each of the above series.

158. It will be well, while discussing theories, to consider how the Tombic theory of the Great Pyramid stands affected by the results of accurate measurement and examination.

In the first place, all the other Pyramids were built for tombs; and this at once throws the burden of proof upon those who claim a different purpose for the Great Pyramid. In the second place, the Great Pyramid contains a coffer, exactly like the ordinary Egyptian burial coffers of early times; like them both in its general form, and also in having grooves for a lid, and pin holes for fastening that lid on. Very strong evidence is therefore required, if we would establish any other purpose for it than that of receiving and safe-guarding a body.

What evidence, then, has been produced?

1st. That Khufu was not buried in the Great Pyramid, according to Strabo.

2nd. That the passages are well defined, and would lead explorers straight to the chambers, instead of concealing them.

3rd. That the coffer could not be taken in with its lid.

4th. That the coffer is unusually deep.

5th. That the grooves are not dovetailed to hold a lid on (since retracted).

6th. That no lid has ever been seen.

7th. That in no other case is a coffer devoid of ornament or inscription.

8th. That "in no other case are the neighbouring walls and passages of the Pyramid so devoid of hieratic and every other emblem."

9th. That the upper passages are unique, and also the above-ground place of the coffer.

10th. That the coffer is not built around to protect it, as others were.

11th. That the chamber has ventilating channels.

12th. That the lid might be a later addition to the coffer.

13th. That the coffer has certain cubic proportions, which show a care and design beyond what could be expected in any burial-coffer.

Now, of these objections to the Tombic theory, the 1st, 2nd, 3rd, 7th, and 8th, would be equally forcible in the case of the Second Pyramid ; yet in that is a coffer whose lid has been finally fastened on, and which undisputedly contained the body of Khafra.　The 4th objection is met by several cases of coffers equally deep, such as the splendid one of Khufu-ankh at Bulak.　The 5th has been retracted, owing to the groove being proved to be undercut.　As for the 6th, it is plain that there are grooves, &c., for a lid ; hence whether such a lid can actually be found, after the various destructions, is of little consequence.　The 10th is of no value, as other coffers are not always built up, *e.g.*, that of Menkaura and that of Pepi.　The 12th point, that the lid (or the grooves for it) might be a later work, is only a hope without any evidence.　That the pin-holes are Egyptian work is certain, by their being cut with a jewelled drill, such as the Pyramid builders used.　It is unreasonable to imagine any later king having intended that his body should be ignominiously tumbled up the long narrow irregular passage of the so-called well, which was the only pre-Arab way to the coffer ; and also that any later king would have altered the coffer without putting his name upon it.　The habit of later kings was rather to smash than to utilize.　The 13th point has been already answered by the fact that the supposed accuracy of the relations is by no means transcendent ; and that the workmanship is decidedly inferior to that of other parts of the Pyramid, and to that of Khafra's burial coffer.

That in a building, whose design appears on good evidence to include the π proportion and the use of areas, some design of cubic quantities might be followed in the principal object of the structure, is not at all improbable.　But any claim to even respectable accuracy and regularity in the coffer, is decidedly disallowed by its roughness of work.　It cannot be supposed that a piece of granite, rough sawn, with the saw lines remaining on its faces, has any special significance in the waves and twists of its sides, any more than in the other faults of cutting, where the saw or drill have by accident run too deeply.

The damaged remains of this theory of accurate proportions, and the fact of the upper passages and air-channels not being known in other Pyramids, are then the only evidences which are left to reverse the universal rule of Pyramids being tombs, and coffers being intended for coffins.

159. The Second Pyramid has not been theorized on to any large extent. The theories of the base length are—

Actual mean length　...　　　...　　　...　　　...	8474·9±·8
6 × modulus (mod. = 30 passage heights, see below)	8467·2±2·4

420 cubits of 20·2208 ...	...	...	...	8492·4
700 " Greek or Egyptian " feet		700 × 12·16		8512
7″ of arc ...	...	...	...	8494·5 to 8521·8
The angle of the Pyramid is actually ...		...	...	53° 10′ ±4′
33 slant height on 20 base	...	...	...	52° 41′ 41″
5 slant height, or 4 vertical height, on 3 base			...	53° 7′ 48″

Here there can be scarcely any doubt that the 3 : 4 : 5 triangle was the design for the slope ; and therefore any explanation of the lineal size should involve dividing the base by 6, or height by 4. This ⅙ of the base is the modulus above mentioned, and the only quantity with which it seems to have any connection is the perpendicular height of the passages. The entrance-passage is evidently intended to be of the same size as that of the Great Pyramid, which, as we have seen, is derived from the King's Chamber courses. Referring to the King's Chamber for its most accurate value, the result is 47·040±·013 ; 30 times this is 1411·2±·4, and ⅙ of the Second Pyramid base is 1412·5±·1. The highest corner of the King's Chamber yields a mean course height of 47·065, and thence a modulus of 1412·0, and ⅙ of the shortest side of the Pyramid is 1412·0. The difference between these quantities, therefore, does not exceed their small variations ; and as there is no unlikelihood in the idea, and no other theory that accounts for the dimensions, this connection may well be accepted until disproved. Some authority is required for multiplying the passage height by 30, but there is good reason for adopting a triple multiple, as the higher passages in this Pyramid are 1½ times the usual passage height, as already described. Hence the modulus is 30 times the ordinary passage height, or 20 times the larger passage height ; and the measured height of the best wrought part of the passage, just behind the portcullis, when × 20 is 1415·2 and 1407·6, just including the modulus of the base, which is 1412·5.

160. None of the dimensions of the inside of this Pyramid have been hitherto explained by theory, hence there are no rival hypotheses to consider in the following cases ; and if the ideas suggested seem too improbable, we must simply confess our ignorance of the design.

Taking the great central chamber as the best wrought part of the inside, it is evident that the height of the sides is 10 cubits, being 206·4 ; but the breadth, 195·8, seems inexplicable, as 9½ cubits is not a likely quantity. In the Great Pyramid we have seen that all the dimensions of the chambers are explainable on the theory of the squares of the lengths being a round number of square cubits. Applying this theory to the Second Pyramid chamber, the

Wall height ...	... 206·4	squared	= 100 square cubits of			20·640
End height ...	... 244·4	„	= 140	„	„	20·656
Breadth ...	... 195·85	„	= 90	„	„	20·644
Length W. from door	412·75	„	= 400	„	„	20·637
Length E. ...	... 144·9	„	= 50	„	„	20·493

The exactitude of the connection of theory and measurement here is remarkable; the only perceptible difference being in the length from the W. side of the doorway to the E. wall. And the value of the cubit required by the dimensions, 20·64, is extremely close to the cubit as best shown in the King's Chamber, 20·632±·004. If any objection be made to dividing the lengths into two parts, it should be noted that it is certainly so divided in the chamber, by the fact of the length of one part, 412·75, being exactly 20 cubits; the wall W. of the door being a double square, 10×20 cubits, equal to the floor of the King's Chamber.

The design of the squares of the dimensions, direct and diagonal, being in round numbers of square cubits, appears then to have been employed in this chamber, as in those of the Great Pyramid.

The rudely-worked lower chamber seems to have been simply designed in cubits. The length 411·6 being evidently 20 cubits of 20·58; and the breadth, 123·4, three times the passage breadth, or 6 cubits of 20·57. The recess opposite the entrance to this chamber is 122·0 to 123·8 long, apparently equal to the chamber breadth.

161. For the coffer of the Second Pyramid there does not appear to be any uniform theory, though it is so carefully wrought. The outer length and width of it might seem as if rougly intended for 5 and 2 cubits, of 20·73 and 20·98 respectively. But it is hard to suppose that such very different values of the cubit would be used in a work so finely equilateral and regular. On applying each of the theories of the Great Pyramid coffer to this, only two of them appear to have been carried out here.

Internal length of coffer 84·73±·02 | 84·75±·01 $= \frac{1}{100}$ of Second Pyramid base.

Thus the Second Pyramid being smaller than the First, and yet its coffer being longer, the relation to $\frac{1}{100}$th of the Pyramid base is produced in the inside, and not on the outside, length.

The only simple relation between the lineal dimensions of the coffer is

Thickness of sides, 7·64±·01 | 7·62=¼ of outer height.

But on applying the theory of the squares of the dimensions, some of the dimensions seem accounted for thus, taking $\frac{1}{1000}$ of the Pyramid base, =8·475, as a unit :—

Outer length	... 103·68 (max. 103·73)	103·79 squared	= 150 square units.
Inner length,	... 84·73	84·75 "	= 100 " "
Inner width	... 26·69 (max. 26·79)	26·80 "	= 10 " "
Outer height +lid,	46·34	46·42 "	= 30 " "

This theory agrees fairly with these dimensions; and, comparing the similar theory of the squares of the Great Pyramid coffer dimensions being multiples of square fifths of a cubit, the theory seems not improbable, though it does not apply to all the dimensions.

There do not appear to be any volumetric relations intended in this coffer, for though the outer volume over all is 2½ × the contents, true to $\frac{1}{100}$ (or twice as accurate as the relations claimed by the theory of the Great Pyramid coffer), yet as this difference is 7 × the probable error, it renders such a design unlikely. Two million times the contents is equal to the volume of the Pyramid, true to $\frac{1}{100}$; but here again the difference is against such a relation being intentional.

It is only then by the execution of this coffer being superior to that of the Great Pyramid coffer, that we are saved from being encumbered with accidental coincidences, which have found such a wide shelter in the irregular work of the coffin of Khufu.

162. The Third Pyramid has been commonly reputed to be just half the size of the Second, but accurate measures disprove this—

> Its actual base is ... ... 4153·6 ± 1·8
> Half of the Second Pyramid base is 4237·4 ± ·8
> 200 cubits is ... ... 4126·2

It seems most probable that it was designed to be 200 cubits long; for the length of the cubit required, 20·768, is far within the variations of the cubit of the Granite Chamber, and other parts inside. The first design of the Pyramid, before its expansion, appears to have been a base of 100 cubits, like some of the small Pyramids.

The angle of 51° 0′, or more likely 51° 10′, may be designed by a rise of 5 on a base of 4, which would produce 51° 20′; but the whole of this Pyramid, inside and outside, is so far less accurate than the two larger, that no refinement of work or of design need be looked for.

The first chamber appears to be 6 × 7½ cubits; the 6 being divided by the passage into 3 spaces of 2 cubits each. The length is 153·8, or 7½ × 20·51; and the breadth 124·8, or 6 × 20·80, varying in its divisions between 20·4 and 21·1 for the cubit. The most accurate-looking piece of work here is the granite lintel of the doorway, which is wrought to 41·23 to 41·35 wide, yielding a cubit of 20·61 to 20·67, which agrees with the true value.

The second chamber is divided in its length into spaces of 416·1, 41·5, and 102·2, in which we cannot fail to recognise 20, 2, and 5 cubits of 20·82, 20·75, and 20·44 respectively; and the width 152·8 being similar to 153·8 in the previous chamber, seems to be intended for 7½ cubits of 20·3.

The Granite Chamber is from 103·2 to 104·0 wide, or 5 cubits of 20·64 to 20·80; and 258·8 to 260·7 long, or 12½ cubits of 20·70 to 20·86, the length being thus 2½ times the breadth.

The loculus chamber is so extremely rude that nothing certain can be concluded from it; but it seems to have been intended to be 3½ × 10 cubits, and the loculi each 5 cubits in length.

Thus it appears that in the Third Pyramid the design was merely in even numbers of cubits; and that it had none of that refinement of the design in areas, which prevailed in the Great Pyramid, and partly also in the Second. The evident irregularity and want of attention even to mere equality, shows a similar decadence in its character; so that from every point of view its inferiority is manifest.

163. It may be asked, Why is more value to be attached to the present measures of the Pyramid bases, than those of any of the various other observers? Why should not a simple mean be taken, and the present and past measures be all lumped together?

This is a perfectly sound question; and unless a difference of trustworthiness can be shown to exist between the different results, a simple mean is the only true conclusion. But if the measurements vary in accuracy, they must be weighted accordingly; and it must be remembered that the weight, or value assigned, increases as the square of the accuracy; so that an observer probably 1 inch in error, has 9 times the weight of one who is probably 3 inches in error.

But by what are we to assign weights, or to estimate the accuracy of the observers? With observations that have no checks by which they can be tested, it is useless to depend on their professed or stated accuracy; for, as any one knows who has ever used check measurements, the unexpected sources of error are often far larger than those known and recognised. Therefore all observers who have not made distinct and separate checks (by repeated measures of angles or of lengths) can only have some value given them, where, from their agreements with other checked measurements, they appear to have some likelihood of accuracy.

Into this category of observers who worked without checks, or at least who have made no mention of them, fall four of the six measurements yet made of the Great Pyramid; those of the French expedition, of Perring, of Inglis, and of the Royal Engineers. The only two surveys made with check observations (and those are abundant in both) are (1) that of Mr. Gill and Prof. Watson, in 1874; and (2) that here published, which was made in 1881.

When I reduced Mr. Gill's observations, it was on the understanding that he reserved the publication of them to himself; and hence I am not at liberty to give their details, but will only state how nearly they are in accordance with my own.

Unfortunately, so many of the metal station marks fixed in 1874 had been torn up, and the stones in which they were inserted, shifted or broken, that I had not many points of comparison. The screw-caps of other marks were set tight; and though I made inquiry at Cairo, I could not get the key which fitted them; even if I had had it, it seemed doubtful if they could be unscrewed, because the Arabs had battered and punched the caps so much. Others of the stations had been but uncertainly fixed by Mr. Gill, owing to their positions, and his lack of time for completing the circuit of triangulation. Finally, but three stations are really common to both triangulations, and fairly fixed. The result of comparing these is a mean variation between the two surveys of 2″ of angle, or $\frac{1}{100000}$, equal to $\frac{1}{10}$ inch. This is a variation such as professedly may exist in either of the surveys; and there is no reason therefore for doubting the professed accuracy of the survey of 1881, which results from the combination of dozens of check observations. Beside the agreement in angles, there is the other question of an absolute value for a base; in this there is far more difference, the 1874 measures of length yielding a result $\frac{1}{1000}$ longer than those of 1881.

Turning now to the other observations, which are without checks, and judging of their value by their difference from the two concordant and checked triangulations, the French expedition result is beyond all probability, being 33 inches too long; Perring's result is rather worse, being 38 inches too long; Inglis's varies in its error on different sides from 10 to 29 inches too short; but the Royal Engineer's results are only from 2·0 shorter to 2·1 longer than the triangulation of 1881. There is therefore no need to consider the first three results, which vary from 10 to 38 inches, on one side or other of the 1881 survey; seeing that we have the three intrinsically best surveys (the R.E., the 1874, and the 1881) all agreeing within an inch or two.

As the R.E. survey* agrees so closely with the later ones in its proportions, it becomes of value in determining the question of the absolute length of the lines, in order to decide between the 1874 and 1881 surveys, which differ $\frac{1}{4000}$ in the base. The R.E. and 1881 measurements in detail are thus:—

Sockets.	R.E.	1881.	Difference.
N. side	9127·5	9129·8	— 2·3
E. „	9129.5	9130·8	— 1·3
S. „	9122·5 †	9123·9	— 1·4
W. „	9121·0	9119·2	+ 1·8

Here the mean difference in the scale of R.E. from 1881 is only — ·8, ± ·6 for the absolute length; whereas the 1874 base differs + 2·0 on the same length. The R.E. therefore confirms the 1881 result.

The relative advantages of the two bases of 1874 and 1881 are as follows.

---

* I have heard, on the best authority, that the method for this survey was by transferring the socket points outwards by theodolite, and measuring along the quasi-level ground between the transferred points; thus the absolute *scale* value is given by four independent measurements.

† This is stated as 9,140; but as the other sides agree so closely with the 1874 and 1881 measures, this would seem to have been measured from a different point. Now the outer W. edge of the socket-block at the S.W. is 17·5 beyond the drawn line (which really defines the socket), and it is therefore about 9,140 from the S.E. corner; hence this was probably taken as the corner, and 17·5 must therefore be deducted from the R.E. measure of this side in comparing it with the other surveys.

The 1874 base was read from the national Egyptian standard of 4 metres, with great care, by microscope micrometers; two readings were taken of each bar length, and the temperature bar was also read. The resulting base of 3,300 inches had a probable error of about ·01 inch, which was far more accurate than the observations of the ends of it by the theodolite. The observations were unhappily not reduced till five years after; and then by an entire stranger to the apparatus. The 1881 base was read from a steel tape which had been accurately compared both with the English public standard, and with a private standard connected with the primary yard (see section 9). The readings of it were made to $\frac{1}{100}$ inch on 100 foot lengths; and thermometers were continually read, both on ground and in air; cloudy sky, and nearly equal temperature of ground and air being obtained. Not only were three or four readings of each length taken in each set, but three entirely separate sets of measurements were made on separate days; and the resulting mean value of 7,900 inches, has a probable error of only ·03. The transferrance apparatus was very simple, and free from a chance of shifts or errors. The observations were all reduced by one of the observers, on the days when they were each made. Though therefore the instrument, and probably the observations, were superior in 1874, yet the three independent series in 1881—the immediate reduction of the observations—and the agreement of the R.E. survey—combine to render it more likely that an error of ·7 inch exists by shift, by transferrance, or by misinterpreting the note-books, in the 1874 observations, than that an error of 1·7 exists in the 1881 observations.

There does not seem then to be any reason for not accepting the 1881 observations as they stand, as being the most accurate survey yet obtained; with the proviso that in no case is it the least likely that the true scale differs from it more than $\frac{1}{4000}$, or that the proportional distances are $\frac{1}{60000}$ in error.

CHAPTER XXII.

A SKETCH OF THE HISTORY AND DESIGN OF THE GREAT PYRAMID.

164. AT the close of the period of the third dynasty, the hill of Gizeh was a bare stretch of desert ground, overlooking the Nile valley. In ages long before this dawn of living history,* that valley had been deeply scored out in the great tract of limestone rocks through which it passes; scored by the deep and rushing stream† which filled the whole width of it from cliff to cliff. This stream was fed along its course by cataracts, dashing down through gorges on either side of it; and thus forming a series of cascades, which continually ate further back into the cliffs of the great river.‡ The present stream, meandering slowly in a channel washed out amid its mud flats, and covering its ancient limits with a few inches or feet of water but once a year, would seem a mere ditch if compared with its former grandeur.

In the days when the fourth dynasty arose, these changes were long past; and the valley would probably seem as familiar now to Prince Merhet, Semnefer the architect, and the rest of the court of Khufu, as it did in the days of their power. Above the then growing city of Memphis rose the low hills and cliffs of the desert on the Libyan side; and one of the higher parts of the edge of the desert, a bare wind-blown rise of hill, attracted the attention of Khufu for the site of his great monument. It is certainly the finest site for miles on either side of it; and probably the happiness of the blessed West in contrast to the filthy East, and the nearness to the capital, Memphis, induced him to build here, even though the materials had to be brought from the higher and more commanding cliffs of the eastern bank.

It may seem strange that the site chosen was not rather further from the edge of the cliff, and thus on a higher part of the rock. But the principle in the early days seems to have been to place the tomb as near to the home as possible; the tomb was looked on with pride and satisfaction; it was the place where a man would be periodically remembered and honoured by his descendants; it

---

* See Climatic Changes, section 111.   † See the banks of scoured *débris* at Beni Hassan.

‡ See the cliffs at Masara, Tehneh, Girgeh, Thebes, &c.; and particularly the gorge south of Beni Hassan, which ends in high waterfalls, with deep basins scooped out at the feet of them.

was—as Aseskaf called his Pyramid—the " cool place," or " place of refreshing," where the body would rest in peace until revivified ; a character of the deep rock-hewn chambers most pleasing in such a climate.   Hence we find the tombs clustered as thickly as possible, where they actually look on the valley at Gizeh ; and scattered less closely where but little of the sacred stream could be seen ; and similarly Khufu placed his Pyramid on a slight rise of rock, as close to the edge of the cliff as possible.

To understand the purpose of the erection of the Pyramids, it should be observed that each has a temple on the eastern side of it.   Of the temples of the Second and Third Pyramids the ruins still remain ; and of the temple of the Great Pyramid, the basalt pavement and numerous blocks of granite show its site.   That Khufu's temple is more destroyed than the others is easily accounted for by the causeway of it being larger and more accessible from the plain than are the causeways of the temples of Khafra and Menkaura ; hence it would naturally be the first attacked by the spoilers.   When in all the tombs of the Pyramid age, we see that the kings are called the Great Gods (" nuter aa "), and had more priests than any of the original deities, it is easy to understand the relationship of a sumptuous temple to each of the royal Pyramids.   The worship of the deified king was carried on in the temple, looking toward the Pyramid which stood on the west of it (the " blessed West," the land of souls) ; just as private individuals worshipped their ancestors in the family tombs, looking toward the "false doors," which are placed on the west side of the tomb, and which represent the entrances to the hidden sepulchres.

165. It has always been assumed that only the finer stone, used for the casing and passages, was brought from the eastern cliffs, and that the bulk of the masonry was quarried in the neighbourhood.   But no quarryings exist on the western side in the least adequate to yield the bulk of either of the greater Pyramids* ; and the limestone of the western hills is different in its character to that of the Pyramid masonry, which resembles the qualities usually quarried on the eastern shore.   It seems, therefore, that the whole of the stones were quarried in the cliffs of Turra and Masara, and brought across to the selected site.

166. The great amount of labour involved in quarrying and transporting such a mass of masonry as even the casing, has always been a cause of astonishment.   But an expression in the traditions reported by Herodotus,† and a consideration of the internal economy of the country in the present day, seem to explain it.   In describing the transport of the stones, Herodotus expressly

* I have repeatedly examined the edge of the desert from Abu Roash to Dahshur, and walked over all the district behind the Pyramids for several miles in each direction ; some very slight quarrying just behind the barracks at the Second Pyramid is all that I have seen, beyond mere tomb excavations.   † See Section 120.

states that 100,000 men worked at one time, " each party during three months ;" now the inundation lasts rather more than three months in the present day, and during that time the inhabitants are almost idle, the land is covered with water, the cattle are fed on dry fodder, and wander on the barren desert ; but few hands are needed to regulate the flow of water into the dammed-up basins of the country, and the greater part of the population turn willingly to any employment they can get, or dream away their time in some cool shade. Here, then, is the explanation of the vast amount of labour extracted from a country of limited area. It was during the three months of the inundation that the idle hands were set to all the mere routine of unskilled labour ; and while the Nile was at its full height, rafts were busily employed in floating over the masses of hewn stone, from the causeways at the quarries, across the five miles width of waters, to the Pyramid causeway, about seven miles further down the stream. It is noticeable that the period of three months is only mentioned in connection with the removal of the stones, and not with the actual quarrying or building ; on these labours probably a large staff of skilled masons were always employed, though they were helped on by an abundance of unskilled labour, for the heavy work of lifting and transport, during the three months when the general population was out of work.

The actual course of work, then, during the building of the Pyramid, would have been somewhat as follows :—At the end of July, when the Nile had fairly risen, the levy of 100,000 men would assemble to the work. Not more than eight men could well work together on an average block of stone of 40 cubic feet or 2½ tons ; and the levies would probably be divided into working parties of about that number. If, then, each of these parties brought over 10 average blocks of stone in their three months' labour—taking a fortnight to bring them down the causeways at the quarries, a day or two of good wind to take them across the stream, six weeks to carry them up the Pyramid causeway, and four weeks to raise them to the required place on the Pyramid —they would easily accomplish their task in the three months of high Nile. They would thus be at liberty to return to their own occupations in the beginning of November when the land was again accessible.

Of course the actual distribution of labour would be more specialized ; but this outline will show that such a scale of work would suffice for the complete building of the Great Pyramid in twenty years as stated by Herodotus.* We thus see that the whole of the material, and not merely the casing, could readily be obtained from the eastern shore ; and that the levies need not have been

---

* The Great Pyramid contained about 2,300,000 stones, averaging 50 × 50 × 28 inches, or 2½ tons each. If 8 men brought 10 stones, 100,000 would bring 125,000 stones each season or the total number in less than 20 years.

employed during more than the three months when all ordinary labour was suspended.

Beside these hosts of unskilled hands, there must have been a smaller body of masons permanently employed in quarrying the stone, and in trimming it at the Pyramid. And it is likely that a year's supply of stone would be kept on hand at the Pyramid, on which the masons would work; and so the three months' supply of labourers would put up the stones which had been trimmed and arranged during the nine months' previously, while other labourers were engaged bringing over a supply for the masons' work of the ensuing nine months.

This system of employing all the unskilled labour of the country on public work, when the lands were inundated, private labour was impossible, and the Nile was in the fittest state for transport, is almost certain to have been followed in all the great works of the Egyptians; and the peculiarity of the country may go far toward explaining their capacity for executing vast public works.

What the number of skilled masons was we may well guess from the accommodation provided for them in the barracks behind the Second Pyramid (see section 72). These barracks were used by the workmen of Khafra; but those of Khufu must have been equally numerous, and have occupied a similar space, if not, indeed, these identical dwellings. These barracks would hold 3,600 or 4,000 men easily; and as about 120,000 average blocks were required to be prepared every year, this would be only one block of stone prepared in a month by a party of four men, which would probably be the number of masons working together. Hence this accommodation is really more than enough; and most likely a good deal of lifting and building work would be going on throughout the year, beside the great supply of labour during the inundation.

Thus we see that the traditional accounts that we have of the means employed in building the Great Pyramid, require conditions of labour-supply which are quite practicable in such a land, which would not be ruinous to the prosperity of the country, or oppressive to the people, and which would amply and easily suffice for the execution of the whole work.

167. The site being chosen, it was carefully levelled, and the lengths of the sides were set out with great exactitude (see section 21). How the angles were made square within 12″ average error is difficult to see; the rock rising up irregularly in steps inside the masonry, to some 25 feet high, would render accurate diagonal measurements very difficult; unless, indeed, narrow trenches or passages were cut from corner to corner to measure through.

The setting out of the orientation of the sides (see section 93) would not be so difficult. If a pile of masonry some 50 feet high was built up with a vertical side from North to South, a plumb-line could be hung from its top, and observations could be made, to find the places· on the ground from which the pole-star was seen to transit behind the line at the elongations, tweve hours apart. The mean of these positions would be due South of the plumb-line, and about 100 feet distant from it ; on this scale 15″ of angle would be about $\frac{1}{10}$ inch, and therefore quite perceptible.

168. From several indications it seems that the masons planned the casing, and some at least of the core masonry also, course by course on the ground. For on all the casing, and on the core on which the casing fitted, there are lines drawn on the horizontal surfaces, showing where each stone was to be placed on those below it. If the stones were merely trimmed to fit each other as the building went on, there would be no need to have so carefully marked the place of each block in this particular way ; and it shows that they were probably planned and fitted together on the ground below. Another indication of very careful and elaborate planning on the ground is in the topmost space over the King's Chamber ; there the roofing-beams were numbered, and marked for the north or south sides; and though it might be thought that it could be of no consequence in what order they were placed, yet all their details were evidently schemed before they were delivered to the builders' hands. This care in arranging all the work agrees strikingly with the great employment of unskilled labourers during two or three months at a time, as they would then raise all the stones which the masons had worked and stored ready for use since the preceding season.

169. The means employed for raising such masses of stone is not shown to us in any representations. For the ordinary blocks, of a few tons each, it would be very feasible to employ the method of resting them on two piles of wooden slabs, and rocking them up alternately to one side and the other by a spar under the block, thus heightening the piles alternately and so raising the stone. This would also agree with the mysterious description of a machine made of short pieces of wood—a description which is difficult otherwise to realise. This method would also be applicable to the largest masses that we know of in the Pyramid, the 56 roofing-beams of the King's Chamber and the spaces above it. These average 320 × 52 × 73 inches, or 700 cubic feet each ; weighing, therefore, 54 tons, some larger, some less. No simple system but that of rocking would enable men to raise such a mass with only the help of crowbars ; if such a block was put on two supports, say 30 inches apart, only 5 tons would have to be lifted at once, and this would be easily done by 10 men with crowbars. Six such parties might raise the whole of these blocks in one year.

170. That sheet iron was employed we know, from the fragment found by Howard Vyse in the masonry of the south air channel ; and though some doubt has been thrown on the piece, merely from its rarity, yet the vouchers for it are very precise ; and it has a cast of a nummulite on the rust of it, proving it to have been buried for ages beside a block of nummulitic limestone, and therefore to be

certainly ancient. No reasonable doubt can therefore exist about its being really a genuine piece used by the Pyramid masons; and probably such pieces were required to prevent crowbars biting into the stones, and to ease the action of the rollers.

The tools employed have been described in the chapter on the mechanical methods; they comprised bronze saws over eight feet long, set with jewels, tubular drills similarly set with jewels, and circular saws. These were employed on the granite work, and perhaps saws of a less costly nature on the limestone The casing blocks were dressed by very fine picking or adzing. The system of using true planes smeared with ochre, for testing the work, shows with what nicety they examined their work, and what care was taken to ensure its accuracy and truth.

The masons' waste chips were thrown away over the cliffs, on both the north and south of the Pyramid; and they form banks extending about 100 yards outwards from the original edge of the rock, and reaching from top to bottom of the cliffs; taking them altogether they are probably equal in bulk to more than half of the Pyramid. This rubbish is all stratified at the angle of rest, about 40°; and the different qualities of it thrown away on different days may be clearly seen. In one part there will be a layer of large chips, up to the size of a hand; a foot above that a lot of fine dust and sweepings; above that perhaps more large chips, and here and there a layer of desert flints and sand, showing when a piece of desert ground had been cleared to get more space for working. Among all this rubbish are pieces of the workmen's water-jars and food vessels, of which I collected a hundred or more fragments, mixed with chips of wood, bits of charcoal, and even a piece of string, which had probably been used in patching up a rubbish basket. All these were obtained from pits which had been lately made in the oldest part of the heap, close to the edge of the cliff, and beyond which a thickness of some dozens of yards of waste had been shot out; there is thus a certainty that these remains show us the true masons' waste and rubbish, as thrown away by the builders, and stretching out from the cliff in lines of "tip," like a modern half-finished embankment.

By means of this bank of waste, the space around the Pyramid was largely increased in appearance, though it was not solid ground for building; and the tops of the rubbish heaps were smoothly levelled down in the nearer parts, so that their junction to the rock can hardly be traced.

171. During the course of building there was evidently a great change in the style of the work; a change, however, belonging more to the builders than to the masons. The pavement, lower casing, and entrance passage are exquisitely wrought; in fact, the means employed for placing and cementing the blocks of soft limestone, weighing a dozen to twenty tons each, with such hair-like joints (section 26) are almost inconceivable at present; and the accuracy of

the levelling is marvellous (section 26). But in the higher parts, the gallery, for instance, is far from such excellence ; and the upper part of it is very skew and irregular, the ramp surface being tilted more than an inch in a width of 20 inches. In the Antechamber the granite has never been dressed down flat, and defective stones are employed ; where the limestone was very bad, it was roughly plastered over, and many parts are strangely rough. In the King's Chamber the masonry is very fine, both in its accuracy of fitting and in the squareness and equal height of all the blocks ; but the builders were altogether wrong in their levels, and tilted the whole chamber over to one corner, so that their courses are $2\frac{1}{4}$ inches higher at the N.E. than at the S.W., a difference much greater than that in the whole base of the Pyramid. An error like this in putting together such a magnificent piece of work, is astonishing, for the walls are composed of nearly $\frac{1}{10}$ of a mile length of granite blocks about 4 feet high, and probably as thick, all of which are gauged to the same height with an average variation of only $\frac{1}{20}$ of an inch. As it would be difficult to suppose any architect allowing such errors of building, after so closely restricting the variations of masons' work, it strongly suggests that the granite had been prepared for the chamber long before it was built, and that the supervision was less strict as the work went on, owing to more hurry and less care, or owing to the death of the man who had really directed the superfine accuracy of the earlier work.

172. Beside these signs of carelessness, there are several points in which work that has been intended has never been carried out. The stone was left in the rough where it was liable to damage, and was to be finished off after it was safe from injury. Over the N. doorway of the gallery the stone is left roughly in excess ; and in the Queen's Chamber the vertical edge of the doorway is left with an excess of an inch or more, and as a guide a short bit was drafted to the true surface at the top and bottom of each stone (section 42). From these points we see that not only was the work hurried about the middle, but that some parts never received the finishing strokes.

The plan of the passages was certainly altered once, and perhaps oftener, during the course of building. The shaft, or "well," leading from the N. end of the gallery down to the subterranean parts, was either not contemplated at first, or else was forgotten in the course of building ; the proof of this is that it has been cut through the masonry after the courses were completed. On examining the shaft, it is found to be irregularly tortuous through the masonry, and without any arrangement of the blocks to suit it ; while in more than one place a corner of a block may be seen left in the irregular curved side of the shaft, all the rest of the block having disappeared in cutting the shaft. This is a conclusive point, since it would never have been so built at first. A similar feature is at the mouth of the passage, in the gallery. Here the sides of the mouth are very well cut, quite as good work as the dressing of the gallery walls; but on the S. side there is a vertical joint in the gallery side, only 5·3 inches from the mouth. Now, great care is always taken in the Pyramid to put large stones at a corner, and it is quite inconceivable that a Pyramid builder would put a mere slip 5·3 thick beside the opening to a passage. It evidently shows that the passage mouth was cut out after the building was finished in that part. It is clear, then, that the whole of this shaft is an additional feature to the first plan.

Another evidence of altered plans is in the Queen's Chamber floor. This is not merely left in the rough core, but it has actually had another course of the rough core masonry built, or at least fitted, on to it; and this upper course has been removed, or omitted, in order to build the chamber there. Of the Subterranean Chamber, all that can be said is that it is wholly unfinished, and hardly more than sketched out; so that a change of plan with regard to that also seems proved, since it was the part first begun.

173. Having now pointed out various mechanical considerations on the history of the building, we will consider the history of the closing of the Pyramid.

There can be doubt that the entrance passage was left clear and accessible (sections 125–6), the door closing it on the outside against mere chance curiosity, but being readily swung on its pivots when regularly opened. The upper passages, however, were well concealed, though they had probably been surreptitiously entered before the Arabic forcing (section 58).

It has often been said that the Queen's Chamber was intended to contain the blocks for plugging the ascending passage, until they were required to be let down. But there is an absolute impossibility in this theory; the blocks are 47·3 × 41·6 in section, while the Queen's Chamber passage is but 46·2 × 40·6, or too small in both dimensions to allow the blocks to pass. Hence the blocks must have stood in the gallery until they were wanted, since they could never be got upwards through the ascending passage, as that is but 38·2 at the lower end, and the existing plugs are 41·6 wide above that. Neither could the plugs be brought up the well shaft, as that is but 28· square; nor out of the King's Chamber, as the passage is but 43·6 high. Now, though it is most likely that there never were many plug-blocks (see section 125), yet the existing ones land us in a further conclusion. The broken end of the upper block, and a chip of granite still remaining cemented to the floor of the passage a little above that, show that it was probably 24 inches longer than it is now, judging by marks on the passage. Thus the total length of plug-blocks would be about 203 inches, or very probably 206 inches, or 10 cubits, like so many lengths marked out in that passage. Now, the flat part of the Queen's Chamber passage floor within the gallery, on which blocks might be placed, is but 176 long ; and the whole distance, from the N. wall of the gallery to the vertical cut down, is but 199·4 : so in no way could 203 inches of blocks stand on the horizontal floor, and certainly any passage through the gallery door would be impossible, to say nothing of the difficulty of pushing such blocks along a rough floor, so as to tip them down the passage. Thus the plug-blocks cannot have stood in any place except on the sloping floor of the gallery.

For them, then, to be slid down the passage, it was necessary that the opening to the Queen's Chamber should be completely covered with a continuous floor. The traces of this floor may still be seen, in the holes for beams of stone, across the passage ; and in fragments of stone and cement still sticking on the floor of the Queen's Chamber passage at that point. It is certain, then, that the Queen's Chamber was closed and concealed before the ascending passage was closed.

But we are met then by an extraordinary idea, that all access to the King's Chamber after its completion must have been by climbing over the plug-blocks, as they lay in the gallery, or by walking up the ramps on either side of them. Yet, as the blocks cannot physically have been lying in any other place before they were let down, we are shut up to this view.

The coffer cannot have been put into the Pyramid after the King's Chamber was finished, as it is nearly an inch wider than the beginning of the ascending passage.

The only conclusion, then, is that the coffer was placed in the King's Chamber before the roof was put on ; that, if Khufu was finally buried in it (and not in some more secret place), then the inner coffin, and any procession accompanying it, must have gone up the gallery, on the narrow-side ramps or benches, past the plug-blocks four feet high standing between them ; that before or after this the Queen's Chamber was blocked up ; then the plug-blocks were slid down the ascending passage; and, finally, the workmen retired by the well shaft down to the entrance passage, closing the way by a plug of stone not cemented in place, and probably removable at will (see section 58). Finally, the lower mouth of the well shaft was closed, probably by a plugging-block not cemented in ; and then visitors of later times crawled in under the outer flap-door in the casing, the stone that could be " lifted out," and so went down to the empty and unfinished Subterranean Chamber in the rock.

174. It may be an open question whether the Queen's Chamber* was not the sepulchre of Khnumu-Khufu (section 113), the co-regent of Khufu. Edrisi, in

---

* These names, King's and Queen's, were given by the Arabs, in conformity with their custom of making the tombs or niches for men flat-topped, and those for women with a sloping gable roof.

his accurate and observant account of the Pyramid (1236 A.D.), mentions an empty vessel in the Queen's Chamber; and that this was not a confused notion of the coffer now known, is proved by his saying that in the King's Chamber "an empty vessel is seen here similar to the former." Whether any fragments of a coffer remained there, among the great quantity of stone excavated from the floor and niche, it is almost hopeless to inquire, since that rubbish is now all shot away into various holes and spaces. Caviglia, however, did not find a coffer when clearing the chamber, but fragments might have been easily over-looked.

175. When, then, was the Pyramid first violated? Probably by the same hands that so ruthlessly destroyed the statues and temples of Khafra, and the Pyramids of Abu Roash, Abusir, and Sakkara. That is to say, probably during the civil wars of the seventh to the tenth dynasties (see section 119). At that time the secret opening of the Pyramid, by which the workmen retired, would still be known; and while that was the case, and before any forced openings had been made (section 58), the coffer was lifted up to see if any hidden passage existed beneath it; then probably was its lid broken off, and the body of the great builder treated to the spite of his enemies. Then also may the Queen's Chamber —the *serdab** of the Pyramid—have been forced open, and the diorite statue torn from its grand niche, broken up, pedestal and all, and carried out to be smashed to chips, and scattered on the hill opposite the Pyramid door, so that no one should ever restore it. This is more of a guess than an inference; and yet a guess, so far harmonious with what we know of other monuments, that it perhaps deserves to be used as a working hypothesis.

In classical times we know from Strabo that the subterranean parts were readily accessible; though the supposed proof adduced by Caviglia, from I A" M E R (M E joined) which he found smoked on the roof of the Subterranean Chamber, has nothing to do with the question; if he had noted the graffiti around the entrance of the Pyramid, he would have found I Aᶜ MERCATOR 1563 (M E joined), which completely explains the smoked letters.

176. With regard to the many records of inscriptions on the outside of the Pyramid, a few words are necessary. From the time of Herodotus down to the 15th century, inscriptions are continually mentioned, and their great abundance is described with astonishment by travellers. This has led to the supposition that the builders had left records inscribed on the outside, although not a letter is to be found on the inside. But against the possibility of this view, it must be remembered that no early inscriptions are found on the casing remaining at the Great Pyramid, nor on any of the innumerable fragments of those stones, nor on the remaining casing of the Second Pyramid, nor on that of the Third Pyramid, nor on the casing of the South Pyramid of Dahshur, nor on the casing of the

* Serdab is the Arabic name for the secret hollow in tombs in which the statue was placed.

2 F

Pyramid of Medum, nor on occasional blocks uncovered at the Sakkara Pyramids. In fact, not a single example of hieroglyphs has ever been seen on any casing, nor on any fragments of casing. The truth then about these numberless inscriptions appears to be that they were all travellers' graffiti. Strabo says that the characters were like old Greek, but were not readable; this points to Phœnician or Cypriote graffiti. The accounts of the inscriptions given by the Arabs also show that they were mere graffiti; Abu Masher Jafer (before 886 A.D.) mentions Mosannad (*i.e.*, Himyaritic) letters; Ibn Khordadbeh (10th cent.) also mentions Musnad letters; Masudi (11th cent.) describes them as being in various different languages; Ibr Haukal (11th cent.) says they were in Greek; Abu Mothaffer (*alias* Sibt Al Jauzi, died 1250 A.D.) gives the fullest account, mentioning seven sorts of writing: (1) Greek, (2) Arabic, (3) Syriac, (4) Musnadic, (5) Himyaritic (or Hiritic or Hebrew in different MSS.), (6) Rumi, (7) Persian. William of Baldensel (1336 A.D.) mentions Latin; and Cyriacus (1440 A.D.) mentions Phœnician. Whether these travellers all understood exactly what they were talking about may be doubted; but at least none of them describe hieroglyphs, such as they must have been familiar with on all the tombs and other monuments; and they agree in the great diversity of the languages inscribed. The earlier travellers also do not describe such a great number of inscriptions as do the Arabic writers; suggesting that the greater part recorded in later times were due to Roman and Coptic graffiti.

Now among the hundreds of pieces of casing stones that I have looked over, very few traces of inscription were to be seen; this was, however, to be expected, considering that the pieces nearly all belonged to the upper casing stones, out of the reach of mere travellers. Three examples of single letters were found, two Greek and one unknown; and on the W. side, in one of the excavations, a piece was discovered bearing three graffiti, one large one attracting lesser scribblers, as in modern times. The earliest inscription was probably of Ptolemy X., showing portions of the letters Π T O .... C ω T ....; the next was a Romano-Greek of a certain M A P K I O C K......; and over that an Arab had roughly hammered in ......m a j...... This is the only example of continuous inscriptions yet found, and it belonged to one of the lowest courses; it is now in the Bulak Museum. Thus, all the fragments and the descriptions point to the existence of a large body of graffiti, but do not give any evidence of original hieroglyphic inscriptions.

When one considers the large number of graffiti which are to be seen on every ancient building of importance, it seems almost impossible but that the Great Pyramid—one of the most renowned and visited of all—should not have been similarly covered with ancient scribbles, like the host of modern names which have been put upon it since the casing was removed.* The statues of

* Described and figured in "Archæological Journal," 1883.

Ramessu II., at Abu Simbel, bear quantities of Greek graffiti, in fact, some of the earliest Greek inscriptions known, besides Phœnician and Roman ; the top of the temple of Khonsu at Karnak is crowded with the outlines of visitors' feet, with their names and particulars appended, in hieroglyphic, demotic, and Greek ; the inscriptions on the colossi of Amenhotep III. (" the Memnons ") at Thebes, and on the Sphinx at Gizeh are well known ; the long scribbles in demotic on the temple walls at Thebes have lately been examined ; the corridors of Abydos bear early Greek graffiti ; the passage of the S. Pyramid of Dahshur has two hieroglyphic graffiti, besides Greek ; and there is scarcely any monument of importance in Egypt but what shows the scribbling propensities of mankind ; be they Egyptians, Phœnicians, Greeks, Romans, or the worst sinners of modern times, Hellenes and Americans.

177. The history of the destruction of the Pyramids really begins with the Arabs. They first, under Khalif Mamun, forced the great hole through the masonry, from the outside to the part commonly called Mamun's Hole, at the beginning of the ascending passage. Had it not been for their shaking of the masonry, which let fall the stone that concealed the plug-blocks, perhaps the upper chambers would have remained yet unknown. Hearing the stone drop, they turned aside their southward progress, and burrowing some twenty feet eastwards they broke into the entrance passage, and found the fallen stone ; here they saw that it had covered the beginning of another passage, and so they forced out of their hole a continuation southward and upward to get behind the granite plug ; finding they only hit the side of the plug-blocks, they tracked along them in the softer limestone, until they reached the upper end, and then they rushed freely up the hitherto unused passage. Probably they found the plug at the top of the well not replaced, after the earlier destroyers ; and so got down the well and forced out its lower closing, which must have been in position for the Greeks and Romans not to have been aware of the passage. Such, from the statements of historians, and the details of the place, seems to have been the history of the attack on the interior of the Great Pyramid.

After the time of Mamun the exterior was used as a quarry ; the casing was apparently stripped off by Sultan Hasan for his mosque in 1356, since he is said to have brought the stone hence, and William of Baldensel* in 1336 mentions both the large Pyramids as being " de maximis lapidibus et politis." It was also Hasan, or a near successor of his, who stripped the Second Pyramid ; as I found a coin of his deep down in the S.E. foundation. The top was not much denuded in the 17th century ; Lambert (Trois Relations de l'Ægypte) in 1630 mentions 12 stones as forming the top of the core, and says that the platform was 20 spans wide ; by his span measures of the coffer, this would be 230 inches ; among these 12 stones was " une qui surpasse en largueur et longeur la

---

* Canisius, " Thesaurus Monumentum," iv. 342.

croyance des hommes." Greaves in 1638 found 9 stones, and reports two as missing. Thevenot in 1667 reports 12 stones ; but as he understood Arabic well he probably accepted a statement of what had been there thirty years before. Other stones of the top and edges of the core were thrown down at intervals, until the beginning of the present century, as is evident from the weathering marks, and the dates of the graffiti.

178. Having now sketched out its history, it is desirable not to close this account of the Great Pyramid, without summing up those theories of its design which seem most likely, and which are consistent one with the other. In the following sketch, then, no theory will be mentioned which is not well within the facts of the case, and no dimensions will be required to do double duty for two theories which do not coincide. It is possible that some parts may have been made intentionally varying in size, in order to include two different relations to other parts ; but such is scarcely provable ; and in a general statement like the following, it is better to omit some things that may be true, than it is to include a number of dubious theories which are not supported by a system of coincidences in different parts of the structure. And if some judge that this summary includes too much, and others think that it states too little, it must be remembered that the whole of the materials for forming an opinion are impartially provided in the previous chapters of this work.

For the whole form the π proportion (height is the radius of a circle = circumference of Pyramid) has been very generally accepted of late years, and is a relation strongly confirmed by the presence of the numbers 7 and 22 in the number of cubits in height and base respectively ; 7 : 22 being one of the best known approximations to π. With these numbers (or some slight fractional correction on the 22) the designer adopted 7 of a length of 20 double cubits for the height ; and 22 of this length for the half-circuit. The profile used for the work being thus 14 rise on 11 base.

The form and size being thus fixed, the floor of the main chamber of the building—the King's Chamber—was placed at the level where the vertical section of the Pyramid was halved, where the area of the horizontal section was half that of the base, where the diagonal from corner to corner was equal to the length of the base, and where the width of the face was equal to half the diagonal of the base.*

The Queen's Chamber was placed at half this height above the base; and exactly in the middle of the Pyramid from N. to S.

* The employment of square measure, which appears to furnish the best solution of the Pyramid design, is singularly parallel to the use of square measure mentioned in the " Sulvasutras ;" from those writings it appears that Hindu geometry in its origin sprung from the religious ideas of the building of altars, differing in form but equal in area. (See Prof. Thibaut in the Second " International Congress of Orientalists.")

Beside the level of the King's Chamber signalizing where the area was a simple fraction of $\frac{1}{3}$ of the base area, thicker courses were perhaps intentionally introduced where the area of the course was a multiple of $\frac{1}{20}$ the base area : this system accounts for nearly all the curious examples of a thick course being suddenly brought in, with a series above it gradually diminishing until another thick course occurs.

The angle of slope of the entrance passage is 1 rise on 2 base ; and the other passages are near the same angle, probably modified in order to bring the chambers to the required levels.

The length of the entrance passage, the ascending passage, the antechamber passages, and perhaps the Queen's Chamber passage, are all in round numbers of cubits ; while the gallery length (horizontal) is equal to the vertical height of its end above the base, which is determined by the King's Chamber being at the level of half the Pyramid area.

The height and width of the passages, gallery, and ramps are all determined by the form of the end of the King's Chamber, of which the passages are $\frac{1}{5}$, the gallery $\frac{2}{5}$ and the ramps $\frac{1}{10}$ the size in each direction.

The King's Chamber walls are determined by the same π proportion which rules the exterior of the Pyramid ; the circuit of the side of the chamber being equal to a circle described by its width as a radius ; and further, the length of the side of the chamber is equal to diameter of its circuit. Thus the circuit of the side has its radius at right angles across the chamber, and its diameter the length of the side along the chamber.

But the floor of the chamber is raised above the base of the walls ; a peculiar arrangement for which some reason must have existed. It gives in fact two heights ; the wall height we have just seen is required for the π proportion ; and the actual height from the floor agrees to another system, which is found to run throughout all the chambers. After the attention shown to square measure in the various levels of the Pyramid, it is not surprising to find something of the same kind in the chambers. Though the idea of making the squares of the lineal dimensions of a chamber to be integral areas, may seem peculiar, yet the beauty of thus making all the diagonals of a chamber to be on one uniform system with its direct dimensions, would be perhaps a sufficient inducement to lead the builders to its adoption. Practically it is the only consistent and uniform theory which is applicable to all the chambers and coffer, and even to the Second Pyramid chamber. By this theory, then, the squares of the dimensions of the King's Chamber, the Queen's Chamber, the Antechamber, and the Subterranean Chamber, are all even numbers of square cubits, and nearly all multiples of 10. From this it necessarily follows that the squares of all the diagonals of the sides of these chambers, and their cubic diagonals, are likewise multiples of 10 square cubits ; and the King's and Queen's Chambers are so arranged that the cubic diagonals are in even hundreds of square cubits, or multiples of 10 cubits squared.

For the coffer it it hard to say what theory is most likely; its irregularities of form and faults of cutting, are such that many theories are included in its variations; and certainly no theory of very great complexity or refinement, can be expected. Taking most of its dimensions at their maximum, they agree closely with the same theory as that which is applicable to the chambers; for when squared they are all even multiples of a square fifth of a cubit. That the cubit was divided decimally in the fourth dynasty we know (see section 139); and as this theory is also the only one applicable to all the chambers, there is very strong ground for adopting it here. There is no other theory applicable to every lineal dimension of the coffer; but having found the π proportion in the form of the Pyramid, and in the King's Chamber, there is some ground for supposing that it was intended also in the coffer, on just $\frac{1}{5}$th the scale of the chamber; the difference between the requirements of this theory and that of the squares is only $\frac{1}{1500}$. Consistently also with the above theories, the outer length at an extreme maximum, may have been $\frac{1}{100}$ of the length of the Pyramid base; and as the inner length of the Second Pyramid coffer has the same relation to its Pyramid, this is rendered the more likely. Finally, it is not impossible that some rough relation of the cubic bulk and contents may have been aimed at, along with the foregoing designs; and the lineal dimensions required above, being nearly all maximum dimensions of the actual coffer, renders it more likely that some other object was in view. In any case the cubic relations were not very exactly attained, and it would have been impossible to run them closer by merely sawing the granite, somewhat skew, somewhat curved, and somewhat too deeply, without any adjustment afterwards by polishing. The design of a coffer which should include more than one idea, would not be unlikely in the Great Pyramid; that structure being so remarkable for the care and precision shown in the arrangement of its chambers, and particularly for the accuracy of the chamber in which the coffer is enshrined.

Such is the outline of what may be considered the tolerably safe theories of the origination of the Great Pyramid; others may by some further discovery be shown to have been intended, but most of these will probably bear the test of time, and certainly bear the test of exact measurement.

APPENDIX I.

ON THE ARRANGEMENT OF A TRIANGULATION.

179. In arranging the course of a triangulation, for a survey in which the distances are short, many questions require to be considered, which never arise in ordinary cases of delicate observing. The lineal errors of centreing the instrument and signals become in many, perhaps most, instances as great as the angular errors of the observations. And further, as some of the stations are merely needed in the course of the triangulating, while others are required to permanently fix certain ancient points, the different character of the classes of the stations have, therefore, to be taken into consideration.

Of course, in every survey, the number of observations is limited ; and the question therefore arises how to distribute the observations so as to obtain the most accurate results. As a general rule, if there be a number of equally determined stations around a point which has to be fixed, it will be best to distribute the observations to and from it, equally among all the stations, as thus their individual errors of position will be neutralized and not transmitted. But, if among the stations around the point, some are much better fixed than others, it will be best to take more observations to and from those superior stations.

Hence it is concluded that every station must have a certain weight of observations (or accuracy) assigned to it, to be aimed at ; and a suitable number of observations to—and from—it ; giving it, of course, a greater number of observations if the conditions are bad, as when there is a want of good cross-bearing in the directions of the observations.

180. Having, then, a given weight of accuracy, and a corresponding number of observations, assigned to each station, how should this be distributed ? In considering this it must be remembered that shifting the instrument and signals takes time equivalent to a certain number of observations ; hence it is desirable to limit the number of instrumental stations, or *from*-stations ; and make some to be only *to*-stations, on which signals are observed. Again the time of putting up observing signals (or testing the adjustment of them) over the stations, is equal to making several observations ; hence only those stations really required should be observed *to*.

The distinction should also be kept in mind, between (1) stations *required-for-themselves*, to fix points needed in the plan; and (2) stations *required-for-others*, to complete triangles, carry forward triangulation, &c., but which are of no further value when the results are obtained. If stations are only required-for-themselves, observations *to* them are sufficient, and save time in moving the instrument: beside this, observing *from* a station requires extra observations; a point may be fixed by two observations *to* it, as there are two unknown quantities; whereas it needs three observations *from* it, as there are three unknowns—the two co-ordinates and the zero of azimuth of the circle. But, on the other hand, if a station is required-for-others, observations *from* the station are best, as thus the rotational stiffness of the azimuth of the instrument is increased.

Another consideration is that if the distances are short, and lineal errors of centreings are greater than angular errors of instrument, all stations should be observed *from* as much as possible, so as to increase the number of centreings, and diminish their uncertainties; on the other hand, in long distances, observations *to* are the best, as more can be obtained from a smaller number of stations in a fixed time.

In actually arranging, then, the distribution of observations, after assigning the number proportionate to the accuracy required at each station, the considerations are:—(1) Whether the station is required-for-itself, or required-for-others; (2) whether the station may be only a *to* station, and not a *from* station; *i.e.*, whether the observations to the signal upon it will suffice, without placing the theodolite upon it; and (3) the distance of the stations apart, and the consequent relation of angular to lineal errors between them. Keeping these considerations in view, the number of observations to be taken from each point to each other point is to be allotted, and entered in a table of cross-columns; and then the field book is to be prepared, reading in accordance with this system of distribution.

181. Beside the distribution of the observations, the order of them is most important. Reference to one station at intervals, in order to detect any shifting of the instrument, is but a poor check, as the epoch of any rotational shift cannot be precisely defined. Observations should be broken into small groups, so that there shall be immediate repetitions of allied stations; since any undetected shift will be far more important between the azimuths of two stations close together, than if between those far apart. Supposing, then, the stations A, B, C, near together, K, L, M, another set, and R, S, T, another set, the observations to these stations should be distributed thus:—A, B, C; A, K, B, C; A, K, L, B, C; K, L, B, C; K, L, M, B; K, L, M, R; L, M, R, S; M, R, S, T; R, S, T. Now if a shift is suspected at any point, the values of the azimuths to each station are divided into two groups, one before and the other after that epoch; and the mean value of each group is taken, with its probable error.

Then if there be a constant difference between the first and second groups, in each of the azimuths, which is well beyond the range of the probable errors, the shift may be taken as proved ; or at least as having a certain and calculable probability of its truth. As examples, the following were the shifts detected and eliminated in the course of the 700 observations of the whole triangulation (or a shift on an average at each 80 observations), with the probable errors of each shift ; $1\cdot9''\pm\cdot4''$; $2\cdot4''\pm\cdot2''$; $3\cdot6''\pm\cdot4''$; $3\cdot8''\pm\cdot5''$; $4\cdot2''\pm\cdot4''$; $4\cdot6''\pm\cdot7''$; $6\cdot0''\pm1\cdot5''$; $9\cdot2''\pm\cdot2''$; $11\cdot0''\pm1\cdot0''$. Thus the shifts are on an average over 10 times the extent of their probable errors, showing a probability of their reality, which would run to 12 places of figures. The first reduction applied was always a search for shifts in the series of azimuths, by tabulating all the observations ; and from one cause or other—heating of the instrument, vibration by the wind, accidental touches in handling, &c.—these shifts thus occur to a perceptible amount once on an average of 80 observations. If the observations are treated in the usual way, without eliminating shifts, either they will be vitiated to some extent, or else if the shift be large, they would be lost altogether by the rejection of the whole of a set of observations as " inaccurate."

From the various considerations above mentioned, the distribution and order of the observations were arranged, and then entered in blank form in the field book ; thus in field work the order of the stations as entered had simply to be followed, and the observations filled in as they were made. Such an arrangement may perhaps be set down as too complex for " practical " men ; but a couple of days spent in planning out the work may easily double the value of a month's surveying, and so save a great amount of time on the whole.

Of course, the physical features of the ground generally modify the arrangements to some extent ; as, for instance, if a station is much below the range of sight, the observations then require to be nearly all taken *from* it, since one very accurate centreing of the theodolite, by cross-transiting with an auxiliary theodolite, would suffice, instead of occupying time by setting up a signal with similar accuracy on several different days. In many other ways the irregularity of the field alters the arrangement of the observations, though the distribution of accuracy allotted to each remains unchanged.

APPENDIX II.

THE REJECTION OF DISCORDANT OBSERVATIONS.

182. THIS subject has been so warmly argued, and is at the same time looked on with so much disfavour by some workers, that it may seem presumptuous to discuss it in brief here. But some common-sense considerations seem to have been overlooked, while results were being deduced by more elaborate methods. And, as Airy says, " The calculus (of probabilities) is, after all, a mere tool, by which the decisions of the mind are worked out with accuracy, but which must be directed by the mind."*

In the first place, errors are of two classes : (1) *Continual, i.e.*, present in every observation of a series ; and (2) *Occasional, i.e.*, only present in a few observations. Both these classes presumably, from theory and experience, follow the law of the distribution of error, well known as the Probability Curve.

But, further, to take the continual errors first : this curve of the continual errors is in reality a curve of the sums of the errors due to various independent causes ; for instance, the probable error of judgment in reading a circle might be $\cdot5''$; of judgment in bisecting the object, another $\cdot5''$; of judgment in placing the signal, $=\cdot3''$; of judgment in placing the theodolite, $=\cdot2''$; of flickering of the air, $\cdot6''$; making a probable error on the complete observation equal to $\sqrt{(\cdot5^2+\cdot5^2+\cdot3^2+\cdot2^2+\cdot6^2)}=1\cdot0''$, without reckoning various unobserved sources of error. And as all these sources of error are always present for certain in every observation (only varying in amount), it is plain that it is impossible that they should give rise to discordant observations, in the proper sense of the term, as meaning beyond the normal distribution of the Probability Curve.

But the occasional errors are those which *need* not occur, and which, occuring but seldom, may be to a large extent eliminated from the observations. They doubtless follow the same law of probability as the continual errors ; but owing to their rarity, and the many causes of different extents and different varieties which give rise to them, their regular distribution is not seen. Among these

* " Errors of Observation," 2nd edition, p. 106.

causes are (1) absolute mistakes in reading, generally integral amounts, but sometimes of complements ; (2) mistakes in identifying the signal, and mistakes due to irregular background and illumination of it ; (3) instrumental defects of accidental character, bruises, expansions, &c. ; (4) shifting of the instrument, or of the clamping ; (5) constant lateral refraction in one line of sight, due to a column of heated air from a black stone, a wall face, &c.   There is no place for these occasional errors in the usual classification, except with the continual errors before mentioned.

183. Now the recognition of the difference between these two classes of error will clear away a confusion which has arisen ; one writer claiming that discordant observations should be rejected, while another says that errors of extraordinary extent are recognised by theory as possible, and therefore should never be rejected.   In reality, both views are right ; for though discordant observations should be rejected, if due to occasional errors, yet in continual errors any extent of error has some small amount of probability, decreasing with a diminution of the number of observations.

How, then, are occasional errors to be detected ?   Solely by the application of the law of distribution of errors.   We have no other guide.   If among observations varying only a few seconds, one occurs differing by many minutes or degrees from all the others, no computer could be found to include it in a general mean ; and yet it is rejected solely on account of its improbability, notwithstanding that extraordinary errors are recognised by theory as possible. What theory does *not* recognise, is an erratic distribution of errors ; and it is precisely that which makes a computer throw out such a case as the above, by intuition.

But the occasional errors, as I have said, most likely follow the law of probability, because in all cases in which a smaller error is more likely than a larger (as in all the causes of occasional error noted above), it is plain that the distribution will be like that due to continual errors.   The real distinction between the two classes being that (practically) only a small portion of the observations are affected by occasional errors, and the greater part are absolutely free from them.

If, then, the occasional errors follow the law of probability, they will (as being generally of much larger amount than the continual errors) be distributed over the whole range of continual errors, and far beyond that as well.   But we can only eliminate the affected observations when they lie beyond the range of continual errors ; and we cannot reject them when they lie within those limits. Hence, as they are more evenly and widely distributed than the continual errors (their Probability Curve being much wider), they will, on the whole, raise the probable error and its functions, which are deduced from the observations, even *after* the *apparently* discordant observations are omitted ; in fact, they broaden the Probability Curve of the whole.   Hence the true probable error of the continual errors alone is really less than it appears, even after so-called discordances are removed ; and it is therefore proper to reject observations as being discordant to the full extent of this criterion, and not to save any cases that are near the boundary of acceptance.

184. We should note parenthetically in this section, a system which has been strongly advocated for the treatment of observations. This is by weighting them according to their distance from the simple mean of them all ; and then employing the mean thus found as a fresh starting point for weighting, and so on *ad infinitum*, until a practically stable result is reached. This is so clearly fallacious when worked, that it is strange that it was ever proposed. The impossibility which it involves is seen thus :—Any increase of weight of one observation over another, dependent upon its distance from the mean, must result in displacing the calculated probable error and all its functions in the curve of distribution of the set of observations in question, bringing the probable error much nearer to the centre ; this is at once a denial of the truth of the law of probabilities, and a contradiction of terms which it is useless to discuss further.

Beside this, the practical result of weighting observations inversely as their distances from the mean, is that if the number of observations be even, the mean is eventually thrown in a position anywhere between the two central observations ; as its position is indifferent, provided it only have any equal number of observations on each side of it. Or, if the number is odd, the final mean is immovably fixed to the central observation. If otherwise the weighting is inversely according to *square* of the distance of the observation from the mean, the successive means are attracted more and more to whatever observation is nearest to the first mean, and the final result sticks to this observation ; like a south pole of a magnet, which has taken its choice of a lot of north poles. Thus, both in theory and practice, the idea of any weighting dependent on the distance from a mean is inadmissible.

185. The best practical way of applying the law of probabilities to a group of observations, for the elimation of the occasional errors, will now be considered. A usual method is to extract the probable error, and then (knowing the number of observations) to find from a table what multiple of the probable error the largest variation should be, and reject all beyond that. Of course, this process requires repeating until constant results are obtained, as the first probable error is increased by the discordant observations which are afterwards rejected. The defect of this method is that as the distribution of the most divergent observations is very irregular, owing to their rarity, it is therefore not suitable to regard their *extent*, so much as their *number* in relation to the whole.

On looking at the Probability Curve, it is seen that the point in which its range is best defined (*i.e.*, in the direction of the magnitude of errors) is, of course, at the point of maximum inclination. And this point is identical practically (if not also theoretically) with the square root of the sum of the squares of the differences, divided by the ²√ number of observations, *i.e.*, the " error of mean square " below.

As the various functions have received rather different names, it will be as well to state them here, to avoid confusion. A, refers to Airy in " Errors of Observations ; " D, to De Morgan in " Essay on Probabilities ; " and M, to Merriman, in " Method of Least Squares." The notation adopted is Σv=sum of differences from mean ; Σv^2=sum of squares of differences ; n=number of observations.

" Probable Error" of A.* D. M.	" Mean Error." A. " 2 × mean risk." D. " Average Error." D.	" Error of mean square." A. " Mean Error." M.	" Modulus." A. $\frac{1}{\sqrt{\text{weight}}}$ D.
$\cdot6745 \times \sqrt{\dfrac{\Sigma v^2}{n-1}}$	$\dfrac{\Sigma v}{n}$	$\sqrt{\dfrac{\Sigma v^2}{n-1}}$	$\sqrt{\dfrac{2\Sigma v^2}{n-1}}$
1·000000	1·182946	1·482603	2·096717 × probable error.
·845347	1·000000	1·253314	1·772454 × mean difference.
·6744893	·797884	1·000000	1·414213 × error mean square.
·4769360	·5641906	·7071068	1·000000 × modulus.

These formulæ of course refer to the functions for a *single* observation, and must be $\div \sqrt{n}$ to obtain the functions for the *mean* of a series.

The maximum inclination of the curve being, then, at the error of mean square, the most accurate method of testing observations is to extract this error of mean square from them by the formula ; and then (by the tables of the Probability Curve) ·682 of the number of observations, or a little over ⅔ of all, should have their differences from the mean less than this amount. Or it is nearly as satisfactory to take the simple average of the differences, and then (by the tables) ·575 of the observations, or 4/7 of all, should differ from the mean less than this function, If on testing the observation thus, by either method, it is found that more than the due proportion of all are within the limit stated, it shows that the limit is too wide ; and hence that the most divergent observations should be rejected, and a fresh limit computed from the remainder, until the proper proportion of all the observations is within the limit of the function calculated. This system of weeding may thus be done by using any function of the curve; but the error of mean square is the most accurate in results, occurring at maximum inclination ; and the average error is the most easy to work.

---

* The values of probable error stated in Airy's " Errors of Observation," pp. 23, 24, are all slightly wrong ; this is owing to simply proportioning from a table, for the relation of probable error to modulus, instead of properly interpolating. The above values are by strict interpolation, and agree with De Morgan.

186. To take a practical example, the following are the angular differences between the observations and the mean stations, on distances between 10,000 and 20,000 inches, in the survey around the Great Pyramid. The limits of distance are necessary, as the relation of lineal to angular error is otherwise too variable, and so affects the character of the distribution; the differences requiring treating in groups according to the distances involved. The following is the largest group, and thus best exhibits the method of weeding.

Data.				Working.			Result.	
Diffe-rences.	Squares.	Diffe-rences. (Continued.)	Squares.	Sum of squares, at successive points in the list of Differences.	$n-1$, at successive points.	∴ Error of mean square, at successive points.	Number of observations within the limit of these errors of mean square.	
$''$	$''$.	$''$	$''$				Normal number, ·682 of all the obser-vations.	Actual number in the series of differences.
0	0	1·5	2·25					
0	0	1·6	2·56					
·2	·04	1·6	2·56					
·2	·04	1·8	3·24					
·2	·04	2·0	4·00					
·3	·09	2·0	4·00					
·3	·09	2·2	4·84	[Earlier	values	need	not be	computed.]
·3	·09	2·4	5·76					
·4	·16	2·6	6·76	$''$		$''$		
·5	·25	2·6	6·76	— 51·10	26	1·40	18·4	17
·6	·36	3·3	10·89	— 61·99	27	1·51	19·1	18
·8	·64	3·5	12·25	— 74·24	28	1·63	19·8	20
1·0	1·00	3·7	13·69	— 87·93	29	1·74	20·5	20
1·0	1·00	5·4	29·16	— 117·09	30	1·97	21·2	21
1·2	1·44	6·2	38·44	— 155·53	31	2·24	21·8	24 ⎫
1·2	1·44	7·5	56·25	— 211·78	32	2·57	22·5	25 ⎬ Reject.
1·3	1·69	9·4	88·36	— 300·14	33	3·02	23·2	27 ⎬
(Continued in next column.)		9·6	92·16	— 392·30	34	3·40	23·9	28 ⎭

Here all the earlier differences are certainly within the range of continuous errors, and it is not until within the last 8 observations that there is any need to search for the limit of rejection. Accordingly, the sum of the squares is only taken after each of the last 8 observations; i.e., each horizontal line of figures of "Working" and "Result" shows what the result would be if all the observations below that line were cut off and ignored. We see, on looking to the last two columns, what the results are: that up to within four observations from the end, the theoretical (or normal) and the actual number of observations, within the limit of "error of mean square," are closely in accordance; the actual being rather too few in the first two, shows that some regular or continuous observations have been cut off. Then, after that, the actual and normal numbers agree within less than one number on three successive lines, showing that the limit of continuous observations is nearly reached. After this point, if any more observations are included, the limit rapidly becomes too large, and includes too many observations in the actual series. For instance, including all the observations, the error of mean square is 3·40″, and looking in the series of differences in the column of " Data," it is seen that 28 of the differences are less than that amount; whereas rather fewer than 24 differences should exceed it by the regular law of errors (*i.e.*, ·682 of the total number of 35 differences), and this proves that the limit given by the mean square is unduly increased by reason of including some discordant observations, affected by occasional errors.

Thus in the above example we see that 4 out of 35 observations are affected by occasional errors, and are detected by their lying beyond the range of the distribution of continual errors. These four are accordingly to be rejected, as being influenced by some of the various occasional causes of error indicated before ; and as nearly all of the quantities to which these differences belong, are the mean of several observations repeated at intervals, it shows that the causes are probably those not affected by the instrument or observer, but arising from local conditions of refraction, deceptive view of signal, &c. In the whole of the mean observations, on 108 sides of triangles around the Great Pyramid, only 9 are rejected by the above criterion, as being vitiated by occasional errors.

187. A difficulty which has been raised against the universal application of the law of distribution of errors (or Probability Curve) is that + and − errors cannot be equally likely in certain cases. This may possibly be true in some peculiarly conditioned cases of physical impossibility; but the objection was applied to a class of cases which really present no such difficulty. The type which has been discussed is that of guessing the area of a field ; the truth being, say, 2 acres, it was objected that a man might guess 4 or 6, but could not guess 0 or −2. But this difficulty is due to a wrong statement of probable error. It is true that in general, for convenience (and the probable error being but a small fraction of the whole quantity), we usually denote it as + or − ; but in reality it should be written × or ÷. It is a factor, and not a term. For instance, a probable error of a tenth of the whole is not ±·1, but is really ⅹ 1·1.

This true expression of probable error becomes of great importance where the probable error is large in relation to the whole. Suppose we write the angular width of an object as 2″±1″, the limits then are 1″ and 3″ ; but if we state its distance in terms of its lineal breadth, we write 100,000±50,000, which implies limits of 50,000 and 150,000, or angularly of 1⅓″ and 4″. Thus it is impossible, writing + or −, that the limits shall be the same in stating a quantity, and in stating its reciprocal. Hence our notation, + and −, must be defective. If, on the other hand, we write 2″ ⅹ 2, the limits are 1″ and 4″; and writing 100,000 ⅹ 2, the limits are

50,000 and 200,000, equivalent to 1″ and 4″, just as they are given by the angular probable error. Or again, in a rather different view, suppose in stating the average distance of a 1st magnitude star, it were put at 10^{15} miles; and suppose its superior limit of probable error to be 10^{16} miles, then its inferior limit is evidently 10^{14} miles; *i.e.*, it is 10^{15} ×÷ 10. If it were $10^{15} \pm 9 \times 10^{15}$ miles, as it must be to have limit at 10^{16}, then its inferior limit would be 8×10^{15} less than nothing. Thus, if the probable error was + and − on the amount, and was not a multiple of it, we should be landed in the absurdity of saying that if the supposed distance is 10^{15} miles, it could not possibly exceed double that distance, because it could not be, on the other hand, less than 0.

It is clear, then, that probable errors must be really multiples of the quantity; and therefore they can only be expressed by + and − when using the *logarithm* of the quantity.* Similarly the factor $\sqrt{n}$ in the probable error of a mean, must really be applied to the *logarithm* of the probable error of one observation, and not to the probable error itself. Suppose, for instance, the probable error of one observation is ×÷ 5; then, by obtaining 100 observations, the probable error must be reduced by being $\div \sqrt{100}$; but we could not write it ×÷ $\frac{5}{10}$, since that would be the same result as ×÷ 2, which would be the value for only 6 observations instead of 100. The *logarithm* of the probable error must, therefore, be $\div \sqrt{100}$, and we must write Log. of mean $\pm \dfrac{\log. 5}{\sqrt{100}}$; and it will thus be Mean ×÷ 1·175. Wherever the probable error is then a large fraction of the whole quantity, it becomes necessary to work rigorously, and to perform all operations on the logarithm, instead of on the probable error itself written as + and −. The practical need of noting these distinctions is shown by the above difficulty of the acre question, which was discussed at length a few years ago without a satisfactory conclusion; and the use of a correct notation will also be seen in the discussion of the following sections.†

188. One class of cases might be supposed to illustrate the impossibility of both + and − errors occurring; namely, that of soundings, or measurements with a flexible measure, and the adjustment of one object to fit within another. Here it might seem as if errors could only exist in one direction. But, to take the case of soundings, if we merely suppose the − half of the Probability Curve abolished, we must expect by theory to find the greatest number of observations nearest to the truth, no matter how slack the line, or how strong

---

* A similar example of the use of × and ÷, rather than + and − (*i.e.*, of logarithmic scales), is given by Lord Rayleigh, in an article on the normal spectrum in "Nature," xxvii. 559. The need of a logarithmic scale is there arrived at, from considering the irrationality of a + and − scale, and its reciprocal scale.

† An algebraic development of the same principle, by Mr. D. McAlister, is given by Mr. Francis Galton, F.R.S., in Proc. Royal Soc., No. 198, 1879.

the current; whereas it is manifest that in practice we shall always have some deflection of the line, never getting it quite straight, and seldom even nearly straight. Hence there must be *some* amount of error which we are more likely to make than none at all; *i.e.*, the curve of observations has not its maximum at 0 difference. The explanation is, that what we really measure is not one quantity, but two combined. The length of the line is equal to the invariable distance measured, $+$ the shortening of the line due to deflection. This last quantity is the variable; and its mean amount depends on the tension of the line, the length, area, and friction of the line, and the strength of the currents. And we have no reason to suppose that the variations, from this mean amount of deflection, do not follow the law of probabilities. For instance, if in sounding to a certain depth, the mean shortening of the line is 100 feet, then a variation of $\times$ or of $\div 5$ is equally unlikely; *i.e.*, a shortening of only 20 feet, or of 500 feet, is equally rare. We can see instantly that the amount of shortening can never become 0 nor ∞; and (in the absence of experiments) our intuitive judgment would certainly not rebel at the idea of a mean shortening of 100 being as unlikely to vary up to 1,000, as to be diminished to only 10 feet, by the run of casual circumstances. Precisely the same principle applies to one object inside another. If, on an average, a shake of $\frac{1}{100}$ inch is made (say, in filing a nut-spanner), anyone accustomed to do delicate mechanical work will allow that a fit to $\frac{1}{500}$ inch is as unlikely to occur as a misfit of $\frac{1}{20}$ inch.* The value of the true view of the probable error as a multiplier, and not a term, is seen in these considerations; and it is very doubtful whether any physical case can be found which, when properly stated, does not involve an equal probability of the observations being both $+$ and $-$, or, rather, being multiples and fractions of the true amount.

189. In stating the probable error of our knowledge of a quantity, we really state the exact unlikelihood of the quantity exceeding or falling short of a certain amount; we introduce a second quantity to define the uncertainty of the first. And this second quantity is liable to be in error, just like the first quantity; its exact amount, or the chance of the truth exceeding certain limits, is only a fallible statement derived from a series of observations; and it may, therefore, be incorrect. In short, the probable error itself has a probable error, and this secondary probable error has a tertiary probable error; so that the series of probable errors is infinite, though rapidly diminishing. In the following discussion, which is limited to secondary probable errors, p.e. I denotes the primary probable error of the datum; and p.e. II the secondary probable error, or probable error of p.e. I, its limits being rigorously stated as a multiple of p.e. I.

* A similar application of the principle was arrived at by Herschel, in his essay on Target Shooting; "Familiar Lectures," p. 495.

Now looking at the p.e. I of a single observation (deduced from the divergencies between the observations), it is plain that it will be known more and more accurately the greater be the number of observations; *i.e.*, there will be a diminution of the p.e. II of a single observation, by increasing the number of observations, exactly as there is a diminution of the p.e. I of the mean by increasing the observations. Hence log. p.e. II of one observation varies as

$\frac{1}{\sqrt{n}}$. But log. p.e. I of the mean also varies as $\frac{1}{\sqrt{n}}$. Therefore log. p.e. II of

the mean varies as $\frac{1}{n}$ in relation to the whole quantity.

The arithmetical method for determining the value of p.e. II is precisely like that for working out p.e. I. When the observations are all the same, *i.e.*, when the *first* differences vanish, p.e. I vanishes; similarly, when the first differences are all the same (irrespective of sign), *i.e.*, when the *second* differences vanish, p.e. II vanishes. To practically exemplify these two statements, we take two examples. The observations on the position of rest of a pendulum will be all the same, and there will be no probable error, apart from mechanical irregularities: in this case first differences have vanished, and p.e. I vanishes. With a coin tossed up, its mean position when at rest again will be on edge (since heads and tails are equally likely), and the difference from its mean position will be constant, 90°: in this case, first differences being all equal (*i.e.*, 90°), the second differences have vanished, and p.e. II vanishes. This result we can see to be true, since there is no uncertainty about p.e. I, but it is absolutely known that the chance of heads or tails is exactly $\frac{1}{2}$, and can never be anything else: hence there is no p.e. II; it has vanished, as theory shows us.

From this it follows that as there is a normal distribution of errors (the Probability Curve), so there must also be a normal p.e. II. And this normal p.e. II, thus deduced, is=p.e. I $\frac{x}{4}$ 1·825 on *one* observation (log. = ·2612); therefore on 9 observations, for instance, the p.e. II is = p.e. I $\frac{x}{4}$ 1·222, or roughly $\pm\frac{1}{4}$; on 25 observations p.e. II is = p.e. I $\frac{x}{4}$ 1·128, or roughly $\pm\frac{1}{8}$; and on 100 observations it is = p.e. I $\frac{x}{4}$ 1·062, or roughly in vulgar notation $\pm\frac{1}{16}$ of p.e. I.

Now this theory is open to actual test thus: take a large series of observations casually arranged, and break it into groups, each containing an equal number of observations, say 5, 10, or 25 in a group; then take the probable error of the mean value of each group, this is its p.e. I. So far the process is usual enough; but now compare these probable errors of the equal groups together, see how much they vary, and take the mean p.e. I for each method of division; the amount of variation from the mean p.e. I shows the uncertainty of the p.e. I in each method of division; and from this we can calculate the p.e. II, just as we calculate the p.e. I from any other set of differences from a mean. In this way the theory can be checked; and on working out five complete cases of this check, consisting of from 4 to 10 groups in each case, the p.e. II was practically found to average = p.e. I × 2·03 ; with a probable error of this multiple (or a *tertiary* probable error) of p.e. III = p.e. II × 1·115 ; *i.e.*, p.e. II of a single observation is as likely to be within the limits p.e. I × 1·82 and p.e. I × 2·26, as to be beyond those limits.

This is such a satisfactory approach in practice to the theoretical value p.e. I × 1·82 (especially as it is all reduced to the extreme case of a single observation), that no doubt can remain as to the correctness of the theory of Secondary Probable Errors, and of its details here discussed.

190. The practical result of the recognition of the secondary probable error is, that it is needless to employ rigorous formulæ, or to spend any extra time, in order to obtain the exact value of the primary probable error of the determination in question : and, that the fewer the observations the more useless is an accurate formula, since the probable error has a much larger uncertainty inherent in it.   This fact is so far contrary to usual views that it is needful to point it out ; one treatise, when mentioning the less rigorous formulæ for probable error says : " For values of n less than 24 it is best to hold fast to the more exact formula ;" and then, half recognising the increased uncertainty of the probable error with fewer observations, it continues, " and even that cannot for such cases be expected to give precise results, since the hypothesis of its development supposes that enough observations have been taken to exhibit the several errors in proportion to their respective probabilities" (Merriman's " Least Squares," p. 189).

Now of the approximate formulæ sometimes employed for probable error, one of the simplest and most useful is that formed by the mean difference, instead of the error of mean square.   By the law of distribution this mean difference × ·845 = probable error ; *i.e.*, in a normal distribution of errors, the one value above and below which are an equal number of errors, will be ·845 × the mean of all the errors.   The variation of the result by this formula from that by the formula on the error of mean square, will seldom be of any importance in view of the secondary probable error ; for if there be much difference between the two results it shows an irrationality of distribution, which implies a large secondary probable error.   Therefore time would be better spent in carefully searching for " occasional " errors, rather than in taking the squares of the quantities, in order to obtain a statement of probable error, with a fallacious appearance of accuracy.   In fact, the usually pretentious regard for rigorous formulæ of probable error, while ignoring altogether the secondary probable error, is only another form of the old fallacy of stating a mean result to an absurdly long row of figures, regardless of the primary probable error.   While showing due honour to the system of observing the probability of the main result, computers have fallen into just the same fallacy over the probable error itself, through sinking the common-sense of the work in an unthinking regard for rigorous methods.

Beside the formulæ for probable error from mean square and from mean difference, there is also the simplest formula of all, *i.e.*, selecting such a value as shall have half of the differences larger and half of them smaller than the amount of probable error. This definition is the fundamental meaning of the expression; and as a formula it has the advantage over all the others, that it does not depend mainly on the amounts of the largest and most variable of all the observations, but it gives equal value to every observation in the formation of the result. It is true this method does not turn out a neat value to three places of figures, but, on the contrary faces the computer with the naked uncertainty which there is in the amount of the probable error; the fewer the observations, the more doubt he must feel as to the exact value. But this is rather an advantage than otherwise, as no man can shut his eyes to the secondary probable error when he has the vagueness of the primary error so plainly before him.

191. One other point of practice may be noted. It is usual, if a series of differences are to be compared with the law of distribution, or Probability Curve, to require that the total number shall be very large; and to compare them by taking the sums of all between certain successive limits. Or, graphically speaking, to draw the curve of the heap of observations, and see how that coincides with the normal curve.

But a more satisfactory method—which does away with the irregularity of successive steps, and which may be applied to any number of observations —is that of forming a table of the value of each difference (in terms of probable error of one observation=unity) according to the normal distribution. Thus suppose it is wished to test 8 observations by the law of distribution. Dividing the whole area of the curve in 8 equal parts, take the difference due to the middle of each part: at ·0625 area (middle of 1st ⅛th) difference is ·116 × p.e.; and so on to ·9375 area (middle of 8th ⅛th), when difference is 2.76 × p.e.

	probable error		× ·116
Table	,,	,,	× ·325
of	,,	,,	× ·596
Normal	,,	,,	× ·860
Distribution	,,	,,	× 1·150
of eight	,,	,,	× 1·496
observations.	,,	,,	× 1·952
	,,	,,	× 2·762

Such a table, for any given number of observations, may be readily constructed from a curve formed by the number of observations (or area of Probability Curve) as one ordinate, and the multiple of the probable error as the other ordinate. By such normal tables occasional errors can be readily searched for;

as, if a few of the more discordant observations ought to be rejected, it will be found that the final entries in the normal table agree with the observed differences a few lines higher up.

In this Appendix some exception may be taken by the reader to the consideration of every question by means of its practical applications; and to the absence of proofs deduced from the more elaborate processes of algebraical deductions from the fundamental theories. But since these fundamental theories have never been completely demonstrated, apart from all practical experience; so there is nothing unsuitable in referring directly to the practical working of a method. With respect to the fundamental law of probability, Merriman writes: "In the demonstration of this law of error ... there are two defects ... and they cannot be bridged over or avoided, but will always exist in this mathematical development of the law of probability of error" ("Method of Least Squares," p. 196–7). Airy writes, of the same law, "Whatever may be thought of the process by which this formula has been obtained, it will scarcely be doubted by any one that the result is entirely in accordance with our general ideas of the frequency of errors" ("Errors of Observation," p. 15). And after giving at the end of the same book, a practical example of the distribution of errors in the N.P.D. of Polaris, he concludes thus, "the validity of every investigation in this Treatise is thereby established" (p. 119). After these appeals to the ultimate dependence on experience, it can hardly be thought objectionable to take the shortest road to the practical demonstration of each question.

APPENDIX III.

THE GRAPHIC REDUCTION OF TRIANGULATION.

192. IN the foregoing Appendix, on the Rejection of Discordant Observations, the method for eliminating those observations affected by occasional errors, has been pointed out. It is needless to enlarge on the importance of some correct and universal rule for the discrimination of errors which may lie beyond those of the normal distribution ; extreme cases are always rejected arbitrarily by every computer, and the question where to draw the line of selection should be determined by some law, rather than by caprice, or even intuition.

But in the reduction of triangulation by least squares, when once the equations are formed, the whole process is in a mill ; and the computer turns the handle, and grinds out the result, without the chance of seeing anything until it is finished. When completed, and the differences of the observations from the mean azimuths are worked out, then if some of the differences are seen to be due to occasional errors (or " discordant observations ") they ought to be rejected, as certainly vitiating the result. Yet this implies a re-working of the whole calculation, a matter perhaps of weeks ; and this would probably need to be done several times, until the differences conformed to the normal distribution. Yet unless some search is made for occasional errors, the apparent accuracy of the results cannot be trusted for a moment ; and a few observations—which if varying as much in a simple set of unentangled observations would be summarily rejected by probabilities—will render useless the elaborate care spent on the reduction of the whole.

What is needed, then, is some way of knowing how the results are going during the working ; and above all some way of quickly seeing what difference will be made by the rejection of some one discordant observation, and whether omitting it will enable all the others to be easily reconciled. As no possible clue to this can be obtained in the course of equational reduction, some graphical method is the only apparatus which will suffice. Whether, then, we finally adopt a rigorous equational reduction, or no, still a graphic reduction is needed in all cases to point out the locality of the larger errors, and their approximate amounts.

193. Graphic reduction, as generally understood, means simply drawing the results of the observations on sheets, and fitting them together. In the case of angular observations, the angles are drawn radiating from a theodolite centre on each sheet ; and then these sheets can be superposed, and moved in the unknown elements of azimuth and position, *i.e.*, shifted about in rotation and translation, until the observations fit together with the least divergences. Now though this is a very rude method in general, it contains the principle of a method which is capable of being worked with any amount of accuracy. The rudeness of it only results from the necessarily small size of the sheets, in relation to the whole extent of the survey ; since this makes the errors of the graphic drawing on the sheets far greater than the errors of the observations in any accurate work.

If then we could have sheets, each as large as the whole ground of the survey,—a furlong, a mile, or a hundred miles across,—and draw on each sheet radii corresponding to the observed mean azimuths, or the *traces* of the observations, around some one station ; and then if these sheets were superposed, and shifted in translation and rotation, until the traces coincided as nearly as possible one with another, and with the theodolite centre, at each point ; then we should have the most probable system of resulting stations, and differences of observations from these stations.

Now, if instead of the sheets covering the full size of the ground (which would be physically impossible to realize), they are reduced to a fraction of that size, and all the distances of the stations apart are similarly reduced, it is plain that rotation or translation of a sheet (within a small angle), will affect all the traces as before ; only if the reduction is, say, to $\frac{1}{60}$th of the lineal distances, then a rotation of $1°$ of the sheet, will shift the traces lineally as much as a rotation of $1'$ on the full scale on the ground.

194. The practical method, then, for graphic reduction on any scale, is to assume a provisional place for each station, and calculate by co-ordinates the differences of the observations from the assumed places, exactly as in the first step of the reduction by least squares. It is generally best to adopt a scale of $\frac{1}{3600}$th (or some simple multiple of that) for plotting the sheet with the provisional places of the stations.* Then, with this reduction, if the angular differences are plotted with a protractor, reading $1°$ on it for every $1''$ of actual difference, the traces will be drawn on the same scale as they are on the actual

* As too great a translation or rotation of the sheets, involves secondary errors, it is best to require that the distances between the stations shall be at least 8 or 10 times the largest differences of observations. Taking 10 times the largest angular difference of any observation from a provisional station, and converting it into actual lineal distance, we obtain the minimum distance allowable between each station, and hence the smallest scale for the whole reduction. Sometimes, if differences are large, a preliminary reduction (not drawing the differences their actual size) is desirable to get nearer values for the provisional station co-ordinates.

ground. Thus the traces of the mean of the observations of each of the azimuths around one station, are all plotted on one sheet (marking also the place of the central station, *i.e.*, of the theodolite) ; all the azimuths around another station, on another sheet, and so on, using as many separate sheets as there are theodolite stations in the survey. These sheets being then all superposed, all the traces to any one station are seen crossing one another ; and the theodolite centre of each station will be seen on the sheet of that station, among the traces which are drawn on the other sheets. Practically the traces are drawn on some transparent substance (as mica), in order to see through a large number of sheets together.

Then the actual work of reduction consists in shifting these sheets in translation and rotation, until the most probable adjustment of all the traces is reached. This is a work taking some hours or days ; but it is the equivalent of some days or months of work in the reduction of simultaneous equations. Many hypotheses have to be tried ; each sheet is shifted about in turn, and any apparently erratic observation is disregarded for the time, and a fresh trial of adjustment is made ; if no great improvement ensues in the adjustments, the observation is taken into the general mass again ; also the likelihood of various eccentricities of the theodolite setting over each station, can be investigated. In short, the causes of all apparently abnormal discordances, can be felt for in different directions ; and they can thus be generally tracked down to some one observation, the elimination of which reconciles many others. Some hesitation may be felt at such a rejection of observations ; but it must be remembered that the omission of the most discordant of, say eight, really normal observations, would not diminish the mean divergence of them by more than $\frac{1}{8}$;* an amount not very striking, and making a difference which would certainly not lead the adjuster to reject one observation in eight. If an average improvement of the adjustment greater than $\frac{1}{8}$ (or, say, $\frac{1}{4}$), can be made by omitting 1 in 8 of the observations, then the computer is bound to omit it by the laws of probabilities, as being due to some occasional error.

Having thus adjusted these sheets to apparently the most probable arrangement, the mean stations to be adopted from the traces should be marked; and the difference of this, from the provisional places of the same stations, is then read off. Applying these corrections to the co-ordinates of the provisional places, we have the finally adjusted co-ordinates. The sheet of provisional places of the stations may be applied in any position to the adjusted points of the traces, for reading off the corrections ; its position is of no consequence, as it affects all stations alike.

* See table in section 191 ; the mean of the differences there is 1·157 ; but the mean after rejecting the one most divergent is only ·928 ; a reduction of $\frac{1}{5}$ of the total divergence by mitting $\frac{1}{8}$ of the observations.

Finally, the differences of the observations from the adjusted positions of the stations should be calculated; just as at first they were calculated from the provisional stations. Then these differences may be plotted all on one sheet, and they represent the variations of the traces as finally adjusted, from the finally adopted places of the stations.* If, then, the graphic adjustment has not been satisfactory, or if an error has been made in any part of the computations, it will be shown by the position of the station not being in the midst of the plotted traces.

195. Such a delineation of the traces may be seen, for the most important part of the present survey, in the diagram of "Traces of the Actual Observations," Pl. xvi. To have included all the stations of the survey, would have made the sheet unmanageably large to print ; hence, only those around the Great Pyramid are here shown.

But beside the traces themselves, their probable errors must also be considered ; for it is needless to shift a sheet so as to bring one trace nearer another, if the probable errors of the two traces already overlap, while perhaps the shifting separates still further two traces, whose probable errors are already far apart. Accordingly, instead of drawing lines to represent the traces on the adjustment sheets, bands should always be drawn, extending in their widths to the limits of the probable error ; and the distances of the traces apart should always be regarded in terms of their probable errors. These bands of probable error are represented as they cross at station U, on Pl. xvi. ; only in actual working they are a thin transparent wash of ink, through which other bands can be easily seen ; and which is made thinner the wider it is, and the less the observation is worth. At W, here, only the halves of these bands are drawn, to avoid confusion. And at all the other stations the half traces, without probable error bands, are drawn, as the diagram would be otherwise too crowded to be intelligible.

Another change in this diagram, from the actual appearance of the working sheets of reduction, is that instead of a spot representing the position of the theodolite at each centre, here the *reflex* traces are marked ; these are the lines in which the theodolite should lie, in order that the direct trace from it should coincide with the adopted station. These reflex traces are dotted ; and it should be remembered when looking at the diagram, that the theodolite station is the mean of the dotted traces on any station ; and in so far as this does not coincide with the mean of the direct traces, it shows an error of observing the eccentricity of the theodolite position.

196. This diagram (Pl. xvi.) shows practically how nearly the observations of a survey may be adjusted, by a single process of graphic reduction. No alteration in any respect has been made from the results obtained by the first

---

* Of course this should tally with the positions of the traces on the adjustment sheets as finally arranged.

graphic working (in which all corrections for levelling, eccentricities, &c., were duly made), except that the ultra-discordant observations, due to occasional errors, are here omitted ; as, owing to their great divergence, they would become confused with the wrong stations; but the 154 traces which agree to the law of errors are all shown here. In no case could any improvement be suggested in the adopted places of the stations, beyond the limits of their probable errors. But in Z and *a* some change may be still needed, by a second process of graphic reduction ; *a* going further north, and Z further south, and somewhat west. This has not, however, been altered here, as the westing of Z is the only change of importance, and it would diminish the base of survey by about ·08 (or ·09 inch on Pyramid base length) ; and a re-comparison of the standard tape used for the measurement of the survey-base, shows a similar change of distance = ·12 ; these errors therefore balance one another, far within the limits of probable errors. Hence no notice has been taken of these insignificant amounts in stating the results.

The base of survey was measured on three different days independently ; each length in each operation being read four or five times. The probable error of the final value of the base, is shown by the breadth of the black terminal band at Z, with an arrow at the end of it ; and the actual differences between the three days' results are shown by the three short lines above the terminal band. It will be seen that the uncertainty of lineal measure is not much less than that of angular position ; this is as it should be, for in all surveys the error of the length of the base should be nearly of the same amount as the errors of observing on it in triangulation ; otherwise either lineal or else angular accuracy is wasted.

The probable errors of the positions of the stations, as deduced from the adjusted traces, is here shown by the radius of a small circle around each station. It was calculated from the divergences of the traces ; and though this is not entirely a rigorous method, yet it gives results quite as near as is necessary, if we neglect the ellipticity of the probable errors. Strictly the probable error limits of all stations in planes are elliptic, and cannot be expressed by fewer than three elements ; describing it in the two co-ordinates being insufficient, unless another element is added. The formula for probable error in two dimensions differs, of course, from that for ordinary probable error in one dimension. Instead of n we must take $2n$, as only half the traces on an average are available in any one direction ; and for $n-1$ we must take $n-2$, as two traces are needed to fix a point.

The general results of the differences of the traces from the mean stations adopted, in the diagram here given, are as follow. The mean of the differences in the various groups being :—

	All observations	After rejecting 1 in 17, affected by occasional errors ; as by probabilities.
On distances over 20,000 inches	2·22″ or ·28 inch	·75″ or ·106 inch
Between 20,000 and 10,000	2·10 ,, ·13 ,,	1· 43 ,, ·081 ,,
Between 10,000 and 5,000	2·62 ,, ·09 ,,	2· 62 ,, ·090 ,,
Under 5,000 inches	4·15 ,, ·08 ,,	3· 81 ,, ·079 ,,

Hence it may be generally said that there was an average error of $\frac{1}{50}$ inch lineally in the azimuths; and in distances over $\frac{1}{4}$ mile this error was exceeded by the average angular error of ·8″.

197. Such, then, is the method of graphic reduction, as applied to observations on plane surfaces ; adaptable to any scale of representation, and to showing any amount of accuracy. If meridian observations be taken, they may be marked as lines (or ends of lines) on the sheets ; and one element of the adjustment will then be the parallelism of these lines, or rather of their probable error bands. For observations on a sphere, the same method of reduction is equally applicable to co-ordinates of latitude and longitude, plotted on a suitable projection ; provided the curvature is not extensive enough to modify the distances, so that a rotational shift does not affect the various stations proportionally. This error could not occur in terrestrial observations, and so the method is applicable to all geodetic surveys.

It should be observed that the graphic reduction is equivalent, not merely to the usual system of reduction by least squares, from equations of shift of the points ; but it is equivalent to a system of equations which allows not only of lateral shift of the points, but of rotational shift of all the observations around each centre, and also of disseverance of the centreing of the theodolite over a station, from all the other observations *to* that station ; beside this, it takes account of the probable errors of all the observations. Thus it is equivalent to the determination of five unknown quantities for each point ; *i.e.,* the two station co-ordinates, the two theodolite co-ordinates, and the zero of azimuth of the circle. And any system of reduction which does not include all of these five unknowns is defective, and cannot impartially render the truest results. Hence the graphic reduction of a network of a dozen stations, which is easily performed, is equivalent to the elaborate formation and solution of 60 normal simultaneous equations, with cognizance of all the probable errors of the observations ; and equivalent not only to doing that once, but to doing it many times over, until all occasional errors have been weeded out. In short, a few days' work with graphic reduction will master a mass of observations and unknown quantities, so complex that its solution by least squares would only be attempted for such an object as a national survey. In any case it is desirable to employ the graphic method ; as, if the method of least squares should eventually be used, still the graphic work takes but a small fraction of the labour; and it is invaluable for showing the places of occasional errors, which would otherwise vitiate the result from the least squares. And it is almost certain that in all cases the graphic results (especially by a repeated process), are well within the probable errors of the most accurate determination obtainable; and thus practically as accurate as any result that can be procured. Hence the graphic method will in most cases obviate the necessity for far longer processes; and also bring the adjustment of check observations within the range of practical work, to a far larger extent than is the case at present.

INDEX.

PRINTED BY FIELD AND TUER, AT YE LEADENHALLE PRESSE.

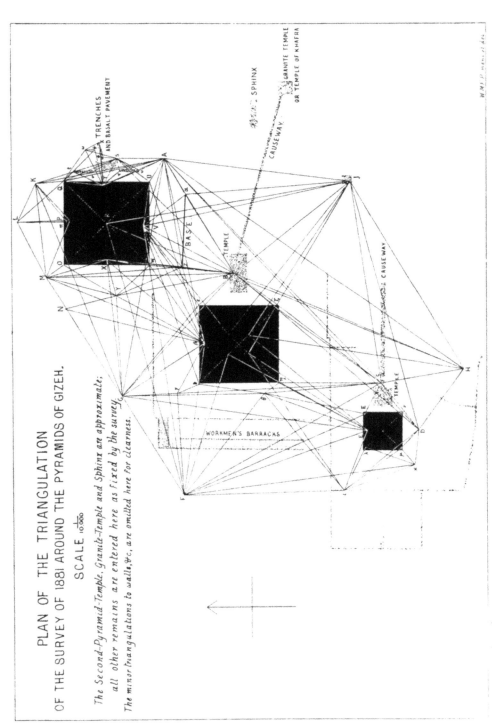

PLAN OF THE TRIANGULATION
OF THE SURVEY OF 1881 AROUND THE PYRAMIDS OF GIZEH.
SCALE 1/10,000

The Second-Pyramid-Temple, Granite-Temple and Sphinx are approximate;
all other remains are entered here as fixed by the survey.
The minor triangulations to walls, &c, are omitted here for clearness.

TRENCHES
AND BASALT PAVEMENT

SPHINX

CAUSEWAY

GRANITE TEMPLE
OR TEMPLE OF KHAFRA

CAUSEWAY

BASE

TEMPLE

TEMPLE

WORKMEN'S BARRACKS

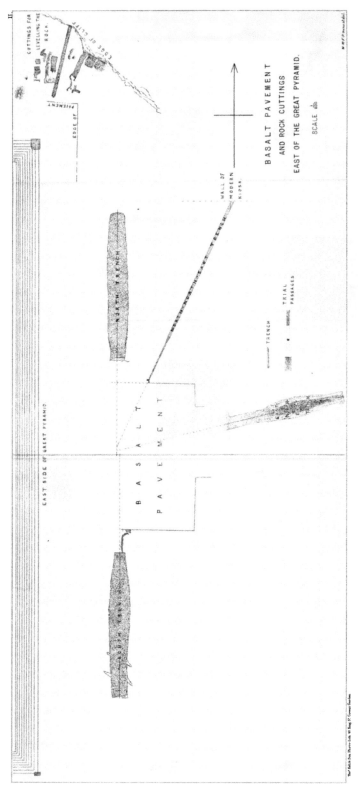

The material originally positioned here is too large for reproduction in this reissue. A PDF can be downloaded from the web address given on page iv of this book, by clicking on 'Resources Available'.

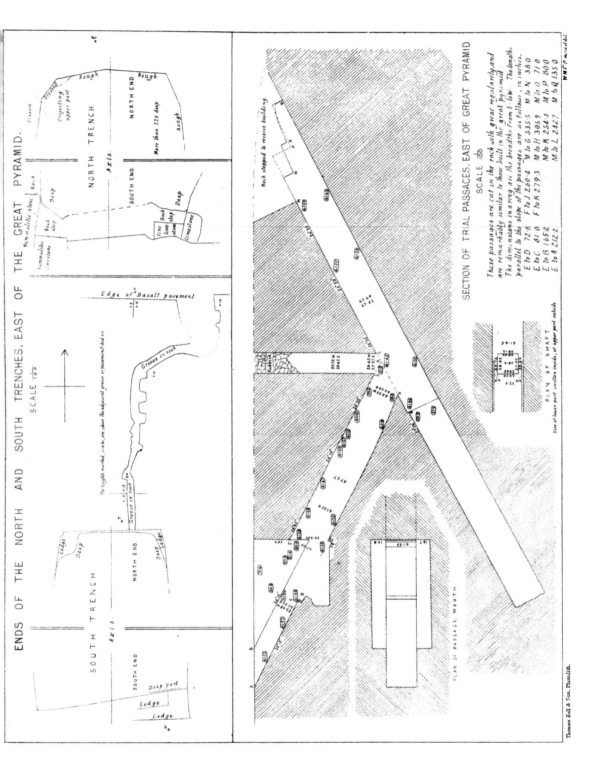

ENDS OF THE NORTH AND SOUTH TRENCHES, EAST OF THE GREAT PYRAMID.

SECTION OF TRIAL PASSAGES, EAST OF GREAT PYRAMID

The material originally positioned here is too large for reproduction in this reissue. A PDF can be downloaded from the web address given on page iv of this book, by clicking on 'Resources Available'.

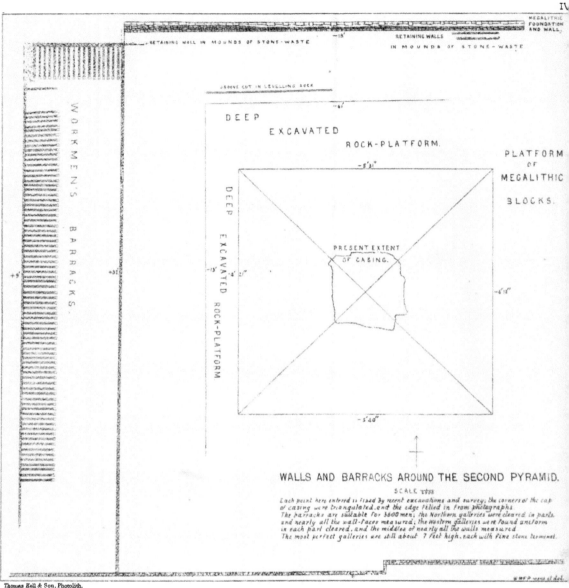

MEGALITHIC
FOUNDATION
AND WALL.

RETAINING WALL IN MOUNDS OF STONE-WASTE

RETAINING WALLS

IN MOUNDS OF STONE-WASTE

GROOVE CUT IN LEVELLING ROCK

DEEP

EXCAVATED

ROCK-PLATFORM.

PLATFORM
OF
MEGALITHIC

BLOCKS.

DEEP EXCAVATED ROCK-PLATFORM

PRESENT EXTENT
OF CASING.

WORKMEN'S BARRACKS.

WALLS AND BARRACKS AROUND THE SECOND PYRAMID.

SCALE

Each point here entered is fixed by recent excavations and survey; the corners of the cap
of casing were triangulated, and the edge filled in from photographs.
The barracks are suitable for 3600 men; the Northern galleries were cleared in parts,
and nearly all the wall-faces measured; the Western galleries were found uniform
in each part cleared, and the middles of nearly all the walls measured.
The most perfect galleries are still about 7 feet high, each with fine stone terminal.

W.M.F.P. mens. et del.

Thomas Kell & Son, Photolith.

The material originally positioned here is too large for reproduction in this reissue. A PDF can be downloaded from the web address given on page iv of this book, by clicking on 'Resources Available'.

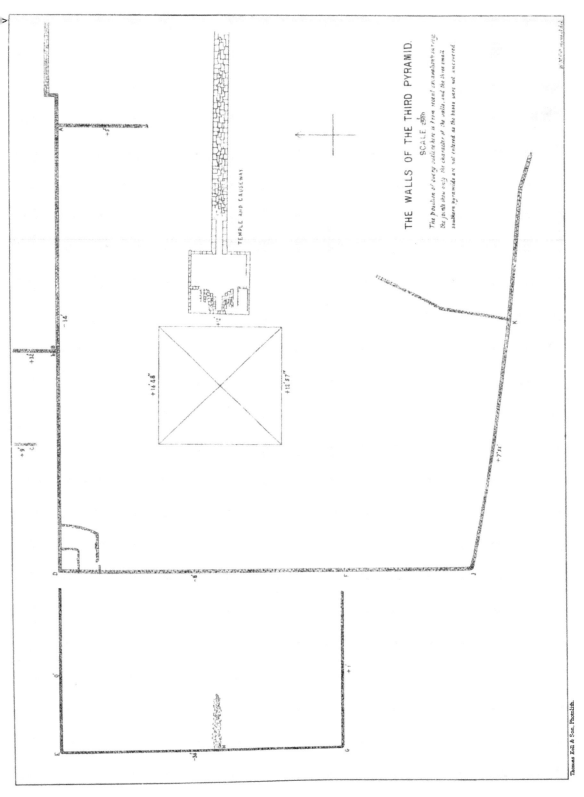

THE WALLS OF THE THIRD PYRAMID.
SCALE

TEMPLE AND CAUSEWAY

The material originally positioned here is too large for reproduction in this reissue. A PDF can be downloaded from the web address given on page iv of this book, by clicking on 'Resources Available'.

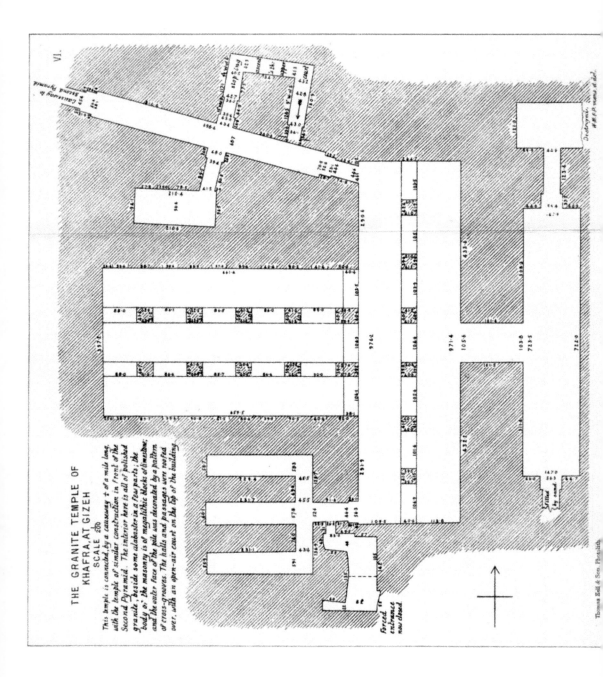

VI.

THE GRANITE TEMPLE OF
KHAFRA, AT GIZEH
SCALE 500

This temple is connected, by a causeway ⅓ of a mile long,
with the temple of similar construction in front of the
Second Pyramid. The interior here is all of polished
granite; beside some alabaster in a few parts; the
body of the masonry is of megalithic blocks of limestone,
and the outer face of the pile was decorated by a pattern
of cross-grooves. The halls and passages were roofed
over, with an open-air court on the top of the building.

Thomas Kell & Son, Photolith.

The material originally positioned here is too large for reproduction in this
reissue. A PDF can be downloaded from the web address given on page iv
of this book, by clicking on 'Resources Available'.

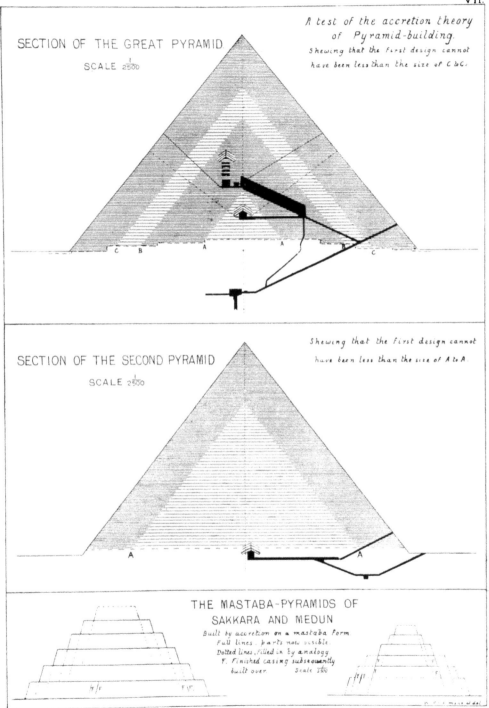

SECTION OF THE GREAT PYRAMID.

SCALE $\frac{1}{2500}$

A test of the accretion theory
of Pyramid-building.
Shewing that the first design cannot
have been less than the size of C to C.

SECTION OF THE SECOND PYRAMID

SCALE $\frac{1}{2500}$

Shewing that the first design cannot
have been less than the size of A to A.

THE MASTABA-PYRAMIDS OF
SAKKARA AND MEDUN

Built by accretion on a mastaba form.
Full lines, parts now visible.
Dotted lines, filled in by analogy.
F. Finished casing subsequently
built over.   Scale $\frac{1}{2500}$

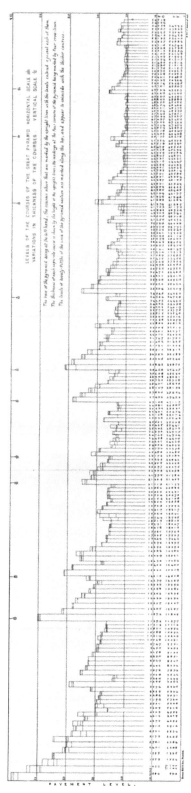

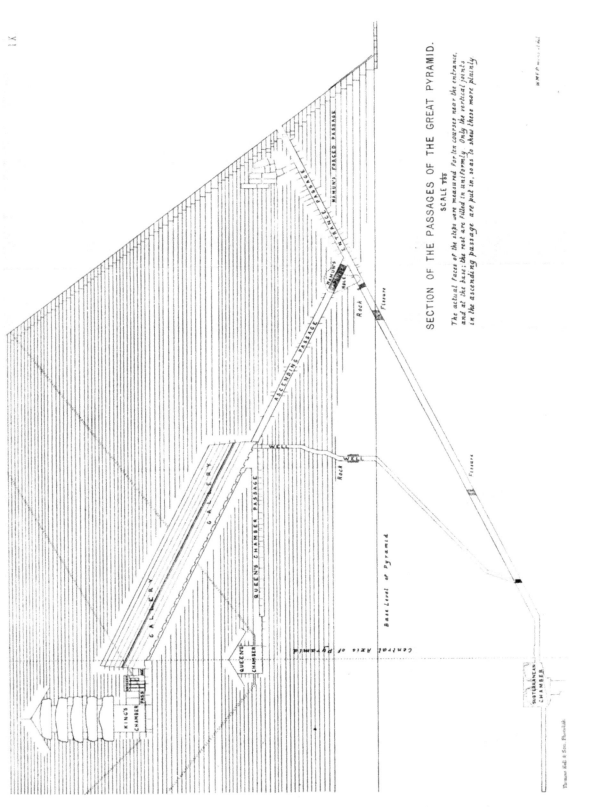

SECTION OF THE PASSAGES OF THE GREAT PYRAMID.

SCALE 1/85

The actual faces of the steps were measured for ten courses near the entrance, and at the base; the rest are filled in uniformly. Only the vertical joints in the ascending passage are put in, so as to shew these more plainly.

The material originally positioned here is too large for reproduction in this reissue. A PDF can be downloaded from the web address given on page iv of this book, by clicking on 'Resources Available'.

THE RELATIVE POSITION OF THE SOCKET-EDGES, CASING, AND CORE-MASONRY,
AT THE CORNERS OF THE GREAT PYRAMID

SCALE $\frac{1}{50}$

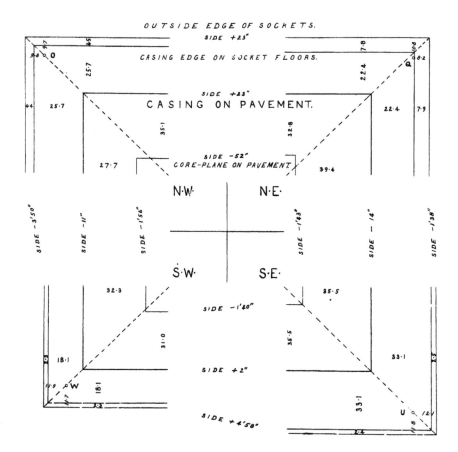

The azimuths of the sides stated are from the mean azimuth of the casing on pavement, which is −3′43″. ie. W. of N. The station-marks O·Q·U·and W· are marked in position.

WMFP mens. et del.

XI.

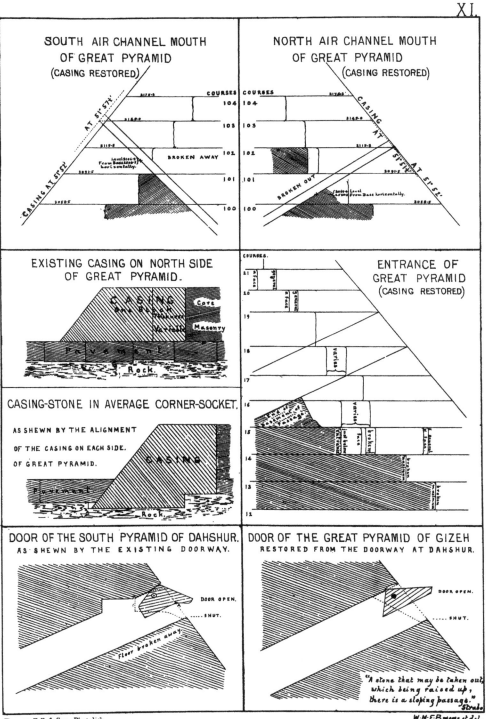

SOUTH AIR CHANNEL MOUTH
OF GREAT PYRAMID
(CASING RESTORED)

NORTH AIR CHANNEL MOUTH
OF GREAT PYRAMID
(CASING RESTORED)

EXISTING CASING ON NORTH SIDE
OF GREAT PYRAMID.

ENTRANCE OF
GREAT PYRAMID
(CASING RESTORED)

CASING-STONE IN AVERAGE CORNER-SOCKET.

AS SHEWN BY THE ALIGNMENT
OF THE CASING ON EACH SIDE.
OF GREAT PYRAMID.

DOOR OF THE SOUTH PYRAMID OF DAHSHUR.
AS SHEWN BY THE EXISTING DOORWAY.

DOOR OF THE GREAT PYRAMID OF GIZEH
RESTORED FROM THE DOORWAY AT DAHSHUR.

"A stone that may be taken out
which being raised up,
there is a sloping passage."
— Strabo.

Thomas Kell & Son, Photolith.   SCALE 1/100   W. M. F. P. mens. et del.

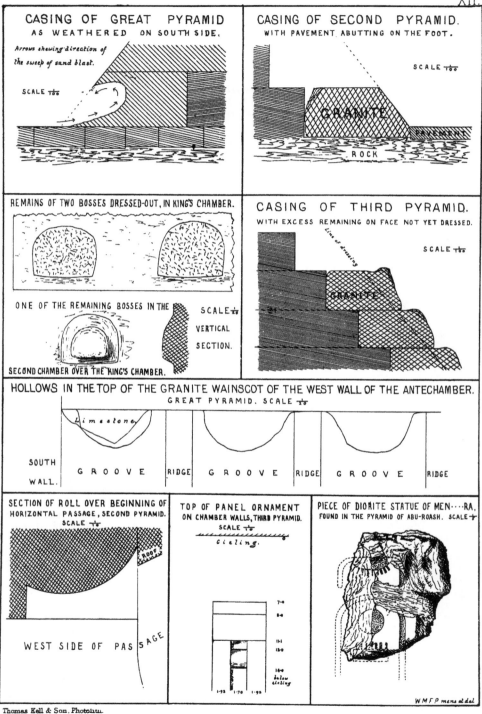

CASING OF GREAT PYRAMID
AS WEATHERED ON SOUTH SIDE.

Arrows shewing direction of
the sweep of sand blast.

SCALE 1/100

CASING OF SECOND PYRAMID.
WITH PAVEMENT ABUTTING ON THE FOOT.

SCALE 1/100

GRANITE

PAVEMENT

ROCK

REMAINS OF TWO BOSSES DRESSED-OUT, IN KING'S CHAMBER.

ONE OF THE REMAINING BOSSES IN THE

SCALE 1/12

VERTICAL

SECTION.

SECOND CHAMBER OVER THE KING'S CHAMBER.

CASING OF THIRD PYRAMID.
WITH EXCESS REMAINING ON FACE NOT YET DRESSED.

SCALE 1/100

Line of dressing

GRANITE

31

HOLLOWS IN THE TOP OF THE GRANITE WAINSCOT OF THE WEST WALL OF THE ANTECHAMBER.
GREAT PYRAMID. SCALE 1/10

Limestone

SOUTH

GROOVE   RIDGE   GROOVE   RIDGE   GROOVE   RIDGE

WALL.

SECTION OF ROLL OVER BEGINNING OF
HORIZONTAL PASSAGE, SECOND PYRAMID.
SCALE 1/4

ROOF

WEST SIDE OF PASSAGE

TOP OF PANEL ORNAMENT
ON CHAMBER WALLS, THIRD PYRAMID.
SCALE 1/10

Cieling.

7·0
8·0

11·1
13·0

14·0
below
cieling

1·93   1·70   1·92

PIECE OF DIORITE STATUE OF MEN····RA.
FOUND IN THE PYRAMID OF ABU-ROASH. SCALE 1/

WMFP mens et del

XII.

Thomas Kell & Son, Photolitu.

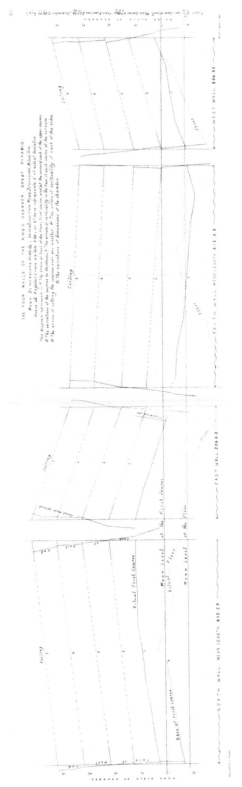

The material originally positioned here is too large for reproduction in this reissue. A PDF can be downloaded from the web address given on page iv of this book, by clicking on 'Resources Available'.

All half actual size.

A. Alabaster.   B. Basalt.   D. Diorite.   G. Granite.   L. Limestone.

XV.

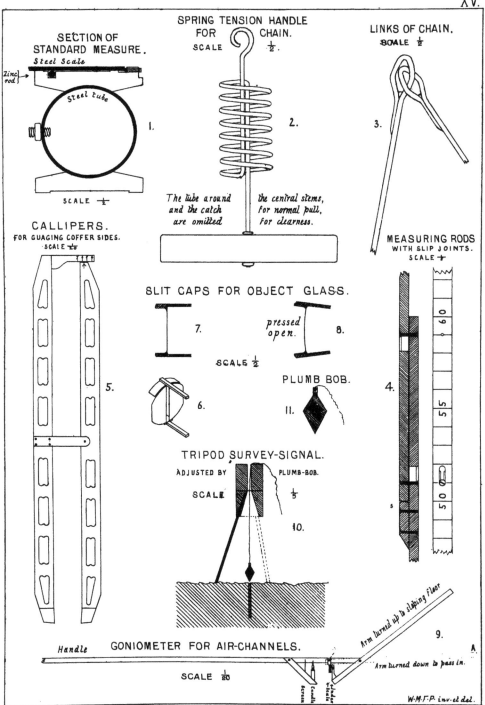

SECTION OF STANDARD MEASURE.

Steel Scale

Zinc rod

Steel tube

SCALE ½

1.

SPRING TENSION HANDLE FOR CHAIN.

SCALE ½.

2.

The tube around and the catch are omitted the central stems, for normal pull, for clearness.

LINKS OF CHAIN.

SCALE ½

3.

MEASURING RODS WITH SLIP JOINTS.

SCALE ¼

4.

CALLIPERS.

FOR GUAGING COFFER SIDES.

SCALE 1/10

5.

SLIT CAPS FOR OBJECT GLASS.

7.

pressed open.

8.

SCALE ½

6.

PLUMB BOB.

11.

TRIPOD SURVEY-SIGNAL.

ADJUSTED BY PLUMB-BOB.

SCALE ⅕

10.

GONIOMETER FOR AIR-CHANNELS.

Handle

SCALE 1/20

Arm turned up to sloping floor

Arm turned down to pass in.

9.

A

W·M·F·P· inv·et del.

Thomas Kell & Son, Photolith.

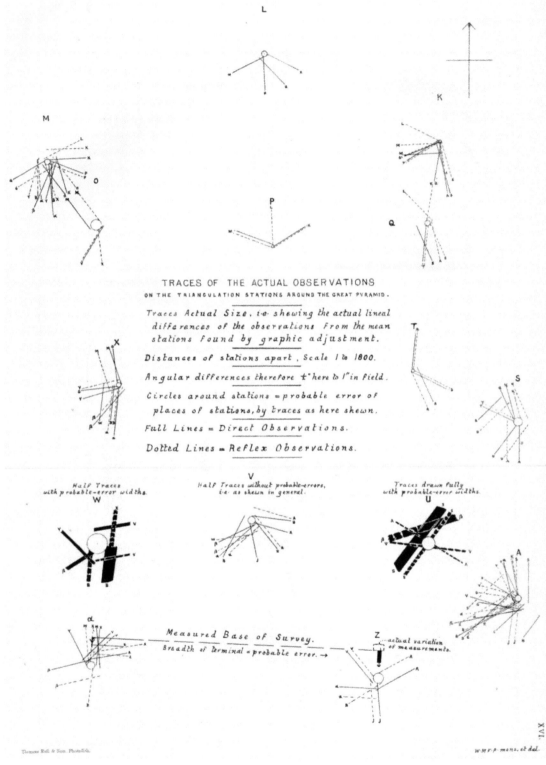

The material originally positioned here is too large for reproduction in this reissue. A PDF can be downloaded from the web address given on page iv of this book, by clicking on 'Resources Available'.

For EU product safety concerns, contact us at Calle de José Abascal, 56–1°,
28003 Madrid, Spain or eugpsr@cambridge.org.

www.ingramcontent.com/pod-product-compliance
Ingram Content Group UK Ltd.
Pitfield, Milton Keynes, MK11 3LW, UK
UKHW030900150625
459647UK00021B/2717